FROM DOGFIGHT TO DIPLOMACY

A Spitfire Pilot's Log
1932–1958

FROM DOGFIGHT TO DIPLOMACY

A Spitfire Pilot's Log
1932–1958

A. R. D. MacDonell

Pen & Sword
AVIATION

First published in Great Britain in 2005 by
Pen & Sword Aviation
an imprint of
Pen & Sword Books Ltd
47 Church Street
Barnsley
South Yorkshire
S70 2AS

ISBN 1 84415 320 7

A CIP catalogue record for this book is
available from the British Library.

Typeset in 10/12 Times New Roman by
Concept, Huddersfield, West Yorkshire

Printed and bound in England by
CPI UK

Pen & Sword Books Ltd incorporates the Imprints of Pen & Sword Aviation,
Pen & Sword Maritime, Pen & Sword Military, Wharncliffe Local History,
Pen & Sword Select, Pen & Sword Military Classics and Leo Cooper.

For a complete list of Pen & Sword titles please contact
PEN & SWORD BOOKS LIMITED
47 Church Street, Barnsley, South Yorkshire, S70 2AS, England
E-mail: enquiries@pen-and-sword.co.uk
Website: www.pen-and-sword.co.uk

FROM DOGFIGHT TO DIPLOMACY

being the memoirs of
Air Commodore A. R. D. MACDONELL CB, DFC, RAF (Ret'd)
(*MAC'IC ALASDAIR*)
22nd CHIEF OF GLENGARRY

As edited by Lois MacDonell and Anne Mackay

Written during the years of my retirement in Scotland, these memoirs are offered in loving gratitude to my wife Lois who worked with me; corrected mistakes in syntax and fact; and advised me, quite fiercely at times, on the suitability of certain passages in relation to the people concerned. For what they are worth, I dedicate them to her in the hope that she and the family will be better able to understand some of the eccentricities of me, the author.

Donald MacDonell of Glengarry
Fortrose 1989

Acknowledgements

Without the skill, encouragement, sheer dogged determination and hard work of Anne Mackay I doubt these memoirs would ever have been published and I am enormously grateful to her, with whom I so much enjoyed working.

The other key person, James Miller, not only typed the original text from the hand-written manuscript, but being eager to read the next 'instalment', he also encouraged my husband to continue. I should also like to thank him for his subsequent enthusiasm for its publication.

All five of Donald's children – Ranald, Patrick, Lindsay, James and Penelope – have been unfailingly supportive and helpful and have shown great generosity, which is truly appreciated. They already have the full text – with many more family details, particularly when their father was a child – but I hope that they will value having this edition brought into the public domain.

Many other people have helped in whatever way they could with their individual memories and expertise. They include members of No. 64 Squadron: Richard Jones, Trevor Gray, J. H. C. Sykes and M. T. Wainwright. Also friends from Moscow days, most notably John Deverill, and Christopher and Helen McAlpine.

Towards achieving publication with illustrations, I am particularly indebted to Francine Raveney, Sheena Clarke, Carolyn MacDonell, Lynsey Wynton, and Dorothy Morgan, as well as Mary MacDonell, Jim Mitchell, Alasdair Gow, Karen Green, Margaret Macdonald, Rosa McDonald, Emma Lavender, Gerald Laing, and Graham Harvey.

The helpfulness of the Battle of Britain Fighter Association, and of the Air Historical Branch (RAF), the Royal Air Force Museum, Royal Air Force College Cranwell, the Imperial War Museum and the Muzeum Lotnictwa i Astronautyki, Krakow, is also greatly appreciated.

Innumerable people have given me help and encouragement – and indeed the imperative – towards getting this story published and it is impossible to name them all individually, but I really do value the tremendous support I have received and hope that everyone's varied expectations will be fulfilled and even at times exceeded.

Lois MacDonell
Fortrose 2005

Contents

CHAPTER ONE

A Career Begins

I left my home in Swanage in September 1932, having spent an evening
in a pub with my friends from the garage where I, Donald, had been
working as a mechanic since leaving school. I made my journey to
RAF Cranwell a few days later. My cousin Maurice Hartford – who had
been brought up with us – was at the Imperial Service College with the
intention of getting into Sandhurst and the Army and my brother Peter
was still at Bryanston, a new avant-garde public school in Dorset, based
on a German model, which suited his unconventional behaviour. The
family had begun to split up and Mum was slowly dying.

Dad saw me off from London on the train to Grantham. Groups of
parents were on the platform bidding farewell to their sons. Elderly men
wearing regimental ties, rocked back and forth on their heels and made
strange military sounds like 'Yeah! Ah-ah! Uhuh! Jollygoodluck' and
'Bashonoldson!' Thank God Dad didn't; he said very little, smoking a
cigarette and just being there. The Mums were badly thrown. A few flung
their arms around their embarrassed sons and kissed them emotionally.
Others stood back and shook hands in a way which Mums find difficult,
and had tears in their eyes when their offspring climbed aboard the train
as the whistle blew. It was awkward and undignified. The boys weren't
going to war. Not for several years.

Most of us were relieved when the train pulled out. We began to
consider each other and started to talk, except the few from the upper-
crust public schools, who merely gave their names. Later, when Cranwell
absorbed us into the classless regime of its two-year process of officer
training, we found no difference in the merits of those from public schools
or grammar schools. Though Hurstpierpoint was a public school, I was
completely at home with the young men of my entry regardless of background or status. However, on the whole we broke the ice on the train to
Grantham.

On arrival, the thirty-odd cadets were met by Warrant Officer Joe
Beresford, the Cadet-Wing disciplinarian and drill instructor. He was on

the platform when the London train drew in; immaculate in his uniform, relaxed and welcoming. Without bullshit or bluster, he projected his personality and, during the coach drive to Cranwell, he established a companionship and authority which was to sustain us throughout the time he held office. Joe was unique. He was tough, human, supportive and yet a strict disciplinarian. To him we were 'Sir' or 'Gentlemen' and he cared for us as a pastor for his flock. We revered him and would drill and parade to our best endeavour to receive his, 'Thank you, gentlemen – well done'.

After his retirement our squad was marching down to the hangars for flying training when we saw Joe, in plain clothes, with his daughter, standing by the entrance to the Guard Room. The cadet sergeant in charge of our squad ordered, 'Eyes right!' and saluted Joe as we passed. He took off his hat and said, 'God bless you, and thank you'. There were tears in his eyes and his voice was shaky. To me Joe was an inspiration. I have not met many men like Joe, in or out of the Service. To a man from a humble background the ordering and upbringing of a succession of teenage youths from varied walks of life must surely have been a daunting prospect. That Joe succeeded reinforces my belief that leadership and example are not always factors derived from privilege and class. It is the Joes of the armed forces who really forge the affinity and understanding between the officers and 'other ranks' which characterise the unique camaraderie of the Royal Air Force. A democracy of common purpose. In my time I commanded a fighter squadron in the Battle of Britain. I was privileged then – as on subsequent commands – to lead a classless complement of men and women. It was Joe Beresford who showed me the way.

Academically Cranwell was more than an equal to any technical college of the day. The universities, by virtue of the range of faculties they offered, obviously had the edge on us. But at Cranwell, while the emphasis was, of course, on developing officer qualities and flying ability, the cadets were given a remarkably wide ranging education. The technical thesis which we were required to present halfway through our course was a stimulating challenge for us, destined as we were to become leaders in a technical service. I chose streamlining, an interest dating from my early fascination with racing cars.

I got much information and encouragement from the Royal Aeronautical Society and other organisations affiliated to aircraft design and the RAF. My graduation report made special mention of my thesis as it had been awarded a one hundred per cent mark. It was recommended that I pursue this particular aspect of aeronautics – a follower perhaps of Frank Whittle, but in aerodynamics?

At Cranwell the transition from first to second year was marked, as far as flying training was concerned, by graduation from the basic training aircraft to an operational front-line aircraft bereft of its guns or bomb rack. The more promising cadets were creamed off to complete their second year as fighters; the rest continued their flying training on less rewarding aircraft. Both the fighters and the also-rans flew obsolescent, often obsolete, aircraft. Though I hate to say it, the duffers who were not awful enough to be thrown out were usually destined for flying boats.

Cranwell was an enchanted two years. I responded to drill and ceremonial. I made many friends and my batman became more of a chamberlain than a servant. I can remember the distress when my father came to my graduation ceremony and slept in a spare room on my corridor. He found petty faults with the cleanliness of the room and was arrogant and offensive to my batman. But that was Dad – sublimating the failures of his post-war life which contrasted so strongly with the importance of his Intelligence role in Baku, the place on the Caspian Sea where Peter and I were born.

For the first two terms we were taught on basic training aircraft. In my first term this was an Avro 504N, the offspring of the 504K of the First World War. The only difference between the two was that the earlier Mark had a Glerget rotary engine and a sort of ski protruding ahead of the landing wheels, while our Mark had a Lynx radial engine and no 'toothpick' in the front. It was a two-seater biplane, the instructor occupying the front cockpit with his pupil in the rear. Communication was by a 'Gosport tube' which connected each cockpit by means of earphones in our helmets, and a voice tube through which we could speak to each other. The cockpits were open, the engine was noisy and it was difficult to hear properly; particularly if one's instructor, often a sergeant pilot, was heavily accented in his local dialect. Alas, I never had one with a Dorset brogue.

One of the drills on approaching to land is to wind back the tail trim or actuator. When flying with a sergeant who was making splendid efforts to master the 'King's English', I forgot to do just that. His voice, grossly distorted by wind and engine noise, came through the Gosport tube: 'Wind back the actuating gear'. I said, 'What?' He repeated his instruction. Again I couldn't hear properly and said, 'Sorry, can you say that again?' Whereupon a splendid North Country accent came through loud and clear: 'Wind the fuckin' wheel back!' I understood this at once and did what I was told.

A week or two later, after I and my flying instructor had spent half an hour practising forced landings, he said: 'Right. Back to Cranwell and land close to A Flight'. Nothing unusual. I flew the Avro back to Cranwell and put her down some three hundred yards from A Flight's apron. My instructor then told me to throttle back and stop. To my surprise, some two hundred yards from the apron, he undid his straps, stepped out of the front cockpit, locked his seat straps and said to me, 'Okay, off you go. Do a couple of circuits and landings. I'll be watching you'. As he stepped to the ground he gave me a big grin and a thumbs-up. He was a great flying instructor!

Ye Gods. I was entirely on my own. I knew this was what it was all about. Pride fought with fear on fairly equal terms. In somewhat of a daze I taxied out and joined the queue of aircraft moving to the downwind end of the airfield. I recognised many of my team-mates with their instructors. But I was alone. I was obviously taxiing far too slowly. I was frequently overtaken by others in the queue until I pulled myself together and accelerated to the take-off position. I swung into wind. I went through my pre-take-off checks. I held my breath. I steadied my hands on the controls. I centralised the controls. I slowly opened the throttle. We moved forward. More throttle. Check your rudder as speed builds up. Ease stick forward. Tail comes up. Speed 60 mph. Ease back on stick. Keep straight with rudder. Then suddenly: no bumping and controls seem light. We are airborne: me and my aeroplane! I have reached for the sky and I have found it on my own.

I relax. I become a pilot. I conform with the circuit pattern for landing. I throttle back and manage a remarkably smooth landing a long way down the airfield, far from the A Flight apron. For a moment I sit in my cockpit without the accustomed solid frame of my flying instructor occupying the front one. 'Do two circuits and landings,' he had said. So be it. I went through the take-off drill consciously and without fear. We became airborne. I flew a full circuit of the airfield and judged my landing approach to put me down reasonably close to the A Flight apron. I was supremely happy. My approach was well judged but the landing was not one of my best. I bounced twice before I taxied to where I saw him standing near the apron. I switched off and climbed out. 'What do you think you are?' he said 'A bloody kangaroo?' But he grinned at me and slapped me on the back. 'You're okay,' he said.

The September 1932 entry was lucky in several ways. First, the new College building, a real architectural triumph, was finished by the beginning of my second term. The first term was spent in wooden barracks with five in a room; one cadet from each of the four entries with a 'senior' in charge of each room. All right, if he was all right, but bloody hell if he wasn't. I was lucky. Also, by the beginning of my second term, the old Avro 504Ns were phased out as basic trainers. They were replaced by a sturdy little biplane, the Avro Tutor, also with a Lynx engine but with a better turn of speed, dead easy to land, open cockpits and the inevitable Gosport tubes. We all fell in love with the Tutor which was fully aerobatic, virtually idiot-proof and relatively quiet.

I ended my first year at Cranwell as an above-average pilot, a centre three-quarter in the College 'A' Rugby team, and with an encouraging general report on my progress towards a commission. Mum was delighted, though Dad was unable to refrain from a characteristically snide remark to the effect that he didn't imagine the competition was very great. After all, he had opposed my joining the RAF because he regarded it as being made up of 'garage mechanics', which of course is what I was at the time!

We moved into 'the College'. Ceremonial and discipline went up several notches. Burberry's had a pitch in the College and they tailored our uniforms and messkits. There was a resident hairdresser whose fingering of our heads rather suggested he enjoyed the physical contact. He always asked us when he was done whether there was anything 'special' we required. A half-open drawer explained what he meant. Some of us bought from him until the buzz went around that 'they' were a lot cheaper from the chemist in Grantham.

We had our own rooms and six of us shared a long-suffering civilian batman. We were paid 7s 6d a day with food and accommodation all found. I think there was a standard rate we paid our batmen who, poor chaps, were more often than not forking out loans for our excesses in Grantham and elsewhere. In the long run they were probably not out of pocket. To have our buttons shined, our shoes cleaned, our rooms scoured and beds made was, to me, a new and luxurious dimension in life.

At the end of each of the four terms was Graduation Day. This was preceded the evening before by a formal ball to which parents, sisters and girlfriends were invited. The younger women swayed around the ballroom and then slunk guiltily towards the bar which served soft drinks and a mildly intoxicating fruit cup. I had fallen in love shortly before I went to Cranwell and so Phyl came to my first graduation ball. Her aunt had taken rooms in a Grantham hotel and had lent me her Morris saloon for the ten-mile drive to Cranwell. Phyl was an excellent dancer. I was not. But we spent a very happy evening in a party with the father and sister of Peter Hackforth, a cadet of my entry, whose elder brother Norman became well known on BBC radio as 'The Voice' in *Twenty Questions*.

Dad came to my Graduation. I met his train at Grantham during the afternoon before the ball. The passing-out parade was on the following morning. The ball took its toll and most of the cadets on parade were green-faced, semi-conscious and suffering the wrath of Hell. But we survived, and parents and well-wishers clapped as we finally marched off.

We were commissioned as Pilot Officers in the Royal Air Force and that was really what it was all about.

I left Cranwell with a good report, and a record of excellence as a rifle shot; a near miss for the Rugby First XV; and a qualified fighter pilot with an 'above average' assessment in my pilot's logbook. I had also grown a silly little moustache and had bought a 250cc Cotton motorbike from a senior cadet for £5. I was qualified, commissioned, adult and mobile but still growing up.

CHAPTER TWO

No. 54 (F) Squadron, RAF

My first posting in the autumn of 1934 was for flying duties with 54 Squadron, equipped with obsolescent Bulldog, single-seater fighters. The Squadron was based at Hornchurch in Essex, within a few miles of the Ford works at Dagenham. We were commanded by a spry little Squadron Leader, George Daly, who had been awarded a DFC in the First World War. The Squadron Adjutant was Flying Officer John Grandy, who befriended and guided me. He rose to high rank and retired with a knighthood and the rank of Marshal of the Royal Air Force and Chief of the Defence Staff. I probably owe more to John Grandy than to any other officer in the RAF.

George Daly was an efficient, kindly and respected commanding officer, and his wife 'Dot', quite a bit younger, was a favourite with the officers. The Dalys had no children, so we young ones were brought under her protective wing. John Grandy, with his great charm and outrageous good looks, was the front runner.

To me, aged twenty, to have my own aircraft, my own ground crew and by now my own car was to step over the threshold from youth to manhood and to taste, for the first time, the challenge of responsibility and the sense of freedom and independence which went with it.

As I was a 'regular', I was appointed understudy to John Grandy as Assistant Squadron Adjutant. Thus I was privy to the assessment of officers and NCOs in the Squadron and began to develop a judgement of people which, as I grew older and held more senior rank, stood me in good stead when it came to selection, promotion and suitability for appointments. Some forty years later, after I had retired from the RAF, I found myself in a close-knit partnership of recruitment consultants in London, where my service experience in personnel assessment was of very real commercial benefit.

At Hornchurch, 54 Squadron was joined, several months after I was appointed, by a re-formed squadron, No. 65 Squadron. This squadron had been disbanded after the First World War. Its commanding officer was Squadron Leader 'Mongoose' Soden, a jovial extrovert who quickly built up a team of eager and slightly superior pilots. Superior because the Squadron was equipped with the relatively new Hawker Demon, a two-seat biplane with a rear gunner and a performance that could outmatch that of our ageing Bulldogs. Inevitably, inter-squadron rivalry built up.

In the Officers' Mess we mixed amicably and without jealousy until the occasional 'guest night' when, after dinner, the anteroom became an arena and 54 Squadron competed against 65 Squadron in jousts which I can only describe as reminiscent of Roman games. No one suffered serious injury but the mess which the domestic staff was confronted with the following morning was pretty awful.

We attended the Station Parade at 08.30 each morning. This consisted of an odd combination of a roll call by squadrons and prayers read by the Station padre. For reasons which I have never understood, the Roman Catholics and the Jews were not subjected to the ritual. They were given the order by the Station Adjutant, an elderly and humourless Flight Lieutenant, 'Fall out the Roman Catholics and Jews'. Whereupon those of such persuasions would 'about face', take four paces out of the ranks and stand at ease with their backs to the proceedings. Following a particularly riotous guest night, the Station Adjutant was compelled to spend the night in the Mess as the plug leads of his car had all been changed around. The following morning he came on parade looking like death, called the parade to attention, reported to the Station Commander and then faced us all and croaked: 'Roam out the fallen Catholics and Jews!' The parade collapsed in hysterics.

One of the Flight Commanders who helped to develop my ability as a fighter pilot was Arnold Christian. Christian had an admirable disregard of the petty restrictions of the rule book. During the course of a perfectly proper Sector patrol, he and I came back to base low over the Thames estuary. As we approached, skimming the flat fields, we noticed a blonde girl standing on a white houseboat waving to us. We swooped low over-head and then, to my surprise, Christian's Bulldog nosed down to a flat field alongside the river. He landed and taxied towards the houseboat. I followed. The blonde was wearing a red sweater. She was very attractive and invited us to tea. Back at Hornchurch, the Duty Pilot logged our 'patrol' as one hour thirty but was persuaded to reduce the time to an acceptable one hour. Of course, the Royal Air Force, was – and is – a highly professional Service, yet I often look back on those days as belonging to a free flying club. Within a few years we were to be put to the test . . . .

With 54 Squadron I learned to perfect my aerobatics and to 'dogfight', to fly in a tight and symmetrical squadron formation, to practise dive bombing with small smoke-bombs, and to fire my two guns at a towed target over the sea and at a ground target on the ranges near Lydd on the coast of the English Channel. I also became aware of what we all owed to our ground crew and, because of an affinity with mechanics, I spent time, when the weather was unfit for flying, assisting my own crew in cleaning, inspecting and servicing my Bulldog.

I was appointed officer in charge of the Corporals' Club, a group of junior NCOs who met once a week in the NAAFI and played darts and snooker. I helped the club raise a small team of musicians; I played an accordion just well enough to be included. We sang bawdy songs and the 'comics' performed their solo and topical acts. It was fine until we took part in the NAAFI concert. Alas, our pianist was pissed out of his mind. But we got through with a substitute from the audience. I was hauled up before the Station Adjutant the next day, but was allowed to continue in charge of the Corporals' Club more or less on remand.

The morning of 1 April, All Fools' Day, was foggy, overcast and unfit for flying. John Grandy and I sat in the office checking logbooks and other documents until the coffee break. We could then find nothing further to do. Inevitably, perhaps, our thoughts turned to setting up an 'April Fool' before the morning ran out. We settled on a splendid ploy which, unfortunately, went awry.

Flying Officer Price, 65 Squadron's Adjutant, was a pompous and humourless individual who took his appointment very seriously. In a sense he epitomised the attitude of his Squadron, he was ambitious and flew unimaginatively. John masterminded our April Fool. We wrote a draft signal as if from Headquarters Fighter Area, posting Price to Cranwell for Cadet Wing administrative duties. I had no difficulty in persuading the Flight Sergeant in charge of our station signals unit to commit this to an official signals form which was duly delivered to 65 Squadron.

John Grandy and I sat in our office and waited. Nothing happened for quite some time. The telephone rang. It was Price, clearly upset. What, he asked me, did Cadet Wing Administration at Cranwell involve. I said it was rather like being a housemaster at a boarding school. Was it a flying post? No, I replied, though you could scrounge an occasional flight if you were lucky. Why was he asking? His reply was terse: 'I've just received a signal posting me to Cranwell. I've given it to my Squadron Commander, who is furious. He is taking it up with the Station Commander.' John and

I looked at each other as I rang off. What the hell to do now? John grabbed the phone and called Squadron Leader Soden, the Commanding Officer of 65 Squadron. The orderly who answered said the CO had gone to Station Headquarters to see the Station Commander. This was no longer a joke!

John thought I should call the Station Adjutant and confess and I did so, explaining it was an April Fool. His reply was characteristic: 'I fail to see anything humorous in this practical joke. I shall inform the Station Commander.' John and I fell silent and waited. It was Soden who phoned. He was obviously amused by the whole thing. He said: 'Mac, I recommend you put an atlas in the seat of your pants.' It was not long before I was summoned to Station Headquarters.

It seems that Soden had brought in the signal to the Station Commander and protested that he was trying to form a new squadron; that Price was essential and for him to be posted away less than six months after he had joined the Squadron was absurd. The Station Commander immediately got onto Command Headquarters who stoutly denied having sent any such signal regarding Price's posting and were quick to point out that the reference code was nonsense. Sticking to his guns the Station Commander demanded to speak with the Air Officer Administration, considerably more his senior, and was spluttering his concern when the Station Adjutant came into his office where Soden was standing by the desk. According to Soden, the Adjutant broke in with a hesitant, 'Excuse me, sir, but I understand this has something to do with today's date.' The truth filtered through to the Station Commander who disengaged apologetically from Headquarters, dismissed Soden and shortly afterwards demanded my presence.

He was beside himself with fury, gripping the arms of his chair; his knuckles were white. I have never seen anyone so angry. To say that I was frightened would be an understatement. I had been commissioned a mere six months. I was terrified. Thoughts of courts martial, dismissal and ignominy ran riot through my mind. I stood before his desk at attention with the Station Adjutant staring unhappily at the ceiling.

'How dare you make a fool of me!' ... 'You impertinent little upstart.' ... 'You are a disgrace to Cranwell ...' and so on and so forth. Eventually the tirade subsided. He had, to give him his due, always been supportive and friendly. He looked hard at me and said something about not playing schoolboy games in the Service. I was then dismissed. He sentenced me to a fortnight's Orderly Officer duties which effectively confined me to camp. A pity, as I had a date with Phyl a few days later. Orderly Officer was tedious. On duty twenty-four hours each day; inspecting the airmen's barracks, their meals, their attendance at the Sick Quarters – always the same malingerers – and taking the evening roll before lights out. The Orderly Officer wore parade kit which was breeches and puttees – damned uncomfortable. He was also required to deal with any minor emergency or official telephone calls in off-duty hours. It was a pretty tedious fortnight: with no flying.

I think it was that fortnight, grounded at Hornchurch, that really brought home to me the extent to which the flying bug had bitten me.

NAZI GERMANY

My generation, born just before, during or shortly after the First World War, was brought up in the unshakable belief that the defeat of the Kaiser's Germany and the conditions of the Versailles Treaty which followed were just desserts for a dangerous and outrageous nation which, with God's help and supportive allies, was put down after four years of unspeakable horror.

I was commissioned into a Service trained in air warfare: the idea that we might be called to war was far from our thoughts. Flying was our life. We were young, adventurous young men with normal pursuits, girlfriends and personal preoccupations which the relatively relaxed routine of squadron life allowed us to enjoy.

It was a chance meeting with an old friend who had recently been appointed to the Foreign Office that opened my eyes and made me look beyond my narrow horizons and to consider seriously what was going on in Europe and in Germany in particular. Thanks to my friend, I became more and more aware of the European scene. The Weimar Government of Germany had been overturned. A man known as Adolf Hitler, whose name was in fact Schickelgruber, had mesmerised the youth of Germany by his oratory and leadership of the Hitlerjugend, the youth of the country. He loathed Jews. Dolfuss, the Chancellor of Austria, had been murdered by German agents and the country annexed. Hitler was repudiating – in mass rallies – the Versailles Treaty. He bellowed against the clause which gave Poland access to the Baltic through the 'Polish Corridor'; an obvious bone of contention since it sliced Germany in two with a smaller section to the east of the Corridor and the main mass of Germany to the west. Hitler's movement was known as the National Socialists, or Nazis. The British Government, totally unprepared to back any disapproval with even a veiled threat of armed intervention, pre-varicated.

In London, Oswald Mosley had recruited a formidable following of 'Black Shirts' – the British Union of Fascists. I was disturbed and curious. I attended a well advertised rally in Hyde Park and was horrified at the parade of black-shirted, arrogant young men and women goose-stepping to the hysterical rhetoric of Mosley's minions, whose theme was fight Communism and down with the Jews. It so happened that a rally of the British Communist Party was being held at the same time, also in Hyde Park: a bad mistake on the part of the Home Office. Before long the Communists had infiltrated the spectators lining the route of the Black Shirts: trouble was inevitable. The Police were unable to contain the threat from the rear. Their ranks broke. A mêlée ensued. The women in the Black Shirt parade were hustled into vans and fisticuffs broke out among the opposing factions. I sought safety in retreat but was twice knocked down on my flight to Park Lane. Oswald Mosley stood his ground until a posse of police led him away to safety. The rally broke up in disarray and many arrests were made. Politically I was growing up.

CHAPTER THREE

The Fleet Air Arm: Conversion and Joining

I was posted to RAF Leuchars in Fife for a conversion course leading to a two-year secondment to the Fleet Air Arm as a Fleet Fighter Pilot to operate from aircraft carriers. I didn't like the idea at all. John Grandy and Squadron Leader Daly both supported me, but the powers that be had made up their minds.

I reported to Leuchars, not far from St Andrews. We were required to fly training aircraft – which I found humiliating – and to bring them in to land on an area of the airfield marked out to simulate the flight deck of an aircraft carrier. Those of us who passed this absurd course – we all did – were earmarked for a tour with the Fleet Air Arm, which had equal numbers of RAF and Royal Navy pilots. Although I was not best pleased at first, the spell in Scotland was a lot of fun. I made new friends and found an unexpected affinity with a number of Naval pilots who shared my concern about the situation in Germany.

I had disclosed this to Dad in letters at the time. Mum had died. Dad and Peter continued to live in Swanage. I wrote frequently to Dad, not only to support him in his loss but also because I was beginning to understand him and to acknowledge his understanding and experience of international affairs. His replies were reasonable but unconcerned: let Germany do what it wished, so long as it didn't pose a threat to France and Britain. He disapproved of Hitler's attitude to the Jews, but hedged this by pointing out the extent to which the Jews were in control of the government and economy of our country – the Press, the Cabinet, the major industries. He was honest in his views but I don't remember taking them very seriously.

Then Benito Mussolini – 'Il Duce', the self-appointed dictator of Italy –
while acknowledging the sovereignty of his pathetic little King, invaded
Abyssinia in 1935 and inflicted atrocities on Haile Selassie's people,
dropping mustard gas from the air. This invasion followed hard on the
heels of the Spanish Civil War in which both Germany and Italy actively
supported the Fascist movement in Spain. It was the success of the
illegally created German Luftwaffe in its bombing offensives against
defenceless towns in Spain like Guernica that finally persuaded a supine
and pacifist British Government that we had a role to play. The disgraceful, so-called agreement between Sir Samuel Hoare and Pierre Laval
of France not to impose oil sanctions on Italy – which would almost
certainly have ended the conflict – finally confirmed me in my belief that
what the British Government said was one thing: what they were prepared
to do was another. Mussolini roared, fulminated and threatened war
against Great Britain.

So, I found myself posted to 'an unknown destination' as a Fleet Air
Arm pilot. I was given a travel warrant, a detailed list of medical injec-
tions, a catalogue of totally useless advice on 'what to avoid' when overseas and a clothes list that included tropical uniform. I, and a number of
other FAA servicemen, were instructed to take a certain train on a certain
date from London to Liverpool and to report to a Movements Officer in a
specified corner of the station. Revealing our destination was taboo and
the order ended with the injunction: 'You are not to discuss this
movement with anyone outside your family.' Fancy! Our baggage was
taken over at Liverpool and marked 'Destination Z'. There must have
been about sixty of us, all in plain clothes. We were led to one of the docks
where the *Cameronia* of the *Anchor Line* lay alongside. Inevitably, it
became common knowledge that we were off to the Middle East; either
Malta, Alexandria or Port Sudan.

We were allocated to four berth cabins and, after a delay of two hours
while the catering staff walked out at being refused extra pay for sailing
into an unknown and possibly hostile part of the world, the dispute was
settled and the *Cameronia* sailed. I sent a mildly dramatic telegram to Phyl
and then joined my colleagues at the bar.

The British Government's response to Mussolini's bluster and threats
amounted to a reinforcement of our Naval presence in the Mediterranean.
The Home Fleet carrier *Courageous* joined the *Glorious* in Alexandria. A
number of additional destroyer flotillas, a light cruiser squadron, three
additional battle cruisers and a number of support vessels were dispatched
to the Mediterranean. Two extra RAF squadrons were sent to the area
and the odd armoured car unit joined in the reinforcement.

Our Naval strength and potential were overwhelmingly superior to the small Italian fleet which remained in Taranto throughout this period of tension. But from what I have since read, I doubt whether we could have offered Haile Selassie's nomad army adequate support against the Italian invaders. The British Government under Baldwin, with Sir Samuel Hoare dismissed as Foreign Secretary in favour of Eden, was not disposed to indulge in anything more effective than the age-old 'gunboat diplomacy'.

The good ship *Cameronia* sailed from Liverpool with a reserve pool of pilots trained for the Fleet Air Arm, a couple of land-based squadrons, a battalion of gunners and an odd assortment of the inevitable administrative 'tail'. Life on board was free and easy. It seemed to me odd that we, the officers, should have to attend the evening meal in Mess kit. As we entered the Mediterranean, the heat became such that we were allowed to wear a modified form of dress which didn't include a Mess jacket. Even so, we perspired freely and obviously. Some, like me, probably smelt.

One instruction was intriguing. It was to the effect that, while uniform was to be worn during the voyage, all Service personnel were to be prepared to change into civilian clothes immediately when so ordered. We regarded this as official crap and paid little attention to it. We spent our time on deck or in the bar. The Purser introduced us to a venomous cocktail which was a knock-out. We played deck tennis and quoits or swam in the overcrowded and over-chlorinated pool on the after deck. Then an odd thing happened. We were off Portugal when, one morning, our cabin staff brought in two ladies' dresses and wide-brimmed sun hats. We asked what the hell all this was about, but the steward, who was very embarrassed, said we would be told later and that he had to leave two sets of dresses and hats in each officer's cabin. Shortly all was to be revealed.

A day or so later the loud-hailer ordered: 'All personnel in military uniform to proceed below decks and to change into civilian clothes. Those with dresses and sun hats to dress accordingly and mingle with others on the port side of the ship.' We changed into 'civvies' and the 'ladies' looked fine except one who had a moustache and was sent below to become a man again. The reason for all this was that an Italian destroyer had been identified on the port bow.

So, we trooped giggling onto the promenade deck where, clad in male and female clothes, we were encouraged to lounge on the railings or sprawl in deckchairs as the Italian destroyer closed with the *Cameronia*, circled from astern and sped away south. The idea that Italy was not all too well aware that the *Cameronia* was carrying reinforcements to the Middle East is of course ridiculous. But we played our part in the pantomime and it was a lot of fun. I shall long remember the large Flying Officer striding along the deck in a flowered frock and a jaunty hat, puffing a pipe. I wonder if the Italians spotted him through their telescopes.

We stopped at Gibraltar just long enough to go ashore and wander through the town. Then on again through the Western Mediterranean to Malta. Here we crept in late in the evening past the promontories of St Angelo and Bighi into Grand Harbour where we moored alongside Parlatorio wharf as the sun went down and the myriad lights of Valetta broke through the darkness like candles on a Christmas tree. Malta was then an important naval base in the Mediterranean. Grand Harbour had a large dry-dock and berthing facilities for ships from battle cruisers to destroyers. The Maltese economy was dependent on the British presence and the whole life of the island was essentially that of a British colony. There was an RAF airfield at Hal Far, mainly for shore-based Fleet Air Arm squadrons, and a seaplane station at Kalafrana in the south of the island. Lloyds Bank and Gieves had established themselves in Valetta and 'medically approved' brothels were doing a roaring trade in the red-light centres of the island.

It was common knowledge that most of us were destined for Alexandria but that a few were going on to Port Sudan. Whether it was the vicious antibiotic jabs that the MOs administered at this stage or simply a virus that invaded the *Cameronia*, I know not, but most of the passengers, including the cabin staff, went down on the passage to Egypt with severe sore throats and high temperatures. We were in pretty poor shape when the ship crept into Alexandria harbour late one night.

CHAPTER FOUR

The Fleet Air Arm: Egypt

I had taken whatever it was badly and was feeling terrible, but I can still remember the unforgettable smell of the harbour, indeed of Egypt: a mixture of ordure, spice and probably just people. We berthed at dawn and those who were classed as 'walking wounded' disembarked. I was among them. We were driven in coaches to the RAF Middle East Headquarters at Aboukir, a few miles from Alexandria. Those unable to travel remained on board for a few days. Two died.

The RAF medical staff were taking no chances and tents had been erected in the Headquarters compound. We were effectively in quarantine. Rumours were rife – yellow fever, typhus? In the event we all recovered within a few days. A week later we were installed in the luxurious Officers' Mess, but we had really nothing to do. This is common to an emergency overseas movement when there isn't a war. As reserve pilots for the two carriers which had no casualties, how were we expected to occupy our time whilst on standby?

We flew a motley selection of aircraft during the morning, by which time the temperature had gone off the clock. So we went to the beach, bathed and acquired a tan or sunburn. There was a bar on the beach run by shrewd Egyptians who plied us with 'White Ladies', a drink which was reasonably harmless when taken in moderation. Not all did. They slept on towels in the Mediterranean sun and paid the price. We soon discovered that the girls in Alexandria didn't care for peeling foreheads and noses.

Because flying was to me an essential ingredient in my life I scrounged flights with the resident units in Aboukir; mostly very ancient twin-engined bombers like the Vickers Valencia or the single-engined Fairey 111F. I was never really content on the ground unless whooping it up in the Officers' Mess of an evening. I did all the things that young men did and probably still do. We took taxis into Alexandria and visited the bar in the Excelsior Hotel where we ate and got mildly sloshed. We then went to one of the many 'exhibitions' which consisted of a variety of sexual activities between the most unlikely partners. But I had a cultural and civilised anchorage in Alexandria – the British Consulate.

The Consul General, Clifford Heathcote-Smith, had been a colleague of my father in the Foreign Office. I was frequently invited to the Consulate for formal and informal occasions. With the Heathcote-Smiths I learned diplomatic protocol: I became familiar with the manner in which visitors from foreign nations were addressed, received and engaged in conversation. I graduated to international receptions and was always encouraged by Jocelyn, Heathcote-Smith's elder daughter, who was four years older than me. She played the piano beautifully and could have become a concert pianist. Gradually she and I became emotionally involved. We wanted to become engaged. Heathcote-Smith and my father exchanged letters: Dad's attitude was one of non-intervention; Heathcote-Smith's was to endeavour to break up this affair. Jocelyn and I stuck to our guns. We announced our engagement in the local paper and the London dailies.

I do not remember any sense of guilt about Phyl. She had obviously been fond of me but a year after my departure from Liverpool she had married a man called Roger Newton. However, she wrote me a very loving letter saying that I would always have a special place in her heart.

Although I was a mere Flying Officer, Heathcote-Smith accepted our engagement and talked to me about my future, about a marriage settlement and – in a thinly veiled allusion to my wardrobe – suggested I buy a 'well-cut', lightweight suit. He hinted that he would foot the bill and recommended an Egyptian tailor in the main street of Alexandria. At the age of twenty-three, I was proud and probably somewhat defensive. I did not take at all kindly to Heathcote-Smith's implied criticism of my appearance and, for the first time, I rebelled against him. He was stuffy and offered me a loan: this I refused.

The monotony of life at RAF Aboukir was broken when we had orders from Middle East Headquarters that all Fleet Air Arm pilots, both RN and RAF, were to be deployed to a desert airfield, El Amirya, some twenty miles south of Alexandria. The airfield, which dated from the First World War, had been sufficiently rehabilitated to provide hangars for the aircraft, a clear piece of desert for the operation of our aircraft and a makeshift Officers' and Sergeants' Mess. We were to be accommodated in tents. I had qualified as an RAF Transport Driver, so I was put in command of the MT convoy.

Among the motley assortment of vehicles which ground and scrunched their way into the desert was the sullage lorry. It was of 1918 vintage, with solid tyres and a vicious gearbox which baffled almost everyone. It backfired when started on the handle – no self-starters in those days. Most of my MT crew were terrified of the thing, so my splendid Flight Sergeant and I between us tamed the brute and drove it to El Amirya. In the absence of sewage drainage in the desert, its presence was essential. Somehow the two of us got it there, where it stood for weeks stinking and refusing to stop backfiring until we drove it to the native village which had been commissioned to dispose of its contents.

Amirya was good. I enjoyed the endless desert, the relentless sun and the fascinating Senussi who had migrated north from their normal habitat following the rains to raise their barley crops. They were nomads, living like us in tents, and we engaged the men to complete the reconstruction of the stone buildings. I had acquired a smattering of colloquial Arabic – I have an ear for languages – and I fell under the spell of their philosophy, their beliefs and their intrinsic dignity and hospitality. They camped, with their camels, half a mile from the airfield. They were working on the dilapidated buildings by six o'clock each morning and returned to their camp twelve hours later. They were friendly and appeared satisfied with what they were paid.

Once, a Senussi father and his wife brought in a very sick child. Our Medical Officer said the child needed immediate hospitalisation. My afternoon was free. I had a dilapidated old car. Somehow we contacted the international surgery in Burg el Arab, a relatively civilised village some twenty miles across a desert track. I drove the parents and the child to the surgery. It took me the better part of an hour. I spent the night lying across the front seats while the child was operated on, and the parents prayed in the waiting room. She lived and, against the surgeon's advice, I drove them back to their camp. I had grown to understand and love the Senussi. They are a proud people.

Flying from Amirya was not without its hazards. We carried out Met (meteorological) flights which consisted of climbing to maximum altitude each morning at first light, recording temperatures, wind direction and velocity, cloud formations and any evidence of low gusting with sand-storms. They were our enemies. We had no homing equipment and our desert base had no beacon. At best, if we overflew the airstrip during a sandstorm, the ground crew on hearing our approach, fired rockets in the hope we could circle and make a safe landing. Most of us did but there were those who were not good at dead reckoning and failed to locate the base. They were forced to give up when their fuel was exhausted. Several force-landed or baled out in the desert and were subsequently rescued, exhausted and suffering badly from dehydration. A few came down in the Mediterranean and were never seen again. The local Senussi, who gave us invaluable advice about the location of desert forced landings, helped to save several of my comrades and their crews.

I am no Lawrence of Arabia but I began to understand his staunch emotional stand for the Arabs. The grace, dignity and beliefs of the Senussi had a deep effect on my search for spiritual truth. Possibly my impatience with the prevarications and in-fighting of the various denominations of the Christian churches stems from the many days I spent with our local tribe of the Senussi.

Our commanding officer was a splendid Naval officer, Commander Tidd, and, as a mixed bunch of RN and RAF pilots, we all got along fine. I became friendly with Flight Lieutenant Derek Syder, the Unit's Equipment Officer, who shared my admiration for the Senussi and who spoke fair colloquial Arabic. It came about that, following my help with the sick child, he and I were invited to a reception held by the tribal chief of the Senussi settlement at Burg el Arab. We drove over the dusty track to the desert village. We were received with great dignity by the village headman, a bearded, white-haired Senussi who bridged the language gap by sheer warmth and gestures which made us feel both welcome and important. We sat cross-legged in his tent on a beautiful Egyptian carpet. We drank a strange potion which was non-alcoholic and were then served with a variety of dishes, mainly farinaceous and highly spiced, followed by unspeakable portions of sheep and camel. We just managed to avoid being sick. There were prayers and dances by dusky nubile girls and then we left. Derek threw up on the way back, but I managed to contain our meal. It was many hours before I fell asleep in my tent. My mind was too preoccupied with our day with the Senussi.

The long-awaited day arrived when I was posted to the aircraft carrier *Courageous* in Alexandria Harbour. She left harbour frequently and at long last I was flying a Nimrod, a Fleet Air Arm version of the front-line RAF Hawker Fury. This was what I badly needed. I enjoyed flying with a fleet fighter squadron and being a member of the wardroom in one of HM ships. The whole mode of life suited my need to pull myself up in matters of protocol. I shall always be grateful to the Royal Navy for having helped me to formulate standards and a self-sufficiency based on confidence and the social graces.

Flying over the Mediterranean and landing back on the flight deck was sheer joy. We tried it at night with limited success. Though we didn't lose a single pilot, a number of Nimrods ended up on their noses or in the crash barriers. But we were learning all the time and, bearing in mind the pitiful inadequacy of our radio control, it is surprising that our casualties were so low. Our progress as fleet fighters improved significantly.

I was temporarily replacing a naval pilot who had been invalided home with TB. He was replaced by a naval officer a few months later and I was then transferred to HMS *Glorious*, also in Alexandria Harbour, as a permanent replacement for an RAF pilot who had been killed in a crash overboard. I joined *Glorious* shortly before she sailed for her base in Grand Harbour, Malta.

But I sailed as a casualty. My friend Derek Syder was getting married to a sweet girl whose parents were in business in Alexandria. Derek asked me to be his Best Man. I was delighted but daunted at the thought of having to propose a toast. However, a few days before the wedding I began to feel unwell with a lot of pain in my left chest. I took aspirin and did my stuff during the service, standing 'commendably still' to quote Heathcote-Smith's words of approval. Derek and I were in RAF Full Dress, now no longer worn but it was indeed impressive. Gieves hired us the uniforms and we looked the part – young and bronzed.

I managed to survive the reception in the Consulate but later that evening felt so ill that I excused myself, was driven to the *Glorious* and sought my cabin and bed. The next morning I was in such pain that the Surgeon-Commander was informed. He examined me, pronounced severe pleurisy in my left lung and general infection of the pleura in the right one. He said that, were I a naval officer, I would be in front of the Commander for not reporting to the sick bay twenty-four hours before we sailed for Malta. I remember very little of the voyage: I was seriously ill.

I was transferred to the Royal Naval Hospital, Bighi, where I slowly recovered and very nearly fell in love with a beautiful blonde nurse. Jocelyn's letters prevented me from making a fool of myself. Eventually, I was discharged with three weeks' sick leave before facing a medical board upon which would depend my fitness to return to full flying duties. Jocelyn decided to join me and was welcomed by the family of the Harbourmaster of the Royal Naval base.

CHAPTER FIVE

The Fleet Air Arm: Malta

Together, Jocelyn and I toured Malta and the tiny island of Gozo just off its north-west coast. We visited the beautiful towns of Citta Veccia, the ancient capital, on its granite hills; Mosta with its incredible mosque and huge unsupported dome; and Valetta where administration, commerce, religion and vice flourished side by side in apparent harmony. We went to the opera. With other members of the Services and their ladies, we were entertained to receptions by the Governor. Here we met and became friends with Stewart Perowne, the eccentric secretary to the Governor, and possibly the strangest but most erudite man I have met.

Jocelyn returned to Alexandria but, possibly with the intuition of a woman, returned to Malta a few months before the end of *Glorious'* commission. She was there with a host of wives and loved ones when, with the crew dressing ship, bunting and ensigns flying, and every ship in the harbour hooting farewell and *bon voyage* on her siren, the guns at the mouth of Grand Harbour fired their valedictory salutes and we steamed slowly into the Mediterranean and home. I thought I saw Jocelyn waving with the others but I knew in my heart that it was leaving Malta that brought the lump to my throat.

But I have jumped ahead. I passed my medical check and was back in the air with 802 Squadron now based at RAF Station Hal Far. These were good days. The small airfield was adequate for our pre-War aircraft and the weather was wonderful. We really got down to training as a squadron: formation, air to ground firing, dive bombing and mock interceptions. We had our tragedies. A Marine captain took off in an Osprey, a two-seater Fleet Air Arm version of the Demon of 65 Squadron at Hornchurch, with an airman in the rear cockpit. It was a flight test following a routine servicing. He had reached about 700 feet when the engine shuddered and stopped.

The inflexible law on such occasions is never to turn back to the airfield but to land straight ahead using what gliding speed is left and, if necessary, make gentle turns to avoid, for example, going smack into a building or some such solid obstruction. Unhappily, he turned back and tried to make the airfield. He stalled from about 200 feet and went straight into a low stone wall. He was in poor shape, unconscious with both legs broken. Miraculously his passenger was only bruised and badly shocked. The pilot died in the Station sick quarters an hour later. He had been the Squadron Adjutant and I, as his Assistant, assumed his role and experienced for the first time the sad duty of arranging a Service funeral.

The second fatal accident was a complete mystery. A young but reasonably experienced RAF pilot took off on a routine mission in an odd aircraft called a Wildebeest, a torpedo bomber. A three-seater, single engined, clumsy and ungainly aircraft that was reliable and easy to fly. At the end of its mission it made a perfectly normal approach to Hal Far. At about 200 feet, just over the downwind edge of the airfield, it reared up with engine running, stalled and crashed nose down on the airfield. The two members of his crew were dead. The pilot was alive and screaming. The Medical Officer came out in a car and administered pain-killers. It seemed ages before the pilot's cries died down. I did what I could to support the pilot but he was in a dreadful mess and died in the cockpit before we could cut him loose. I don't remember being shaken or affected: I appeared to be strangely unmoved by death and mutilation, yet, I cannot watch a live operation on TV and have to turn away.

For my own part, I was running up my Nimrod after a minor inspection when at full revs the engine clattered to a smoking halt. I was out of the cockpit in a flash, but there was no fire. It was found that the overhead valve spur gearing had been cross-threaded and had sheared. Had I taken off, who knows the result? It was not possible to pin the blame on any one of the ground crew. The Flight Sergeant in charge of the technical work was admonished at the subsequent enquiry, but I was not happy. We had a handful of Maltese civilian technical assistants. It was said that their sympathies were with Mussolini's fascists.

Once, when we were to carry out a patrol over a small convoy some fifty miles west of Malta, we got an ambiguous Met report. In effect it predicted fair weather for a while, followed by low cloud with sandstorms approaching from the south. But we took off as a squadron with our CO in the leading Osprey and a naval lieutenant in the rear cockpit with radio and a pretty elementary navigation set. We got caught. We failed to locate the convoy, the weather deteriorated rapidly and the R/T (radio transmission) between Hal Far and the Osprey became indistinct. To his great credit our leader and his navigator got us down to what I thought was a dangerously low level, some 100 feet above a misty sea. When my fuel gauge was alarmingly low, I saw land ahead. I had no idea what it was. Thoughts of forced landings in Sicily excited me. An international crisis! But then below us we saw Valetta and, safely and gratefully, we all landed, very short of fuel, at Hal Far with a cloud ceiling of a few hundred feet.

I enjoyed our life on Malta. Perhaps to me the old Maltese women weaving their lace in their cottages, the hard-muscled, brown farmers with their goats and fields of crops, and the fishermen in their open, high-prowed boats were the features of Maltese life with which I identified, particularly during Jocelyn's absence. For she preferred the musical and literary activities, including the operas and the concerts in the beautiful Opera House in Valetta, later destroyed by bombing during the War.

When Jocelyn was away, I was with the boys, visiting pubs or sun-bathing at Sliema, where there was a bar on a ledge above the blue creek that nestled between bare granite rocks. I joined the Malta Amateur Dramatic Company. We staged a variety show. We had a troupe of chorus girls from the young Service wives; instrumentalists, 'comics' and an orchestra. With John Casson, Sybil Thorndyke's son, who was in 802 Squadron with me, we enlisted a few others to put on a burlesque of the glee singers of the Victorian era. We included in our repertoire the song 'Sweet Lass of Richmond Hill'. Perfectly acceptable under normal circumstances. But Edward VIII had abdicated in order to marry the twice-divorced American, Mrs Wallis Simpson. There is a line in the song that runs 'I'd *crowns* resign to call thee mine, sweet lass of Richmond Hill'. It just wasn't on; one mustn't poke fun at Royalty. So we changed the wording to 'I'd *worlds* resign to call thee mine . . .'. Splendid! Good show! But this proved to be far too obvious. The audience roared with laughter. This I attribute largely to John Casson's hilarious grimace as he sang the line.

There were cocktail parties: too many. The 'fishing fleet' – possibly an unfair description of the young, unmarried women on Malta – set these parties. Not all the girls were British. Malta had an indigenous population of wealthy and influential families such as Mifsud, Camilleri, Mama and Mintoff. Tania Mifsud, slim, bronzed, dark haired, with a superb figure and magnificent eyes, was the belle of every party and the toast of the young men as well as of the not-so-young. After a couple of seasons which she dominated with her beauty and charm, she fell for a young naval lieutenant, and the blood pressure of the youth of Malta was restored to normal.

Jocelyn's return to Malta was something of an anti-climax. I was happy to see her but the company she enjoyed didn't really represent my basic interest – flying. I don't believe Jocelyn ever thought of me as a long-term

RAF officer. I felt that she was indulging a hobby of mine. She gave me splendid books to read; encouraged my emergent interest in the philosophies of Kant and Jung, the post-Impressionist painters and modern writers such as Jean Paul Sartre and St Exupéry. I began to write: not just letters to my father and friends but prose and poetry which stemmed from an affinity with Malta.

CHAPTER SIX

The Fleet Air Arm: Return Home

When leaving Valetta I remained on the quarterdeck of *Glorious* watching Malta fade over the horizon before I went to my cabin. We were the only squadron on board. The others had been left at Hal Far as an earnest of the United Kingdom's defiance of Italy's aggression in Abyssinia. There was no flying on our voyage home. Boredom set in. Our Captain, Bruce Fraser, suggested that we might enjoy watch-keeping under the guidance of the Officer of the Watch. In turn we stood on the bridge and were instructed in keeping watch both by day and night.

I did two spells under instruction by day and was then scheduled for night watch-keeping with Commander Tapper-Carey as my mentor. We ploughed on through the night and somewhere on the approach to the Straits of Gibraltar he left the bridge 'for a few minutes'. Everything was fine: a slight swell, good visibility, and the comforting throb of the engines. I paced the bridge. I held the voice-pipe to the helmsman below and felt pride in the knowledge that whatever instruction I gave him would be obeyed. I was virtually in charge of a 30,000-ton aircraft carrier of the Royal Navy. It was good while it lasted.

Then I saw to starboard what I thought was a red light and a saying of the uncles rang a bell in my mind: 'Should to starboard red appear; 'tis your duty to keep clear'. Red to starboard! I grabbed the voice-pipe. 'Port 20,' I ordered. The helmsman below repeated my instruction with a note of alarm in his voice. He asked me to repeat. 'Port 20,' I said. 'Aye, aye, sir,' he replied.

I had not been told of the top-heavy nature of *Glorious*. Within a minute we were swinging to port and listing alarmingly to starboard. Tapper-Carey clambered up the ladder to the bridge and ordered 'Midships steady', to the great relief of the helmsman. He explained to me, kindly, that the light to starboard was not red and was some twenty miles away off the coast of Spain.

A number of drinks had been lost in the wardroom, sliding off the tables as *Glorious* performed the first part of a slow roll! I was much mocked – which I richly deserved.

As we entered the English Channel our squadron was flown off to Eastleigh which was known as Southampton Airport. It operated short-haul flights, but presumably the Air Ministry had leased the hangar and parking area. And so to the prelude to the Coronation Review of May 1937, with the Fleet assembled at Spithead and a fly-past of Fleet Air Arm and RAF squadrons.

The naval review was magnificent. The might of the Royal Navy crammed the Solent. But the fly-past was a disaster. Bad weather and bad management resulted in squadrons running chaotically in and out of low cloud. We met a gaggle of RAF flying in the opposite direction. What this must have looked like to those who could see it, heaven only knows. However, the whole event became historic when Commander Woodroffe – a retired naval officer commissioned by the BBC – having spent most of the day boozing in the wardroom of one of his old ships, hit the air waves with his famous introduction – 'The Fleeth's lit up! The Fleeth's lit up!'

The Heathcote-Smith family was home on leave. Dad had left Swanage and was established in Barn Close, a small house on the outskirts of Christchurch designed by Uncle Bertie, Mum's eldest brother. Dad had 'adopted' a twenty-four-year-old girl who lived with him. Nancy – known as Nan – would become an essential and under-rewarded custodian and partner in the bringing up of my first family.

I hired an ancient Morris Cowley saloon and introduced Jocelyn to Dad, uncles and aunts and friends. In turn she took me to spend weekends with her friends. Dad didn't like her. Nan was non-committal. Generally speaking, Jocelyn was a disappointment.

I drove Jocelyn to Uncle George and Aunt Ebbie Hartford's house in Botley for supper. It was not a success. After the meal, Ebbie led Jocelyn to the drawing room. Uncle George delivered a swingeing sermon on duty to one's parents! What support was I prepared to give my father and brother? Marriage, at my age and in my circumstances, was irresponsible – and so on. I had more of this by post for the following months. This was the beginning of Uncle George's interference in my life which continued until his untimely death as Senior Naval Officer, Sheerness, in 1941. I wrote him a strong letter which he returned to me with the words 'totally unacceptable' scrawled across the first page. From then on, his letters to me remained unanswered.

But the truth was I was having second thoughts about marriage. After a succession of emotional letters, our engagement was broken off. I knew in my heart that what I had done was right. Subsequently she was happily married to a successful naval officer, now a Baronet, and had a family.

From Eastleigh, I was posted to an appointment as Flight Commander of the Fleet Air Arm Pool at Gosport in Hampshire. This suited me fine. First, the Unit was equipped with a catapult for simulating those fitted forward of the flight deck on the carriers. Second, it consisted of a motley collection of aircraft: Buffins and Swordfish, which were torpedo bombers; Ospreys and Nimrods, which were standard so-called Fleet fighters; and then an assortment of oddments such as a Tom Tit, a lively little two-seat biplane, a Miles Magister, a rather nasty two-seater monoplane with unpleasant stalling habits, and an Avro Tutor, of fond Cranwell memories. To a twenty-four-year-old Flight Lieutenant this was great.

The Royal Navy was anxious to operate its carriers with naval pilots but there were not enough in the pipeline. The RAF had a substantial cadre of 'Short Service' commissioned officers who were of suitable rank and were pilots. They were offered a further service as naval officers in the Fleet Air Arm and several accepted. It was a great joke in the Mess when previously-mustachioed RAF officers, suddenly bereft of their upper-lip adornments and dressed in naval uniform, joined us in the ante-room. I had never realised just what a moustache does to change the appearance of its wearer!

I somehow coped with this hybrid group of officers, some ex-RAF, others Navy, all within my charge to become competent in flying and operating Fleet Air Arm aircraft and, above all, qualified to be launched by the catapult. The catapult was clearly the 'raison d'être' of the Fleet Air Arm Unit of which I was in command. There was no other land-based unit with a catapult. Fleet Air Arm pilots were required to have experience of catapult launching before joining a carrier-borne squadron. I had to give them that experience. The catapult at Gosport became my responsibility, my pride and joy.

I worked with the technicians on this strange, cordite-operated device, which had a fascination for me. Basically, it was a powered trolley on which the aircraft was secured to the launching ramp. The undercarriage straddled the ramp. The aircraft was positioned at the rear end of the ramp. It remained secured while the pilot went through his drills which included, emphatically, 'Ensure that your brakes are released'. He then opened up his engine to full throttle, braced his head back against his head-rest, raised his arm and then lowered it smartly. Whereupon, the catapult hurled his aircraft along the ramp and threw it into the air. To the uninitiated it was a hair-raising experience. Once launched, and with just enough forward speed to be airborne, the temptation to gain height was well-nigh irresistible. But it had to be resisted. The catapult was sighted with an arc of movement of about 45 degrees. Usually it faced the prevailing, south-westerly wind.

I briefed every pilot, personally. I described the incredible sense of loss of control when the catapult shot them into the air. I stressed the importance of trying not to gain height until they had sufficient airspeed, and I instructed everyone to observe the drills which I had written from my own experience. One after another, my pupils were launched from the catapult. Most of them tried to gain height too soon but, happily, the far end of the airfield was free of trees or buildings and they all survived. After a few launches they got the hang of it and droned away until they had enough airspeed to climb safely. But 'Rastus' Carnduff, a Naval officer, knew it all. He outranked me and his attitude to being instructed in what was essentially a Fleet Air Arm operation by an RAF flight lieutenant was somewhat condescending.

He was swung onto the ramp and winched back to the take-off position. I checked he was securely strapped in. But that was all. He went through the drills. He raised his arm, then dropped it. He was launched and sailed sedately towards the Solent. Perfect. He made a few circuits of the airfield before getting the green light to land from the control tower. He came in throttled back. He touched down halfway across the airfield. His tail lifted – and lifted; his nose went down and slowly, with great dignity, his Swordfish nosed over and came to rest on its back with its undercarriage motionless and pointing to the sky. Rastus had omitted to release his brakes! He paid me the courtesy of apologising for having damaged one of my aircraft.

I bought an elderly MG tourer for £20. It cost me a deal more to restore to reasonable serviceability but it made it possible to spend a weekend away or drive from Gosport to Christchurch to visit Dad. Dad and Nan had set up home together and there was a lot of local tut-tutting. We had a number of friends in Christchurch. Dad was nudging sixty but looked older. Nan was twenty-four. I never knew how much Dad had to live on, though I suspect he was still dependent on the bounty of his brothers-in-law. I made him my small monthly allowance which cannot possibly have contributed much to his overheads. Nan had no money, so far as I know. She smoked a great deal, and dressed and looked like a gypsy with her shoulder-length dark hair, her face without make-up and a slouching, listless presence which belied the very shrewd intellect which sheltered behind this strange and defensive exterior. I was to discover the complexities of this extraordinary woman many years later.

The MG needed constant attention and, when I spent a weekend with Dad and Nan, I was usually busy with the engine, the gearbox, the transmission or the brakes. Nan joined me in my oily work and gradually we got to know each other. I would take her out to a pub for a drink and a snack. We hired a sailing dinghy from the Sailing Club and messed around on the river. But we always came home to feed Dad. It was much later that I was told he had proposed to Nan, who had said no but that she would remain with him.

CHAPTER SEVEN

A Qualified Flying Instructor: Back with the RAF

In September 1938 I was selected for a four-month course at the Central Flying School at Upavon in Wiltshire. This was a compliment to my flying ability. The Central Flying School – CFS – was the university for flying instructors in the RAF and only those who graduated were let loose on the entry of pupil pilots.

I regarded myself as a well-above-average pilot. I was arrogant and unsympathetic to the dreary briefing of 'Student Reaction', 'Engine Failure', 'Forced Landings' and – with an almost apostolic hush – 'Baling Out'. But I very soon discovered at the hands of my instructors my shortcomings as a pilot over the previous five years. I swallowed my pride and learned. Indeed I relearned much of what I had taken for granted and was soon aware that my future role as a flying instructor required me to teach from basic principles as well as from personal experience. This, to a fighter pilot, took a lot of digestion, but digest it I did, and in four months I became a qualified flying instructor with the highest category awarded.

This was in March 1939, at the time of the belated and frantic expansion of the Royal Air Force as the folly of appeasement with Hitler had at last been accepted by our supine and crass Government. New operational stations were being set up. Thanks to Dowding's unstinting and unrewarded persistence, radar stations were being established along the south-east coast of England. Fighter Command was reinforced and the Hurricane and Spitfire were in volume production. An expanding Air Force required an increasing number of pilots, so new flying training schools were needed. No. 13 Flying Training School was being constructed at Drem in East Lothian, not far from Edinburgh and within a few miles of Gullane. John Grandy had been appointed as the Chief Flying Instructor.

Grandy asked that I should join him as one of his three Flight Commanders. Of the other two, 'Scottie' Pryde was a great character with his roots in Glasgow, and Peter Gibbings was a pleasant but somewhat withdrawn Flight Lieutenant who didn't seem to fit his uniform. Possibly his rather flabby physique gave him the impression of lacking authority. We all wore forage caps in those days, tilted over the right side of the head. Gibbings wore his – a large one – straight over his large head and pulled well down to his ears. He was a well-liked colleague in the Officers' Mess and I got to know him well. Gibbings was a good Flight Commander. As it turned out, many years later, I was to marry Peter's niece, Lois, as my second wife.

My brother Peter was a student at the Edinburgh College of Art. We often met in town with his current girlfriend, Barbara. They would join our pub crawls and meals in a favourite restaurant off Princes Street and they would come to the Officers' Mess for cocktail parties and summer 'open days'. Barbara was a favourite among the junior officers – Peter knew how to pick them – and a group of us dallied frequently in Edinburgh and became regular attenders at the Powder Hall, the greyhound racing stadium.

About a month before No. 13 FTS became operational, Peter Gibbings and I each commanded a training flight of Oxford, twin-engined training aircraft. They were produced by Airspeed in Portsmouth and for several weeks we ferried them up from the south. The Oxford was a good, twin-engined trainer and though I was basically a single-engine pilot I took to the Oxford, which was stable, manoeuvrable and reliable.

So we flew down to Portsmouth, checked our Oxfords and flew them back to Drem. On one occasion I approached Drem in fine weather and good heart. As an aerobatic pilot, I had an impulse to demonstrate that I was not just a twin-engined flying instructor. So I went into a barrel roll almost over the airfield – simply because I wanted to. Concorde has since done one! The Station Commander and John Grandy were on the tarmac when I arrived and I was then confronted with the Station Commander who said, 'MacDonell, you are not a fighter pilot but a flying instructor'. Humiliating. John Grandy said nothing but his wink was all I needed. John and his wife Cecile were wonderful friends: he was also an excellent Chief Flying Instructor and commanded the respect and admiration of all in the Flying Training Squadron.

I found a new excitement in teaching during my tour of duty at Drem. My pupil pilots were varied in both aptitude and social status. Often, the NCO pupils showed more promise than those who had been commis-

sioned. I was to find this staring me in the face when I took command of
a Spitfire squadron in 1940. We trained several pilots who were to
distinguish themselves in the Battle of Britain. I have in mind 'Dutch'
Hugo from South Africa and Anthony Bartley, who married Deborah
Kerr the actress. Anthony became a POW, following a distinguished
period of action as a fighter pilot with Douglas Bader.

The weather in East Lothian was usually ideal for flying training, but
our enemy was the haar, a thick, low-lying fog which inhabited the inner
waters of the Firth of Forth and developed with surprising speed, masking
everything from ground level to a height of 1,000 feet. I had an interest in
meteorology and I was concerned with the combinations of temperature
and pressure variations which produced a haar. It was not good enough to
say, 'Behold the haar' because in all probability a number of our aircraft
would be airborne and some could well be flown solo by pupil pilots. It
was of the utmost importance to be able to predict a haar, preferably at
least an hour before the fog blanket crept in to envelop the airfield.

We were served by nearby Met offices in Leuchars and Dundee and
together we worked out a chart based on temperature and pressure varia-
tion which came to be known locally as the 'Drem Haar Detector'. In
effect it was a forecast of haar probability within about 45 minutes. We
had found that a simple thermometer hoisted onto a mast on the roof of a
hangar gave an early warning of temperature change which proved to be
the key element in haar detection. I am sorry for the two or three airmen
who took it in turns to climb onto the hangar roof and read the
thermometer but I am sure it prevented aircrew without radio contact
with base from finding themselves lost and unable to land safely. We did,
of course, have our casualties but they were modest in comparison with
those of other flying training schools, such as Montrose.

In mid-June 1939 I was granted a fortnight's leave. I had sold my MG,
so I flew an Oxford-load of others going on leave down to Portsmouth to
take trains to their leave destinations. At our refuelling stop in the
Midlands I got a weather report from Gosport. Not good. In fact, pretty
bloody. Knowing the terrain like the back of my hand, I decided to press
on. We lost contact with the ground about fifty miles north of our
destination, but I had worked out a very careful time and distance chart
and did not begin my let-down until I was certain we had cleared the
600-foot escarpment to the north of Gosport and were approaching the
Solent. Everyone had stopped talking. I dropped slowly and steadily
through the overcast to about 500 feet, flying on instruments alone. No
R/T contact with the ground. Then, heaven be praised, a break below and
clear water. We had broken cloud above the Solent. I turned north and
flew a few hundred feet above the water. Conversation began again.

We were over Lee-on-Solent. I decided not to go for Airspeed at Portsmouth but settled for Gosport. I skimmed over the well-known hangar with the catapult on the tarmac and bounced rather clumsily to a halt before taxiing in to the control tower to report our unheralded arrival. Nan had agreed to meet me at Airspeed, but I got a message to her that I was at Gosport, which meant an hour's delay before she was at the Mess. By that time I had drunk quite a lot and she was not best pleased as she drove me the forty-odd miles through the New Forest to Barn Close and Dad. The following day I received a telegram which read 'Congratulations on your scraper ring. Signed: John Grandy'.

The 'scraper ring' was the thin stripe worn between the two broad ones of a Flight Lieutenant to denote the rank of Squadron Leader. My promotion was gazetted in *The Times* the following day. So we celebrated. I was twenty-five. Telephone calls came and even Uncle George sent me a letter of congratulation. He took the opportunity nevertheless of reminding me of my increased responsibilities as a commissioned officer, of the importance of personal discipline and, above all, example. He got another dig at the obligation I had to help support my father and brother and had even gone to the trouble of finding out what my new rate of pay was as a Squadron Leader. He ended his letter by hoping that I would take more interest in my brother Peter and encourage him to drop this 'modern facade' of pseudo-intellectualism and get down to doing a man's job!

So, I returned to Drem to find that my splendid old batman Moran had taken my tunics home where his wife had sewn on the 'scraper rings' of my rank as a Squadron Leader. The Officers' Mess threw a party in celebration and the Station Commander informed me the next morning, hung over and under-slept, that I had been appointed to the Air Ministry in Adastral House, Kingsway, as a Staff Officer in the Directorate of Flying Training. I was in effect to sit behind a desk, pushing a pen. It was, I suppose, inevitable. Since graduating from the Royal Air Force College in 1934 I had had a succession of purely flying appointments. The time had come for me to experience the less exciting role of a staff officer.

CHAPTER EIGHT

London, the Air Ministry, the Phoney War and Romance

The Edinburgh to London night-sleeper operating on the east coast route called at North Berwick on request. Virtually the whole of the Officers' Mess with their wives escorted me to the station. There was also a surprising number of student pilots. As the guard was blowing his whistle, we surged onto the platform. To shouts, yelps and a positive cacophony of valedictory advice and injunctions, the guard blew his whistle for the last time, the engine blasted off and Squadron Leader MacDonell began his journey to London and pen-pushing.

Beaufort Gardens is a well-preserved and well-presented cul-de-sac off the Brompton Road, some five minutes walk from Harrods. Numbers 38 and 39 were run by Mr and Mrs Pace. It was a bed and breakfast deal – and what a breakfast. Mrs Pace's attractive assistant Moira would bring me my breakfast each morning, smiling and chattering happily, hips swinging and breasts barely concealed. An open temptation which I resisted. I took up residence in No. 39 in August 1939. I had never lived on my own before, nor had I lived in London.

The physical impetus of life in London hit me like a huge wave, enveloping and yet uplifting. While the traffic crawled, the people – the humans who were the life-blood pumping in and out of the heart of the city day in day out – ran, jostled, thrust and wove their way to work by the Underground, the buses, the pavements, escalators and lifts. In the morning the pulse thrust inward and in the evening outwards. Only on Sundays was there no perceptible flow either way.

Following the weekday evening exodus, the tempo of life in London gradually changed. There was a more ambling, fluid traffic: restaurants, pubs, theatres, cinemas and night clubs swallowed their nightly diet of young and old, male and female. Later – fulfilled according to their tastes, whether gastronomic, exotic, theatrical, artistic, sexual or any combination of what was on offer – they gradually drifted away to homes, pads, hotels or even the Thames Embankment.

My appointment in the Air Ministry was with the Directorate of Flying Training. The Director of Flying Training was a forty-year-old Wing Commander called 'Tishy' Groves. Tishy was tall and thin with smooth dark hair, dark eyes and clean shaven. The Groves Memorial Prize for flying had been presented to RAF Cranwell by one of Tishy's close relatives. Tishy was impressive in appearance, clear-headed and straight-forward in his leadership of the Department.

He oversaw my work efficiently and somewhat paternally. He apologised for the nature of the work but said it was of importance and had to be carried out with meticulous attention to facts and detail. How right he was. My job, it transpired, was to study every fatal flying accident report; to produce a summary of each report and make recommendations as to whether the cause of the accident required attention to or modification of any aspect of the appropriate flying training manual of instruction. Within a month I was sickened by what I read and the photographs I had to study. The dreadful charred skeleton of a crashed Tiger Moth with the civilian passenger still strapped into the rear seat, his face unrecognisable, his mouth charred in a final agonised scream and his body burnt to a cinder, still haunts me. Surely to God this job wasn't what a twenty-five-year-old Squadron Leader in full flying practice was expected to contribute to an international situation which was escalating.

Tishy and I got on well and he was sympathetic. He said he would do what he could to get me moved, even though he was pleased with my work. He took me to lunch at Romano's in the Strand where he had a reserved table each day. We drank champagne and ate extravagantly. Back in the office I realised that Tishy – who for the first half-hour after the lunch break always appeared to be absorbed in reading my and others' reports, his head in his hands and his elbows on the desk – was fast asleep.

To be in the Air Ministry during the summer and early autumn of 1939 was to be privy to the evidence – as opposed to propaganda and media conjecture – of the imminence of war with Nazi Germany. This overlaid every other consideration. My own distaste for my role was subordinated by the enormous military and constitutional problems which the inevitable war would create.

Then, in August, a non-aggression pact was signed in Moscow between Nazi Germany and the Soviet Union. Though few realised it at the time, Stalin – at a stroke of his pen – had revoked his widely trumpeted anti-

Fascist pact merely to buy himself time. For Europe it was to prove catastrophic, freeing Hitler's hands for an immediate invasion of Poland. So I continued with my gruesome analyses of fatal flying accidents, with my mind on what I now believed to be unavoidable.

During the last week of August, Dad had been admitted to a London hospital for a prostate operation. The following week was to rock virtually the whole world.

Dolfuss had been assassinated in Austria, which had then become a vassal state of Hitler's Germany. Czechoslovakia had been annexed on the pretext of defending the interests of the Sudeten Germans who occupied the south of the country. Next was Poland. Hitler invaded in the last week of August, secure in the German–Soviet non-aggression pact and confident that the British–French alliance with Poland would amount to nothing. He had Neville Chamberlain's concession over Czechoslovakia to support his judgement. So, Poland was invaded and with Hitler's hitherto invincible *Luftwaffe* and the armoured might of the *Wehrmacht*, Poland was swiftly bombed and blasted into submission.

Hitler now had an open door to France through Belgium and the Low Countries and ready access to Scandinavia. The British response was surprisingly swift. On 1 September 1939, Neville Chamberlain, the 'Dupe of Munich', having spent the previous week consulting our French allies, delivered a 48-hour joint ultimatum to Hitler, demanding the withdrawal of all ground forces from Poland and an end to hostilities. As we all expected, this ultimatum was rejected. On 3 September, Prime Minister Chamberlain announced to the world that a state of war existed between Great Britain and Germany.

There was one day left before the expiry of the Anglo-French ultimatum. We wore plain clothes in the Air Ministry but had been instructed to report for duty in uniform if war was declared. So I polished my buttons, cleaned my shoes and dusted off my peaked uniform cap. I bought a new black tie and uniform shirt from Gieves. London was more or less holding its breath.

THE PHONEY WAR

September 3rd 1939 was a Sunday. Shortly after eleven o'clock the Prime Minister made his historic announcement over the radio. I went to bring my uniform in from the long section of the L-shaped wardrobe on the half-landing of my civilian digs in Chelsea. The other end of the wardrobe was for the room next to mine. The door of that room opened and an extremely attractive girl – tall, long-limbed, with huge hazel eyes and shoulder-length straight golden hair – emerged. We looked at each other.

'Hello.'

'Hello.'

'I'm Donald MacDonell.'

'I'm Diana Keane.' An upper-class English accent. 'You're in the RAF.'

'That's right. What are you doing?'

'I'm working in a canteen: lunches only.'

An impulse grabbed me. 'Are you doing anything this evening if we aren't all blown sky-high?'

'No, I'm not.'

'Would you have dinner with me in the RAF Club? I'll be back here about 6.30.'

'Yes, thanks. I'd like to.'

We smiled at each other and returned to our rooms.

I left in haste, hoping to find a taxi but no sooner had I turned into Brompton Road than the air-raid sirens broke into their first and terrifying wail – a sound we were to come to live with. Most people ran hither and thither. Some stood like statues, gazing up into the sky like crowds at an air display. My concern was to get to the Air Ministry at Adastral House, Kingsway, as quickly as possible. Buses roared by, taxis didn't stop. I stepped off the pavement as an open two-seater sports car raced up Brompton Road. It must have been my uniform that brought the driver to a screeching halt a few yards ahead of where I stood. 'Where do you want to go?' the driver shouted. 'Kingsway.' 'Okay, jump in, I'm trying to reach the City.' Middle-aged, red-faced, expensive suit, broad grin, ginger hair all over the place. I jumped in. He drove like a man possessed, but confidently and competently. We overtook everything, roared up Piccadilly with horn blaring, swerved anticlockwise round Piccadilly Circus, and were doing well over 60mph past Charing Cross and up the Aldwych. He dropped me at Adastral House and was off again almost before I had climbed out.

The main door was closed. I banged on it until it was opened by a frightened-looking guard who, seeing my uniform, let me in. 'They're all downstairs in the basement,' he said. 'But you're not to use the lift. That's the order.' So I went down the stairs where a motley crush of uniformed officers and civil servants, clerks and typists thronged and jostled. 'Where's the bombing?' someone asked. 'What bombing?' A frightened, elderly woman cut in: 'There's bombing going on. You can hear it.' 'It's been going on for half an hour.' 'It sounds close. You must have heard it.' 'That's right, heavy bombing,' asserted a fat man in a shiny suit. 'I know heavy bombing when I hear it.' He offered no explanation for his superior knowledge. 'Heavy bombing,' he repeated, 'That's what it is.' At that moment a young male clerk with a spotty face joined us. 'Them's not bombs,' he said, 'them's a door bangin': that bleedin' metal door on the file store,' he announced with a triumphant grin. 'It always bangs in the draught if it's left open. I know 'cos I works there, see'. He smirked and moved off. There was no more 'heavy bombing' and shortly afterwards we were told the 'All Clear' had been sounded and we made for our offices.

The first day of the War had started like a damp squib. The 'enemy' proved to be a civil aircraft on an unscheduled flight from France to Hendon. As it was Sunday, the Director said we could go home after lunch but we were to remain on telephone call until 6.30 pm.

Shortly after five o'clock, I heard Diana go into her room next to mine. I waited impatiently until six when I crossed the half-landing and knocked on her door.

'Come in.' She was sitting reading and rose as I entered. She wore a short black dress with a golden girdle casually gathered round her waist. In high-heeled shoes she looked taller than I had expected. Her hands were long and well shaped. She had beautiful legs and her hair was groomed and gleaming, her long page-boy cut suiting her long neck and square shoulders. We exchanged pleasantries and moved into my room, where I poured drinks. We found a taxi which took us to the Royal Air Force Club where the restaurant manager gave us a corner table for two.

We talked about ourselves. Her family was Anglo-Irish. Her father had died in a shooting accident a few years before. Her mother was of the English aristocracy. Their home in Ireland was Belleville Park in Cappoquin, County Waterford. Diana's mother owned a flat in Draycott Avenue, Chelsea, which was let at the time. She intended to come to London in a few weeks. Meanwhile, Diana was lodging in 39 Beaufort Gardens. I was not surprised when she told me she had been a model in Harrods for two years before the War. She was twenty-four when I met her. I was twenty-five.

We said goodnight formally. I think we shook hands. I had a better night but Diana was much in my mind.

So began the 'phoney war'. Following general mobilisation, those of us in the armed forces wore uniform.

'*You must see London under a blackout,*' wrote my father to my brother the following Saturday. '*It would be dreadful not to be able to have seen the ultimate result of the two Cs (Civilization & Christianity). After dark London is like some boggy grotto with little blue, red and yellow glow worms (taxi and bus lights) floating through space. ...*

Later he describes how we all dined at the Royal Air Force Club and were turned out at 9.30.

'... *We pulled the taxi up at a spot where used to be the hospitable double doors of the Club. Donald pushed furtively on a closed door. Half the door opened exposing a dim light such as issues from the door of a Russian church at the midnight service, ghostly figures groped this way in the distant corridor. The door snapped to behind us. I was pushed up a darkened staircase and one entered the Ladies Lounge. Half a dozen standard lamps burning bluish lights gave the impression of a spiritualistic séance. After Pimms for the others and a glass of cold water for me we stumbled along a dark corridor to the dining room where we consumed an excellent dinner which we could not see. On a cold night when all windows can be closed the bright light is promised again but with open windows the heavy dark curtains are apt to flap and expose a shaft of light that might tell Hitler where we are if he cares to know. The drive home was an experience. I could not have driven that car and during the short mile we heard two crashes. Vivian says he walks a mile rather than cross the road. Experts tell us that in ten years time we shall have developed a special mole sense or long whisker like a blind moth. No war news. I have, just 12.30 pm, got Warsaw on the wireless and they were still talking Polish, so the German (sic) are not yet there.'*

Diana and I went out together and we went to parties held by her friends and mine. I found that my hosts and particularly my young hostesses regarded me, a uniformed squadron leader, as adding lustre to their parties. I became much in demand and was frequently introduced as 'Have you met our "Squew El"?'

We were both lovers of ballet, so we went to Covent Garden. We liked dancing and often frequented the Café de Paris which later got a direct hit by a bomb during the night raids in the winter of 1940, killing a large number of merrymakers, 'Snake Hips' Johnston and most of his Band. We were young, carefree and not too committed. We kissed spontaneously.

CHAPTER NINE

The Outbreak
of War

THE WAR BEGINS IN EARNEST

By June 1940 the phoney war ended. The German army had invaded Belgium and outflanked the northern wing of the Maginot Line. The British Expeditionary Force had put up stiff resistance; the French army, demoralised and disaffected, fell back and began to crumble. The Germans, with the full support of the *Luftwaffe*, swept westward. The retreat of the British force to the Channel ports began. France pleaded for additional Hurricane squadrons to be sent out to augment those we had provided in support of the Allied forces. Churchill required Fighter Command to fly out eight squadrons which Dowding stated emphatically would reduce the fighter defences of the United Kingdom to an unacceptable level. At an historic and bitter meeting with Churchill, the Chief of the Air Staff, the Air Minister and other Service chiefs, Dowding, a taciturn man, known as 'Stuffy', laid the plain truth in terms of simple mathematics on the table. He then placed his pencil on his pad and sat back, silent. Churchill havered but eventually accepted what he saw before him. He compromised with a smaller reinforcement of Hurricanes for France, but from then on he was Dowding's enemy. Dowding suffered accordingly but he won the Battle of Britain, for which Churchill took most of the credit.

By now I was busy exploiting my contacts with the Postings department in Adastral House. With Tishy's full approval, I openly lobbied my colleagues for a posting to a fighter squadron. Week followed week and nothing happened.

The evacuation from Dunkirk had somehow been accomplished. The 51st Highland Division had been surrounded and most of them made prisoners of war. The Hurricane squadrons in France had been decimated, their remnants returned, disillusioned and demoralised to be rested and re-formed in the UK. Our situation was desperate; our plight unimaginable.

And then I got it. No. 64 Squadron, equipped with Spitfires, had lost its commanding officer over Dunkirk. He was replaced by a small, oldish Squadron Leader who, for medical reasons, was unfit to operate at high altitude. He too needed replacing. I got the job.

After a short conversion course onto Spitfires at Aston Down, I was ready to take over command but I was informed I wasn't to take over 64 Squadron. I was to be the first CO of an entirely new concept in fighter aircraft. In short, I was to work up a squadron equipped with a single-seater, twin-engined fighter, the Westland Whirlwind. So, I was 'converted' to Blenheims to give me experience of twin-engined fighters. I was furious.

The Whirlwind proved an unmitigated disaster which was quickly recognised by the Air Staff. It was taken out of the front line. At low altitude it was fair enough. Its armament was equivalent to that of the Spitfire and Hurricane but, above 15,000 feet, its performance fell off dramatically. It would have been suicide to have used it in the ensuing Battle of Britain and mercifully it was relegated to a night-fighter role. I pleaded limited night-flying experience which was borne out by my log book and, after further lobbying and string pulling, I succeeded in recovering 64 Squadron, which was still without a serviceable commanding officer. So, with enormous relief, I was despatched to Kenley, a front-line fighter sector station near Caterham in Surrey.

While at Aston Down I had met and become friends with Art Donahue, an American civilian pilot. He had somehow joined the RAFVR in Canada and was, I believe, the first American citizen to volunteer for flying duties in the RAF. In June 1940 the United States was neutral. After I had left to command 64 Squadron, Art asked if he could be posted to serve with me. He served me with great loyalty and gallantry. He became the 'pet' of the Squadron. He was a little over five feet tall with close-cropped, blond hair and bright blue eyes. He was killed in 1942. His book *Tally Ho* is dedicated to me.

At that time Kenley was a two-squadron station. Wing Commander Prickman was the Station Commander, a first-class officer and leader. Squadron Leader Norman was the Sector Controller. There was an elderly and eccentric Flight Lieutenant in charge of airfield discipline and safety. He was a Christian Scientist and preached his beliefs incessantly, off duty and on. I was to meet his son in the British Embassy in Moscow when I was appointed Air Attaché some sixteen years later.

My arrival at Kenley was not auspicious. The CO whom I was to relieve was an ill man and looked it. He was courteous enough but unwelcoming.

He introduced me to the Squadron officers in the Mess that evening. I was none too happy with what I saw. No. 64, a pre-war squadron, had recently been re-equipped with Spitfires in replacement of obsolescent Blenheims. The Squadron had been badly mauled during the Dunkirk patrols where it had lost its leader. Morale was low and there was no corporate spirit in the Officers' Mess. I was told by the CO that I would meet the NCO pilots and ground crew on the following day. The Squadron consisted of two Flights of six aircraft, each with a Flight Lieutenant in command. One Flight Commander had recently returned from hospital with wounds in his head from a cannon strike. The other was suffering from nervous exhaustion.

One or two of the junior officers were showing signs of bloody-mindedness. One was insolent and bordering on the insubordinate. The CO and I went to talk privately in his room. He explained that until he himself was posted as unfit to fly I was to be supernumerary. He would continue to lead the Squadron. This suited me fine. I needed time to get to grips with what was to be my team. Something was wrong and it was imperative I find out the reason as quickly as possible. I asked his opinion but he hedged. He did explain the tactics he had evolved for the patrols over the Channel and gave me a certain amount of confidential information about the personal capabilities of the pilots. He hardly mentioned the NCOs. I formed the opinion that the whole situation was too much for him. I had one hell of a job to do to pull the team together before the real fighting began.

The Squadron was operating mainly on patrols over the Channel, protecting the slow-moving convoys coming in from the Atlantic. They were sitting targets for the *Luftwaffe's Stuka* dive bombers which attacked them relentlessly but without much success. The number of ships which got through the strait and made the docks at Tilbury was remarkably high.

We were called to 'readiness' at dawn, which was about 4 am. The CO had me as his No. 2. He adopted a pre-war tight formation which required considerable concentration on station keeping, allowing little or no chance to scan outwards, above or below. I didn't like it. We flew Channel patrols for a week: we seemed always to be late over the convoy and only on a few occasions were in time to engage the *Stukas*. We destroyed a few, but the Squadron scattered and engaged the Bf 109s which were always in attendance. We lost two pilots before the CO was posted to a staff job and I was officially appointed as CO of 64 Squadron.

CHAPTER TEN

The Battle of Britain: Early Skirmishes

W e all knew that a massive air assault on the convoys, the port installations and the south-east fighter stations was imminent. During a 'stand down' period, I got the whole Squadron together and we talked the situation through. I didn't like the close formation and said so. Most of the pilots agreed. One, however, a brash, self-opinionated junior officer, disagreed: indeed he disagreed with everything I proposed, and offensively. I smacked him down hard and he looked daggers. I instructed him to report to me when the meeting was over. I noticed the non-commissioned officers looking at him none too kindly.

I laid down the ground rules for the next patrol of my Squadron, No. 64(F). I set out on the wall chart the formation we were to adopt. I appointed a senior NCO pilot to lead one of the Flights, as the Flight Commander was off sick, and I left for my office. The rebellious young officer arrived and saluted insultingly. I took him through what I expected of him, word by word. I let him have it for a good twenty minutes. I instructed him to fly as my No. 2 and to remain with me throughout the next day's patrol. He was to take off with me early to practise a mock dogfight, each one manoeuvring to get onto the other's tail. I told him I should be an easy target for him as I hadn't the experience in a Spitfire that he had.

He and I were in our cockpits at 5 am the next morning. We had climbed into the cloudless July sky over the Thames estuary to 15,000 feet when I said, 'Okay, off we go.' I gave him several chances but he was seldom on my tail. I then turned the tables. Within minutes I had him in my sights. I called him in to station beside me and we returned to base and landed. At first he wouldn't look at me. Later, we spoke. He listened to my advice but his eyes were hard. He never liked me, was a bad influence among the junior officers and contributed little to the battle honours of the Squadron. Until he was posted away several months later, he remained a thorn in my side. In the context of personal relations, he was one of my few failures during the command of my Squadron.

For the better part of a week the Squadron was under no great pressure. We destroyed a few *Stukas* during our Channel patrols but I noticed that, after we had broken off engagement, the Squadron scattered in all directions. I had led them out to the battle area, but they came home in whatever way they wished. So, after we had attacked a formation of *Stukas* over a convoy off Dover, I ordered over the RT, 'Re-form and return to base.' No one appeared but I noticed what I recognised as a Spitfire heading northeast over the North Foreland. I opened up to full throttle and pursued it, a thousand feet below to avoid detection. Gradually I overhauled the Spitfire. I drew abreast and recognised my own Squadron insignia – SH. I closed with him. I recognised the pilot. 'Follow me to base,' I ordered and turned to port, he following astern. We flew back to Kenley. 'What on earth were you up to?' I asked him, 'Why didn't you re-form and return with me when I called? Did you get my message?' 'It was distorted.' I asked him why he had broken out to the North Sea. What was his object in doing so? He answered evasively. He thought there might be other *Stukas* off the entrance to the Thames Estuary.

I lost my temper. I declared my intention to operate a squadron, a cohesive unit, not a gang of individuals doing their own thing. He said he was sorry but you could catch stragglers if you went out and looked for them. The lone rider failed to return from a very hairy engagement with *Stukas* and Bf 109s a fortnight later, by which time the Battle of Britain had begun in earnest.

I believe I had succeeded in pulling my Squadron together. But I was short of a Flight Commander, off sick, and my other one was in poor shape. I concentrated on the NCO pilots. I found them an intelligent, united team with good ideas about fighter tactics and the strengths and weaknesses of the enemy aircraft. I talked with them frequently. They responded openly and I learned much from them. I spotted several who were of commissioned officer calibre and, against all the protocol of rank, I gave the ablest the temporary command of one of my Flights. He distinguished himself.

I made time to visit the Maintenance Hangar and to get to know the NCOs and airmen who were the fitters, riggers, armourers and electricians, without whom we would never have got off the ground.

As a Sector Station, Kenley had its own Sector Operations Room under the control of Squadron Leader Norman. I made it a custom to visit the Ops Room as often as possible, especially following a particularly heavy engagement. Though the plotters might well have been wholly preoccupied with further incoming raids, there was always one very attractive WAAF who brought me a cup of coffee and said, 'Glad it went all right, sir,' even if it hadn't.

Integrating the three officers who were not pilots was also essential. They were the Technical Officer, an able Flight Lieutenant of the RAF Technical Branch whom the ground crew respected and admired; the Intelligence Officer, who was a Flying Officer in his forties with a fascinating background of tea planting in Ceylon; and the Squadron Adjutant, a young and recently commissioned officer who worked tirelessly to keep the administration of the Squadron functioning properly. These three were in the Squadron but not somehow part of it. They were affectionately known as 'the Three Stooges'. I wanted to identify them more closely with the Squadron. We agreed to accord them a pecking order in accordance with their ages, not their ranks. So, the Intelligence Officer, Fagan, became No. 1 Stooge, the Technical Officer Gittens No. 2, and Towers the Squadron Adjutant, No. 3. The idea caught on. The three Stooges greeted each other at breakfast: 'Morning, No. 1', 'Morning, No. 2.' 'Morning, No. 3'. The thing became a custom which other squadrons we were teamed up with found quite incomprehensible.

By now the Battle of Britain had converted the cloudless and wonderful summer of July into a battlefield of bombers and fighters, with the staccato rattle of machine guns and the slower, venomous crack of cannon fire. The war in the air burst over the south-east of England and the approaches to London. Whatever degree of preparedness my Squadron had reached, the time had come and for better or worse we were in at the deep end.

The summer of 1940 burned on, cloudless and intensely hot. Our normal routine, two days out of three with an afternoon stand down on the fourth, was to come to readiness at our Squadron dispersal point at four o'clock each morning, either to be scrambled to intercept an early enemy raid or, more usually, to take off at first light and deploy to Hawkinge, our advance base a short distance north of Folkestone on the Kent coast. Here we would remain at readiness for convoy patrols or any other action called by telephone from Kenley.

Short of sleep as we were, I found a sense of calm during our flights to Hawkinge. The Kent countryside was bathed in a light mantle of morning mist. The low sun was soft and kindly. The eternal pale blue sky above was slowly shedding the gloom of the night and a few stars still shone before they grew dim and disappeared. It was peace – not war.

It was 4.30 in the morning. I looked at my Squadron in formation behind and beside me, each Spitfire seemingly motionless in the still, cloud-free sky. I looked with affection more than pride. The sheer beauty of the Spitfire, a poem of grace which contained a fighting man and an armoury of devastating destruction. They belonged to me.

We floated south-east at 15,000 feet. We maintained RT silence and I relaxed in my cockpit, lulled by the deep, muted pulse and thrust of the Merlin engine which swept me onwards to the Kent coast. We broke into 'Flights' over Hawkinge and landed on the grass airfield where the ground crews were ready with the refuelling bowsers.

Too short the flight; the benison of silence and quiet contemplation. On the ground we slumped into chairs in the dispersal hut. Most of us snoozed off. Usually, a second squadron landed shortly after us, either Spitfires or Hurricanes. They taxied to the other end of the airfield and refuelled, and we all settled down for the telephone to ring.

I was still not entirely happy about the battle-worthiness of my Squadron. True they had become a far more cohesive fighting unit. They were all brave young men. There were, however, a few who sought glory in individual exploits and found it well nigh impossible to stay with the tactics we had worked out and agreed. All but one paid the price of their recklessness. This upset me a great deal and I talked over my troubles with No. 1, who had become a wonderful ally.

The success of my Squadron was due in no small measure to the counsel, advice and caution of No. 1. He became more than my Intelligence Officer: he became a close and valued friend. We would talk at the end of the day in my room in the Mess, discussing our effectiveness as a squadron. We shared confidences and he and I identified the weak links in the chain. From his position as an observer and an interrogator, No. 1 became invaluable to me in more ways than I realised at the time. It was he who drew my attention to a Sergeant Pilot who was breaking up, though determined not to quit. I took the pilot off operations and he went to a 'convalescent' unit. No. 1 also confirmed my suspicions that a junior officer was 'playing safe' and breaking off when the going got too hot.

Most of the non-commissioned pilots had enlisted before the War: they had discipline, guts and a loyalty to me which was both uplifting and humbling. My officers were a mixture of talented individualists who related closely enough in the Mess but were 'way out' in the air, and a cadre of less high-spirited young men, most of whom were married. Until I fell for it myself, I regarded marriage as none-too-welcome. As the battle over the south-east of England gathered in intensity, we became an effective fighting unit. Our 'score' began to build up but casualties inevitably occurred and losses on both sides grew heavier. Our maintenance team, under the unremitting guidance and leadership of No. 2, worked round the clock making good the damaged aircraft that had succeeded in landing back at Kenley. Many didn't and replacements were flown in by ferry pilots, both male and female.

My losses in pilots were mounting and their replacements seldom maintained my front-line strength of eighteen. Few of them had more than twelve or fifteen hours in Spitfires. None had flown in battle formation and one, a nineteen-year-old Canadian sergeant, had never fired his guns. There simply wasn't time to train them. I sneaked the odd thirty minutes from our Sector Controller when there was nothing on the plotting table and took the newcomers up with me to let them get on my tail. I took the minimum of avoiding action to build up their confidence. But it was pitifully inadequate.

For their first few sorties I flew them as number three pilots under an experienced Section Leader who instilled in them the vital need to stay with him whatever happened. Thus we probably saved a number of totally inexperienced newcomers from becoming casualties.

We were forced back to Kenley when the *Luftwaffe* switched their attacks from convoys to our fighter bases and radar stations. We were scrambled on 25 July to deal with one of the last *Stuka* attacks on a large convoy off Dover. I had a young Sergeant Pilot as my No. 3 and Art Donahue as my No. 2. We found the convoy under heavy *Stuka* attack escorted by a fair number of Bf 109s, with the *Stukas* coming in from about 10,000 feet. I brought my Squadron in from up-sun at 12,000 feet and attacked first as the *Stukas* began their dives. With air brakes out, the *Stuka* could dive vertically at a relatively low speed, far, far slower than a diving Spitfire. I and my two wingmen rolled over, cut back on power and dived after a gaggle of *Stukas*. We plummeted down, got in a quick burst, did no harm and dived past them. But the *Stuka* was a dead duck after it had released its bombs and pulled screaming out of its dive.

We levelled out at 3,000 feet and circled over the convoy. Only one ship appeared to have been hit and a skein of *Stukas* was waddling back towards France. We got three of them. I went for the one in the middle, leaving the others for my No. 2 and No. 3. I knocked mine down but felt a thump while I was firing. A lot of tracer was snaking up at me as I closed. The *Stuka* turned over and plunged into the Channel. I called my Squadron and ordered them back over the convoy where further *Stuka* attacks were being made. The Bf 109s now came down and mixed it with us. It developed into a dogfight.

I lost sight of Art, but my No. 2 was still with me. I gave him a thumbs up. I then became aware of an uncomfortable smell and fumes in my cockpit. We were about twelve miles off Dover. I scanned my instrument panel. The oil temperature gauge was climbing alarmingly and the coolant was at maximum. I had obviously been hit somewhere in the engine. I throttled back, radioed that I was making for Hawkinge and watched things getting worse and worse on the instrument panel. I made Dover at about 3,000 feet. The ack-ack opened up at me but, as usual, missed. I throttled back again and was just maintaining height as I approached Hawkinge. Then the engine clattered to a halt and things began to look very awkward indeed. Somehow, with my cockpit full of fumes and unbearably hot, I succeeded in gliding powerless over the trees on the downwind edge of the airfield. I lowered my undercarriage at the last moment but left the flaps up to help maintain height. I was unable to open the cockpit canopy. I plonked down halfway across the airfield with my airscrew motionless. I applied brakes, which worked, and came to rest about 50 yards from the far boundary.

Get out quick! Things were smelling extremely hot and clouds of fumes were coming into the cockpit. I grabbed the hood-release handle and pulled hard. It didn't move. I yanked as hard as I could with both hands. It was jammed. Nothing I could do would move it. I hit at the perspex hood with my fists but that didn't work. I was gripped by cold terror. Not this, dear God – not fire. I tried to attract attention from the ground crew at the other end of the airfield. Then a small truck came out from the dispersal area but it headed towards the northern perimeter.

Things were cooling off in the cockpit. I began to relax.

A Hurricane came limping low over the hangars, wheels and flaps down. It made an approach across wind and was too low and flying too slowly. It hit the top of the generator station, crashed just inside the perimeter and burst into flames. I watched helplessly as the fire tender, ambulance and other vehicles rushed to the blazing wreck. It was soon over. The pilot had been the Squadron Commander of our sister squadron. They said later that he had been mortally wounded over the Channel in combat with an Bf 109. They said he had probably passed out just before he crashed. I hope to God they were right.

I was released unharmed from my cockpit some ten minutes later. I jumped out, thanked the fire team and was violently sick.

My Spitfire was towed to the maintenance hangar. The Flight Sergeant in charge diagnosed a bullet strike in the coolant system. He said it would require an engine change. How long to complete the work? 'Ready by midday tomorrow, sir.' They had a couple of spare Merlins in crates. I thanked him warmly and said I would have a pilot available to fly the aircraft back to Kenley some time during the following forenoon. I then contacted Kenley Operations Room by landline and spoke with Norman, the Sector Controller. He was relieved that I was okay. There were still two of my Squadron missing. It looked as though we had destroyed at least six enemy aircraft, possibly more. How was I to get back to Kenley? Norman suggested I stay overnight at Hawkinge.

No, I didn't like that at all. Was the two-seater training Magister available? Yes. Could he send it down? He hesitated. It was unarmed and still painted in orange 'Dayglow'. But there was nothing on the plotting board; he would get one of my pilots down to Hawkinge in the Magister which I would fly back. The pilot would stay overnight and bring back the Spitfire when the engine change was completed. An hour later, a sensible Sergeant Pilot landed in the Magister which he had flown at tree-top height, dumped his overnight kit, grinned me a good-luck farewell, and I took off for Kenley.

I hugged the Ashford main line and was so low that the smoke and steam from the locomotive of a London-bound train actually threw my little yellow aircraft about like a leaf. The flight seemed endless. At last the white chalk quarry just short of Whyteleaf station; turn 90 degrees to port, over the Kenley hump and touch down at last on the short runway.

There was no further news of my two missing pilots, one a Pilot Officer recently posted to the Squadron and the other a Sergeant Pilot.

No. 1 was adamant that I take the evening off. There had been a sudden deterioration in the weather with a blanket of low cloud over Kent and Sussex. We were at stand down from four o'clock, other than a midnight patrol which was flown by my most experienced night-flying pilot. No. 1 insisted that I go to London. He was aware of my interest in Diana. I phoned her.

We met at her mother's flat soon after seven o'clock. Mrs Keane had returned to London and Diana occupied her very comfortable bedsitter in 8 Cadogan Court. She looked particularly beautiful when I arrived. We were becoming very attached to each other.

Mrs Keane approved of me, having been assured by Diana that I was suitable. She was a Lumley-Smith before her marriage to Henry Keane, an Irish landowner and entrepreneur in County Tipperary. He had succeeded in avoiding having his house, Belleville Park, destroyed during the 'bad times' by giving refuge and accommodation in turn both to the Black and Tans and the Irish rebels. He was commissioned as a Colonel by the British and made a CBE which was, to say the least, extraordinary.

Diana and I had become very close indeed but we agreed not to make love. While I had an extraordinary faith in my own invincibility – a sort of 'it can't possibly happen to me' – I knew deep down in my heart that any day might be my last.

In the months of July and August we lost several pilots, among them O'Meara – an Irishman. One of the mavericks, Dawson-Paul, from the Fleet Air Arm, was picked out of the Channel by the Germans, very badly wounded and he died in captivity. He was an outstanding young man who walked like a panther and struck like a snake. His mother lived in a flat close to Mrs Keane. I visited her to offer such comfort as I could. She wept in my arms. When I joined Diana in her room I too collapsed and cried in her arms like a child.

Mass daylight bombing raids with fighter escorts occurred daily and often three or four times a day, we were stretched to our limits. Replacement aircraft and pilots were put into the air almost before they had been checked out. Once we were scrambled late in the day. I had nine aircraft, four of which had been delivered that day and were without our Squadron letters, and had not had the synchronisation of their eight guns checked. Their pilots were barely able to handle their aircraft. Mercifully we were not engaged and for the following two days the weather broke with heavy overcast and nothing on the Operations Room plotting board.

During the first fortnight of August 1940 we were engaged two or three times a day. Once we were scrambled five times. I was credited with four more enemy aircraft destroyed, all Bf 109s – and our Squadron tally began to look pretty healthy.

The new pilots were beginning to settle down. Their morale was splendid and they were being looked after and given invaluable advice by their elder brethren. A few of them began to chalk up victories. One came home to Kenley with over six cannon strikes in his fuselage and was over the moon at his 'wounds'. No. 2 was not so pleased but his team patched up the Spitfire which was serviceable at first light the following morning. As a Squadron we had never felt fitter or more confident.

I went to London a few evenings later. Diana and I went to a ballet in Covent Garden and had a late supper in Soho. We said goodnight under the station clock before I caught the last train back to Whyteleaf. I said, 'Diana, will you marry me?'

She paused and then replied, 'Do you really mean it?'

I said yes, I did, and she smiled her broad and lovely acknowledgement.

'Yes,' she said, 'I would like to very much.'

I slept like a log that night.

We decided not to announce our engagement for a while. I think we were both aware that emotions could be out of control under the stress of war and that we hadn't really thought out our future, always assuming I survived the War. So we kept our secret, though I suspect Diana's mother knew what was afoot. I didn't tell Dad but I hinted to No. 1 (who had met Diana) that I was thinking of asking Diana to marry me. He thought it was a splendid idea but quite sternly counselled me to ease up and not burn myself out. I was twenty-six and he thought, and hoped, that before long I would be promoted and moved out of the front line.

My log book shows that I shot down a *Stuka* and a Bf 109 on 29 July. It was also our best Squadron record to date. In all we accounted for ten enemy aircraft and the total broadcast by the BBC for the whole of Fighter Command was around eighty, for the loss of thirty-odd of our own. I was in London that evening with Diana. We were walking down Park Lane when a group came up to us and cried, 'Eighty of the bastards shot down.' Diana said, 'Yes, and he was one of the Spitfire pilots in the battle.' They hoisted me onto their shoulders and carried me to the RAF Club. I couldn't invite them in as they were fairly drunk, but it was quite an occasion.

I shot down another Bf 109 on 5 August. This was a life and death joust. Our mounts were pretty evenly matched though the enemy's cannon was a devastating weapon. We met after a mêlée involving *Heinkel* III bombers, which were attacking the docks off Tilbury, and a substantial escort of Bf 109s. I spotted him in my rear mirror as I broke away from a flank attack on one of the bombers. I broke away hard and he crossed over me and I turned in, unsure where he was. We then met head on, both firing but with his cannon shells luckily passing over my cockpit. I don't think my head-on attack hit him. It was all too quick and impulsive. We then took stock of the situation and circled each other warily. We were pretty equal in a dogfight. The 109 could outdive the Spitfire but this wasn't an occasion for evasion. My opponent was clearly bent on knocking me down. We circled, closer and closer. Once he opened fire with his cannon in a beam attack. I ducked under his fire and found myself below him and turning fast. I managed a few seconds burst with my eight Brownings and I think I hit him. For a moment he hesitated but I was past him and on his beam. Not a healthy situation.

I pulled up with full boost and flattened out with him climbing and turning towards me. He then made his fatal mistake. He flicked over into a half-roll and began a steep climb to my starboard and slightly astern. I pulled up and over and for a moment had him in my sights. I gave him a five-second burst and saw the tracer raking him. He began to smoke and then went into an inverted dive. His cockpit canopy flew off and shortly afterwards the pilot fell out, His parachute opened and he fell away below. We had fought over Kent, so I hope he was taken prisoner.

His aircraft dived vertically into a field in Kent, shearing the branches off one side of an oak tree before it buried itself deep in the ground at its base. Some twenty-five years later, I and my daughter Lindsay, with a team of young enthusiasts, excavated most of the Bf 109. My thoughts were largely about what happened to the pilot.

CHAPTER ELEVEN

The Battle of Britain: Baling Out over Sussex

August 16th broke overcast and raining. I went into the Operations Room, drank my coffee and looked at an enemy-free plotting board. Norman and I chatted for a while. I returned to the Squadron, who were at 'thirty minutes available'. We were almost immediately brought to readiness. Sector Operations said there was a large build-up of enemy aircraft over Calais and already several plots were moving north.

Our sister Squadron, No. 615, Hurricanes, was already airborne and I got the Spitfires into the air some fifteen minutes later. As usual, I gained height over Kenley and then, still climbing fast, reached 15,000 feet over the Canterbury area. We had penetrated some 5,000 feet of cloud and were somewhat scattered when we broke through but were quickly back in battle formation. Then we saw them: three large formations of *Heinkel* III bombers. They were about a thousand feet above us and to the west, heading presumably towards London. We were down-sun and still climbing.

I could see the Bf 109 escorts weaving above the bombers and liked the situation even less. I ordered 'Buster' which was full throttle without the final surge of going 'through the gate', which gave the engine maximum boost and was an emergency extra for only a few minutes. We climbed and turned level with the nearest bomber formation.

Then the leading *Heinkel* group altered course slowly to the west, followed by the rest. We closed on the rear formation and had spread out to attack when my rearguard called 'Snappers', the code word for attack by enemy fighters. We broke and faced them just in time. There were dozens of them. Their formation had its engine cowlings painted bright yellow back to the cockpit. I instinctively fed this into my mental computer and then we were fighting for our lives. Outnumbered and down-sun, it was amazing that we weren't all knocked out of the sky.

But the German regimentation probably saved us. They were flying 'finger four' formations. Basically, this consisted of two pairs making up the four. The leader was covered by his number two who flew wide and slightly astern. The next pair adopted the same formation abeam of the leading pair. Only two of the four were attackers; the other two were defensive. It was relatively easy to knock down the supporters but not that easy to avoid the attackers, who were usually seasoned and excellent fighter pilots.

We were lucky. We lost three aircraft and two pilots but took a substantial toll of the yellow-nosed group, who seemed bent on retaining their formation. We accounted for six confirmed destroyed and several 'probables' and 'damaged'. The bomber swarm had been attacked by at least two Hurricane squadrons and had continued to turn to port. The cloud over the south-east of England remained unbroken and the attackers swung round south towards France apparently without dropping their bombs. I just had time to note a number of the *Heinkels* falling out of formation with smoking engines. One blew up like a bomb. Another turned turtle and plunged into the cloud. There were several parachutes falling towards the cloud and a Hurricane ablaze below me as I swerved away from a very aggressive 109. He fired his cannon, missed me and dived away.

Then suddenly all was still. The fight was over. The bombers with their escorts had disappeared into the cloud and a mixed assortment of Spitfires and Hurricanes put their noses down and scattered in a north-westerly direction to their bases. It was pointless trying to unite my Squadron so I joined the queue. It had been a good engagement. Bombs had in fact been dropped at random but with little effect. The bomber force had been severely mauled and their fighter escort had taken a real pasting. Allowing for the inevitable over-estimates on both sides, we had undoubtedly come out on top. I was credited with another Bf 109 destroyed and one 'probable'.

Pride goes before a fall, so they say. That afternoon I came to grief. We had counted our gains and our losses and given brief verbal combat reports to No. 1, our Intelligence Officer, and were having something to eat when at about two o'clock we were called to readiness. I had nine aircraft serviceable, armed and refuelled, and flown by my best remaining pilots. We were scrambled and vectored south to intercept a second bombing raid at 12,000 feet.

Again, we broke through the cloud at about 8,000 feet and this time there was no need for ground control. We were about 3,000 feet below and behind another large formation of *Heinkel* III bombers with the usual formidable fighter escort. But the whole circus had clearly decided that blind bombing was useless and was heading south for France. A repeat performance of the final act of the morning's show. We were in a hopeless tactical situation. We climbed fast behind the *Heinkels* and I gave short instructions to my sections. I decided that with my No. 2 we would go for the rear group. I deployed my other two sections to attack the stragglers who were out of the main formation. Again we heard the warning 'Snappers' and the 109s poured down on us, guns blazing and cannons pumping. My No. 2 and I were able to knock down one *Heinkel* which fell away with an engine on fire and parachutes erupting from the crippled aircraft. I attacked another which had closed in to take its place and it began to lag astern with a white spume of glycol from one of its engines and no response from the rear gunner.

The two of us then broke into half-rolls downward and went hell for leather for the cloud cover. Maybe I was too slow. I had tried to keep RT contact with my Squadron. I was within 1,000 feet of the safety of the cloud and had expended all my ammunition when I glanced in my mirror and saw an extremely unwelcome yellow-nosed fighter opening fire with its cannon. I was hit good and proper. There was a lot of smoke, oil and glycol pouring into the cockpit and then an explosion in the engine. Just before we hit the cloud layer, I opened my cockpit hood, released my side panel, and my trusty D-SH and I parted company as I went over the side.

My parachute opened in the cloud. I felt suspended in a weird world of mist, motionless. I dropped out of the cloud into daylight. I heard a crash which must have been my Spitfire but then I had to concentrate on how best to plan my landing. I had about 2,000 feet in hand, was drifting towards a row of bungalows with gardens in front and behind, a wood across the other side of the road, and fields immediately beneath me.

The steady drone of aircraft overhead brought home the reality of my situation. I tried to remember the drill for side-slipping to land where one wanted.

In 1935, I had done three 'pull off' practice parachute descents from the lower plane of an ancient Vickers Victoria bomber. Now, in 1940 and having to do it for real, I aimed for the fields but drifted too far downwind. I plummeted earthwards, caught the heel of my flying boot in the gutter of a red-tiled bungalow and landed unceremoniously on my bottom in the rose border of the front garden. This shook me a bit. I got up slowly, released my parachute harness and began to gather in the canopy and rigging lines. I realised that I was shaking like a leaf.

With my parachute bundled up in my arms, I rang the front-door bell. No response. I looked into the windows and saw no one. I walked round to the back and banged on the door. Still no response. I dropped my parachute on the path and tried to figure things out. Of course: an air raid! Everyone would be in shelters, taking cover as best they could. As if to confirm this blinding glimpse of the obvious, a man appeared from an Anderson shelter a few paces down the garden, with a double-barrelled shotgun pointed straight at me. 'Put your hands up!' 'But I'm RAF ...' 'Do as you're told.' So I did. A woman appeared beside him and then a girl in her teens. We stared at each other. 'Would you like to see my identity disc?' I made a movement to pull it from under my shirt. The shotgun was jabbed at me. 'No you don't. You put your hands up!' Back to square one. Then the girl said, 'Dad, I'm sure he's one of ours. The way he speaks, I mean.' Dad was beginning to have doubts about his doubts. 'You get his disc,' he said to her. 'I'll keep him covered.'

She got my disc and read it to her parents. The gun was lowered and we all began to laugh. In a moment I became a hero. Was I all right? Had I been wounded? Better have something to drink. I didn't look too good. Apologies for holding me up. They didn't recognise my black flying suit with my rank stripes on the shoulder straps. Please come in. Was that my parachute? Perhaps bring it inside.

In the sitting room, the husband took over. He poured me about half a pint of brandy, then produced an ARP directive which gave instructions in the event of an aircraft or a 'parachutist' landing or crashing nearby. It ended by saying, 'Do nothing but stay calm and phone your local police station'. This he did, most efficiently. He readily let me phone Kenley, who were jubilant that I was okay. My No. 2 had landed, very badly shot up, with a report that I had gone down in flames. Kenley suggested sending a pick-up to collect me from Uckfield police station in about an hour. I drank my brandy and began to feel better. Twenty minutes later, when a young police officer arrived in an open MG, I was well away and feeling no pain at all. I thanked the family warmly and, quite without authority, suggested that I send the silk canopy of my parachute to the daughter, who was making quite an impression on me.

The young police officer took the situation in at a glance and on the way to Uckfield he told me that an aircraft had crashed in the paddock of a house some two miles away. He thought it was a Spitfire and wanted me to take a look at the wreck. No one had been hurt. I agreed, and we drove down country roads to a sizeable house with a gravel drive. On the way he informed me, with the discretion and understatement for which the police force is renowned, that the owner of the house was a retired Captain in the Royal Navy who was known locally as 'the Admiral'. He also implied that

I might find the Admiral somewhat peculiar. Recovering slowly from shock and the effect of the brandy, I don't think I took this in.

The door was opened to our ring by a maidservant in a black dress and white apron. She led us through the house to a verandah where we met 'the Admiral', an ageing grey-haired man in a blue blazer. On a glass-topped table was a half full bottle of whisky and an empty glass. He was gloriously drunk. The young police officer handled the situation with commendable tact. Twice he explained that I was probably the pilot whose aircraft had crashed in the paddock and that he thought it best if I inspected the wreckage. The Admiral muttered his approval and added, 'Bloody fine body of young men. I do hope the pilot's all right.'

The policeman explained once again that I was the pilot but, when a gardener arrived and led us out to the paddock, the poor old Admiral was knocking back another whisky and mumbling, 'I just hope the pilot's all right.'

The wreck was without doubt D-SH, my aircraft. No rounds were in the guns. It had crashed at about 45 degrees slap into the middle of the paddock which contained no stock and was some two hundred yards from the house. The engine was completely buried; the cockpit had disintegrated and only the rear end of the fuselage bearing my letters D-SH remained recognisable. The wings and the tail plane had smashed to smithereens and the gun packs and ammunition containers lay spread on the paddock.

The lobby of the police station at Uckfield was piled with German flying kit-helmets, RT headsets, flotation waistcoats, flying suits – the lot. We went into the office where a sergeant sat behind a heavy desk. He looked up as we entered: 'Not another of the buggers?'

My escort explained who I was and asked me to produce my identity disc. The stunned sergeant apologised profusely, offered me a cup of tea and invited me to join his wife in their sitting room which was part of the flat they occupied over the station. I told my hostess what had happened. She hung on my every word. Then the pick-up arrived from Kenley and I was on my way back to base. After the formalities of submitting my combat report and exchanging experiences with my Squadron, I rang up Diana who suggested I come up to Cadogan Court.

CHAPTER TWELVE

The Battle of Britain: 'The Hardest Day'

My Squadron was unconditionally released until 12.30 the following day – the heavy overcast weather persisting – and my Squadron relaxed in the Mess. Kenley Operations had my telephone number. As Diana's mother had gone down to her sister's house in Sussex, we had the flat to ourselves. I was still a trifle shaken but we talked long and got to know each other a great deal better. We became confident that our engagement was for real.

That morning off was a blessing to all of us. I was back with my Squadron by 11.30 am and at once went into the Operations Room to see what plots were on the board. There were none: ominous. The Luftwaffe usually laid off minor raids before a major build-up. Norman confirmed my views and my favourite WAAF plotter gave me an even more generous smile when she brought me my coffee.

I got my team together and told them that a full-scale bombing raid was expected. We made our dispositions accordingly and No. 1 looked tired and serious and told me that Command had it that Kenley and Biggin Hill, both Sector Stations, were likely targets. We sharpened our swords, as it were, and had an early lunch. An hour later we were at readiness and soon after were scrambled to orbit base at 15,000 feet. The overcast of the past two days had disappeared and we were back with the cloudless blue of that extraordinary summer.

I had only eight Spitfires. We climbed as fast as we could, circling the Kenley area. I saw two squadrons climbing up beside me from Croydon, and a formation of Hurricanes coming up from the north-east, probably from Biggin Hill. We were at 16,000 feet when we got a very brief and cryptic call from base – 'Bandits overhead!' I looked up into the unbroken blue of the autumn sky. Nothing. I looked down. For a moment my mind didn't register. Then all became clear. Grey mushrooms were appearing around and on our base, the centre of each a bright ball of fire which was instantly covered by the mushroom. Something much larger was ablaze in the hangar area and was pouring black smoke across the airfield. All this went through my mind as I called my Squadron and we went into a screaming dive. Kenley was under a heavy bombing attack. On the way down we tore through a group of *Junkers* 88s, but I continued to dive with my pilots following. Something convinced me the 88s were heading for Croydon and Kenley had been bombed by a much lower enemy raid.

We levelled out at about 5,000 feet and there they were – *Dornier* 17 bombers, known as 'Flying Pencils', heading south as fast as they could. Hurricanes, Spitfires and Bf 110s, twin-engined fighters with a longer range than Bf 109s, were all tangled up and I let my seven followers loose to attack any targets they chose.

I closed first with what I thought was a *Dornier* 17. I closed right in from astern and below and overtaking much too fast. I fired a long burst. The enemy aircraft rocketed vertically upwards, black smoke pouring from its port engine. I passed beneath it, pulled up into a steep climbing turn, lost a lot of my surplus speed and then circled as I watched it fall away downwards in a smoking spiral. I 'goofed' at it like a novice who had shot down his first enemy aircraft. I pulled myself together with a start; checked in my mirror. Nothing, thank the Lord. I spotted one of my Squadron to my right and slightly below. I waggled my wings to bring him in. He closed up and I recognised one of my best Sergeant Pilots. I called him by his name as I couldn't remember his call sign in our formation. We went after what we could see of the *Dornier* 17s, well ahead of us now but many in bad shape, judging by the smoke trails they were leaving in their wakes.

A sudden call: 'Bandit above 3 o'clock, Leader!' Okay. I saw him about 2,000 feet above. A *Junkers* 88, almost certainly one of the raid we had raced through on the way down. The two of us broke hard and fast to port and climbed flat out until we had his altitude; and then a bit more.

All was confusion. The RT was crackling with enquiries from base. That was reassuring and meant that our far from bomb-proof Operations Room was still operating.

We had got up-sun of the *Junkers* 88 when he must have seen us. He put his nose down and went hell for leather towards the coast. I was afraid that, being a dive bomber, he would make his escape by descending vertically before we were in range but he simply used his immense engine power and ran for it.

We caught him. I put a five-second burst into his 'office' which effectively silenced his rear gunner. My acting No. 2 followed suit and hit the *Junkers'* starboard engine which began to smoke. No. 2 then said, 'Sorry,

Leader, no more ammo.' So he was unarmed. I told him to stay with me, which he did. I emptied my guns into the enemy and I too ran out of ammunition. So we dived out of trouble and headed back to Kenley. Control came through loud and clear. 'All Freema Squadron pancake at Bye-Bye One.' This was repeated twice. In plain language, it meant all 64 Squadron to land at Redhill, a satellite airfield alongside the North Downs. Six of us landed and I immediately ordered refuelling and rearming. A Warrant Officer seemed to be in command.

The petrol bowsers took over twenty minutes to appear and the ammunition was loose and had not been belted. In effect the whole support was inefficient and chaotic. I raised the roof, rang Kenley and told Norman that the War would be over before my aircraft were rearmed and refuelled.

I was under a lot of stress, which he understood. He told me that the Operations Room had not been hit. But two hangars had gone up, the Officers' Mess had been damaged and an air-raid shelter outside the Sick Quarters had received a direct hit which had killed the Station Medical Officer and most of his nursing staff. The main runway was badly pitted but was being filled in and repaired temporarily. There were unexploded bombs on and around the airfield and, if I cared to, I was free to bring my six back to base but for God's sake to be careful. Two of my Squadron had landed back safely. That was good news indeed. None had been lost.

I delivered a final broadside to the Warrant Officer who was at least trying to make amends. But he was having the War too easy and I had more important matters on my mind. I got my pilots together and explained that when we reached Kenley I would land first with whatever advice I could get from Sector Control.

Norman was splendid. He recommended the short cross-wind runway which had only one bomb crater at the far end, which had been filled in. The main runway was not to be recommended. I came in slowly with a lot of power and flaps and wheels down. I landed as short as I could and turned off the runway well before its end. I called in my five others and told them what to do. All landed successfully and the original eight of us met up in the dispersal hut to give our combat reports to No. 1. He seemed remarkably composed considering he had been at the receiving end of a low-level raid by a squadron of *Dornier* 17s which had attacked by flying at a few hundred feet, below our radar screen along the same path I had followed in the yellow-painted Magister two days earlier.

We were trying to piece together the events of the day. We heard that Biggin Hill, Croydon, Tangmere and Hornchurch had all been bombed, as well as radar stations and port installations. Somehow we were rearmed and refuelled. Two hangars had gone up, one containing the M/T section with its vehicles and a number of private cars. The bomb shelter outside the Sick Quarters had received two direct hits, one on each of its entrances. Everyone in the shelter was killed. The façade of the Officers' Mess was damaged but the Sergeants' Mess and the airmen's barracks were mercifully spared.

The hero of the hour was an airman who was manning a 'secret device' in a round, sand-bag bunker. The device consisted of a rocket projectile which, when fired, shot vertically to a height of a few hundred feet dragging with it a chain attached to a parachute. When the rocket reached its maximum height and expired, the parachute opened and the chain came slowly to the ground. When the air-raid alert was sounded, the airman and all others operating the airfield defences came to readiness. The first of the low-flying *Dorniers* passed overhead dropping their bombs on the airfield. The 'secret weapons' were then fired as the rest of the enemy formation appeared over the airfield boundary. A *Dornier* flew into a chain and fell to the ground several hundred yards outside the airfield. Another secret weapon damaged a *Dornier* which, according to German reports, just managed to creep back to France before making a forced landing near Calais.

But then we were scrambled again. Patrol base at 12,000 feet! But we were down again among the bomb craters half an hour later without having made contact with the enemy. So ended our operations of 18 August, the day during the Battle of Britain on which several authorities claimed more aircraft were engaged and more casualties suffered by both sides than on any other. All I know is that we were bloody tired.

The BBC put out the number of enemy aircraft claimed as shot down. It was a tremendous score and though it was exaggerated it was a great morale booster to us and the public rejoiced.

That evening we and our sister Squadron made ourselves as comfortable as possible in the Mess, part of which was out of commission. We drank and talked. We were joined by our Station Commander, Wing Commander Prickman, while bomb disposal squads defused unexploded bombs and the occasional time-bomb shattered the late evening. I phoned Diana and said I was okay. She sounded lonely.

CHAPTER THIRTEEN

The Battle of Britain: Pilot Training

T he Station Commander was called to the phone. He was back ten minutes later, beckoned me to follow him and we made our way to an empty room. First, he congratulated me on the award of a DFC. He had been called by Group Headquarters who confirmed that, while his recommendation that I be awarded a DSO had been regarded as premature, a DFC had been approved.

My award would be gazetted in the national press within a few days. He said many kind things about me and my Squadron, and then told me that Fighter Command had decided to withdraw the Squadron from the front line and redeploy us to Leconfield, a fighter airfield in Yorkshire for rest and training of new pilots who were to be posted to us. The movement, Prickman explained, was part of an overall plan to rotate squadrons from the front line to the rear areas and vice-versa. I was very upset but I saw the wisdom of the decision. Too many of our casualties were due to lack of experience and sheer mental and physical fatigue. We were desperately short of serviceable aircraft and reliable pilots. He asked me not to inform my Squadron until the following day. I had a few more drinks and went to bed with very mixed feelings.

Prickman, together with the Senior Air Staff Officer from No. 12 Group, sent for me at about eight o'clock the following morning. He introduced me and the SASO said complimentary things about our operations. He explained that the Yorkshire and Lancashire areas were under threat and that he proposed to keep one Flight at Leconfield and deploy the other one to Manchester. He suggested that the Manchester Flight should consist of my most seasoned pilots and the Leconfield Flight be reinforced with new pilots for training, and replacement Spitfires. He said that Fighter Command had proposed this arrangement as part of the overall plan to prevent too much pilot exhaustion and erosion of aircraft. I was told that I could let my Squadron know. We were to move to Leconfield at noon on the following day.

In fact, I had consulted No. 1 the night before. He was already privy to the move and spent a long time reassuring me that I had not been withdrawn from the front line for incompetence. My hackles were up and I was not entirely sober. He made it all sound reasonable, and suggested I tell No. 2 and No. 3 early the next morning and get the Squadron together immediately afterwards. He despatched me to bed quite fiercely and said he would see me first thing on the morrow.

No. 3 called all ranks to the one remaining hangar and I said my piece. I set out the movement programme and set our take-off time as 1300 hours. I told everyone to have a proper meal and reassured them that we would all be back in the front line after a few weeks. They gave me three cheers, at which I nearly broke down. It was No. 1 who led me out of the hangar.

Nine Spitfires took off at 1300 hours. Two were being repaired to be flown up later. We hoped the shortfall would be replaced when we were redeployed at Leconfield. The Station Adjutant ran to my aircraft as I was being strapped in by my ground crew. He shouted that my DFC had been gazetted in the morning papers. I could have the ribbon sewn onto my tunic as soon as possible. It didn't somehow signify. I think I must have been pretty near the end of my tether.

I had said goodbye to the Station Commander, to Norman our Sector Controller and to my favourite WAAF plotter. I had phoned Diana at her mother's flat but had got no reply. We took off from bomb-scarred Kenley and I led my team north to Yorkshire and Leconfield.

We were made welcome by the Station Commander who told me that the squadron I was replacing was on its way to Kenley. My ground crew and technical personnel were on the way up by train and Nos. 1, 2 and 3 were expected shortly in an Anson from the Communication Flight from Hendon, a courtesy arranged, so I understand, by my friend Norman.

The Squadron ground crew arrived about midnight but were comfortably accommodated after a square meal in the NAAFI. We were at readiness at six o'clock the following morning. Our sister Squadron at Leconfield was a non-operational Polish one, commanded by a bovine Squadron Leader, Satchell, whose looks clearly belied his qualities as a leader. He was awarded a DSO before the Battle of Britain was over.

I accepted the role I had to play. I re-formed A Flight and appointed a competent Flight Commander and an experienced team of fighter pilots. They left for Ringway (Manchester) next day and I awaited the arrival of replacement Spitfires and new pilots. Nothing happened.

I asked to see the Station Commander, who undertook to speak to Group Headquarters. The Group Commander was an ambitious Air

Vice-Marshal, Leigh-Mallory, who detested his front-line counterpart in No. 11 Group, from where we had come. AVM Park, a New Zealander, was fighting the air battle in the south-east of England extremely skilfully and in accordance with Dowding's (his Commander-in-Chief) direction. Dowding has been criticised for his tactics, but they prevailed and his strategy and tactics gave us the victory. Leigh-Mallory fulminated and resented his role as a back-up group providing air cover to the front-line airfields when they were committed to battle. Douglas Bader was his protégé and stirred the pot.

So, we were not received with open arms by the 12 Group staff though, to give him his due, Leigh-Mallory was sensible and positive when I was summoned to his presence a few days later. Replacement Spitfires arrived in dribs and drabs. Young pilots with little more than six or seven hours flying experience on the type were posted in.

We made friends with our Polish messmates who were a splendid group of excitable and unpredictable pilots. They were eager to understand our culture and attitudes, striving to learn our language, particularly our slang and invective. Few of them had more than a smattering of English. I didn't relish Satchell's job of controlling them in the air when they were fit to join combat with the Germans, whom they loathed and detested. We had a Station Medical Officer who was unpopular in the Mess. He was a bit pompous and loud-mouthed. One lunchtime he came into the Ante-room and one of the Station Staff muttered, 'Here comes the fucking quack.' A Polish officer was within earshot. That evening when the MO again came into the Ante-room, the young Pole rose to his feet, bowed politely and greeted him with 'Good evenings, fuckings quack'!

We settled in at Leconfield. I gave the replacement pilots all I could in counsel, instruction and practice in air combat. They were intelligent young men but at times I despaired of their chances in combat. They hardly knew their way around the Spitfire cockpit and I spent several hours trying to explain the technique of deflection-shooting to the nineteen-year-old who had graduated with an Honours degree in History. Surprisingly, he survived the War and ended up as a Squadron Leader, twice decorated.

Diana said she would come up to Yorkshire and stay in a local hotel in Beverley. We announced our engagement in the national press on the same day as I had a local tailor sew my DFC ribbon on my tunic and battledress. This was in August 1940.

My Squadron took to Diana, spoilt her and said what a lucky so-and-so I was. The Poles beamed at her, bowed and took over. The Station Commander threw a party in the Mess. I don't remember seeing much of Diana who was swept up by the Poles and given far too much to drink. I got her back to the hotel in Beverley. She had to be undressed and, as I 'laid her to rest', she murmured, 'Please let's get married soon.' She was alive the next morning when I phoned her at eleven o'clock.

Congratulations came in by mail and telephone. Dad sent me a particularly warm telegram congratulating me on both counts.

In retrospect our deployment to Leconfield was sensible. I began to recover my balance which had begun to wobble during the last fortnight at Kenley. My pilots lost their look of strain and the relative calm of our Sector gave us a badly needed opportunity to pull ourselves together, put the past behind us and re-form as a fighting unit.

The division of my Squadron into an experienced, battle-hardened Flight based at Ringway and a group of virtually inexperienced young men at Leconfield was a major problem. I appealed to the Station Commander to allow me to unite my Squadron, train it as a fighting unit and make it possible for the experienced pilots to lead the inexperienced. I knew what I asking was difficult but that, if the present arrangement continued, I would never have a squadron worthy of its name. The Commander took it well. He said he would talk to Group. Still nothing happened.

Our mark of Spitfires was being fitted with metal ailerons which made the aircraft much more stable and manoeuvrable in a dive. But we didn't get them. The Station Equipment Officer was unsympathetic. We were not in the front line; we could wait our turn. I blew my top. We were re-forming so that we could get back into battle as soon as possible. I wanted metal ailerons and quickly. I phoned my contacts at 11 Group, who suggested I contact Fighter Command Headquarters. I did so. Within a week we had our metal ailerons, but I had made an enemy of the Station Equipment Officer. So what!

CHAPTER FOURTEEN

Marriage to Diana

Suddenly things took a turn for the better. I had been granted seven days leave from the following day. Diana and I left by train for London to see her mother and then to Swanage to visit Dad. We reached Swanage two days later to be greeted by an officer of the Swanage police force who told me they had received a message that my Squadron was being moved to Biggin Hill – a front-line station – on the following day and would I join them tomorrow afternoon. My Squadron was due to land at 1600 hours.

So bang went our leave. Diana and I decided to get married. We drove in a hired car to Salisbury where it had been agreed that we could obtain a special licence. This took time. When we arrived back at Swanage the Rector, who had undertaken to marry us at 9 pm, had given up and suggested ten o'clock the next day. We were too exhausted to argue the point.

Dad's companion, Nan, gave Diana a sleeping pill. She was all over the place the following morning but we made the church with Dad, Nan and John – an eccentric electrician-cum-mathematician and an old friend of mine – as 'Best Man'. My mother had died five years earlier, in 1935. John produced a bottle of champagne, which we subsequently demolished in Nan's flat before Diana and I set off in the car for Sevenoaks where I had booked a room. I left Diana at the hotel and drove to Biggin Hill where I found my Squadron well settled in. The Station Adjutant thought it best if I spent the night on the station. I phoned Diana at the hotel in Sevenoaks. She was very upset.

That night there was a heavy raid on London and its surrounding fighter airfields, so I spent my wedding night in an air raid bunker until four o'clock in the morning. We were back in the front line with a vengeance. A few hours later I was asked to report to the Station Commander. He appeared ill at ease. How many experienced pilots had I?

I told him seven, including myself. What was my strength of serviceable aircraft? I had checked this the evening before. Eight, I replied, with three expected down from Leconfield later during the day. Eight, he mused. Possibly eleven by this evening. He then looked me very straight in the face. 'MacDonell,' he said, 'it's not your fault in any way but we are taking the hell of a pasting and we must have fully experienced squadrons if we are going to survive, let alone keep our fighter stations operational.'

I fought back as hard as I could. I assured him we had enough seasoned pilots to take care of the inexperienced ones; that I had pressed Command to send us back to the front line; that we were a fresh, rested if not wholly tested Squadron and that what we needed was a chance to prove our worth. Why, otherwise, had we been posted to Biggin Hill? He was clearly upset. We drank coffee and the Station Adjutant, an elderly school-masterish type, came in and said that Group wanted to speak to him. I made to get up but the Station Commander motioned me to remain. His conversation was brief. The signal calling us down from Leconfield was incorrect; the squadron number was wrong. We had not been intended to join the front line; another fully trained squadron was on its way to replace us. So we were told to remain at 'stand down' while our destination was decided. It was to be Coltishall, alongside the Norfolk Broads and not far from Norwich: out of the front line. I told my Squadron the news, which they received in silence. I had no stomach for consolation or promise of an early return to the battle.

I worked out a movement order for our ground staff with Nos. 2 and 3 and called Leconfield to send our remaining Spitfires to Coltishall. They were already airborne and Biggin Hill undertook to refuel them and send them on. We reached Coltishall in bad weather and landed over trees on the short arm of the airfield. A squadron of Hurricanes was dispersed below our let-down path. A young Sergeant Pilot clipped it too fine and struck the airscrew of one of the Hurricanes and bent it badly but landed safely.

I got on the phone to apologise to the Squadron Commander but was told he was on his way to our dispersal area. Sure enough a staff car arrived at high speed and an enraged Douglas Bader staggered out and wanted to know 'who the ... these clumsy buggers were and who was I anyway?' I apologised, introduced myself and explained what had happened to my Squadron. He stumped up to me on his tin legs, put out his hand, grinned and said, 'Okay, let's forget it. Let's meet in the Mess this evening and have a noggin'. This was my first meeting with Bader. We were to become friends until his untimely death from a heart attack long after the end of the War. He was an outstanding man.

Douglas had lost both legs in a flying accident in 1931, after which he had been invalided out of the RAF. At the outbreak of the War he had been turned down as a pilot. He bludgeoned his way through official red tape and medical reports and was eventually accepted for flying duties. He became one of the finest Fighter leaders in the RAF and a legendary figure.

At Coltishall we became a Squadron. We grew to know each other and I was able to reassess my team, decide with my Flight Commanders who should lead whom and discuss the strengths and weaknesses of the newcomers. It was a far more rewarding deployment than our previous one to Leconfield. We flew a few patrols to cover fighter airfields further south and we mixed very happily with Bader's Squadron, who gave us a great deal of advice and encouragement. Douglas and I got on fine. The Squadron was happy, relaxed and steadily becoming fighting fit. As far as combat was concerned it was something of a non-event. We were scrambled occasionally but never made contact, we flew standing patrols and had plenty of opportunity to practise battle formations and generally polish up our tactics.

Domestically, for Diana and me, it was bliss. A very charming middle-aged couple lived in a large house on one of the Broads a few miles from the airfield. They extended the warmest hospitality to the officers of the squadrons, indulged our pranks and threw splendid parties for us, one of which ended in a conga swaying and yelping along the Broad with a large number of the local villagers, male and female, young and old, following behind. Learning that I had been married for only a fortnight, our hosts immediately insisted that Diana and I stay in their gardener's cottage which was unoccupied but fully furnished. The rent they asked was £1 a week! I couldn't find words to thank them. We settled in and were very, very happy.

CHAPTER FIFTEEN

Further Sorties into France

Now I had no Polish competition but Douglas Bader and his boys were a gang to be reckoned with! My flying log book records that nothing of particular significance was happening. I began to fret. Having crossed swords with me before the War, the Station Commander didn't like me. He refused to ask Group to return us to the front line and quoted a few incidents when bad landings had resulted in minor damage. He was offensive and I nearly hit him when he said something to the effect that he hoped I was enjoying my 'love nest' on the Broads. So I put my foot in it good and proper. I wrote him an official letter setting out the reasons why we were wasting our time at Coltishall, stating that we were a competent fighting unit and that I requested a posting south as soon as possible.

Douglas Bader, who also disliked the Station Commander, gave me full support and apparently phoned Leigh-Mallory, the Group Commander, and suggested that I was a rebel and ought to return to the front line as soon as possible. This, coupled with the fact that I had also phoned the Senior Air Staff Officer at No 11 Group, sparked off a first-class row. The Station Commander was furious but he had to give in when the longed-for signal arrived, posting my Squadron to Hornchurch.

Hornchurch, with memories of Bulldogs and John Grandy and the April Fool prank that had gone too far. It was hard to believe. I said goodbye to Douglas, was refused an audience with the Station Commander, organised my ground crew and took off for the last time from Coltishall.

I had called on our kind hosts who were sad to see us go. She told me to take care in a motherly way; he offered the cottage to the Commanding Officer of my replacement squadron and his wife.

Hornchurch was shrouded in low cloud. The Control Tower wanted us to divert to North Weald but I knew the Hornchurch approach like the back of my hand. I said I would make it to Hornchurch where the cloud base was 400 to 500 feet. I got an 'okay, it's up to you' sort of answer. We let down over the Thames Estuary. The cloud base was broken but unpleasantly low. I put my Squadron into line astern and we flew slowly up the estuary until the Ford works at Dagenham came up ahead and on the right. The London balloon barrage was a few miles up the Thames. I saw the Dagenham Creek beneath the murk under my right wing. I swung round to follow it with my Squadron strung out behind me. Almost immediately I spotted the camouflage of the Hornchurch hangars. I told my Squadron to 'follow my leader' down and they all circled Hornchurch in a string. We landed safely, all of us; but, to use a modern expression, it was a very hairy experience. We were back again in the front line.

The squadron we were relieving was No. 222 whose CO was Jonnie Hill, a friend of mine. Jonnie told me that they had been very badly mauled during the previous month and he and his pilots were all suffering from nervous exhaustion and a shortage of Spitfires. I confess I was none too happy. The *Luftwaffe* had stepped up the day bombing on the airfields, the docks and the East End. By night the City was getting hammered very heavily. Jonnie was clearly in need of a rest. I told him of the cottage at Coltishall and he suggested he send his wife ahead by train two days before he flew his squadron up to Norfolk. He had several unserviceable aircraft and had been given forty-eight hours to get his act together.

So Jonnie's wife and Diana spent a couple of days together in the cottage. Jonnie left and Diana came down to the quarter which had been made over to us. It all seemed somehow unreal to me. Diana arrived looking tired. She had found Jonnie's wife distraught and full of gloom and doom – the casualties, the pilots who were all suffering from battle fatigue, the sleepless nights due to the air raids, and the constant fear that Jonnie wouldn't come back. From what Diana told me, I suspected that Jonnie's wife had gone to pieces. Was it right for me to have Diana with me at Hornchurch? But she slept through the air raid that night, and was her old self again the next day, said goodbye unemotionally when I left for the airfield, and seemed cheerful when I returned in the evening.

This was in November 1940.

During the month we were engaged mainly with Bf 109s. The bombers were left to the Hurricanes. I destroyed two Bf 109s and damaged another. Our Squadron score was mounting satisfactorily and I judged our effectiveness as being better than I had known it since I took command in June. Then the *Luftwaffe* attacks virtually ceased by day. The weight of the bombing raids was concentrated by night on London in particular and other industrial centres in the Midlands and the West. By the end of 1940 our Squadron score tailed off because there wasn't much to shoot at.

On New Year's Day 1941, a conference was convened by 11 Group for the Squadron Commanders of the Group, together with the Group Commander of a day-bombing squadron commanded by an old friend. The substance of the conference was to spell out a new operation, designed to bring the War to enemy territory. A Wing of three Spitfire squadrons would escort twelve Blenheim day bombers over the Pas de Calais where they would bomb enemy installations in the Forêt de Guine. We were not told, despite frequent questions, what these installations were. Reception was very mixed. What the Hell was it all about? To provoke the enemy fighters to give battle? Over their own occupied territory where they could crash-land or bale out safely? The top brass were not, I am sorry to say, very convincing. But this was what had been decided, so we reluctantly told our squadrons what was afoot. They took it very well.

The first of our 'sweeps', as they were called, was not until March and a complete flop. We flew out, a Wing of three Spitfire squadrons escorting twelve Blenheims. They dropped their bombs on the Forêt de Guine. We turned for home and landed, having met no opposition whatever, neither enemy fighters nor flak.

Earlier, in the New Year, we had been deployed to Rochford, a grass airfield on the Estuary not far from Southend-on-Sea. It had been Southend Airport before the War. Our operations from Rochford were mainly routine patrols over the Estuary and the Canterbury area. We tangled on a few occasions with small formations of Bf109s off Sheerness and two of my Sergeant Pilots had a splendid chase after a *Dornier* reconnaissance aircraft which they eventually caught and destroyed halfway across the Channel. We decided to leave the very high-flying photo-reconnaissance aircraft which came over usually once a day. We tried several times to reach them but our Spitfires took too long to gain their altitude.

Diana and I moved into a small semi-detached house with an ack-ack battery at the bottom of the garden! But before our move I heard that No. 1, Arthur Fagan, was to be promoted and posted to the Intelligence staff at the Air Ministry. This was a sad blow, particularly to me. While happy for his promotion, I had come to regard Arthur as a fixture, an essential ingredient in the cohesion of my Squadron. Respected, admired and indeed treated by all ranks with real affection, he had become my mentor. He always called me 'Sir', even when we were alone in my room or office discussing personal problems or, more usually, operational ones. He was to become my firstborn son's godfather.

I took No 1's going too much to heart. That I admit. We gave him a farewell party which got slightly out of hand. Diana and I had a few of my senior pilots to a supper party and our ground personnel took him over to the NAAFI. If his going was a sad day for the Squadron, the arrival of his successor was a disaster. From the moment my new Squadron Intelligence Officer reported to me in my office I took a dislike to him. About thirty-five, tallish with a slight stoop, he had a mean mouth, wore large spectacles and had a loud arrogant way of speaking. I asked him to sit down. He looked at the chair opposite my desk, flicked its seat with his uniform gloves which he held in his hand, pulled up his trousers at the knees, sat and then crossed his legs. We looked at each other. I asked him about himself.

He removed his cap, put it on his lap and placed his gloves in it. He produced a cigarette case, opened it, looked at me and raised his eyebrows. I said nothing. He snapped it shut, returned the case to his pocket and started talking. I think he said he had been with the BBC. There was also a lot of crap about not graduating from university due to illness, freelance journalism, then being called up, a commission and a short Intelligence course before being posted to my Squadron. He had no previous experience of squadron life. I then told him what his duties were and what I expected of him. Did he have any questions? Oh yes, lots, but perhaps they had better wait until he had found his way around.

I called in No. 3 and asked him to introduce the new arrival to as many of the Squadron as he could, to see to his accommodation, and to have him read and sign the Squadron standing orders and other documents which were mandatory. I foresaw trouble.

I was contacted by the Group Intelligence Officer whom I knew well. He asked me how my newcomer was making out. 'Too early to say,' was my reply. 'Quite so. Oh, by the way, your Station Commander will be briefing you tomorrow on something of importance. Just be sure you are around, will you?'

Next morning the weather was atrocious. I asked No. 3 to get my two Flight Commanders and No. 2 to come to my office as I wanted to discuss a technical matter with them. 'They are at the Intelligence Officer's meeting, sir.'

'What meeting? Whose Intelligence Officer?'

'No. 1's replacement, sir. He's called a meeting of all pilots and No. 2.' 'Bloody hell! Where?'

'In B Flight's dispersal hut.'

I told No. 3 to get into my staff car and drove like mad round the perimeter track to our Squadron's dispersal area. I stormed into the meeting and asked what it was all about.

'Intelligence briefing from Group ... Sir.' He had an insulting habit of leaving a long pause after he had finished speaking to me before adding 'Sir'.

'Intelligence briefing about what?'

'Offensive sweeps over France ... Sir.'

I told the meeting to disperse and, with No. 3, I drove him back to my office. I took a very deep breath. This time I didn't invite him to sit down, and I had No. 3 remain behind my desk. Bearing in mind that that this was my new Intelligence Officer's first experience of his duties, I kept my cool and I asked him why he hadn't informed me. His reply was that Group had told him the night before that the Station Commander would brief me. He saw no reason why he, my Intelligence Officer, shouldn't do what was no more than his duty. He was required by Group to keep my Squadron informed of all intelligence matters that affected them. I felt No. 3 snort behind me. It was a near thing but somehow I managed to keep control of myself. I explained once more, as I should have done when he first arrived, that his duty was to pass to me or, in my absence, my deputy all and every bit of intelligence that he received from Group; that never again was he to divulge intelligence matters, whether conjectural or factual, to anyone on the Station before he had seen me or my deputy. I rammed home to him that I was in command of 64 Squadron in every sense of the word, that I would decide what intelligence should be passed down the line and what should not. He was my adviser: the decision whether or not to act on his advice lay fairly and squarely on my shoulders. Did he understand?

'Yes, Was that all?'

'No,' I said, 'I want to speak to you alone.' No. 3 withdrew. I told him to sit down, which he did. I said he could smoke, which he did. I was in the process of telling him that he wasn't making a very good impression, and was thinking hard and fast of examples of lack of cooperation and sheer bad manners, when No. 3 came through on the phone. The Station Commander, Harry Broadhurst, wanted me right away. That was that. As I already guessed, he had a brief from Group to let me know in advance of the conference what they had in mind regarding offensive sweeps across the Channel. Broadhurst and I had known each other for several years. We had always got on well. He was an excellent Station Commander, a first-class fighter pilot and a deadly shot.

It was not a long interview. He wanted 64 Squadron to provide top cover to the fighter Wing which he would lead. There would be a Polish squadron below us and above and astern of the one he would lead. The Blenheims would be in close formation below the fighter Wing. We would have an opportunity of hearing more and exchanging views at the conference. I took the opportunity of apologising for my new Intelligence Officer's gaffe. He was bound to hear of it if he hadn't already. Broadhurst grinned his crinkly grin. 'Bloody silly twit, Hope you chewed him up, Mac.'

I went back to my office and wished the weather would lift. I needed some fresh upper air.

I had no further obvious trouble from the new Intelligence officer. Significantly he wasn't often called by his Christian name. All the officers and NCO pilots used each other's Christian names or nicknames. I saw no reason why they shouldn't. This sort of democracy worked very well both on the ground and in the air. A fighter squadron is a unique blend of skill, courage, quick thinking and, above all, team reaction. A weak link, a 'difficult' personality or simply a bloody fool can wreck the effectiveness of the team. I knew nothing about group psychology or 'deviants' but if my leadership erred on the side of the loose rein it was nevertheless effective with the young men under my command. Little did I know then that their nickname for me was 'Bonnie Prince Charlie'!

In an attempt to thaw our relations, although I felt we were mutually incompatible, I invited my new Intelligence officer to have a flight with me in our Magister. He hesitated and then agreed. We got the okay from Hornchurch for local flying and took off. I asked him on the Intercom if he was all right and he said he was. We had fluttered around a bit over the Estuary and Sheerness when I felt the rudder bar being kicked. I looked round. He was holding on to his glasses with both hands and his flying goggles were trailing behind his head in the slipstream, held only by a thin strap. I told him to take off his glasses and grab his goggles. He replied that he couldn't see without his glasses and could we please land as he was feeling sick. I throttled back and we drifted home to Rochford where I switched off and helped him out. He muttered his thanks and made off unsteadily towards the old clubhouse which served as our Squadron dispersal and rest area. I had a few words with him to make him feel less of a fool but I don't think I achieved very much. He continued to spend rather too many evenings with four young officers, boozing in the local pubs. On more than one occasion I arrived at our crew room to find some of the party asleep in chairs and clearly badly hung over.

Perhaps I should have spent more evenings with the pilots but Diana and I had not long been married and I cherished our evenings and nights together. We had Squadron parties in our semi-detached, but closed them up reasonably early. On one occasion I invited the 'problem child'. He took centre stage, made much of Diana and dropped names continuously. He drank a lot of my whisky and was difficult to get rid of. Diana didn't like him one bit.

The Squadron called Diana 'Mrs Mac'. We learned how to sleep through the booming of bombs and the crack-crack of our neighbouring ack-ack battery.

On 12 March 1941, we were briefed for another sweep over France on the following afternoon. No. 64 Squadron was to rendezvous with the two Hornchurch squadrons over Rochford at 10,000 feet with Broadhurst leading as before. The Wing, with 64 Squadron again providing top cover, would deploy above them. In short, the mixture was as before.

That evening there was a Guest Night in the Hornchurch Mess. Keith Park was the Guest of Honour and the three squadrons of the Hornchurch Wing were hosts, Broadhurst presided and I drove up from Rochford with my two Flight Commanders and Nos. 2 and 3. There was a limit on the number of officers from each squadron as I think the whole of 11 Group were invited to send representatives. It was a splendid evening with wartime rations obviously augmented from 'private sources' and plenty to drink. Talk was incessant and the morrow's sweep was on most people's lips. Arguments broke out. Opinions were stated loud and clear – for and against. By midnight I should think the whole *Luftwaffe* knew what was afoot. The AOC and Broadhurst suggested that those on the sweep should pack it in and get some sleep.

I collected my four (No. 3 most indignant at having to break up the party), said thanks to Broadhurst and said we'd be waiting for him over Rochford in the afternoon. 'You better had,' he grinned. We drove down the Southend road with our dimmed lights.

Diana turned over in the bed and asked drowsily if I was all right and had I enjoyed myself. I reassured her on both counts and she was asleep before I was undressed and in bed beside her. I awoke early. Our Squadron was at stand down until 10.30 so I lay gently dozing for a while, then got up to find Diana downstairs with breakfast ready. I was in fair shape considering. I drank two cups of coffee, felt better, ate some toast and said bye to Diana. She smiled her wide, warm smile and said 'See you this evening.' I got into my car. She was not aware of the sweep: I didn't tell her those sorts of things.

CHAPTER SIXTEEN

Shot Down over the Channel

Back at the airfield there was a lot of good-natured banter about our state of health following the night before. No. 3, who had a twisted ankle – from playing football in the Ante-room – and an obvious hangover, came in for most of the charlie-poking. My two Flight Commanders were in good shape and I was fine, but busy. I ordered an early lunch from the Catering Officer, chalked up our formation plan on the blackboard and noted a bank of cumulus building up from the northeast.

We had an hour before take-off. We ate our lunch. There were prunes again. They came up on the menu far too often. I had complained to the Catering Officer but that had had no effect. At 30,000 feet a plate of prunes does extraordinary things in your stomach. You fart continuously and feel as though you have swallowed a football. I didn't eat my prunes.

We made a final check on our aircraft. There were only ten serviceable for the operation but that wasn't too bad. I did my deep-breathing relaxing exercises and went back to join my pilots in the crew room.

I am not sure to this day what my new Intelligence officer said that got up my nose, but as we left to climb into our Spitfires he got in another snide crack accompanied by a derisive laugh. That did it. I rounded on him, 'You're suspended from duty. I'll deal with you when I come back.'

I was in a bad temper as I climbed into my cockpit and accepted the usual help from my ground crew to fasten my parachute harness and fix my straps. I managed a smile and a 'thumbs up' in acknowledgement of the 'best of luck, sir' from the airman who looked after me, checked my cockpit, closed the side panel and waited until he had moved under the mainplane to the chock rope. I fired the Koffman starter and the Merlin burst into life. I waved away the chocks and taxied slowly out of the dispersal area towards the downwind edge of the airfield. I looked back and the nine aircraft of my Squadron were moving in a long crocodile behind me. We processed to the far end of Rochford, keeping RT silence. It had become so much of a routine, there was no problem.

I turned into wind, checked my airscrew pitch control, adjusted my headset, saw my No. 2 coming up behind me and on my right, and my No. 3 swinging in on the left. I raised my hand. They raised their hands and I opened my throttle. We climbed low over the dispersal area, retracted our undercarriages and swung left-handed in a climbing turn with the others following in the formation we knew so well. The cloud bank to the north-east was dispersing and at 5,000 feet the visibility was good. We climbed steadily in a wide circle over the airfield. I reckoned to be at our rendezvous height of 10,000 feet slightly ahead of schedule, so slowed our rate of climb.

I looked round at my team as they rose and fell in the slight turbulence of the afternoon sky. The comforting growl of my Merlin and the crackle from its exhausts helped me to relax. I felt clean inside and purged of rancour. I had my team of nine young men, nine separate personalities each with his own thoughts, hopes, fears. A surge of pride tinged with emotion overcame me. I deliberately carried out a meticulous check of my cockpit instruments and dials.

We reached 10,000 feet spot on time, But I couldn't see Broadhurst with the two Hornchurch squadrons. We throttled back and loafed around in a wide sweep. Then I saw them. They were lower than I expected but we slid down into position above and slightly astern of the second Squadron and then, as a Wing of three, climbed again fairly steeply towards the French coast. I never saw the Blenheims throughout the whole sweep. They were well ahead of us and much lower. But we weren't expecting trouble.

Our Spitfire cockpits, though enclosed, were neither pressurised nor heated. We had oxygen masks and were dressed as warmly as possible for high patrols. Diana had bought me a pair of silk pyjamas which I wore under my heavy submariner's sweater and my tunic. We wore fur-lined flying boots and leather flying gauntlets.

At 15,000 feet I turned on my oxygen. I closed the radiator and sat comfortably at my controls. Broadhurst's two squadrons were deployed below and ahead of mine like a pattern woven round the bottom of a dirndl – I thought the theme would appeal to Diana.

I wasn't expecting any trouble but as we climbed to 20,000 feet my left hand, the one which rested on the throttle lever, began to get cold, At 30,000 feet when we crossed the French coast I was smacking it on my left knee in an attempt to restore its circulation.

Broadhurst turned the Wing south-west. We had lagged behind due to our reduced performance at this altitude. I opened up but my Squadron began to straggle. They closed up and we carried on. I continued to bang my left hand on my knee. I was beginning to feel cold inside and out.

The Polish squadron below us disintegrated. One after another they simply dived headlong towards French occupied territory leaving a gap between us and Broadhurst which I did my best to fill. Then I saw them. A large gaggle of yellow-nosed Bf 109s climbing steeply to the south of us. I broke RT silence. At least I attempted to, but my microphone seemed dead.

My No. 2 fell away and dived south. I heard later that he had severe overheating, so fair enough. My No. 3 was a young Canadian Sergeant Pilot. The 109s were fast outclimbing us. I turned towards a straggler and hand-signalled to my No. 3 to have a go. We lost 1,000 feet in the turn but were still in a position to attack. I tried time and time again to contact Broadhurst on the RT but without success. Too late I found that I had disconnected the lead from its socket while banging my hand on my knee. I was trying to reconnect when there was one hell of a bang somewhere below my cockpit. Instinctively I went into a steep turn and then slowly I passed out.

Anoxia is an extraordinary experience. I had been through the decompression chamber at the School of Aviation Medicine at Farnborough, when four of us had been seated round a table playing cards. The pressure had been reduced slowly and progressively. I became fuddled but was conscious of two of us falling asleep, then a sense of drowsiness overcame me and I knew no more until the pressure was restored and I came to without my tie on and minus my watch.

It was a valuable experience because for about five minutes after recovering consciousness I wasn't really with it. And this was the point of the exercise. I came to that afternoon in a spin at about 7,000 feet. I regained my senses sufficiently to recover from the spin and realised that I had been shot up and had better get home as soon as possible. My oxygen was out.

With somewhat laboured precision I locked my compass to stop it spinning and then set a course which I reckoned would get me back to the English coast. I stooged on, dazed and dismayed. A few minutes later I realised that I had set a course due south! I was flying at 6,000 feet into France.

I swung round violently and opened my canopy to get fresh air. The cockpit was beginning to smell unhealthy. I set a north-westerly course on my compass and flew slap bang over the Calais flak, which mercifully did me no harm, and began to assess my situation. Obviously my oxygen supply had been ruptured. My flying controls appeared to be responding satisfactorily but my oil and coolant gauges were climbing alarmingly.

I tried my guns, which didn't fire, and rather desperately called base on my RT, which was evidently out of commission. I think that it was at about this stage of the proceedings that I became sufficiently clear-headed to recognise that I was in real trouble.

I flew on and on. The temperature gauges went off the clock but still the Merlin gave me hope. I remember passing over a small ship some ten miles off Calais and then, with an appalling shudder, my Merlin seized and I sat staring with disbelief at a completely stationary propeller. I was at about 8,000 feet and a quarter of the way across the Channel.

Carry on: there was no alternative. Get as close to home before baling out. Spitfires were death-traps if ditched: they simply porpoised and nose-dived deeply.

With no noise except the wind of my gliding descent, I became aware of the sound of an aircraft astern. I turned and found a Bf 109 on my tail. He fired his cannon at me but missed. I turned beneath him and he was round again. This time I heard his cannon shells whine just over my cockpit. I was down to 3,000 feet. There was no point in carrying on. I opened the side panel, went overboard, pulled my parachute ripcord and floated down towards a nasty-looking sea on the afternoon of Friday, 13 March 1941.

I saw my Spitfire nose down, hit the water and disappear with remarkably little disturbance other than a cloud of spray. A piece of the tail plane broke off on impact, floated briefly and then went under. I inflated my Mae West – we had no dinghies at that time – and as I neared the water I held my nose with my left hand and put my right on the parachute quick release. I smacked into an ugly steep sea with the wave crests breaking viciously.

I probably went under momentarily. I hit my parachute release. The canopy dragged me for a moment and then drifted free, deflated and lay floating some distance from me. I rode the steep waves using my arms as paddles and was immediately soaked to the skin. At first I didn't feel cold, but I seemed to be spending as much time partially submerged as on the surface.

Somehow I managed to take off my flying boots which were water-logged. I kept on my helmet until I decided to be rid of everything that wasn't essential to my survival. I decided to keep my wristwatch which was waterproof and still going. I unstrapped my webbing belt with its pistol in the holster and watched it ride a wave crest and then disappear.

I began to feel bloody cold.

By kicking and flapping my arms I managed to cope for about twenty minutes. I cannot remember fear, though I must have been very frightened, because my senses weren't registering and my physical reactions became automatic while my mind wandered vaguely from thoughts of the Squadron, Diana and Dad to the immediate problem of keeping alive.

Several times I shipped a lot of English Channel and coughed and spluttered as I rode the next wave crest. Then I felt a great weariness and a cold inertia engulfing me. I remember looking at my watch. I had been in the water thirty-five minutes. I stopped fighting and drifted into a strange sort of sleep ...

... I was being pulled and heaved. There were sounds and voices and then I was out of the sea and lying on a solid, hard surface which moved up and down. I was being stripped of my sodden clothing. Something rough was rubbing me and then people dressed me in a heavy sweater, dark blue trousers and thick woollen stockings. I was carried into a small space and laid down on a sort of bed. I passed out.

I came to in full possession of my senses. At once I knew that I was on a boat. I was lying on a bunk, wrapped in a coarse blanket but I was warm. I saw a large man in dark-blue uniform with gold stripes on his sleeves in a covered wheelhouse, and a couple of others I took to be ratings seated on stools behind him. They began to talk in German. I turned over on the bunk and one of the ratings came aft and grinned at me. '*Engländer?*' I had learned German at school. '*Jawohl. Engländer,*' I replied and then for good measure added, 'Major'. He went back for'ard and the Captain came to me. In German he said they had seen me come down by parachute but had had difficulty in finding me, I was being taken to Boulogne to be handed over to the *Luftwaffe*. For me the War was over!

I thanked him for saving my life in halting German. He smiled and called one of his crew who appeared waving my silk pyjamas. The Captain took them, laughed heartily and said, 'The British Air Force leave the beds of their lovers, fly into the sky and then fall into the sea.'

The irony of it was too much. I turned over on the bunk and feigned sleep. We berthed in Boulogne some time later, where I was taken over by a *Luftwaffe* Captain, a Sergeant and two airmen. I thanked my saviour once again. He saluted me and said, 'You will be alive when the War is over. Many others will die.' I was strangely and almost uncontrollably moved.

My sodden uniform was handed to the *Luftwaffe* Sergeant and I was bundled into an open staff car to be driven into the unknown.

CHAPTER SEVENTEEN

Kriegsgefangenschaft: Transit

I was a prisoner of war – a *Kriegsgefangener* or, in the idiom of those behind barbed wire in Germany, a 'Kriegie'.

I sat in the rear seat of the Citroen tourer, painted *Luftwaffe* grey with an identification letter on the rear door. A *Luftwaffe* Captain sat in the front with the driver. A Sergeant, with an open holster in which could be seen a heavy pistol, sat next to me. We moved off from the coast through heavily wooded country. The sky became overcast and I started to shiver. The Sergeant threw a cloak over me. I thanked him and began to consider my situation. The rule book for capture had emphasised that the sooner one made an attempt to escape the better one's chances of doing so. The Citroen, though a four seater, had only two doors. The front door was on the left, the driver's seat. The rear door was on the right, the seat occupied by the armed Sergeant. Short of leaping over my side of the open-top car there was no way of escape.

We climbed a hill into a thick forest. The engine began to splutter, then failed and we came to a halt. The Sergeant read my thoughts. He brought out his Mauser and, with a meaningful grin, cocked it on his lap. I decided not to make a break for it and sat resigned while the driver fiddled under the bonnet. Then he climbed back into the driving seat, started the engine and we moved off into open pasture land.

The Sergeant relaxed, replaced his pistol in its holster and gave me a cigarette. The Captain in the front, who had remained silent during the journey, turned to me and said in excellent English, 'We should not be at war. We are cousins and relations should not fight each other.'

I wasn't able to figure out the relationship, so I remained silent. He turned and looked over the countryside and then stared ahead through the windscreen. He turned up the collar of his greatcoat against the evening chill. A little while later he said, without turning his head, 'We are spending the night at St Omer'. We arrived about an hour later. Our destination was obviously a peace-time estaminet which had been taken over by the *Luftwaffe* as an interrogation centre. The ground floor was still a café with metal-topped tables and a bar. Upstairs was an office and a room with bunk beds, a desk and two telephones. The toilet was on the ground floor and outside the café.

I was escorted into the upstairs room, given an adequate meal, accompanied to the outside toilet and then invited to lie down and sleep. I was tired out and did so. Two *Luftwaffe* airmen, both armed, sat at a table, smoked and played some game with cards. I fell asleep. The lights had been dimmed.

At three o'clock I was awakened. The lights went on and an elderly, bespectacled *Luftwaffe* Lieutenant told me to get up and join him at the table. He spoke tolerable English. He showed me a form headed 'International Red Cross – Geneva' which he told me to fill in so that my family would know very soon that I was alive and a prisoner of war. We had been briefed about this. The Geneva Convention required POWs to give only their name, rank and service number – nothing more. The form I was given required, amongst other details, name and address of next of kin, number of squadron, age, length of service, and private address.

My interrogator, fat, slightly boozy and not too cleanly shaven, assured me that if I filled in the form the International Red Cross would be able to contact me and my family wherever I was during my captivity in Germany. I didn't fall for it. It was a pathetic piece of bluff. I explained that I knew the provisions of the Geneva Convention and completed the sections – name, rank and service number. He was not best pleased and threatened that my family might well not know that I was alive if I refused to give the information required.

At about 3.30 in the morning of Saturday, 14 March 1941 I produced the answer. 'I have no family,' I said. 'I am an orphan and unmarried. No one would be concerned with my whereabouts.' I was given a cup of coffee and two croissants at seven o'clock in the downstairs café. A young French girl with lovely dark eyes brought my uniform, dried and ironed, which she handed to me.

She looked me very straight in the eyes, said '*Bonne chance*' and shook my hand. I felt something hard in her palm. I closed mine on it and put my hand in my pocket. When I changed into my uniform I found she had given me a gold ring. It fitted my left little finger well enough. I put it on and wondered where it came from and to whom it had belonged. I felt very moved and thought about it for a long while afterwards.

I and my *Luftwaffe* escorts drove to Brussels where we waited for an hour until our train drew in. I was handed over to a nasty little *Luftwaffe* lieutenant and a bored sergeant who grinned at me and said it would be a long train ride into Germany. How right he was. For the first half-hour or so the Lieutenant smoked and glanced at me from time to time. We sat opposite each other.

The train was evidently a military one as the corridor was full of German soldiers who peered in at me and made jokes which I didn't understand. To relieve the boredom I asked to go to the toilet. The sergeant accompanied me along the corridor past the soldiers, one of whom said in English, 'Germany will win the War!' I made no reply and went to the toilet. The window was sealed, so there was no possibility of climbing out. I returned with my escort and rejoined the lieutenant in our compartment.

He then addressed me in very indifferent English which I pretended not to understand. This shut him up for another half-hour by which time we had stopped somewhere in a large station. We were brought hot soup and a roll. He tried again. This time I helped him out with my limited German, which proved a mistake as he forthwith launched into a tirade against the Versailles Treaty, explaining that as a professor of history before the War he had made a study of the humiliation to which his country had been put by evil-minded politicians who had themselves connived to wage war against his country for no better reason than to demonstrate that they, not Germany, were the rulers of Europe.

There was much more. It was great rhetorical stuff delivered in staccato English-cum-German which made it none too easy to follow but was quite evidently intended as a prelude to the grand finale which was the enormous guilt which we and our French allies must bear for defying the right of Hitler and the Third Reich to repossess their 'homelands', have access to the Baltic and stabilise (not the word used in 1941, but it expresses what he meant) the splinter groups in Europe who were now under control and no longer causing trouble. Germany was Europe! A pact had been agreed with the Soviet Union and only Britain's folly and cowardice had forced the Fuehrer to resort to arms. Cowardice on Britain's part: she feared for her empire and the possibility that her colonies would explode in her face. After half an hour he was literally spitting and a group of German soldiers had grouped at the compartment door. Occasionally one or two contributed a comment, or a discussion broke out which the sergeant in our compartment usually silenced with a wave of the hand. The lieutenant ended his lecture. He suggested that the sooner Britain came to terms with the Third Reich the better for everyone. I should ponder this and cease to be arrogant. He sat back, wiped his glasses and lit another cigarette. For half an hour or so he remained silent. The sergeant was dozing; I followed his example.

I slumbered on, semi-conscious of the train jolting to a halt at several stations where there were sounds of loud voices and people moving up and down the corridor and then the clanking of the train drawing out from the platform. I fell soundly asleep.

I was woken by the sergeant who jerked his thumb towards the door of the compartment. The train was slowing down, lights appeared and we came to a halt. The three of us climbed down onto the platform, where we waited awhile and soldiers and civilians milled around while a loud-hailer gave messages which I couldn't understand. Then a young, fair-haired, blue-eyed Luftwaffe corporal approached us. He didn't salute the lieutenant. He spoke in a tone of authority. The officer looked at me, clicked his heels and departed with the Sergeant.

The corporal turned to me and in perfect English, with only the slightest German accent, said 'I have come to escort you to your camp. Bad luck your being shot down but you won't be with us for long. The War will soon be over and then we can be friends again. We will look after you well. Come, follow me please.' I said 'Thank you' rather feebly. 'You are surprised I speak English, yes?' I said 'Yes.' He laughed. 'For four years I was an undergraduate at Cambridge. A beautiful place Cambridge. I love the reaches of the Cam with a punt and a pretty girl. Do you know Cambridge?' I said I didn't. 'Pity,' he said. 'You must visit Cambridge when the War is over, yes?' All this frankly took the wind out of my sails. For a day and a half I had held my tongue and kept the traditional 'stiff upper lip'. To find a man of my own age, albeit an enemy, speaking my language and identifying with what I had left behind broke down my assumed dignity and hostility.

We talked as he led me to a car with a *Luftwaffe* driver. We sat together in the back. He said we were going to a transit camp – *Dulag Luft* – at a place called Oberoesel where I would meet several of my friends. He mentioned John Casson who had come to grief over Norway and others whom I had known before the War. He said the conditions were comfortable, the food was good and there was wine from France. It was, he added, a very pleasant place to relax after what I had been through.

Dulag Luft was a hutted camp surrounded by barbed wire and guarded by sentries in watchtowers with machine guns. I was taken over by a *Luftwaffe* captain who led me to a block apart from the main camp, then upstairs where he handed me over to a guard who unlocked a door and showed me into a small room with a bed, a table and a chair. He said something about banging on the door if I wanted the toilet and locked me in.

I spent three days in solitary confinement. I was adequately fed and watered and allowed out to the toilet. Other than that, I had no attention and my requests for a razor and something to read were ignored. Left to myself, I worried about Diana and Dad and the Squadron I had left behind. I became increasingly neurotic and only snapped out of it by reminding myself that this was precisely the effect my treatment was intended to have.

On the fourth day the door was opened and a short, middle-aged Captain walked in. He stared at me and said in good English, 'Good morning, Mr MacDonell. Why haven't you shaved?' I explained why. He grunted and then said we would go for a walk. After that he would see that I was given shaving things. I thanked him and he led the way down to a side entrance leading to a walled garden.

He opened the conversation by asking if I knew London well. Before the War he had many English friends in London. Several of them from aristocratic families, he added. I replied non-committally. We walked on in silence. I then asked him how long I was to be confined alone in a room without even a book to read. He carried a little swagger-stick which he pointed at me. 'That will depend on you,' he replied. It had been reported that I was insolent, uncooperative and had shown no gratitude for being saved from drowning. In short, my behaviour was unbecoming an officer and a gentleman!

We walked back to the building in quick time. At the door of my room I looked at him and said, 'I apologise if I have been uncooperative. You know, as an officer, that prisoners of war should not disclose information to the enemy. I have obeyed my orders. Also, I am Scottish and not English. The Scottish are known to be dour.' He was clearly unable to understand that, so I explained that the Scots were a people who kept their thoughts to themselves!

His attitude became less formal. He ordered my guard to bring me a razor and shaving soap, and a newspaper. He clicked his heels, told me that the Commandant would visit me later in the day, and departed. I had my first shave in four days and felt ten feet high.

That afternoon the Commandant came to see me. He was extremely impressive, tall, slim, erect and very good looking. He spoke excellent English. I was beginning to wonder whether the entire officer class of the *Luftwaffe* had been educated in England. He shook my hand, addressed me by my rank, apologised for my confinement, but there had been no spare bed in the camp; that had now been arranged. He was sorry that I had 'fallen out' with my escorts, particularly as he had a deep fellow feeling for fighter pilots. Perhaps I had been strained to the limit during the great air battles of the summer? Perhaps, I thought.

He was arranging for me to join my comrades in the camp that evening where, he understood, a reception was to be held for me by my several friends. John Casson's name was again mentioned. They had been told that I had been shot down but was now safe and well. I thanked him and called him 'Sir'. Why not? He rose elegantly from my bed on which he had been sitting and handed me a tin of Players cigarettes. From France, he said with a smile. He then gave me a sealed envelope with nothing written on it. I opened it. A sheet of notepaper read: 'Bad luck. For you the War is over!' It was signed 'Werner Molders'.

Molders was one of the *Luftwaffe*'s most successful fighter pilots. His career began in the Spanish Civil War and by the time he became a Wing Leader during the Battle of Britain his personal score was considerable. A devout Catholic, he rose to high rank but was not a favourite of Goering. His death in 1942 in a transport aircraft on the way back from the Russian front was unaccountable and highly suspicious.

The Commandant told me Molders had shot me down. Some consolation perhaps – but not much. I joined the main camp that evening. There was no special 'reception' but those who knew me showed me round and introduced me. The Senior British Officer (SBO) was apparently in bed suffering from flu.

The atmosphere in the camp seemed to me far too free and easy. Security was non-existent. All but a few talked about their experiences before being shot down. Units were referred to by name, number and location and the place was infested by young, blond, blue-eyed 'guards' who all spoke fluent English, fraternised with the POWs and provided unlimited cigarettes and far too much French wine, brandy and cigars.

Dulag Luft was a propaganda camp. And a very useful source of intelligence for the Germans, as was to be proved later. The contrast between my four days in solitary and the holiday camp atmosphere which I now experienced was both unreal and disturbing.

I spoke with John Casson and others I had known. I told them I didn't like what I saw. We were being softened up and the Germans were getting a lot of useful information, particularly during the evening fraternisation with wine flowing. They thought I was over-reacting. The Germans already knew far more than we could tell them. I hadn't any cause to worry. Relax! Meanwhile the evening games of crap and the ever-present, blond, English-speaking guards and adequate rations maintained the status quo. But I found a number of kindred spirits and we exchanged our ideas and concerns.

The SBO, Wing Commander Day – 'Wings Day' as he was called – was too often in the company of the Commandant. However, I am absolutely certain that Wings Day never disclosed anything of importance. Indeed, throughout the War, he distinguished himself as a magnificent leader in a number of camps and was awarded a DSO when he was finally repatriated. He had been shot down in 1939, dropping leaflets by day over Germany! But 'Wings' had a drink problem which the Germans soon recognised. They provided him with too much liquor: his frequent bouts of flu when he took to his bed became a standing joke. I saw very little of him during my few weeks in *Dulag Luft*.

Far more serious, I was to discover, was the presence of a Flight Lieutenant who had been a pilot in the Communication Flight from Hendon and had been captured with an unserviceable aircraft when the Germans overran an airfield in France in 1940. He was a traitor who spoke openly of treating with Nazi Germany, who sneered at the idea that we could win the War, and was far too frequently called to the Commandant's office.

I was warned about him by John Casson and many others. But nothing was done. Later he was removed from the camp by the Germans: he then joined the *Luftwaffe* as an intelligence officer and wore a flash on his shoulders – *Freiwilliger Engländer* – 'English Volunteer'. He surrendered to the Allies at the end of the War.

As more and more RAF pilots became POWs, a proportion of those in the transit camp were sent to stalags – permanent camps in Germany. It was significant that those who were regarded by the Germans as co-operative were retained while those like me, who had not made a favourable impression, were 'purged', as the saying went.

CHAPTER EIGHTEEN

Kriegsgefangenschaft: Stralsund

T wo or three weeks after my arrival at *Dulag Luft* I was among some thirty RAF pilots who were put onto a train for a stalag near Stralsund on the Baltic coast. There was an officers' compound and an NCOs' compound, each separated by barbed wire and the whole complex was guarded by a formidable number of machine guns and sentries in watchtowers. The countryside was bleak. Half a mile away was a German Army flak school. There were four barrack blocks in our compound and about a hundred RAF POWs. Most of them had been captured after the disaster of France in 1940. Morale and rations were low, very low.

The Senior British Officer was a Squadron Leader Geoffrey Stephenson. Small, older than me, he had been shot down during the evacuation from Dunkirk. He was doing a reasonable job under difficult conditions and was not a German speaker. He represented the 'old guard' of the RAF. Most of the other POWs were in their twenties and far less class and rank conscious.

I found it difficult to fit in, being one of the very few fighter pilots who had been through the Battle of Britain. Indeed I think I was the only one. But we newcomers soon settled down to our surroundings and fellow Kriegies, who were an interesting, mixed bag. Apart from the British, there were Canadians, Australians, Poles, Czechs and even a Yugoslavian who for a time was thought to be a 'plant', quite unjustifiably as it proved.

But the camp was disorganised. Stephenson was not a leader. There was no Escape Committee as such, no organised activities, nothing intellectual. The unit was the room and its few occupants. Uncoordinated escape plans were legion and before long the ground under the barracks was criss-crossed with a labyrinth of tunnels almost half of which had been found by the Germans before they had gone more than a few yards. In one instance, two actually intersected each other, the diggers suddenly finding themselves face to face. There was, however, a small group who seemed to be involved in something. I got to know the leader, a Naval Lieutenant, Peter Fanshawe, known affectionately as 'Hornblower'. He struck me as being sound and sensible, and we became friends.

Before I was shot down I had been taught a simple code for sending messages home by means of the two letters and three cards a month we were allowed to write to our families and friends. Hornblower was delighted. Three others in the group had also been taught the code. We began to obtain what local intelligence we could and produced a unified communication system.

At about this time I heard that my name had been broadcast as being a POW and a few weeks later I received my first letter from Diana. It contained three important pieces of news. First, she was expecting a baby in November; second, my father was very ill; and third, she had put notices in *The Times* and *The Telegraph* announcing that I was a POW, giving the official Red Cross mode of address and adding 'friends and relations please write'. I was of course delighted to think that Diana and I had managed to start a family. I also received a letter from Dad before he died in June 1941,

But Diana's broadcast to all and sundry to write to me produced problems. Our coded letters were acknowledged in the same code by a 'pen pal' who signed himself or herself by a nom-de-plume. Within weeks of Diana's broadcast, letters galore came addressed to me, not only from my relations and friends but also from complete strangers, often signing themselves 'Love from Jenny' or Jim, or Molly, or Bertie. Dozens of them from all over the United Kingdom. Some, particularly the females, sent photos and a few were frankly pornographic. God knows how they got past the censor!

Needless to say, I much enjoyed this abundance of letters from unknown writers. But somewhere among them were presumably replies to my coded ones to Diana and my family. I should add perhaps that the code we used in no way affected the general content of our letters. It was simply a matter of maintaining a consistent style as letter followed letter. I was told after the War that virtually none of us gave the enemy cause to suspect our correspondence was coded.

But how were we to identify the 'hot' ones from among the flood that poured in to me when the mail arrived at our camp once a week? We did so in the end, but to this day I remain fascinated by the two-year-long, virtually one-sided, regular correspondence from one Thelma Blewett which drifted through pleasantries and descriptions of her friends and relations into emotional outpourings of unrequited love and an avowal to await my return when the War was over. I think I wrote her one postcard in gratitude for her fidelity! We never met. Little did Diana know what her public notices had produced. There was, however, a sad aftermath.

It was January 1942. The International Red Cross sent me a cable through the camp authorities announcing the safe arrival of our son born on 11 November the year before. Dad had died, Nan had joined the WRNS and my younger bother, Peter, was somewhere in the Western Highlands, working on the land. He never wrote to me. Germany had reneged on the German-Soviet pact and Hitler's armour was pouring east on a broad front, forcing the Soviet armies to retreat, adopting a 'scorched earth' policy as they went. Italy had long since joined the Axis with its navy more or less permanently sheltered in Taranto. The Vichy Government in France was being 'accommodating' to its conquerors. Japan had bombed Pearl Harbor and the USA was now in the War. The Battle of the Atlantic had reached a critical stage and the 8th Army in the Western Desert was taking a heavy hammering. The battleship *Prince of Wales* and the battle cruiser *Repulse* had been sunk by the Japanese. The War news was pretty bloody as far as we were concerned.

Rations remained short, the Red Cross food parcels were not reaching us regularly, and morale remained low.

But we had two successful escapes. Harry Burton was a tall flight lieutenant in his mid-twenties. He was a compulsive tunneller, determined to escape, and spent as much time underground as he did above. We had established an embryo Escape Committee which was recognised as a useful means of coordinating projects but lacked any real authority and was often disregarded.

So it was that one wintry night when the camp was deep in drifted snow, a flying officer clad from head to foot in white shirts, sheets and towels crawled from beneath one of the barrack blocks and began to clip his way through the barbed wire. The sentry in the nearest tower was seen to be shielding himself behind the side of his box, peering out occasionally. We watched through cracks in the window shutters. There was an almighty clang as a particularly strong strand of wire snapped under the homemade wire cutters. The sentry switched on his searchlight, spotted the fugitive well under the barbed wire and swung his machine gun towards him. Hopelessly caught and obviously panicking, the Kriegie raised a hand and shouted what he thought was German for 'don't shoot'. This is *Nicht schiessen*. What in fact he called was *Nicht scheissen* – 'don't shit'! The sentry kept the searchlight on but burst into guffaws of laughter while his victim was extricated from the wire fence and led away to the statutory seven days in the 'cooler'.

There was at that time no continuous watch on the entry and exit of guards – goons, we called them – nor any record of how many, if any, were in the camp at any one time. Because of this, Harry Burton was caught down a tunnel shaft by a roaming guard who entered the barrack block before Harry could get out and cover his tracks. So Harry went to the 'cooler', which was a brick two-celled building with iron bars across the windows. Prisoners serving their 'sentences' were allowed books, letters, extra food from the Red Cross parcels, and half an hour's exercise under armed guard each day. To many of us it was a week's peace and quiet, away from the enforced company of one's fellow Kriegies. Communication between a person in the cooler and his chums in the camp was relatively simple even though the cooler was outside the perimeter and a few metres from the main gate. Guards could be bribed and small objects – compasses, German currency and work passes (forged) – could be smuggled in, not always successfully of course. Harry asked for a change of clothes (not unreasonable), a local map, some currency and – not so easy – a hacksaw blade. We didn't have one in the camp. Harry was evidently planning an escape from the cooler, so we pulled out all the stops and, on the third day of his seven-day sentence, we got a hacksaw blade to Harry. I'm not saying how!

By the night of the fifth day Harry had succeeded in cutting through enough bars of his cell to allow him to squeeze out. The incisions had been made, entirely unsuspected by the patrolling guards, and concealed by margarine mixed with ersatz coffee. Harry slipped out, crawled on his belly under the lowest bar of the main gate and gained the German administration area, where he found a bicycle. He rode it through the night towards the Baltic seaport of Stralsund where he lay up under cover until early in the following morning. A guarded bridge led from Stralsund to the island of Rugen, to the north of which lay Sassnitz, the port which fed Trellebörg in neutral Sweden. Harry mounted his bicycle and joined the stream of workers crossing the bridge to Rugen. He had no identification card or foreign worker's pass (*Ausweis*). He studied the behaviour of the guard at the foot of the bridge. About one in ten were checked for their papers, the rest were waved through. There was no check at the Rugen end of the bridge. Harry continued with the stream. He was clad inconspicuously in dark trousers and a sweater. He carried a rucksack. He pedalled on.

At the foot of the bridge he saw the guard halt a woman on a cycle. He checked her papers and she remounted and rode on. She was six ahead of him. He overtook three stationary cyclists who didn't seem to mind, and dismounted. His turn came. The guard looked at him, said something which Harry didn't understand and waved him on. He pedalled on to

Sassnitz which he reached in the afternoon and spent the rest of the day sunbathing on the beach with many others who had their families running round and splashing in the sea. He fell asleep.

When he woke, the beach was emptying; the evening was drawing in. He rode towards the marshalling yards where the freight trains for Trellebörg were loaded up. He abandoned his bicycle and found cover somewhere where he could observe the yards without attracting attention.

As night fell the floodlights went on and the marshalling yard was fully illuminated. He chose his time when the guard was at the far end of the yard, crept in the shadows to a loaded freight train consisting of trucks covered by roped tarpaulins, found one that was slack and climbed in undetected. Much later, after a cursory inspection by a small patrol, there was a lurch, a clanking and the train steamed slowly onto the Swedish rail-ferry. In the early morning, Harry slipped from under the tarpaulin and gave himself up to the Swedish port inspector.

There seems to have been an argument as to whether Harry was still a German POW or a Swedish internee, but the latter was accepted. The British consul was alerted and within a few days Harry was airborne in the bomb-bay of a Mosquito on his way back to the UK. We got news of his return by a coded letter a few weeks later. Harry ended his career a few years ago as an Air Marshal with a knighthood. He was awarded the DSO for his escape. That was escape number one. The second was possibly less spectacular but none the less remarkable.

The Kriegie was 'Death' Shaw, so named because of his extraordinary and wholly improbable escape proposals, among which was one which involved a levy on every piece of elastic in the camp – braces, the sock suspenders we wore in those days, and even belts. His plan was to construct an elastic-operated man-throwing catapult on the lines of the ancient Roman weapons of war. By night his pals would hurl him over the barbed wire while a diversion at the other end of the camp would distract the guards' attention.

We had a lot of trouble convincing him that this would fail through lack of thrust and, at worst, was suicidal. He went away to brood over his next trick. This in fact succeeded, possibly because of its simplicity. He hid himself in the garbage bunker, which was a substantial one and stood against the wire of the NCOs' compound. We covered his absence during evening *Appell* and by next morning he had gone. I cannot say how he fled the camp, nor how he reached the UK, except that he too got on board a Swedish ferry from a Baltic port. He was also decorated for his successful escape.

Following his repatriation he was sent to a number of RAF stations, dressed as a *Luftwaffe* captain correct in every detail, and introduced as a

Norwegian Air Force officer – to test their security! I understand he passed muster on some four or five but was then identified as being in German uniform by an armed Warrant Officer who was inspecting the Guard Room when the 'Norwegian' pilot arrived. He was held at gun-point until the Station Commander and a security patrol arrived. Death Shaw was quickly unmasked and his charade came to an immediate end.

So, back in camp, week followed week, month followed month and a year passed. We lived for our mail from home, our Red Cross parcels and better news of the progress of the War. By now we had our own radio. It was a masterpiece of ingenuity, scrounging, bribery and sheer technical genius. We could receive the BBC news. Furthermore, the radio was con-structed in such a way that, in the event of a crisis, it could be dismantled in seconds and its components dispersed in safe hands or safe hiding places. The Germans undoubtedly knew of its existence but they were only too ready to get the edited versions of the BBC news: they never caused us any serious trouble.

German POW camps, both Army and RAF, were scattered over a large area of eastern Germany, including Silesia. They conformed to a common pattern. The barracks were single-storied, wooden huts standing some two feet from the ground. Each had a toilet, a washroom, a primitive cooking area and a central corridor off which were rooms of varying sizes, depending on the intended population of the camp. Most rooms had double-decker bunks with bed boards on which was a straw-stuffed mattress. There were two blankets and a bolster. The centre of the room was taken up by a wooden table and benches. There was usually one cupboard and a solid-fuel stove. The windows were fitted with shutters, which were closed after dark when the domestic lighting was switched off. Our daily rations consisted of enough bread (pretty inedible) to provide at most four slices, a small amount of margarine, an oddly flavoured sort of jam which was issued twice a week, ersatz coffee, a very little sugar and, at midday, a ration of hot soup which consisted of boiled water with swedes chopped up in it and the occasional piece of fatty meat which was generally regarded as horse. We were told we were on the same rations as the garrison troops. I doubt it. And, of course, we couldn't buy unrationed food from the village stores. For the first six months in the camp on the Baltic we were hungry – really hungry – and food became an obsession. Hunger is bad. Real hunger is very bad; starvation is catastrophic. There is a minimum calorific intake required to sustain human life, depending on the bodily make-up of the individual, his or her rate of calorific con-sumption. But if the dietary intake remains persistently below the required minimum, the person will slow up mentally and physically and eventually die. Starvation is a hastening of the process of dying. The quickest is dehydration through deprivation of liquid.

We, after I had arrived in the camp on the Baltic, were nowhere near starvation but we were always very hungry. Until the Red Cross parcels began to reach us our world was food obsessed; our quality of life gradually declined, our physical strength ebbed and our willpower and self-respect began to nosedive. That I went through this experience was a humiliation and a personal revelation that has lasted me throughout my life and has brought my philosophy to a sharp focus today. I look at the millions of people, especially those in the underdeveloped countries whose subsistence, under normal conditions, is comparable with ours in the winter of 1941 in the camp on the Baltic. But I also consider how near to starvation they are, and how countless of these millions die every year when their countries are visited by plague, wars or the failure of the rains.

In our camp we had only a vague idea of the death camps in which Hitler systematically and cynically exterminated by starvation, forced labour and gas chambers millions of Jews. Most of them died of starvation. Today I see at best an internationally organised series of relief operations directed to the succour of those unfortunate people of the Third World. How much of the aid, food, medicines, machinery and specialist teams actually penetrate the barrier of national bureaucracy or how much grant-in-aid is siphoned off by the leaders of these 'liberated' countries to be salted away in Swiss banks, who can tell?

But we came through the bad beginning. Red Cross parcels started to arrive and the Germans were honest in their delivery – not easy for them, as much of what the parcels contained was unobtainable in Germany. Real chocolate, Klim – which is milk spelled backwards – powdered and in a tin, real tea, sugar and corned beef. There were other things carefully chosen for their nutritional value. The improvement in our health, stamina and morale was immediate. Where nights had been spent restlessly tossing in our bunks, unable to sleep because of the emptiness of our stomachs, snores and peace took over. We had become men again.

The German staff were courteous and reasonable. The Commandant was a dapper, elderly Major Burchardt who spoke good English, having spent two years as a POW following his capture in German East Africa in the First World War. He liked being with us, enjoyed his cups of tea and was regarded as harmless and slightly pathetic. His *Lager Offizier* – Camp Officer – was an Austrian, *Hauptmann* Hans Pieber, whom we got to know well. He was emotional and clearly unhappy that our two countries should be at war. He didn't like the Americans and evidently hated the Japanese. I think he grieved for us even more than for himself. He was supported by a Bavarian, *Hauptmann* Zimmerleit, who had been a history teacher before the War. He occasionally gave lectures in passable English on the development of the Third Reich following the Weimar Government. The Polish and Czech members present invariably stormed out during the lecture, in protest at the 'bad things *Hauptmann* Zimmerleit said about our countries'.

Some time in early 1942, the rumours about a huge, new RAF POW camp at Sagan in Silesia were confirmed by the Commandant. It was planned to be opened in the summer and we would all be moved down by rail.

Stephenson, the SBO, had been sent to Colditz for possessing an infamous piece of doggerel written by a fellow POW which heaped filth on the Fuehrer. Stupid Stephenson kept it among his papers which were found during a routine search. 'Wings' Day and a number of the old *Dulag Luft* lags arrived, together with several of the senior staff including three squadron leaders, which considerably strengthened and improved the discipline of the camp. Life took on a more meaningful aspect and an authoritative hierarchy was established under 'Wings' Day.

'Hornblower' got into trouble. He had been communicating with a senior NCO in their compound. The messages were relatively inoffensive and in no way involved in intelligence. The Germans pounced and the two were taken off to some interrogation centre. 'Wings' Day showed his mettle. He put what pressure he could on Burchardt and demanded access to the International Red Cross. Some while later, 'Hornblower' and the NCO were returned to the camp, having been held in solitary confinement and regularly interrogated by the Gestapo.

CHAPTER NINETEEN

Kriegsgefangenschaft: *Stalag Luft III* and the 'Wooden Horse'

By the time of our move south to *Stalag Luft III*, Sagan, we were united, fit and prepared for whatever lay ahead. The journey was tedious but uneventful. We were in compartments as opposed to cattle trucks, which made a huge difference to our comfort. For the first and only time in my life, I spent a night in the luggage rack above the seat. It was tolerably comfortable and I slept quite well. During the early hours of the morning the train came to a halt in a small marshalling yard. We were told to collect our belongings and to prepare to get out. There was no platform, so we had to jump.

Our reception committee was formidable and frightening. At least sixty guards with rifles at the ready surrounded the area, with two machine gun positions manned near the front and rear of the train. Two officers were in charge and the whole scene, in the half-light of the morning under the dimmed overhead lamps, was menacing. The Germans were taking no chances with us and the message was all too clear. We were lined up and counted. Eventually we were marched off, carrying our possessions as best we could, though a couple of open trucks accompanied us and later took over most of our heavy luggage. We trudged out of a town where the inhabitants came from their houses and stared silently as the long column of Kriegies passed through.

We were halted twice to relieve nature and eat a snack. The countryside was flat, with groups of coniferous trees and little sign of agriculture. We passed the occasional horse-drawn cart carrying some sort of root vegetable and then, weary, hot and thirsty, we saw ahead of us the familiar cluster of buildings and an immense area consisting of wooden barrack blocks, barbed wire, machine gun boxes and another, but less ominous, reception committee of armed guards. We had arrived at *Stalag Luft III.*

We were kept in the *Vorlager* – the German administrative area – while we were individually searched and then herded into groups for admission to the camp proper. I remember being allocated to a room in Block 68 which was one of the eight blocks nearest the main gate. The furniture was of the standard pattern – wooden double bunks, a long wooden table, benches, a few stools and a solid-fuel stove. Again there was a toilet at one end of the block and a small kitchen at the other. I noticed that each block was a good two feet off the ground, which was a mixture of sand and pine needles. The camp was in a large pine forest.

Ours was one of four compounds, each separated by barbed wire and sentry boxes on stilts. Immediately adjacent to ours the defences were reinforced by a wooden fence. Our neighbours were United States Air Force aircrew. Further down the complex was a third and much larger camp for RAF officer personnel and a fourth lay a short distance away for RAF NCOs. It was, by any standard, a very large concentration of Allied airmen, at one time totalling some 4,000 to 5,000 POWs.

We were assigned to what was designated the East Camp. We met new colleagues, settled down to the usual routine and took stock of the escape potential of the camp. Also, we began to identify with long-neglected intellectual activities. We started a theatrical group and study groups for subjects such as law, accountancy and even theology, for which the International Red Cross provided reading material and guidance on exams and standards required.

In my room alone, among the original eight inmates were Aidan Crawley, a son of the Dean of Windsor, who was to become Under Secretary of State for Air in a post-War Labour government; Marcus Marsh, who trained the King's Derby winner; and David Lubbock, a naval Lieutenant, who was studying for a degree in medical science and was married to Lord Boyd Orr's daughter.

Intellectual, artistic and dramatic interests spread and, from the 600 or so who formed the original population of the East Camp, many young men of unsuspected talents emerged. I joined the Choral Society led by Jacobi, a talented musician and choirmaster. Bruce Organ, from the Stratford School of Drama, produced plays – particularly Shakespeare – in two of which I appeared. We became a civilised community, led by enthusiasts and intellectuals. A small group of Christian believers grew up and though we had no padre, prayer meetings were held each Sunday. I once gave an address which was well received though its base was less theological than down-to-earth reality.

But escape and its supporting services took precedence over everything else. There were two facets to escape: the obvious one being the need to get away and the other – perhaps even more important – the desirability of keeping as many German troops as possible employed in containing us.

Several others, like me, who had been taught the code, formed an intelligence group under a Squadron Leader who was studying for the law. He oversaw our letters and with a small staff coordinated the instructions which we received from the UK and gave us the replies he required us to include in our letters home. I confined my subversive activities to these coded letters, to and fro. Being claustrophobic, I was no use in tunnels. I was appointed Adjutant of the East Camp. As a go-between for the Kriegies and the German camp authorities, I had my hands full. Most of my duties were routine: assembling the Kriegies, other than those who were 'sick in bed', for the morning and evening *Appell* – roll call, dealing with petty disputes between the Germans and ourselves, and organising which rooms the ever-increasing influx of officer aircrew should occupy. All this was relatively straightforward.

My German was much improved. I established a fair relationship with the *Lager Offizier*, Major Züyst, a difficult, elderly reservist who had by then seen the writing on the wall. He disliked the British.

But it was the emotional and psychological problems of those who broke down under the strain of captivity and were referred to me that I found very distressing and almost beyond my competence. There was the young naval officer who had walked round the perimeter track with me for over an hour, talking wildly about a mass break-out. That night he climbed the barbed wire and was shot by the sentry, who had called 'Halt!' at least three times. Another, was a boy of eighteen, who had been shot down on a night bombing raid and had revealed something to his captors which he felt was treachery. It wasn't. I tried to convince him but he didn't want to know. He cut his throat in the potato store, the only private place in the camp. He didn't kill himself. He hadn't severed the jugular vein. But what happened to him when the German medical staff had removed him? What of his mind? A young Canadian went literally round the bend and had to be restrained physically before he could be got out of the camp into the German sick quarters. There were the inevitable 'Dear John' letters which spoke of broken marriages. How did one offer counsel or comfort? What could one do? These were the human problems which wore me down.

At the age of thirty, with no previous experience, I found myself assuming the role of pastor, psychologist and general welfare officer. I did my best, but it took a lot out of me and, as month followed month and despite the tide of war turning in our favour, I found that I needed to distance myself from other people's personal problems, if only to recharge my own batteries. Because once you have reached out to help a colleague in real distress, you can never disassociate yourself from that person.

So, with the agreement of the SBO, I handed over my office as Adjutant to another and either joined a theatre group or the choral society, or just loafed around with chums being an ordinary Kriegie. After a month or so I got my wind back and took over as Adjutant once more.

Escapes from our compound were few and far between, not through want or trying but largely because the Germans had learned from our previous attempts. But we made a nuisance and a name for ourselves, in the escape – which has since been the subject of a book and a film – known as the Wooden Horse.

As Adjutant, I was closely involved in handling the use of the wooden vaulting horse. It was constructed from the three-ply cases in which the Canadian Red Cross parcels were sent to the POW camps. Though light in weight it was strong enough to conceal a maximum of two men or several bags of sand. It was kept in the canteen overnight and was carried out each day with the 'digger' inside and placed precisely over the sand-covered trap of the vertical shaft that had previously been excavated. The sand and the subsoil plus the 'digger' emerged at the end of the working stint; he concealed the trap and was carried back into the canteen inside the Horse.

The sand was distributed in stockings with ends secured by a loop of tape. The stockings were worn down the trousers of chosen helpers, who held the retaining tapes until well clear of the area and then pulled the release tapes and dribbled the sand over the surface of the camp. The Germans knew from the nature of the 'droppings' that they were from a tunnel but were baffled as to where it was.

It was for me to ensure that each barrack block provided a rota of 'jumpers'. Not too frequently and not too seldom. The Germans took this vaulting activity for granted, as they did the joggers round the perimeter track, the footballers, volleyballers and plain crazy physical-jerkers. They did suspect a 'streaker' who, in the dead of winter, ran two circuits of the camp for a bet. But they satisfied themselves in their firmly held belief that all the British were mad anyway!

The Wooden Horse had been given the stamp of approval by the Escape Committee, which had become well organised, well respected and highly efficient. It operated not only a coordinating section but also a highly professional forgery team which produced up-to-date and outstandingly accurate foreign workers' passes, German camp entry passes, photocopies of German or French identity cards and travel documents. A false passport was used successfully for crossing a frontier. All these documents are to be seen in the Imperial War Museum in London.

At first the Wooden Horse was regarded as well worth a try but unlikely to succeed. However, as week followed week and snap *Appells*, with a 'digger' still underground, were successfully covered, confidence in the enterprise grew. This was dangerous. A loose remark overheard by a vigilant guard who had never disclosed his knowledge of English could blow the gaff. You cannot ensure absolute security in a camp of several hundred Kriegies of mixed backgrounds and nationality. But the tunnel remained undiscovered.

The digging went on, the subsoil was trickled out of the trousers and the *Appell* cover-ups remained undetected. A month or so passed. The leader of the trio came to the Escape Committee and announced that they were outside the barbed wire and had started the vertical shaft to the surface. They undertook to poke up a thin rod to establish the exact position of the exit before they broke through at night, hopefully in the edge of the woods surrounding the camp. Their report was disappointing. Their probe had surfaced behind the path used by the guards patrolling the camp, but it was some thirty metres from the shelter of the woods. If they continued digging horizontally, there was a considerable risk that the vertical shaft would result in a total collapse of that vital section of the tunnel.

We pondered this at length. We agreed that they should make their break where they were. They would be in shadow, they could time their individual escapes to when the patrol was at the far end of his beat and the searchlight would be trained into the camp.

All the three men escaped from the tunnel and independently made it back to the UK via Sweden. One, a young army gunner, picked up with the RAF at Tobruk but was subsequently killed in Malaya. The whole escape was his brainchild. The other two are still alive: one, Eric Williams, wrote the bestseller *The Wooden Horse*.

The seasons changed. Rugged, ice-bound winter, when the surrounding pines broke with sharp cracks like rifle fire under the weight of the frozen snow which lay upon them, turned into spring with a welter of melting ice and our pipes unfroze and strange animal and bird sounds came out from the woods. Then the hot summer came when we played cricket on a sand-baked pitch and sunbathed in shallow graves which we dug outside our barracks each day, to find them filled in by the night guards the following morning. Summer gradually drifted into autumn when flocks of migrating birds honked overhead and the window shutters were slammed to before the lights went out in the barracks. And so again into the frozen winter.

Though we were a community, we remained individuals, introspective, anxious to share our problems with each other, yet reluctant to do so, holding onto our few shreds of personal privacy until or unless they proved unbearable. The unity of the room became the confessional though many, indeed too many, often came to me as the Camp Adjutant. I learned to know myself and often, through others' problems, to find how best to come to terms with my own. I also learned a hell of a lot about human nature and perhaps the understanding of my fellow Kriegies which years of close company gave me has been the greatest lasting benefit that I gained from over four years behind barbed wire.

In 1942 Diana had gone to Ireland with Ranald, the name we had agreed for our son. She was living in Clonmel in County Tipperary with Dollie Perry. Diana wrote happily about her life in the country and of Ranald's development. About a year later, I detected a change in her letters. They became repetitive. She sent me photos of herself and Ranald. I thought she looked far from well. Her letters became more and more confused. There was a gap of several weeks and then I received a very guarded letter from Dollie saying that Diana had gone to Belfast where she was in hospital having had a slight nervous breakdown. Ranald was fine and a nanny was looking after him. The news of Diana distressed me greatly.

I learned later that Diana had shown signs of cracking up for the better part of six months. Then she received a letter from an unknown man in Belfast who said he knew me, was travelling south into Tipperary and would like to pay her a visit. With Dollie's agreement, she arranged to meet him. After a few preliminaries he disclosed that he was a British Intelligence Officer who was responsible for decoding my letters when they were filtered through his organisation. They had missed two in a series I had written to her. He gave a rough idea of the dates I could have written them and asked her if she had them. She went to look, found the two he wanted and handed them over. He promised to return them which, in the event, he did. I am not sure what credentials he gave but the day after his visit she suddenly realised what she might have done. She packed a bag, left Ranald with Dollie and, saying she was visiting friends for a few days, took the train for Belfast. Diana had never known that my letters to her were in code.

Two days later Dollie heard that Diana had gone to the police in Belfast, had broken down and begun to talk dangerously. The police had checked her out and she had been admitted to a private ward in a psychiatric hospital. She was there for several weeks. When her letters began to come through again they read more normally and my anxiety lessened. But from then on I was never entirely at peace: I knew too much about nervous breakdowns, both from witnessing the stresses of airborne armed combat and from prisoner-of-war experiences.

CHAPTER TWENTY

Douglas Bader

The arrival of Douglas Bader in 1942 was not unexpected. We heard that he had been shot down over France, that a truce had been agreed between the *Luftwaffe* and the RAF for a new pair of legs to be dropped by parachute and that he had made a bid to escape from a hospital. Within days he made his presence felt. He stomped round the camp followed by a 'tail' of those he had led earlier in the War and was, put bluntly, a bloody nuisance. His aggressive and uncompromising spirit found no outlet in the camp. He scorned the 'softly softly' philosophy we had cultivated to avoid confrontation with the authorities so that we could dig tunnels, write our coded letters and develop our 'contacts' from among the increasing numbers of disillusioned German guards. He wanted overt resistance.

The Germans called an unscheduled *Appell*. Bader, then a Wing Commander, assembled the senior officers of each barrack block and proposed a 'sit-in'. No one was to go out on *Appell*. The meeting broke up in disarray. Only two representatives decided to follow Bader. The rest said he was talking balls. The German guard came into the camp. No one knew what to do and I'm not sure whether the SBO gave instructions. Bader and his followers went from block to block shouting to the inmates to stay put. Quite a lot did. Bader had a commanding personality. But others drifted out to the parade ground in dribs and drabs.

The main gate was opened and a troop of heavily armed tin-helmeted Germans marched in, their tommy guns at the ready. Orders were shouted in English and German. Then tommy guns were opened up at the base of the barracks. Within minutes the 'sit-in' was over and the *Appell* formed up. Bader was led out of the camp. We were counted, the armed troop left and we returned to our rooms. Bader had lost the first round.

I got to know Douglas well. We became friends though I failed to get across to him the extent of the War effort that was being waged unconventionally in the immense complex of the compounds of *Stalag Luft III*. Because he wasn't leading it, he instinctively opposed it and unwittingly created difficulties for the Escape Committee and its numerous ancillary functions. But the Germans had had enough. Bader was removed to Colditz, where perhaps he met more of his ilk. In a strange way I missed him. Our guards relaxed and we settled down to our undercover activities without the constant risk of their being blown by the Germans over-reacting to the Bader-provoked nonsenses.

The whole pattern of the War had changed. The Russians had re-grouped far back east of their European frontier. Leningrad was under siege by the Germans, but was holding and the Soviet counter-attack to the south had surrounded Von Paulus in Stalingrad. 'Bomber' Harris had persuaded Churchill and the War Cabinet that massive night bombing of German cities would break the enemy morale. The United States Air Force was building up a complementary day bombing offensive from a vast number of hastily constructed air bases in East Anglia and vast reaches of the Midlands. Montgomery had begun his successful operation against Rommel's Afrika Korps in the Middle East. The BBC News, which we received daily almost without fail, was reassuring.

Then with twenty-four hours warning, the SBO was called to the Commandant's office and given a list of some sixty or seventy POWs who were to be removed to a camp in Poland for being 'undisciplined and uncooperative'. The camp was at Schubin. It was late autumn. I was among those to be purged, as was 'Wings' Day. I was frankly astonished, though in many ways pleased. A change was a change. It was made clear that we would be under the command of the German Army who might not be as tolerant of our behaviour as the *Luftwaffe*. Rules were different and stricter.

We were in fact to be punished for the oft repeated complaint of being 'uncooperative'.

CHAPTER TWENTY-ONE

Kriegsgefangenschaft: Schubin, Poland

So again by train across Germany, this time into Poland. Transport conditions were as usual, though a lack of supervision resulted in a unsuccessful escape by an elderly Major who had somehow joined the RAF captives in France in 1940 and had been our 'guest' ever since. Major Dodge, following repeated requests to go to the toilet, succeeded in prising open the window and swinging himself out. We saw his anguished face through our window and then he was gone. The train was chugging sluggishly up an incline.

A staccato rattle of machine gun fire burst from the rear. The train jerked to a halt and a breathless and bruised Major was pushed unceremoniously back into our compartment, accompanied by a very unpleasant German guard who, with pistol in hand, stood with his back to the door for the remainder of the journey. No one was allowed to visit the toilet which was, to some of us, unendurable until a bucket was produced. But it stayed in our compartment!

Our camp at Schubin was little different from other German POW camps. It was, however, built on a slope which provided splendid sledging during the coming winter. The Army guards seemed reasonable enough. On our arrival we were counted time and time again. The Commandant was a nervous little Major with a limp. He was clearly uneasy about his RAF prisoners and their SBO, 'Wings' Day, who had earned quite a reputation. We got their measure in double quick time. To them the RAF was a wild, insubordinate and devious service with no traditions and totally 'uncooperative'. How right they were in many respects!

'Wings' Day soon found breaches of the Geneva Convention which he threw at the Commandant. Inadequate basic rations, failure to release Red Cross parcels which were known to be accumulating in the *Vorlager*, and unacceptable delays in having the latrines – *Aborte* – cleared by the sullage lorry. 'Wings' Day went for him with unrelenting regularity. Why, for example, was our mail being withheld? Where were our monthly clothing parcels which we knew had been redirected to our new camp?

Our intelligence on all matters was almost immediately passed to us by the Polish workers who serviced the camp in various ways, many humiliating and degrading. There were amongst us several Poles who had joined the RAF and ended up as Kriegies. To allow such inevitable fraternising between the Poles was an act of crass stupidity on the part of the Germans.

Before long two potential tunnel sites were identified. The outside latrines were ten-seaters in two rows facing each other. The building was a mere couple of yards from the wire. A wooden partition was fitted by the escape team, sealing off the trench of number one seat from its neighbour, creating in effect a ready-made vertical shaft which required a mere three or four feet further deepening before the horizontal tunnelling could begin. A messy beginning but too good an opportunity to pass up.

We were all told NOT to use number one seat. The Polish driver of the sullage lorry – the Krap Kart – and his mate were passed as trustworthy and made privy to the scheme which soon made good progress. Once, a prowling guard felt the urge and used the forbidden seat. The digger was some way along the tunnel at the face and had a messy retreat at the end of his stint. He stank for days. But progress continued.

The second site was behind the altar of a small, disused chapel which contained broken timber and other junk. It was less successful. After several weeks chipping away at stone foundations, the project was abandoned. The Germans found it several weeks later and sealed up the chapel, talking piously of desecration. But it diverted their attention from the *Abort* operation. The day arrived when the tunnel was finished and only a foot or so of vertical digging was required to break through. That night was dark with no moon. Eight went down the shaft and along the tunnel by day before our barrack blocks were locked and blacked out. The team included Major Dodge and a couple of Poles. Evening *Appell* was successfully covered. The German army appeared to be innumerate or plain stupid or both.

Early the following morning soon after first light, the balloon went up. '*Raus! Raus! Raus!* . . .' – 'Out, out, out' – in our pyjamas and overcoats. Literally dragging our feet and taking as long as possible, we shambled out to be counted, once, twice, and yet again. The Commandant limped back and forth accompanied by 'Wings' Day who demanded to know what was going on. Three on *Appell* were genuinely ill with high fevers. 'Wings' insisted they be allowed back to their bunks. The Commandant prevaricated, whereupon a perfectly fit Flying Officer keeled over and began to writhe on the ground. An old trick we had played back in *Stalag Luft III*. 'Wings' towered above the Commandant and produced an admirable imitation of a man about to throw a fit: consternation all round. A mounting growl from the Kriegies of 'Epilepsy' brought two of the guards to the 'patient' on the ground. A stretcher was brought and he was carted off to the *Lazarett* – sick quarters – outside the camp.

The three genuine cases of 'flu' were allowed to return to their barracks. We were then recounted for the umpteenth time and allowed to dismiss. Oddly enough, I felt sorry for the wretched limping Commandant who would, of course, be answerable to higher authority for the escape of eight RAF POWs after they had been committed to his charge for no more than a few months. I was glad I wasn't in his boots.

Dodge was the first to be recaptured. He was courageous and an inveterate 'escapologist' but pretty thick and his plans were hopeless. One by one others were caught. One of the Poles never reappeared. We hoped he had made it among his own folk, but there always lurked the fear that he might have come to a tragic end.

There was no 'cooler' at Schubin. As an example to all of us, we were confined to barracks for a week and allowed out, barrack by barrack, for one hour a day for exercise. The latrines were *Verboten*! We had two in each block, so we got by.

'Wings' Day was splendid. He demanded to see the Commandant. He again invoked the Geneva Convention which stipulated that an individual breach of discipline should not result in wholesale punishment of the POWs in the camp. That this had become common practice, particularly among the army stalags, in no way deterred 'Wings' who, making the most of the disasters suffered by the German forces and predicting the possibility of military defeat or a negotiated peace, suggested that the internationally accepted conduct towards POWs should be observed. The Commandant relented. The following day our confinement to barracks was ended and life returned to normal.

'Wings' was no orator. He was nervous and hesitant when speaking in public but he called an assembly on the parade ground and, in the presence of a number of guards who were there presumably to ensure order if necessary, he told us of his meeting with the Commandant and ended by stating emphatically that while he remained our representative he would brook no breach of accepted treatment of officers. He looked tired and his voice broke once or twice. He was a great man.

Several weeks later a Polish working squad were seen to be digging vertical shafts at intervals around the camp. Mines, we were told by our guards. Any further tunnellers would risk being blown up. But our local informers scotched that one. They were microphones. This seemed much more likely as bales of cable appeared and each 'dug out' was connected with its neighbour. Then, behold, a sentry box facing the camp was erected a few yards outside the wire. Some sort of boxed equipment was installed and finally a seat and what looked like a pair of earphones.

There was some more digging to cover the cable system and a lot of detailed and obviously first-hand information as to the listening equipment that had been installed in the sentry box was passed to us. For it was indeed a listening unit designed to detect the sound of digging through the 'slaves' that were wired into the central reception console in the sentry box.

For a few days it remained unmanned, at least during daylight hours. Then, to our huge amusement, it was reported that the Commandant himself was in the box with headphones over his uniform cap. We trooped round the perimeter track to see for ourselves. Sure enough, there he was.

A prank! Whose idea it was is immaterial. It was a winner! The entire camp walked round the perimeter track for an hour. As each Kriegie passed the Commandant in the box he saluted. The Commandant saluted back. So it went on. The poor man must have saluted a thousand times or more before he was replaced by an NCO to whom we gave the less respectful two fingers up.

A month or so later we were informed that we were returning to *Stalag Luft III*. The German Army, it seemed, had found us more than they had bargained for. The limping Commandant had been pronounced medically unfit and – so the bush telegraph had it – was in a mental hospital.

CHAPTER TWENTY-TWO

Kriegsgefangenschaft: Sagan Revisited

Back in the familiar surroundings of *Stalag Luft III* in Sagan, we had much to tell our old colleagues. It was quite a reunion. The population of East Camp had increased considerably. Rooms were overcrowded and triple-tier bunks had been introduced. Two Group Captains had arrived during our absence. The senior was the SBO. I didn't like him and it was touch and go whether I agreed to resume my old job as Camp Adjutant, but in the end I did. The man who had taken over was at the end of his tether and I was put under a lot of pressure from the new SBO to do so. Schubin had been a playground. Sagan looked like being tough going. It certainly was.

The atmosphere in the camp had changed – and not for the best. Factions had developed. Within a few days I sensed an alien and unhealthy influence that had permeated the overcrowded barrack blocks. I was besieged by requests to remove so-and-so to another room because he was a bad influence; because he never stopped talking; because he was frequently caught helping himself to more than his food ration; because he never washed and stank. So it went on.

The SBO was unpopular. He was not an attractive person though he was a brave man and had been awarded a DSO in Bomber Command. He was pasty-faced, given to favouritism and possessed of a snide criticism of those he didn't like. He 'adopted' a senior NCO whom he employed as a fag rather more than as a batman. He gave him the phoney rank of Pilot Officer to ensure that if and when we were moved his servant would come with the officers. I made a point of getting to know the SBO as a man. I discovered much below the surface which was both sad and lonely. Once he showed me a poem he had written to a lady friend in England. She was not his wife. It was heart-rending in its appeal. I was touched and thrown off balance by the confidence he had bestowed on me. We began to get on together much better.

'Wings' Day had been moved to another camp. The problem of the caucuses, the non-conformists or pure dissidents remained. I did what I could, which was little enough. A well-known awkward bugger was unlikely to be accepted by another room after he had driven his old room-mates to distraction. How do you cope with a man who snores so loudly that the occupants of the next-door room complain?

But our own way of life continued. I was happy to be back in Sagan. The Red Cross food parcels were arriving regularly, news from Diana and friends and relations was encouraging, and 'Operation Overlord', the Allied invasion of Europe, had succeeded. Eisenhower, the Supreme Allied Commander, though quarrelling constantly with Montgomery, had put an immense Anglo-American force ashore in France and, after severe setbacks, was advancing east. The Soviet Army had retaken all its lost territory and was advancing on a massive front. Italy had surrendered and, after a bitterly fought series of engagements by the Germans against the Allies from the south, Monte Cassino fell with appalling casualties on both sides.

THE GREAT ESCAPE

This epic but tragic escape has been so well documented and filmed that I shall not dwell on the details of the planning, conduct and final success of this historic and professional example of tunnelling. The tunnel was lit by electricity from the camp mains. It was so long that it was serviced by a cable railway which carried diggers, air-pump operators and soil from the face throughout its length. It was a year-long operation managed with outstanding skill by a team in the North Camp. Seventy-odd escaped, two or maybe three reached neutral safety, and fifty were shot on recapture. I lost many good colleagues and the shock that went through the entire complex of *Stalag Luft III* was devastating.

We, in the East Camp, knew of the tunnel's existence. The Germans likewise suspected that a major operation was in progress. The better part of 300 metres of cable had mysteriously vanished during a rewiring of an old section of the camp.

Our SBO was summoned to the Commandant who, in obvious distress, told him that many who had escaped had resisted arrest on recapture and had been shot. They had been cremated and their ashes would be sent to the International Red Cross. The SBO expressed his outrage, said that he did not hold the Commandant to blame, but flatly refused to accept the explanation. It was a blatant lie and those responsible would be brought to book when the War was over. He called an immediate assembly on the parade ground. He told us of his interview with the Commandant and of his reaction to the story about resisting arrest. He didn't pull his punches, for which I admired him. He forbade all escapes until further notice.

Piece by piece the truth came out. The fifty selected to be shot were mostly unmarried – I'll say that for the Germans. They were put on a train to a wooded area where they were allowed out 'for exercise'. There they were gunned down by SS troops with rifles and machine guns. Those not immediately killed were given the *coup de grace* by officers with revolvers.

We held a simple memorial service in the camp. We had no padre but the SBO rose to the occasion and we sang 'Abide with Me'. The Germans at first forbade the service but the leaders of all compounds in the camp made it absolutely clear that if a veto were imposed they would not be responsible for the behaviour of the officers in their charge. They suggested that any further bloodshed would fuel the hatred which the murder of the fifty had already generated. We won that round.

Gradually things returned to normal. Our Christmas celebrations were traditionally a somewhat awkward visitation by the Commandant and his officers who wished us 'Good Christmas' and gave us a small Christmas tree. This was followed by those who were so disposed walking round the perimeter track wishing 'Happy Christmas' to the guards and pitching tins of cigarettes over the wire to those on foot patrol. On the orders of the SBO, we had refused to give parole for Christmas Day. It would have meant the release from duty of a large number of guards.

We held a short service, sang appropriate hymns with a small choir led by Jacobi and went to earth in our rooms for the festive meal which those of us who could cook had prepared from a little bit of extra German rations and our Red Cross food parcels.

But the mainstay of the meal was a generous supply of extremely intoxicating schnapps. Our Polish colleagues had taught us to distil this from the dried fruit in our food parcels and the yeast which we had 'bought' from the numerous guards who were by now on our payroll. Illicit stills were operated at night behind the shutters. To produce a pint of 'hooch' took a long while but it was worth it and by the 1944 festival every room in the camp had an adequate supply. To their credit, while acknowledging our refusal to give parole, the Germans allowed us to move from barrack to barrack until midnight, when we were assisted back to where we belonged, the shutters were closed and half an hour later the lights went out.

Shortly before midnight we saw the searchlights focusing on a figure climbing onto the roof of one of the barracks. He had a trumpet in his hand. In the full glare of some four searchlights in the middle of the frozen night, he stood on the roof and played with immense feeling and great beauty – *Stille Nacht. Heilige Nacht.*

To me this is the most moving carol of all time ...

Only one searchlight remained beamed on the trumpeter, who was a Canadian. He ended the carol, by which time the other searchlight had been dimmed, possibly a tribute to an emotion which transcended the barriers of war. He climbed down and went to his barrack. The compound remained silent for a time. It was a deeply moving occasion which I shall never forget.

On the 27 January 1945, with the Russian Army a mere one hundred kilometres to the east, the SBO was instructed to prepare the East Camp for evacuation that night.

CHAPTER TWENTY-THREE

The March to the West and the Unknown

he message went round in a flash. The senior officer in each room was in charge of his unit. Bed boards were converted into sledges, bags of clothes were sewn together by anyone with a needle and cotton. I ran round each of the eight barracks to see how preparations were going. All seemed fine.

We were called out and counted at 6 pm, then sent back to our barracks and told to have a meal. At nine o'clock with the outside temperature at −15°C we were counted again and told to return to barracks. This was repeated at midnight when the SBO refused to obey any further orders to attend *Appell*. We were left alone until about 7 am, by which time the entire East Camp was ready to follow Scott to the Antarctic if necessary.

The evacuation had begun during the previous evening with the NCOs' Camp; then the North Camp during the night, followed by the USAF Camp who – if the stories were true – were hopelessly unprepared for what was to follow. We from the East Camp were the last to go and, though we had a night in our barracks, no one slept and we spent the time reinforcing our sledges and making sure of our essential footwear and clothing.

We got what information we could from our German intelligence but, apart from the fact that we were to march west, our destination remained unknown. Though we didn't realise it at the time, an enormous migration of prisoners of all nationalities was on the move, driven by their captors ahead of the ever-advancing Soviet forces.

At about nine o'clock on the morning of 28 January 1945 – my brother's birthday – a final *Appell* was held; we were given half an hour to prepare ourselves for evacuation and then marched out, some eight hundred Kriegies, through the main gate of *Stalag Luft III*.

It was deep winter. The whole of Silesia was snow-bound.

Our column wound through woods, over long stretches of open moorland and through small villages where the inhabitants had already lost interest in the constant stream of prisoners who had trudged through since first light. A few followed for a while, begging for cigarettes, but were sent off by our guards. Poor guards. Mostly elderly reservists, they had no idea whither we were bound. They laboured under their rucksacks and the weight of their rifles. Their rations were pitiful and we carried their luggage on our sledges and gave them what we could from the Red Cross parcels we had been allowed to collect from the parcel store before our departure from Sagan. We were fit and organised and in high spirits.

It was extraordinary with what efficiency and dispatch the East Camp got its circus on the road. There were the inevitable hitches and arguments but, as the long trail of Kriegies and their sledges wound its way along the track of those who had left during the night, I shared the spirit of adventure, tinged albeit with fear of the unknown, that possessed this plodding, seemingly endless column of young men and their weary, elderly guards.

The SBO had asked me to keep him company in the front. We both had homemade golf clubs which we used as walking sticks. He set a pace which was too fast for the column with their sledges. I suggested we slow up. He agreed and we halted once an hour for five minutes to allow the stragglers to catch up and have something to eat. I used up a lot of energy walking back to the tail of the column to help with breakdowns or give advice or generally be seen to be around. I then had to hurry back to the front and keep the pace down lest the column became too long and straggling.

At one stage, after we had halted at the top of a long uphill drag, I looked back at the men and their sledges slowly climbing the hill. It was a brilliant January day: not a cloud in the sky and not a breath of wind. The temperature was well below zero. From the long, straggling column steam was rising from their bodies. Most had shed their shirts and jackets: many were plodding stripped to the waist. When they joined us, I sent a message back telling them to put on their clothes during the halt. Some refused but most did what I asked. We were beginning to get very tired and the winter sun was slowly slipping down in the west.

The SBO and I resumed the march. We had not seen our German Major Züyst throughout the day: indeed he didn't reappear until the following morning. We were effectively under the command of *Oberfeldwebel* (Warrant Officer) Stühlmeier who had been our camp disciplinarian for some two years. He and I related well and grew to respect each other.

We worked together: me with my elementary but effective German and he with his smattering of English. We both understood that '*Das ist eine Schweinerei*' meant 'that's a bloody mess', and he soon accepted 'Piss off!' as an effective way of ending an argument with a belligerent Kriegie.

The SBO fell silent as we trudged along the snow-bound route. I was not inclined to talk. Instead I let my mind dwell on all that had happened during my time in *Stalag Luft III*. In a strange way, it was as though I was leaving behind something that had become a habitat, a way of life. In a sense our going left me with a feeling of insecurity. I would have walked back to what I had left for ever. Possibly I was more exhausted during the march west than I realised: perhaps emotionally rather more than physically.

The Second Front, Operation Overlord, had succeeded and the British, Canadian and American forces had broken out of the bridgehead and were inexorably forging eastwards.

The Russians cannot have been far behind our exodus, often overtaking other columns of Allied POWs struggling westwards from their camps in central and eastern Germany.

My mind wandered back to the events of the past year and to the first news we had of the German V-1, the flying bomb that had been launched in increasing numbers against London. It created a lot of damage and its nuisance value was considerable. It was, however, vulnerable to the latest Allied fighter aircraft but inevitably many got through.

Diana's mother, together with her sister-in-law and niece, were attending a memorial service for those who had been shot following the Great Escape. The service was being held in the Guards' Chapel when a flying bomb fell on it. Virtually the entire congregation, including Diana's mother, aunt and cousin, were killed. I had Diana's letter with me on the march. It was an amazing example of restrained emotion, written with a philosophic acceptance which I found of immense comfort and encouragement to me.

The Allied forces overran most of the V-1 sites but by then a far more potent weapon was being deployed against south-east England and London in particular, the V-2 – the ballistic rocket which was indestructible once launched from its base. This weapon was extremely effective and had very sinister overtones. The Allies had discovered how to split the atom and produce an atomic bomb of immense destructive power. Germany likewise was well on the way to a similar breakthrough and the Soviet Union, though at the time without the scientific know-how, was going flat out to make good its inferior position and was spying madly wherever there was a sniff of nuclear fission. None of this was known to us as we marched to the west.

Mentally and physically exhausted, I managed to keep the now extended column more or less together, though we had to halt for the better part of twenty minutes each hour to allow the stragglers, those with broken sledges, with broken spirits, or simply suffering from exhaustion, to catch up with us. It was during one of these lengthy halts, when Hornblower had done us proud in preparing a substantial snack, that Major Züyst stormed up to us, ordered us to move at once and said that we had deliberately held up the march. Hornblower explained that we were eating our rations and would be ready to move as soon as possible. Züyst drew his revolver, pointed it at Hornblower and screamed words to the effect: 'If you do not move now, I can shoot you down!' Hornblower looked him straight in the face and began methodically to collect his belongings, while we grabbed what food we could. Züyst seemed to have taken leave of his senses. He waved his revolver and ordered one of the guards to arrest Hornblower. A brave but possibly foolhardy young Canadian in our team said with astonishing calm and deliberation: 'If you murder that British officer, you will die.'

I reckoned it was high time I involved Stühlmeier and went off to look for him. It was as well I did. By the time I found him and we had returned to the scene, the situation looked very ugly. Züyst had put his revolver back in its bolster but was furious. A morose-looking guard stood with his rifle pointed at the ground, with a circle of extremely angry Kriegies surrounding the group and going for Züyst hell for leather. Many had adequate German and when Stühlmeier and I arrived there was a real fracas going on, with the SBO involved.

'What the hell does the Major think he's doing?' 'Does he know that throughout the day we have carried the baggage of his German friends on our sledges?' 'Does he want real trouble?' 'There are eight hundred of us. The War's coming to an end and we're not prepared to be pushed around by a defeated enemy!'

The SBO ordered all German baggage and equipment – this included quite a number of rifles! – to be unloaded from our sledges. A hefty Flight Lieutenant from South Africa said 'Bloody well right!' and set off down the column, by now cold and dispirited, to pass the SBO's order down the line. Within half an hour every piece of German baggage was off loaded and lying in the snow.

We moved on. Presumably the support lorry carrying a heap of potatoes and bread, all frozen solid, had retrieved the German baggage. Züyst marched off, escorted by Stühlmeier. We were not to see the Major again. Stühlmeier took over, with the SBO and me forming an administrative group. It worked very well.

As evening fell we came to a small town. The inhabitants, except for a few who spat at us and called us *Mordbrenner*, came out and offered us eggs, cheese and even chickens – alive – for cigarettes, chocolate and butter. Clearly, those of our colleagues who had preceded us had paved the way for a very useful trade, much to our advantage. We were billeted overnight in a school. I think the SBO got a bunk. We were under cover, the radio was assembled and the BBC news was good. We ate and then fell asleep from sheer exhaustion.

The following day was much like the first. We got into a moderate stride which inevitably slowed towards the afternoon. There was no trouble. Züyst was not to be seen and, though the column stretched behind us for at least a kilometre we made steady progress westward. The SBO relented on his order of the previous day and we took on our guards' baggage, very much to their relief. Poor men, marching across Germany in the dead of winter, knowing little of the truth of the War except that the Russians were behind us and that the Allies were advancing from the west. Small wonder that their numbers dwindled as we plodded on. Desertion was not infrequent and we off-loaded German baggage after its owner had not been seen for two days.

We spent the second night in a church. I may have nodded off in my pew during previous uninspiring and monotonous sermons but I had never prepared myself to pass a night in the second-row pew of a Lutheran church. The radio boys had found a power point in the belfry, so we received the BBC news. The SBO and the 'reporters' devised a plan which involved a mock service conducted by the leader of the radio team. By word of mouth it was made known to us in the church. The news had been written in a sort of Kriegie shorthand with appropriate pauses. The 'reader' mounted the pulpit and the congregation became silent. He read out the headline – 'The Russian forces continue their advance westwards and have today taken ... Allied forces are continuing to advance, particularly on the northern front ...' The congregation then said loudly, 'A ... men'. Thus the news was read, not that I think it would have mattered had any of the few guards present realised the purpose of 'evening prayers'. But we depended so much on our radio that we took quite extraordinary measures to conceal its existence.

The third day we marched slowly. It was bitterly cold and none of us had slept much in the pews. I became introspective and at times close to despair. Alone, I could have given up, but with this great exodus – for which I had a degree of responsibility – my will was strengthened. All of us pressed on.

That night we were billeted in four barns of a sizeable farm. The barns were full of hay. The farmers seemed friendly and we exchanged eggs for cigarettes at a rate agreed after some hard bargaining. The Americans who had preceded us had spoilt the market – as they always do. But we were allowed to use the huge coppers of boiling water in the farm kitchen to cook our eggs. Stühlmeier and those who remained of our guards were sitting around a blazing log fire in the kitchen-diner when I went to thank him and bid him, his hosts and his guards '*Gute Nacht*'. We ate our eggs, climbed into the hay and slept like logs.

The next day was bad – very bad. It was snowing heavily. Several sledges had broken down and we were told that we had to march forty kilometres to our next evening accommodation. The SBO said this was impossible and he demanded that we remain where we were until the weather improved. No dice! March we must and march we did. We covered something like twenty-two miles in ten hours. This may not seem a great achievement but in blinding snow, hauling sledges and short of food and sleep, it was pretty good. Particularly as everyone was still upright.

That day, and on the previous two days, I had a very strange experience. On the march from the school to the church and then from the church to the barns, I had been aware of a 'presence', who seemed to keep pace with us on the other side of the road. Whoever it was never looked at us but was always there. I pointed out the figure loping along the edge of the woods on the other side of the road to someone with me. He looked and then said he couldn't see anybody. I pointed again and said 'Look, there it is'. He looked again and said 'There's no one there, you're imagining things, Mac'. He moved away and I walked on alone – except for the presence across the road.

As darkness fell on that first day's march, the figure faded in the dusk. By the time we had reached the school, it was out of my mind. Indeed I thought no more about it until the following day. The figure was there again: not clearly defined but slightly stooped and walking at our pace.

I found myself becoming obsessed with my unknown companion. I tried to drag my mind away from this phantom, or whatever it was.

Made to march on the right-hand side of the road, we could, accompanied by a guard, leave the column to relieve nature but we were not allowed to cross to the left-hand side. I approached Stühlmeier and asked if he would come with me across the road as I was concerned that someone seemed to be following us. He was at first dubious but then agreed and, with his revolver in his hand, led me over. He watched me very carefully. I looked through the conifers, walked around with Stühlmeier behind me, but found no trace of my companion. There were no footsteps in the snow, no sign of any human presence. I nodded to

Stühlmeier and we rejoined the column. He looked at me strangely and said I was very tired.

Next day was dry, cold and cloudless. Stühlmeier kept close to me, which I appreciated. Again I sensed the presence accompanying us. It disappeared when we passed through villages and became vague and indistinct when we moved through open country. It was absolutely clear to me only when the road ran through woods. By the time we approached the little town and the church where we spent the second night, I had come to accept the person as being identified with me, and me alone. I remember that, when I began to fall asleep in that place of sanctuary, the thought that my companion might be with me on the march of the morrow gave me a sense of peace and hope.

The next day's march was Hell – we marched through another snow-storm – but my companion was there and I found a strange comfort and strength in the fact. Our column was beginning to crack up. The potato wagon was no way suitable to carry casualties. It was uncovered and anyone aboard it and ill would have died of hypothermia in a day. Everybody had to keep going. It was the uncertainty of our daily destinations that broke many spirits. But we had to bash on and do what was expected of us, worn out though we were.

On the fourth night on the march we reached a town called Muskau. Not large but an industrial centre with a glass factory which had been evacuated and into which we were led for the night. Other than the glass-making factory, which we effectively sabotaged, there were numerous warehouses and packing sheds where bales of packaging were available as coverings for the night. There was also a number of Polish female employees, who were more than ready to offer themselves for a tin of cigarettes or butter. We were far too exhausted to show any interest and the women sloped off disgruntled.

We remained in Muskau for two days which gave us time to recover and rest. The women were back that morning. They were trollops and I doubt many of us accepted their invitations. For the better part of four years I and many others had been deprived of normal sex. In the French POW camps, homosexuality was not unusual. In the East Camp of *Stalag Luft III* there was none, to the best of my knowledge. However there was a strange homosexual affinity between those younger Kriegies who had played parts as girls in our various plays and musicals and the 'elder brethren' in the camp who would invite these young men to tea. Thus a pseudo-sexual influence permeated certain rooms where the attractive young men were frequently entertained. Many resorted to the only way of release open to us: masturbation. But when the Red Cross parcels and the

German rations were woefully inadequate, the sexual urge drifted away; when we had enough to eat, it crept back.

On the second day of our confinement in the glass factory in Muskau, we were called to be ready to leave in twenty minutes. We were marched through the town – the snow had stopped – and were halted at the railway station. Here we were separated into groups of twenty and herded into cattle trucks of a train with steam up. The doors were slammed to: it was getting dark and then the train snorted and clanked away. Where to, no one knew.

It was bitterly cold in our cattle truck. We had nothing to lie on except the bare, hard boards and nothing with which to cover ourselves, other than our overcoats, some RAF, others Polish, acquired through a thriving black market run by the 'outside workers' when we were in Schubin. We spent a miserable night, cold and sleepless. I doubt many of us would have contemplated escape even had the opportunity occurred. Such insidious mental and physical erosion was the forerunner of despair.

Despair had to be fought tooth and nail, for it was the harbinger of collapse and death. Few of us were religious or had much understanding of the psychology of mind over matter. But we did our best, individually and in groups, to maintain our morale, even though the bucket provided for our bodily needs stank. Some time early the following morning the train stopped, the doors were opened and we were ordered out 'for exercise'. The bucket, thank God, was removed and emptied but its over-spill remained. We were in open countryside. I think all of us, remembering the murder of the fifty recaptured after the Great Escape, feared the worst. But there were no machine gun squads, no Waffen SS, just a dozen or so of our old guards looking, if possible, rather more depressed and unkempt than we did. We wandered about. No one made a bolt for it. Someone climbed back into our cattle truck and brought out a couple of Red Cross parcels. The filth inside had made eating impossible during the journey. We were then ordered back: the doors were closed once again.

Each cattle truck had a ventilation slat down either side, well above head height. We could not see out unless standing three or four feet above the floor level. We had nothing to stand on. So we took turns at being bearer and look-out, the latter sitting on the shoulders of the bearer and the bearers being changed about every quarter of an hour. The heftier ones were bearers and were given extra food. Observation was for thirty minutes in each hour. We gained a fair idea of the terrain we were passing through. By midday on the second day we were approaching an industrial area: factories; extensive marshalling yards; housing estates; gasometers. The train stopped on the outskirts for about an hour. Nothing happened and our lookout said there were no guards to be seen.

The train began to move again. About half an hour later we were approaching what appeared to be an important railway station. We were diverted into a siding and a while later the doors were opened and we were ordered out onto the platform. Our reception committee, machine guns and all, was there to welcome us! To this day I am not sure what station it was. We were counted, searched and eventually put into a convoy of trucks which set off with a formidable escort of motorised armed guards and an extremely unpleasant *Luftwaffe* captain who gave every impression of being drunk. He brandished a revolver and said, 'Those who do not obey will be shot!' There was no Stühlmeier. We were on our own.

We crossed rough, open terrain, passed through a town and stopped outside the main gates of what was obviously a very large prisoner of war camp. As far as the eye could see was barbed wire with machine gun towers and far too many guards. We were driven into the camp up a long road where we halted. We were ordered out of the trucks and manhandled into squads on the edge of the road, lined with an extraordinary assortment of prisoners. In due course we were led to our barrack blocks and locked in, while some sort of argument took place around the convoy.

Eventually the convoy drove off, having been loaded with a bedraggled, unkempt and hollow-eyed group of prisoners who were treated with even less dignity than we had been. Our barracks were unlocked and we were allowed out.

We didn't like what we saw. Our compound consisted of four large barrack blocks, each accommodating some fifty Kriegies. There were cooking and heating facilities of a sort and an unspeakably filthy latrine at the end of each block. The blocks were open-planned, long wooden huts furnished with double bunks with a passageway down the middle. The camp was a mile from the town of Luckenwalde and some forty miles south of Berlin. To us the camp was simply known as Luckenwalde.

CHAPTER TWENTY-FOUR

Luckenwalde Camp

Whereas I can recall with astonishing clarity episodes and events of previous years as a POW, my memory of our last six months – from the time of our arrival in Luckenwalde in February 1945 to our release in June of that year – is scant. Perhaps it was because we were utterly exhausted and, having consumed our last Red Cross parcels on our march out from *Stalag Luft III*, we had nothing more than the most basic rations on which to exist. Glimpses of what we did remain.

We were a British compound in an enormous camp of many nationalities. Predominant were the British, American, French and a small but exemplary compound of elderly, immaculate Norwegian army officers under their one-time commander-in-chief General Ruge. They had been POWs since the fall of Norway in 1941. There was a handful of others: Polish, Greek, Yugoslavian, Hungarian, Lithuanian and an emaciated group of Russians. Among the British was a contingent of Army other ranks who occupied a separate compound. They were headed by a young, very efficient but absolutely worn-out Warrant Officer.

The cookhouse was run, under the supervision of a German *Feldwebel*, by a group of Southern Irish soldiers who had enlisted in the British Army as 'medical orderlies'. The entire British contingent in the camps depended on them. And they knew it. They operated as a Mafia. If you paid your tribute – so many cigarettes per barrack block – you got your share of the rations. If you paid over the odds, you got that much more. If you didn't pay, the rations 'hadn't come up' or 'the damned Germans have short-changed us again'. You couldn't beat the Mafia. The SBO demanded to see the Camp Commandant who was never available, if indeed he existed. The SBO demanded to visit the cookhouse but was refused. Then the bread ration ran out. For the better part or a week, we existed on cabbage soup and ersatz coffee. I have never been so hungry.

It was the Polish driver of the sullage cart who, following daily protests on my part – I was still regarded as the Adjutant – came to suck out our stinking latrines and told us that he had a friend who went out daily on working parties in the area. He could negotiate bread and even eggs for cigarettes. Were we interested? Yes we were! We agreed to a per capita cigarette levy. We got bread: not much but it kept us going for a few weeks.

The racket run by the Irish cookhouse staff was common knowledge. Within a month the SBO had pinned down the Mafia 'godfather', a Staff Sergeant from Dublin. He was informed that he was to consider himself under arrest and would be court-martialed when we were repatriated. His reply was to the effect that he was not a British subject, so we could stuff our courts martial! But our normal bread ration was resumed.

Our numbers were now down to some two hundred. There were the usual morning and evening *Appells*. The guards were German Army reservists, no great counters of people, and we stood, shivering and hungry, for anything up to an hour each time while the dreary ritual went on. Misery and exasperation drove us to shouting and stamping our feet. The guards eventually agreed the count and we were allowed back to our barrack blocks.

An image which remains in mind is that of the faces of my colleagues on those *Appells* – yellow, strained and almost lifeless with cold and hunger. I could do nothing. My appeals to the *Hauptman* who took the *Appells* were brushed aside. He hated us and made that very clear. The SBO was equally unsuccessful. Small wonder, since day after day we heard the echoes of the bombing of Berlin by the United States Air Force, just forty miles to our north.

Thus we survived the winter of 1944–45.

Probably what kept us going was the BBC news and the knowledge that the War was all but over. In March rumour had it that the Russians were again pushing their armoured columns westward and had reached a position fifty miles east of Berlin. It was also reported by the working parties that a Russian armoured patrol had penetrated to within thirty miles of the camp. Then came the incredible BBC broadcast which carried Churchill's message to us to stay where we were: that the Allied forces would soon release us and that we were not to risk a break-out before deliverance arrived. We were all somewhat stunned. We were still POWs.

The Irish Mafia had stepped up their pressure and were leaning on their proles to extract as much 'merchandise' as possible before the camp was liberated. They had elaborate plans for slipping away with their loot as soon as possible, and held several hostages from among the British soldiers in the camp.

I went sick with bronchial pneumonia.

Thank God we had a doctor with us. He had arrived with one of the columns of Army other ranks who had preceded us in the great trek westward, ahead of the Russian advance from the east. He was a Major in the Royal Army Medical Corps, and not only a doctor by profession but a pastor. For over four years we had never had a padre to whom we could turn for comfort. True we had been told in *Stalag Luft III* that one was shortly to arrive. In due course he did: a sloppy, unshaven nincompoop who styled himself a Captain in the Church Army. Fair enough. We asked him to take an interdenominational service. He said he had never taken a service and wouldn't know what to say. We gave him a prayer book but he chickened out. He didn't shave. We made him do so. He claimed that as a non-combatant he should not be required to attend *Appell*. We made him do so. He complained about not being respected and spent most of the day lying on his bunk. Mercifully, with Stühlmeier's backing, I had him removed to an Army *Stalag* after a few months.

But in Luckenwalde, our MO was a tower of strength. With limited medication, he cared for the seriously sick, succoured those whose morale was breaking and comforted and supported all who turned to him for help. I was very ill and – in my fever – I equated him with the person who walked beside me on the other side of the road. He not only saved several lives but he saved the souls of many who had reached the end of their tether. He was an outstanding man.

I began to recover. It was agreed that I should go into the *Lazarett*, the Sick Quarters, which was about half a mile outside the camp. Under German supervision, it was run by a Yugoslavian doctor, by name Stinkovich – popularly known as Stinkers. There was no question of transport, so our MO with an armed German guard accompanied me and helped me to the *Lazarett*, where I was given a bunk in the ward reserved for TB patients. I was still too ill to register this and fell asleep among some thirty British soldiers who had marched a hundred or more miles from their *Stalags* in the east.

Throughout the first night a young soldier in the bunk next to mine coughed and coughed, and said 'Sorry, sir.' I tried to comfort him. I sat with him until his spasms passed and he seemed to sleep. I too slept but the pain in my chest woke me early. I looked at the boy in the bunk next to me. He seemed to be at peace. An hour later I got up and went over to him. He was dead.

A fortnight or so later, and I was considered well enough to be returned to the camp proper. I was weak on my feet but my German escort was considerate and slowed his pace to suit mine. Poor man, he had left a family and many relatives far behind in eastern Germany. He had no contact with them and was as cut off from his homeland as I was from mine. I had not received a single letter from home for over three months or more.

The day before I was discharged from the *Lazarett*, an elderly German Army Colonel visited us. He was distraught and highly emotional. He said the War was nearly over. He hoped we had been properly cared for and he gave me a card with his name, rank and Army unit and, with great dignity and obvious difficulty, asked 'My friends' to give him a good reference. He grabbed my hand and stared into my face. I disengaged, stood back, saluted him and said in German, 'Good luck'. His escort clicked their heels and saluted, and the group moved on. I felt nothing except a great emptiness at the immense personal tragedies that were unfolding day by day.

We were ordered to prepare for evacuation by train. This created near panic. Then the order was cancelled and we were told that all Germans, including the guards, were to be organised into a company to oppose the Russian advance. We would have no Germans to 'protect' us. It was up to us. We were to be left on our own.

The following day, the guards marched out, the machine gun towers were unmanned and the first of many columns of foreign workers – French, Poles and Italians – began to straggle into the camp, men and women who had marched from the shambles of Berlin down the main road to the south. They came in their swarms and overran the camp, finding accommodation as best they could, rifling the food store and creating chaos wherever they went.

Our SBO and the other Group Captain had been taken out by the Germans. We had no means of knowing what befell them until after the War. They were okay but were, I dare say, regarded as hostages to be used for bargaining if need be. 'Wings' Day had gone north with the group who had left us at Muskau. Our new SBO was a senior Wing Commander, Dick Collard, who was to prove himself a truly great leader and to bring us through the confusion of the last months in captivity. But he was to die tragically not long after we were all repatriated. He was a very brave man.

It took me a while to recover my strength. Collard suggested I rest up and let someone else act as Adjutant, but I wanted the job. There were no more *Appells*. A convoy of Red Cross food parcels had somehow got through. We had enough food to supplement the German rations for a few weeks at least. The cookhouse Mafia had gone to earth exactly where was unknown but it was thought they had bribed their way into the Yugoslavian compound. Rations, however, were running short and within days the entire camp would be without its food supply.

So, the British, the Americans and the French set up a 'Joint International Command Staff' in the camp headquarters previously occupied by the German *Kommandanteur*. I think the Americans fielded a Brigadier; he was elected 'Chief of Staff'. It worked splendidly. I was appointed Officer Commanding Administration and, with typical American love of designation, we soon had Officer i/c Rations, Officer i/c Accommodation, Officer i/c International Relations and Officer i/c Health and Hygiene.

CHAPTER TWENTY-FIVE

Soviet Liberation and American Repatriation

T wo days later, on 22 April, 1945, we were woken soon after dawn by the firing of guns, roars of applause and the clapping of thousands of prisoners as a Soviet column of tanks and armoured personnel carriers burst through the camp gates and growled up the road between the barrack blocks.

The Soviet Army had arrived!

For the remainder of that day pandemonium reigned. The Russians had a liberal supply of vodka which was freely administered, with the inevitable effect on empty stomachs and uninhibited emotions. By midday a large number of prisoners were gloriously drunk. So were most of the Russians.

We of the 'Joint International Command Staff' kept our heads above water. Later in the day an inebriated Russian Captain, accompanied by an extremely attractive English-speaking blonde in uniform, was shown to our headquarters. We toasted each other in vodka and somehow managed to conduct a dialogue through the blonde and an American Sergeant who spoke fluent Russian. We were to stay where we were. Negotiations would take place for our repatriation as soon as the European War was ended. Meanwhile, the Soviet Army would guard us, care for us and feed us. Anyone who attempted to escape would risk his life. The German guards were replaced by Russian ones. The machine gun towers were manned by Soviet soldiers. We were in effect internees of the Soviet Union. So much for liberation!

Bizarre things were to follow. On one occasion the Army Warrant Officer asked to see the British SBO and he had with him a Corporal in battledress. The Warrant Officer saluted Collard with military precision. The Corporal did likewise, but with the left hand. The Warrant Officer, in considerable embarrassment, then explained that the 'Corporal' was in fact a German girl whom he had met when out on working parties; he had fallen in love with her, and wished to take her back to the UK to marry. The 'Corporal', with virtually no English, was only too ready to accept the proposal. Collard agreed to the plan on the understanding that if it was blown, and the Russians grabbed the girl, that was nothing to do with him. Not entirely satisfied, the Warrant Officer and his 'Corporal' left. I don't know what happened to them or to the Flight Lieutenant who slipped out of the camp with his German 'fiancée', went to a minister and was married locally.

Von Rundstedt's final and desperate offensive in the Ardennes was defeated. Hitler had committed suicide in the Bunker. Berlin had fallen to the Soviet Army and the Red Flag flew over the *Bundestag*. The end was very near but we were quite unable to get any satisfaction from our Russian 'hosts' as to what arrangements were being made for our repatriation. Meanwhile the BBC continued to broadcast daily instructions that we were to remain where we were until further orders. However, groups of American infantry POWs were slipping out of the camp each night, intent on moving under cover of darkness through the woods to the Elbe where the Western Allies had set up a line of demarcation. How many American POWs made it we never knew, but I heard later that many did.

Collard reinforced the BBC broadcast to stay where we were, while he demanded daily to see the Russian Colonel who was said to be in charge of the camp. The only Russian officer we saw was the Captain and his blonde interpreter, Valya. Lucky Captain: she really was a smasher – and knew it! They had set up shop in one of the offices of the 'Joint International Command' building. Any excuse was good enough to call on the Captain who spoke neither English nor French, so Valya would interpret and smile at us and toss her locks and open the door for us to leave, standing so close that the impulse to grab her was well-nigh irresistible.

While the nightly exodus continued from the US Army compound, the rest of us grew increasingly fidgety and bloody-minded. Almost daily now, the BBC instructions to 'stay put' came over the air, embellished with assurances that 'We know where you are' and 'Hold on for a little longer. The arrangements for your repatriation are nearly complete'.

We waited.

The camp had a siren. We had notified everybody that short blasts meant an emergency; a long blast of a minute or more was a general muster and would be used, for example, when instructions for evacuation had been received. The Russians understood and approved. The siren was in our Headquarters. A week or more went by. Nothing happened. Then, one morning, a convoy of trucks bearing US Army insignia appeared outside the main gate. An altercation took place between a helmeted US Army Major and several Russian armed guards. The Major was supported by a GI from the passenger seat of each truck and a jeep with a machine gun. The Russians hesitated. Then the siren sounded a series of short blasts.

The Russians gave up, the gates were opened and the US convoy drove in to tumultuous cheers from an ever increasing crowd of POWs. The US Army Major demanded to see the camp Commander. We explained that we had an American Anglo-French Headquarters. The 'Boss Man' was a US Army Brigadier, and perhaps the Major would care to accompany us to his Headquarters? The Major agreed. He took with him a Lieutenant and a Senior Sergeant. All were armed and clearly meant business.

We proceeded to our Headquarters. The elusive Russian Colonel had been summoned and arrived shortly in a staff car with an escort of a Lieutenant and an enormous, none too sober NCO with a sub-machine gun and a face which was typically Mongolian and unshaven. Valya was in for a difficult time. Fortunately our own interpreter was able to take over, though the 'conference' was further complicated by the never-ending supply of vodka which we were enjoined to drink time and time again. At the end of an hour or so the meeting broke up virtually in disorder.

The Major in command of the US convoy produced an order which he said had been agreed by General Eisenhower requiring the Russians to repatriate all American, British and French POWs in the camp. Our Brigadier strongly supported the order. The area between Luckenwalde and the Elbe was clear of the enemy and the evacuation was to take place immediately.

The Russian Colonel asserted that as the war with Germany was not yet over all POWs in Russian-occupied territory were the responsibility of the Soviet Army and no one else. They had a duty to protect Allied POWs and not to release them until after hostilities had ceased and formal arrangements for repatriation had been completed. This made sense to me, unpalatable though it was.

Deadlock! The Russian Colonel agreed to consult 'Higher Command'. Meanwhile the convoy would remain in the camp; the US servicemen could spend the night as 'guests' in the camp and the decision would be taken the following morning. It was, as I had suspected, '*NET*'. The Colonel had been instructed to ensure that the convoy returned at once to the Elbe and that no POWs were to be carried on it. Thus it was. The

Americans moved off empty-handed, having lost that trick to the Russians.

Amongst us, hopes had been dashed. Inevitably there was a good deal of bad feeling towards the Russians, particularly from the American compound. This didn't help cooperation. The Russian Captain sulked and refused any further discussion, and Valya, from what little we saw of her, was tight-lipped and silent. We tried the soft approach. We had a volume of Shakespeare's plays that was in reasonably good shape. We caught her alone in her office and gave it to her, suitably inscribed by our Russian interpreter. She took it grudgingly, then looked at it and burst into tears. I wanted to hug her but prudence restrained me. We won that trick.

A week later we heard the news we had long expected. Germany had surrendered unconditionally. The war in Europe was over. Now, surely, we would be repatriated. The camp went mad. Compounds were no longer guarded and POWs of every nationality mingled in the camp. Foreign workers too, men and women, swarmed everywhere. A brothel was set up in the potato bunker. I forget what the going rate was – in cigarettes, chocolate or tea – but it did a roaring trade.

Russian soldiers, with the inevitable vodka, invaded the camp. They had billeted themselves, together with the elusive Colonel, in a nearby military camp called *Adolph Hitler Lager* – Adolph Hitler Camp. In Russian there is no 'h' equivalent, so the Russians referred to it as 'Adolf Gitler'. We fraternised, we got drunk, we got involved with women who offered themselves to us for free if only we would marry them so that they could accompany us to freedom. Poor creatures.

The Russian Captain turned up with Valya. He said he wanted all of us – the US Brigadier, Wing Commander Dick Collard, and the French Colonel – to sign a document of cooperation and everlasting friendship between the Soviet Union and the Western Alliance. It would be a historic document; he had written it himself and it would be acclaimed by the Soviet High Command. I tended to doubt that, but we agreed to have it translated into English when we would consider whether or not it was suitable as an international document.

The following day we were invited to the Captain's office. From their appearance, he and Valya had passed a pretty rough night. We were presented with the document of everlasting friendship. Our Interpreter translated it for us. It was non-committal, emotional and virtually meaningless. It spoke of the 'Great Patriotic War' successfully waged 'single-handed' against the Fascist aggressor with the help of the Western Allies – something of a contradiction – and of the hope that the Soviet Union and all peace-loving nations would unite to defeat those who opposed the worldwide Socialist revolution. It concluded with the out-moded slogan, 'Workers of the World Unite', but we persuaded him that the Soviet forces had, in fact, repulsed, on their own, the German invaders who had overrun their vast country. In the end we signed the document, handwritten in Russian though it was. Much vodka was expended.

The Captain then declared that he was a cavalry officer and required a horse! Collard said this might be difficult but Valya looked at me and said, 'Perhaps there are horses in the camp?' Indeed there were. I tottered off to the Italian compound and, not knowing the right word for horse in Italian, shouted, 'Eques por Russkies'. Surprisingly it had the desired effect. A man who spoke fair English produced a horse, albeit a very miserable specimen, which I led up the camp road to the Headquarters, up the few steps to the entrance, along the corridor to the office where the Russian Captain was putting some finishing touches to his document. I led the horse up to the desk – I must have been pretty drunk – and it put its nose over the blotter and dribbled on the document. No one seemed to care. It then did what horses do when unsure of their whereabouts. No one seemed to care. Our interpreter said, 'Captain, your horse.' He looked up, replied '*Khorosho!*' – meaning good, and continued with his work on the document. Collard suggested I took the horse back. I got it down the steps, by which time it had had enough. It broke from my grasp and cantered off along the camp road.

The following morning the camp was in no mood for excitement. Then a second American convoy approached and was defiantly halted by the Soviets. This time there was no question of allowing the convoy into the camp. There were angry exchanges. A Soviet tank rumbled up and, within half an hour, the American convoy withdrew. So the 'Joint International Command' demanded to see the Russian Colonel. It was an hour or so before he arrived with his bodyguard. He was apologetic, explained that the Soviet Command and the Western Allies were arranging the exchange of POWs and that we would have to be patient. He understood our frustration but could do nothing about it. Orders were orders. He softened the blow by inviting us to supper in 'Adolph Gitler' Lager that evening. We accepted and agreed a time to be collected. In what uniform we could find we were driven a mile or so to 'Adolph Gitler' Lager. An escort of armed Russian soldiers led us into a large room where some dozen Soviet officers were introduced and we were plied with the inevitable vodka. We sat at a long table. There was black bread and more vodka. Somehow I managed to keep awake. The Colonel's Mongolian bodyguard was hovering in the background. The meal was a good one, Russian style. Borsch, dried fish, spiced chicken, ice cream and a lot of fruit washed down with an acceptable German wine (loot) and the inevitable tipples of vodka.

Toasts galore; long stories from our hosts, which rather lost out in translation; speeches from Collard and the American Brigadier – the latter having had a vodka or two over the odds. Then the Russian Colonel's bodyguard drew his revolver from its holster, said something which was not translated and waved it in the direction of Collard. It was a very ugly moment. Dick Collard, with superb composure, looked at the gunman and with a dismissive wave of his hand said, 'Put that thing away, it might go off'. This was translated. The Colonel ordered his bodyguard to leave the room, and the meal proceeded peacefully.

The American Brigadier was not too happy about the 'single-handed' reference in the 'document of everlasting friendship'. Eventually a group of heavily made-up women came in. They were explained as the 'ladies of pleasure', which we took as our cue to leave. After much handshaking, pronouncements of everlasting friendship and kissing, we were escorted to a car and driven back to the camp and our Headquarters. The American Brigadier passed out and the French Colonel sang a song. Collard, who was badly shaken, began to shiver. We got him to bed as soon as we could.

A few days later there was a 'concert party' in an improvised auditorium in one of the foreign compounds. Halfway through the performance the siren sounded loud and long. This must be IT! We bolted to our Headquarters. We were greeted by a group of Soviet officers we had never seen before. One spoke reasonable English. He explained that arrangements had been agreed for the British, American and French POWs to be evacuated the following day to the Elbe where there was a pontoon bridge. On the other side the US Army would have a convoy to take us to Halle from where we would be flown out to England. Collard asked about the Norwegian officers. They would remain and be repatriated via Odessa. They were elderly, and Odessa was totally unacceptable as a port of embarkation to Norway; they should come with us to England. A long and bitter argument ensued. Collard was joined by the American Brigadier who warned that the United States' armoured forces massed on the Elbe would not hesitate to cross and rescue the Norwegian officers, by force if need be. The responsibility for the consequences would rest squarely on the Soviet Army. A good piece of bluff, I thought, but with the French Colonel standing firm with his British and American colleagues it was agreed to defer any further action until the morrow. The Russians could make our position absolutely clear to their superiors. Meanwhile there would be no movement. It was up to them. We lost two days, but we won. The Norwegians could accompany us and 'registration' of all to be evacuated would take place immediately. The Russian convoy had remained outside the camp since its arrival.

Registration was an absolute farce. There were only four or five Russians who could speak and write English. Valya and her Captain were not to be seen. The American POWs, particularly the GIs, were obstinate and uncooperative. Their Brigadier got them together and gave them hell. Thereafter they toed the line. The RAF and the British Army were fed up, sullen, and on the verge of 'breaking ranks'. The French simply got drunk and caused little trouble, while the Norwegians were on the verge of tears at what had been done for them. Relations between our Command staff and the Russians were very brittle indeed. But somehow the tedious and absurd procedure of registration was completed. We were required to give our name, rank, service number and nationality. Fair enough. But added to this was next of kin and place of birth. We point-blank refused to complete these details. In no way was I prepared to give my place of birth as Baku, southern Russia!

A further hour or so was wasted arguing. Eventually the Russians agreed to the basic details required by the Geneva Convention – name, rank, number – to which we added nationality as British, regardless of whether the individual was Polish, Czech or Free French. The Americans, French and Norwegians agreed with us and a very hostile Russian officer took the documents away and we waited – and waited.

Some time in the afternoon of 19 May 1945, eleven days after the end of the war in Europe, the main gates were opened and a large Soviet convoy crawled into the camp. The drivers were unshaven, slit-eyed and evidently from Siberia. We were counted into the open trucks, nationality by nationality, American, British, French and Norwegian. The convoy was then surrounded by a crowd of other nationals who shouted that they were western Europeans, men and women who tried to clamber aboard until repelled by shots fired by the Russians. I don't think there were any casualties but it was a tragic situation.

We lowered the Union Jack, Stars and Stripes and Tricolour which had flown over our Headquarters and, after a further delay, the convoy moved off. I sat in the front seat alongside the Russian driver who looked at me and then grinned. At least we had established friendly relations.

Engines were run; the convoy moved slowly down a narrow road through the woods and then turned west at a junction with a major well-metalled highway. We passed wrecked vehicles lying on their sides where they had been pushed onto the grass verges. Frequently we had to drive through thick acrid smoke from burning trees. Not all of us had anything to cover our faces and there were several cases of smoke inhalation.

Our route crossed several others by flyovers, all of which had been blown. The road had been constructed on an embankment and the only way to reach the other side of those at a right angle to ours was for our drivers to crawl obliquely down the embankment, their trucks tilted at precarious angles, and then up the other side. I experienced the first of these extraordinary manoeuvres from my seat in front. I decided the risk of capsizing was far too great, as did all in our truck, so at the next hazard we jumped out and crossed the intersecting road on foot, climbed the embankment and rejoined our truck when it had clambered back onto the main road.

This procedure was followed by the rest of the convoy and we escaped injury, though one truck did roll over on the slope and held us up until it was literally manhandled, Russians and Kriegies working together, to the edge of the forest and out of the way of those behind. Thus we proceeded through the pine forests, the debris of war, tanks, personnel carriers, weapons and the inevitable corpse, fire and destruction.

Our driver said something in Russian which of course I couldn't understand. He pointed to the shelf in front of him. I found a small canvas bag; he nodded vigorously. I gave it to him. He took out a flask which he opened and put to his mouth. Vodka, I reckoned. Next he produced a leg of some animal – presumably cooked – which he proceeded to gnaw like a dog at a bone, He offered it to me. I declined politely and he handed me the bag which I replaced in the locker. We carried on. I had reckoned the distance to the Elbe to be about fifty miles. We had covered perhaps thirty. He began to sing a rather lovely Russian song and looked at me invitingly. The song had a repetitive chorus which I tried to follow and, though I had no idea of the words, we sang together. He had a very fine baritone voice and we sang for perhaps half an hour.

We must have been nearing the Elbe by my reckoning. I was bursting for a pee. I made suggestive indications which eventually got through. He stopped and I jumped out and relieved myself. Looking back, throughout the length of the convoy, the edge of the road was lined with an ever-increasing number doing likewise. I rejoined my Soviet driver whose bladder must have had a far greater capacity than mine. We drove on.

Not long afterwards I noticed that his driving was leaving a lot to be desired. He was misjudging corners, crashing his gears and giving every indication of falling asleep. I tried to get him to sing again but unsuccessfully. I made motions suggesting that I take over the wheel. He became angry, pointed at the locker and said '*Napitok*' which of course I didn't understand. I gave him the bag. He took a long swig from the flask, belched and grinned. There was nothing I could do and, mercifully, we reached the rendezvous at the pontoon bridge over the Elbe before he gave up the struggle. We learned later that the convoy had covered seven hundred miles from the east before it arrived at Luckenwalde.

There was an idiotic and exasperating delay before we were disembarked and escorted across the bridge. On the other side was a long, immaculate US Army convoy of trucks, parked at exact convoy interval, with US Army personnel standing beside each vehicle. A tall, loose-limbed US Army Major seemed to be in command. We were allocated so many to a truck in an impersonal, efficient and no-nonsense manner. He had Collard with him who, together with the US Army Brigadier, the Norwegian General and the French Colonel, rode with the convoy commander in jeeps.

The GIs who drove the trucks and provided armed guards were mostly young and expressionless and seemed totally uninterested in what was going on. We poured across the bridge, shouting and cheering and tried to shake their hands until we were bawled out by a Senior NCO who restored some sort of order amongst us. The GIs stood by until we were all aboard, their helmets tipped onto the bridge of their noses and their mouths slightly open as though they all had adenoids.

The Russian convoy backed away from the other end of the bridge. Our convoy commander, together with an interpreter and an armed escort, crossed on foot. There was a short meeting with a group of Russian officers, an exchange of handshakes, salutes and final embraces, and our party returned to the convoy. The Major shouted 'Move!' and in precision, at exact regulation convoy interval and speed, we rolled away in the direction of Halle, our destination for the night.

A strange lethargy seemed to engulf us. We fell silent: we were played out, hungry and experiencing a feeling of anti-climax which I can neither explain nor describe. Nothing seemed to matter anymore. It was all over. We wanted out; peace, quiet and reunion with our families. In retrospect, I imagine we were suffering from a form of shock. Perhaps the expressionless GIs had been told to expect just that. It would explain their remoteness.

We drove to Halle and into a large military establishment flying the Stars and Stripes. It must have been a German base of some considerable importance, judging from its size. We disembarked with our 'belongings' such as they were. It was perhaps about eight o'clock in the evening. We asked for a meal. The cookhouse and canteen were closed, we were told. What we needed was sleep; we could eat early tomorrow. We made a fuss and demanded food. This brought a US Army Captain and a couple of NCOs who made it clear that we couldn't eat that evening and would we get the hell out and go to our quarters and sleep. I had long ceased to carry the responsibility of Adjutant. I refused to be involved. Gradually we accepted the inevitable. We were directed to our quarters in a large two-storey barrack and within an hour or so the mutterings of discontent had subsided. Not long afterwards we were all asleep.

We were woken early next morning by a US orderly who shouted that if we wanted to eat we had best get dressed quick and follow him to the canteen. We did so, and he led us to a large building where we queued for a substantial breakfast which we carried to long tables in what appeared to have been an assembly or lecture hall.

There was a stage flanked by the Stars and Stripes and a screen on which had been attached a notice writ large: EAT AND GET OUT. We did just that and then sought out the Captain and asked what the form was. He was friendly and communicative. We were to be flown out by DC3s – Dakotas – on the following day. The weather in the UK was at present un-flyable but was expected to improve overnight. He would keep in touch with us. Meanwhile he was sorry but we could not leave the base. There was a midday and evening meal and a cinema where movies were being shown more or less round the clock. The base was 'dry' as far as liquor was concerned.

So we fidgeted and fretted through the day and woke early to 'eat and get out'. Inevitably, I suppose, I found myself coordinating and communicating plans and arrangements agreed by our American hosts. Sure enough, very soon after breakfast, we were told over the loud hailer that all 'RAF personnel' were to pack and muster on the parade ground for transport to the airfield. Bedlam and near hysteria!

CHAPTER TWENTY-SIX

The Return

By convoy to the airfield, then counted – we had become used to that – and before long we were seated in the gaggle of DC3s that had arrived at first light.

After what seemed an interminable delay, our aircraft taxied, rattling, to the downwind end of the runway, rolled forward into wind and lurched, shuddering and clattering as it gathered speed, into the air. Speech was impossible. The venerable Dakota was an uninsulated metal shell: draughty, incredibly noisy but trustworthy. The crew on the flight deck cleared the necessary control zones and then set course for Dunsfold in Surrey. We flew above cloud for an hour or more and then the overcast below us broke and we were approaching the Channel. More low cloud, and nothing to be seen. We waited, tense and impatient. The engines were throttled back, we dropped into cloud and hit considerable turbulence.

Then we were clear and below. We crossed the English coast in the late morning of a June day in 1945, almost four and a quarter years since I had done so going in the opposite direction. I was near to tears. I dare say others were, too.

We circled the small airfield, landed noisily and came to a halt in a marshalling area. Aircraft followed aircraft and then all had landed. There were RAF ground personnel who guided us to an enclosure with a marquee, several tents and a reception committee which included a Group Captain, several other officers, a padre and a lot of WAAFs and RAF nursing staff. The welcome was somewhat overdone, with cups of tea, scones, impromptu speeches and lots of laughter and heartiness. But it was genuine, and if one puts oneself in the shoes of those who waited at Dunsfold to receive some two hundred ex-POWs from Germany, surely one must recognise the difficulty and awkwardness of reacting spontaneously to an unknown and unpredictable range of emotions from those so recently liberated. Those who greeted us were splendid, though the padre was clearly unsure of his ground. It was one of our wags who later described his welcome as: 'A packet of cigarettes for us in one hand and the text for the day in the other'.

Gradually everyone relaxed. There was an understandable migration from the refreshment marquee to where the several WAAFs were nervously forming a defensive circle behind the table from which they were distributing pamphlets about food and clothing vouchers and other wartime provisions which were on that occasion of no possible interest to us.

The Group Captain then addressed us over the Tannoy. He explained that we were to be driven by RAF coaches to a railway station – I think it was Guildford – and on arrival at Victoria would cross London, also by RAF coach, to another station where a train would take us to RAF Cosford. We were asked to give our parole not to jump the column on the way to Cosford. There we would be given uniform, food, clothing and petrol vouchers, a medical check and travel warrants for six weeks' leave. We would not be kept at Cosford for more than forty-eight hours and we would be allowed to phone our folk at RAF expense.

This was clearly reasonable and so I spoke on behalf of all of us and gave our word as parole. We had seen nothing of Dick Collard and his colleagues since we had crossed the Elbe three days before. I gather they came home together in a special aircraft and were 'processed' elsewhere. I never saw Dick again. Our train pulled into Victoria. Inevitably our arrival had been leaked to a number of next of kin, who mobbed the train and seriously imperilled our parole. But I believe we remained united and once more in RAF coaches sped off to St Pancras or King's Cross.

What I shall never forget is passing a group of immaculate, red-tabbed senior Army staff officers, probably from the War Office or the Cabinet Office, striding down Birdcage Walk as our coach drew level. It was too good to be true. With our windows down, we roared at them, shouted 'Whitehall warriors' and generally behaved like hooligans. They were halted in their tracks. Their mouths dropped open and they looked at us in utter bewilderment.

Our train was in the station. We left London for RAF Cosford, a large depot in Maintenance Command with ample accommodation and all geared up to deal with the documentation, clothing, medical checking and general rehabilitation of a very large number of repatriated RAF POWs. We were gradually and sympathetically passed from one department to another. I watched while an attractive WAAF sewed my wings and medal ribbons onto my new battledress. And then another gave me my ration card, clothing coupons and travel permit. Yet another quietly took my personal particulars, gave me a railway warrant to London and told me which telephone to use for my free calls. It was all very well arranged with great understanding and compassion. I was cleared by mid-morning on the second day, registered, properly dressed and provided with a ration book, travel permit, identity card and a six-week leave warrant. I also had a wallet with a fair sum of money.

I dialled the number of the London flat in Draycott Avenue which my mother-in-law had occupied until she, with her sister-in-law and niece, had been killed in the Guards Chapel. A woman's voice answered. I said, 'Is that you, Diana?' 'No. This is her cousin, Anne Fummi. Is that Donald? Diana is in Dublin having treatment. Aunt Nellie is looking after her. Ranald is with a nannie at Dollie Perry's in Clonmel.'

Another pause. 'Could you come to London and spend a night or two here before going to Dublin? There are some suitcases of yours here and letters and things.' Obviously, I agreed.

I was alone again and with a heavy heart I packed my few belongings in the kitbag I had been given and joined the group of my colleagues who were ready to travel in the next coach for the station and the London train. I remembered Churchill's final message of comfort which he broadcast to those of us trailing across Germany in the last stages of the War: '... to those of you moving from the unknown to the unknown ....'

CHAPTER TWENTY-SEVEN

A Sad Homecoming

The door was opened by a servant and a dark-haired woman, several years older than me, came into the hall. 'Hello, Donald. I'm Anne.' She was good-looking, well dressed in a simple style, and radiated class and self-confidence. A daughter of the Earl of Crawford and Balcarres, her sister, Lady Barbara, had married Diana's first cousin, Colonel Richard Hurst. She was gracious and suggested it was a bit late for tea: would I like a sherry? We sat in the drawing room where I well remembered my late mother-in-law entertaining friends to morning coffee and afternoon tea. Nothing had been changed; the Degas still hung squint on the wall above the piano. Our wedding photo was on the mantelpiece and a dreadfully posed and fuzzy one of me in uniform, taken by a local photographer in Swanage, stood on the piano. The room smelt – as it had always done, of old furnishings and old people.

Anne told me that Diana had had a series of nervous breakdowns but was in the care of an excellent psychiatrist in Dublin and that 'Aunt Nellie' – Lady Eleanor Keane – was very much in control. She suggested I go to Dublin as soon as possible. We talked about travel warrants and the fact that Ireland had remained neutral, so I would need to wear civilian clothes. I found Anne very much to my liking. We didn't talk about the past but discussed the immediate future.

I phoned Dublin and Lady Eleanor answered. She didn't let me speak with Diana but said my wife was doing well and that Ranald was a lovely little boy and was being well cared for by Dollie Perry in Clonmel. I could stay with her and her husband for as long as I wished. Lady Eleanor conveyed confidence, purpose and comfort in an extraordinary way. I felt enormous relief that Diana was in such capable hands. I went to bed early, but thoughts of the past haunted me. Eventually I fell into a deep sleep.

Next day I went to Lloyds, Pall Mall. The branch manager welcomed me home. My account was well in credit and he gave me a glass of unspeakable sherry. I walked up Lower Regent Street and Piccadilly for the first time in four and a half years. This was before demobilisation: we were still at war with Japan. We were still in uniform. I found being saluted by 'other ranks' embarrassing but realised I had to accept it. On to 128 Piccadilly and through the swing doors of the RAF Club, where I was stopped by a uniformed doorman who asked for my membership card. I didn't have one. He became mildly offensive. I became abusive. He asked the receptionist to call the Secretary. An elderly man in the uniform of a Wing Commander came down the corridor. He wanted to know what proof I had that I was a member. Members were not disposed to be offensive to Club servants: had I been drinking?

I took a deep breath, undid my shirt and shoved my identity disc under his nose. 'Go and check my membership,' I said, 'And while you are establishing it, I am going into the bar and then having lunch. Before I leave I want a new membership card with my original membership number on it. I've been a bloody POW for over four years and I'm not going to be pushed around by my own Club ...'

My membership had been confirmed. The Secretary was overcome with apologies. Would I join him for a drink? You bet. So we went upstairs to the bar which was crowded with members, many of whom were well known to me. There was a 'dud' of my 1932 Entry at Cranwell, who was wearing the stripes of a Group Captain, and other contemporaries of mine who had been promoted way ahead of me, still a Squadron Leader. Fair enough.

I was soon drawn into a group of old colleagues. We had a boozy lunch after which I fell asleep in a deep armchair in the smoking room. The Club servant never forgave me for blowing my top. In October 1984, nearly forty years later, I received a gilt-edged card from the Chairman of the Committee informing me that I had been elected an Honorary Member for Life in recognition of fifty years of unbroken membership! I am no longer required to pay an annual membership fee.

I had decided to catch the late evening train the next day to Holyhead which would give me the day to obtain a travel warrant and documentation in lieu of a passport. Throughout the journey my thoughts were with Diana. My Diana, my wife, the mother of our son. I would be seeing my Diana after four and a half years. I would hold her to me and we would say – I knew not what. But we would be together again and could plan our future and she would help me to forget the past ...

The gangway came aboard ship. A heavily accented Irish voice came over the loud hailer. 'Will Squadron Leader MacDonell come to the gangway, where he will be escorted ashore. You are awaited on the pier, sor.' This message was repeated twice. I made my way through the waiting passengers, who stood aside and smiled and said strange things like 'There's a good man for sure' and 'God bless you, sor'. Embarrassed, I reached the gangway where a ship's officer took my case and escorted me to the pier. Aunt Nellie had surely done her stuff. The officer handed me my suitcase, saluted and said, pointing, 'That's herself, sor.'

Diana and I ran towards each other. She threw herself into my arms, buried her golden head on my shoulder and wept inconsolably. During the brief moment before I clasped her to my body, I saw not my Diana, not the lovely girl whose beauty and body had captured my heart and soul, whose wide and loving smile had welcomed me back each evening and who had whispered drowsily, 'See you later, darling', when I had left her arms four and a half years ago, not to return until today. My world had fallen apart. She was not my Diana but a cruel caricature of what she had been.

All that I had longed for so long crumbled and fell in shreds as I held her fast and tried to still her sobbing.

Her lovely hair was still golden but had been waved unbecomingly, her make-up was atrocious: blotches of colour mingled with clumsily applied powder. Her lovely, warm, wide smile was no more. She looked terribly old.

Diana stopped sobbing. She took my handkerchief and dried her eyes. 'Uncle Jack's car is over there. The black one.' We walked, still entwined, to the car where a chauffeur took my bags and we got into the back. We were soon at the entrance to Sir John and Lady Eleanor Keane's house in Ranelagh.

Aunt Nellie met us: she put her arm round Diana's shoulder, smiled at me and shook my hand. She was a tall, fine-looking woman in her sixties who immediately gave an impression of quiet authority. Her husband, Sir John Keane Bt. DSO, was a character. Extrovert and eccentric, he was a Senator in the Dail. He was erudite and artistic and collected Post-Impressionist paintings which hung, incongruously mixed with conventional etchings, oils and watercolours, all over the house. He commuted weekly between Dublin and London, invariably dressed in pyjamas, a dressing gown and bedroom slippers, to be received at the termini by the harbour- or stationmaster in full regalia who would escort him to or from his sleeper or berth as the case might be.

During the meal, Diana ate very little and smoked, then left the table and, still smoking, went into the drawing room. Aunt Nellie explained that Diana was in the hands of one of the best psychiatrists in Dublin; and was having a course of electro-convulsive therapy or ECT. Aunt Nellie felt that my safe return would make all the difference. She didn't prevaricate or refer emotionally to my years as a POW.

She explained that since Diana's mother's death in the bombing of the Guards' Chapel, the flat in Cadogan Court had been occupied by members of the family. Diana and I and Ranald could use it until the lease expired. Aunt Nellie suggested we could go down to Clonmel to give me a chance to get to know my son and then all return to London. We were to remake our marriage: she would help in any way she could.

Uncle Jack came onto the scene that afternoon. I liked him at once. He had won his DSO in the First World War and was intensely interested in my limited experience of the one that had just ended. He hung on my words when I described to him the Battle of Britain and the war in the air. He told me a lot about his family and left me with a growing sense of trust and understanding. He then asked me about my background.

I told him that on the death of my father I had become the 22nd Chief of the MacDonells of Glengarry and twelfth titular 'Lord Macdonell and Aros' – a Jacobite peerage. The Glengarry clan is part of the great Clan Donald – descendants of Somerled Lord of the Isles, who died in 1164 – which spreads worldwide from North America to the Antipodes. The progenitor of Glengarry was Ranald, the son of John the Good of Islay, who died in the early fifteenth century.

I told him of the outrageous and extraordinary behaviour of Colonel Alastair Ranaldson Macdonell, fifteenth Chief of Glengarry who died in 1828 after a life of legal wrangles and a totally unjustified duel in which he killed his innocent young victim and was then acquitted by the courts. He squandered what dues he could squeeze out of his tenants in an idiotic lifestyle and appeared in public always in full Highland dress. His outburst of fury was legendary and yet, at his death, he was mourned deeply and a huge gathering of the Clan attended his burial at Kilfinan, the family mausoleum near his seat at Invergarry.

My father, Ranald, was working on a tea estate in Ceylon when the sudden death of his father in 1901 brought him home to deal with the family's affairs. This done, he accepted a position with the oil firm of Schibaieff and Co. in Moscow from where he was transferred to the company's office in Baku on the Caspian Sea, thus continuing the connection with the Southern Russian port, first established by his own father. I was born in Baku. My father by then had become the twenty-first Chief of Glengarry and the British Vice-Consul in Baku and an honorary major in the British Army. My mother brought firstly me and then my younger brother, Peter, home to England to live with my paternal grandmother. My father, having lost all his assets in the Russian Revolution, escaped to Persia a year or two later, where he contracted typhus and was invalided home. Following a short period in the Foreign Office, where he drafted much of the Curzon Report, he moved on to journalism, working as a reporter on *The Morning Post*. My mother, Dorah Hartford, was brought up with her brothers and sisters in Christchurch, where her father was a doctor.

Uncle Jack and Aunt Nellie were a remarkable pair and they never gave up their valiant endeavours to help me through the sad years which were to follow my return from being a POW in Germany.

Each day I would spend an hour or so at the nursing home with Diana and then Aunt Nellie and I would talk in the evenings.

Diana's psychiatrist never put a name to Diana's illness. It was always, 'She has grieved and suffered too long, the poor soul. She will soon be well now that you are safely back'. He recommended we resume normal married life and suggested another child would contribute to her complete recovery.

Diana improved quite a lot during the journey south to Clonmel. Only once she seemed to slip away and sat beside me staring fixedly and fiercely at an elderly woman who had joined the train at one of the halts and had seated herself opposite. The woman soon became aware of something wrong and, after ten minutes or so, collected her bag from the rack and left the compartment. Diana relaxed and muttered something about old women 'messing one about'.

We were driven the last forty-odd miles to Clonmel and Woodroof. On the drive outside the front door were a small, elderly woman, a nanny in uniform, and a pink, shining, chubby little boy with fair hair and huge eyes. Diana got out and clasped him in her arms. The driver and I got out together. The small boy looked at us and then in a broad Irish brogue said, 'Mummy, which might my Daddy be?'

Dollie cosseted me, fed me – 'You're all skin and bone, you poor man' – and gave me more than enough Irish whiskey. She managed a large country house with a small domestic staff and the minimum of attention to tidiness and meal times. Ranald was in the charge of an elderly, competent and very Irish nanny who spoiled him and overfed him. He was far too fat and howled his head off until he had his way, which he invariably got.

My two main preoccupations were getting to know our son and gaining his confidence and seeking to break through the tragic barrier to communication which separated the Diana I once knew from the Diana I now found beside me. Ranald came to me spontaneously and joyously. He had a tricycle which no one had taught him to pedal. It took me an hour or so one morning to teach him how to pedal forward so that he was self-propelled. His intake of food was a different matter. He was with us during the morning but had his meals with Nanny. In the afternoons Diana and I rested in our room. I tried to find out what this thing was that had possessed her mind, sometimes to the exclusion of all else. I had no knowledge of, or guidance on, how to handle mental disturbance. Sex gave temporary respite, after which she would relax physically and smile and perhaps sleep for a while. But later the fixed look would return, she would laugh suddenly and then begin to rant, usually against old women who were 'messing her about'.

So my leave was drawing to a close and it was time for me and Diana and Ranald to travel to London and set up home in Cadogan Court. The crossing from Dun Laoghaire to Holyhead was rough and Ranald was sick. Diana seemed to do nothing about it and I spent a very un-comfortable voyage trying to mop things up. Our sleeper to London was filthy and smelled of stale tobacco smoke.

When we arrived at Cadogan Court, we were in pretty poor shape. The janitor gave me two sets of keys and told me of a restaurant across the way where we could get a meal. We ate the standard rationed wartime meal at the controlled price. Diana and I ate everything, whale steak and all. Ranald said he didn't like his food, wanted Nanny and began to howl. He was then sick. I paid the bill with apologies for the mess and we returned to the flat. Ranald was still howling and saying he was hungry. I made him a bowl of bread and milk which I fed to him with a spoon. Diana was on the drawing room sofa and it was left to me to settle us in. I gave Ranald a bath and made him paper boats from the writing paper in the hall. He calmed down and was soon laughing and splashing and playing with his boats.

Diana was unpacking and I left her while I dressed Ranald. It was early afternoon and we had essential shopping to do. She came out of our bedroom in a full-length evening dress, high-heeled shoes and a fur stole. She was heavily made up. I said something about having rather overdone it for shopping. She said firmly that in London one dressed smartly. That was that.

It was at this stage that the stark reality of what lay ahead really began to come home to me: I had to report for a staff appointment in the Cabinet Office in a few days.

I often wonder how we managed. Diana was inconsistent and Ranald was often neglected. I would prepare breakfast before leaving for Whitehall and would return, as often as not, to unmade beds, bedroom curtains still closed and a tactful but disturbing report from the janitor. Eventually we engaged a cook-housekeeper but she left at the end of a week. Friends and relations dropped in, made excuses and left.

Then Diana told me she was pregnant.

We visited the family doctor and I told him that Diana had been in the hands of a psychiatrist in Dublin and had undergone a course of ECT. I was then asked to leave. Diana remained seated hunched up and looking far from cooperative. I sat outside in the lobby until the secretary escorted Diana out and I was asked to go in alone. The doctor looked me very straight in the face, 'I don't like your wife's condition. I don't like it at all. I want her to see Dr ... who is an excellent psychiatrist.'

CHAPTER TWENTY-EIGHT

The Long Haul

Diana saw the psychiatrist. He disclosed nothing that I regarded as positive. After several weeks and three or four visits he sent me an astronomical account for his medical services. Diana's mental and emotional state gradually improved and when, in March 1946, Patrick – Paddy – was born, she was very nearly on an even keel with only the occasional relapse into upset and confusion.

We engaged a daily help who had served with the Royal Army Medical Corps during the War. This worked well but after a few months, the help's mother died and she left us to care for her elderly father. However, it was she who first gave me the first real indication that Diana's condition was mental illness. Stubbornly, I refused to accept this, though I did agree that I would need help. She suggested I write a list of everyone among my family and friends who could be called upon to lend a hand, and what material support I could secure from the health services, the RAF proper and the RAF Benevolent Fund.

The situation was thus. Both my parents and Diana's parents were dead. My mother's brother Uncle Jacko, was shacked up with a 'companion' in Victoria and was penniless and alcoholic. My cousin Maurice Hartford was still in the RAF but about to be 'demobbed'. My brother Peter had a flat in Edinburgh: he wrote a sympathetic letter but was busy acting in the Citizens' Theatre in Glasgow. Arthur Fagan, my dear 'No. 1' of 64 Squadron, was in Chelsea. He and his wife, Kitty, had no children and were nonplussed by Diana's condition, but we were always welcome. Others wrote compassionately or visited, but no one offered anything other than sympathy. There was no National Health Service and the RAF was of limited help.

However, one family did come up with practical support. They probably saved me from cracking up out of sheer loneliness, helplessness and despair. Cecil and Sybil Hurst and their daughter Bardie lived near Horsham in Sussex. Sir Cecil had retired as a judge of the International Court of Appeal in The Hague. Lady Hurst was Diana's aunt. The Hursts took in Ranald and provided an excellent nanny to look after him when Diana went into a London nursing home to have Paddy.

Yet, even with extra help, the strain and anxiety each morning when I left the flat for Whitehall, and the fear of what I might find at the end of the working day when I returned home, began to take its toll. I had been promoted to Wing Commander, in the Cabinet Office, and had come to terms with my future to the extent that I was determined to remain in the Royal Air Force.

I served an Air Commodore who was my Director. He was efficient and also observant. I found my duties interesting and it seems I did a good job. My boss told me I had a flair for it and gave me a complimentary report but said I was looking tired and suggested I take a week's leave to 'sort things out at home'. He had learned of my circumstances and, though he never intruded, he gave me a great deal of unspoken support.

Once, following a dreadful night in the flat, I arrived at the office more dead than alive. The Department had two senior secretaries. I must have looked whacked that morning. They helped me to talk of what I had left in the flat and describe my loneliness and despair without breaking down. They brought me coffee and we turned to consideration of a draft I was writing for the Director. Shortly before lunch, one of the secretaries returned with Ranald, who was over the moon as they had travelled on the top of a bus! Apparently, Diana was being looked after by the lady across the hall and the nanny had Paddy. Ranald was given lunch in their office and then taken to the Zoo. He was brought back in time for me to take him home in the evening.

I record the wonderful help from the Hursts and the completely spontaneous comfort of these two secretaries not only in gratitude but more perhaps as a chronicle of the true bonds of humanity that resulted from the common suffering of all during the years of the War. Here in the Highlands of Scotland – and in other small communities – that fellowship, compassion and understanding are found to this day. They exist, I think, in much smaller measure in the densely populated south-east of England and in large conurbations. There, envy, avarice, one-upmanship and class barriers have eroded the one great social advance that emerged from the horrors of the War.

Sunt lacrimae rerum.

So my life had become a precarious balancing act between the needs of my family and my responsibilities as a Wing Commander on the staff of the Cabinet Office.

My Director then recommended me for a course at the RAF Staff College at Bracknell in Berkshire. He stressed that he saw my future career as secure, despite my domestic problems. A course at the Staff College should not be too much of a strain, would qualify me for further promotion and would, perhaps, help me to relax in the company of my fellow students, many of whom were of my seniority and age group.

So, in due course, we vacated Cadogan Court and moved into the flat in a house in Bracknell which had been requisitioned by the RAF. I had bought a car, a fourteen horsepower ex-police Wolseley saloon which had been thrashed throughout the War and had lost its punch but was, nevertheless, serviceable and large enough for the family.

The Squadron Leader and his wife across the courtyard were friendly but uneasy in Diana's presence. We settled into the new environment and Diana appeared to accept it happily enough. The fact that the Staff College was within walking distance seemed to comfort her. Ranald thought the move was great fun; Paddy was too young to register. I reported to the Staff College for the commencement of the last 'War Course' which was an abbreviated version of the traditional year-long course which had its foundation under the authority and vision of Lord Trenchard and was based at Andover in the pre-War years.

We were a carefree, somewhat laid-back group. Among our number were several who had distinguished themselves in the air but were not inclined to endure six months of reading, lectures, and writing 'appreciations' of theoretical and often esoteric scenarios which simply did not make sense in relation to what they had experienced during the War. But, to me, who had for over a year been privy to the thinking of the War Cabinet and in particular the Air Force Board, it was manna from heaven. I had it all in the front of my mind.

So I sailed calmly through the exercises and the often violent arguments between the students and the senior members of the Directing Staff. I made my contribution but without aggression and I listened with silent despair to what was said in public forum. But I enjoyed the respite from Whitehall and when we were required to write our terminal thesis I found it much to my liking and was given a good rating, while the Commandant, who knew of my domestic problems, was sympathetic and generous with his thanks for my contribution to the course. I was earmarked for a subsequent posting back to the Directing Staff but this didn't come to pass. My posting from the Staff College was to Headquarters Flying Training Command at Shinfield Park just outside Reading. This meant a move from our Bracknell flat.

I was not sorry to leave. Diana's eccentricities had not passed unnoticed by the WAAFs in the other part of the building. One night, late, Diana woke up and screamed. I tried to silence her but had to resort to putting my hand over her mouth. I heard the voices of the WAAFs through the wall and, from then on, I got some very cold looks from them at the Staff

College. The Squadron Leader and his wife tried to help but Diana clammed up and said they were 'messing her about'. When I returned one evening I learned that Diana had gone shopping and had left Paddy in the pram outside the grocers. The police who, mercifully, knew where he belonged had brought him home. This was just another incident in the long trail of domestic difficulties which beleaguered my life. So I was ready to leave behind the embarrassment of the past.

We moved to Camberley for my next posting at HQ Flying Training Command at Shinfield Park. We engaged a cook-housekeeper who left after a month or so, and then another who did the same. The domestic scenario hadn't changed at all, only the location.

I slotted into my new job as a Wing Commander on the Air Staff of HQ Flying Training Command happily and confidently. I was back in the RAF proper. I was responsible for planning the future size, shape and composition of the component parts of the airborne elements of the RAF – flying, navigation and gunnery. I had access to the existing training establishments, the subordinate formations of the Command and the senior staff who commanded them. We had a small Communications Flight at White Waltham, just outside Reading, and once again I was airborne on my frequent visits to our outstations.

In May 1947 Diana was pregnant again. In July she had a very bad mental relapse and was admitted to a special wing of a hospital near Reading. Ranald and Paddy were boarded out in a home for young children and infants.

And then, within a few weeks, Stella Boyd came on the scene. Stella's sister, Marjorie – known as 'Mike' – had been Diana's close friend at boarding school. I remember 'Mike' at several of Diana's parties in her bedsitter in Cadogan Court. When I was posted to the Staff College, Diana, Ranald, Paddy and I would often drive over to the Boyds on a weekend when Mike was there. Mr Boyd, known as 'Pop Man', was good company but a shade withdrawn. Mrs Boyd , 'Lady' – the driving force in the family – always spoke her mind. It was 'Lady' who conceived the idea that Stella should run the Camberley flat until Diana recovered. 'Lady's' offer was a lifeline.

Stella had trained to become a nurse during the War but had failed her exams. She was good with children – and was a capable housekeeper who could cook simple meals and sincerely wanted to play a part in helping us. For five years, Stella sustained my home, espoused my children as her own and gave selflessly of herself. I am conscious that I did not always return in full measure the devotion which this wonderful friend showed to me and my children.

Diana was discharged from the nursing home six months pregnant and for a while we tried to keep the circus on the road. Then she had another relapse and demanded to go back to Dublin and her Irish psychiatrist. I tried to appease her but she fought me tooth and nail and so I took her back to Dublin. In due course, in November 1947, a perfectly healthy daughter was delivered, whom we named Lindsay. I flew over a few days later.

Diana took no interest in her baby. It was decided the infant should go into a crèche which had a good reputation for caring for 'unwanted babies'. I didn't get the message and agreed to the proposal. Aunt Nellie had no objection. But little did we know of the truth – after all the Matron had told me that the 'Sisters of Mercy' would take the greatest care of my little baby.

Lindsay was taken from me by a youngish woman wearing a nun's habit. The small dormitory with about twelve cots in it smelled horrible and almost all the infants were howling. There was a bottle or milk in each cot but out of reach of the babies. They were about to be fed, explained the Matron. There was a strict routine to condition the babes to feeding times. The fee seemed high. I paid the Matron and said my wife's aunt would visit regularly. She didn't like this at all and I left, none too pleased with what I had seen. I doubt whether the Matron belonged to any Holy Roman order whatsoever.

Aunt Nellie and Uncle Jack listened and understood my concern. Uncle Jack undertook to check out the 'Home' through his welfare contacts. I returned home but Lindsay and Dublin haunted me.

Ironically, though I had a difficult job as Wing Commander Air Plans in HQ Flying Training Command, I found a depth of peace and contentment in working on the future shape, size and component units of the Command, based on the Air Staff's forecast of the number of aircrew required for the post-War RAF's contribution to the North Atlantic Treaty Organisation and for defence of the UK.

CHAPTER TWENTY-NINE

Stella

With Stella at the helm, the peace and serenity which enveloped the family in Camberley and the sense of confidence which began slowly but surely to return to me was like awaking from a bad dream. Ranald was becoming a normal, extrovert and boisterous five and a half year old. Paddy was two, mischievous and full of fun. On my return from Shinfield Park each evening, I would give him my uniform cap and gloves which he would put on and strut around the sitting room saying, 'I'm Wing Commander, I'm Wing Commander'.

I began to consider my physical condition. For too long I had been behind desks, so I took to what is now known as jogging each morning before breakfast. Ranald wanted to come with me. Stella put him in a sweater, shorts and plimsolls, and we would set off for a trot up the hill. It set me up for the day and Ranald lost a lot of his puppy fat. We were living as a family. At times Ranald would ask after Mummy and there were occasions when he would call for her at night but Stella was ready to comfort and console.

Then, Aunt Nellie phoned. She sounded worried and asked if I could come as soon as possible, as she was not happy about Lindsay's health. She was very thin and not feeding properly. Could I come over and fetch her? My misgivings about the infants' home came to the surface.

I couldn't get leave. I had a series of presentations around the Flying Training Schools in the Command which I could not delegate to my subordinate, a hopeless speaker, and a conference chaired by the Commander-in-Chief immediately afterwards. I explained my predicament to Aunt Nellie, who said she would bring Lindsay over by air. She added that the sooner Lindsay was seen by a doctor the better.

Lindsay was carried from the aircraft at Heathrow in Aunt Nellie's arms, wrapped in a blanket and a woollen shawl. She was whimpering and looked terribly thin and deathly white. I drove Lindsay to Camberley as fast as I could. At one time I heard sound from the carry-cot on the seat behind me. I pulled up and lifted the shawl. Lindsay was breathing, but weakly. I drove on.

When we arrived at the flat 'Lady' was there with Stella, Ranald and Paddy. Lindsay was immediately taken over; hot water bottles were produced and she was encased in heated blankets in a cot and persuaded to drink some warm milk from a bottle. I watched as she was undressed and was utterly dismayed. She was a little skeleton, literally skin and bones with body sores and an eye infection.

The doctor was in attendance an hour or so later. Then Aunt Nellie rang from London. 'Lady' took the call and was white and drawn when she rang off. Later, 'Lady' explained that Lindsay had been virtually starved for a month. Uncle Jack had suspicions which he was intending to bring to the attention of the Law. I later heard that the home had been closed indefinitely.

For Lindsay it was touch and go for a week or more. It was a month or more before her weight was judged satisfactory, and longer before her skin eruptions were cured. Her eye infection proved troublesome but eventually responded to treatment and by early spring 1948 she was in good shape. Stella was supreme and never neglected Ranald or Paddy.

But I wasn't sleeping. Possibly reaction, possibly the ever-present problem of Diana, still in Dublin on a further course of ECT, possibly the backlash to my years of under-nourishment and tension as a POW all combined to reduce me to a state of partial inertia, a lack of concentration and a creeping sense of hopelessness. Food and clothes rationing had been ended. Petrol rationing also ended soon after and life began to shed the straitjacket of the War and became freer and unrestricted.

But I began to slip.

Seemingly my work continued to be approved. At Command Head-quarters our somewhat laid-back Commander-in-Chief retired. A new, dynamic and initially unpopular hard-hitting man was posted to replace him. Sir Ralph Cochrane turned Headquarters Flying Training Command upside down. His War record was brilliant but ruthless. He spent an hour with me discussing my Five-Year Plan for the Command. He condemned a lot of what I proposed but gave cogent reasons why. He approved many of my recommendations and gave me a month to complete the paper. He stated that he wanted it direct from me and not filtered through the Group Captain for whom I worked. Awkward: but I did what he said. By the time I had completed my task, my posting as Chief Flying Instructor at the Royal Air Force College, Cranwell, was promulgated. My appointment was scheduled to take effect six months later. I had two months' leave in hand and was overjoyed to be going back to flying duties. I wonder to what extent Cochrane had a hand in it, but I was badly run down and depressed.

When 'Lady' suggested that I become her tenant of the four-bedroomed house she owned in Chobham I accepted. The house, with a small garden, was adjacent to their home and was a great success with Ranald and Paddy. There was a junior school close-by which Ranald went to, and shopping in Woking was no problem for Stella with her car.

It was decided that Diana should be admitted as a voluntary patient to St Andrews Hospital, Northampton, one of the largest psychiatric hospitals in England. I met her plane from Dublin, drove her up the A1 and registered her at the Hospital. A kindly Sister took over and said the Deputy Medical Superintendent would like to see me.

Dr O'Connell was a man I grew to like and respect. He had reports from Dublin and he told me frankly and unambiguously that Diana was a paranoid schizophrenic. He explained that Diana could not be a 'certified' patient until they had built up a case history to present to the Board. She had not responded to ECT. The next stage, which he warned me was irreversible, was leucotomy but that could not be undertaken unless the patient's next of kin and a panel of close relations agreed. He told me that leucotomy involved slicing through some of the connections in the brain and the effect this would have on Diana's personality and behaviour pattern. He suggested I come up to see the Medical Superintendent in a fortnight when Diana's case could be discussed more fully. I thanked him and drove out of the extensive hospital grounds into the town for an early meal before the two and a half hour journey back to Chobham.

I was tired and the impact of what O'Connell had told me was sinking in. I remember stopping at an hotel in Northampton for a bar supper and then nothing more until I found myself walking, cold and confused, along a road at the end of which I could see lights. It was dark. I tried to remember who I was, where I was and what had happened, but nothing seemed clear to me. I walked on. I saw a blue light above the door of a building. I rang a bell and a man in police uniform came out. He asked me something. I forget what, and then I was indoors where it was warm and dry. He sat me down and asked questions which I couldn't answer. He then searched me but found nothing to identify me. He asked whether I had a wallet. I didn't seem to know. He called his superior who looked at me very hard and said something to him about 'a hospital'. I was given a cup of tea but was still unable to say who I was, where I lived and why I had mud all over my clothes. I still don't know how that happened.

Some time later a man came in. He asked me how long I had been in St Andrews Hospital. Which ward was I in? Then, suddenly, like waking up from a dream, I came to. It was instantaneous – not like coming out of an anaesthetic, but immediate. I took in my surroundings, I knew who I was; I remembered with absolute clarity taking Diana to St Andrews Hospital, my conversation with Dr O'Connell and the significance of what he had told me. I had forgotten the name of the hotel in Northampton where I had eaten a meal but I remembered the lounge bar and what I had eaten.

The newcomer, I learned later, was a nurse from St Andrews. I addressed my talk principally to him. He used the phone in the outer office. He returned looking friendly and relaxed. Yes, a Mrs Diana MacDonell had been admitted that afternoon. Her husband had driven her up from London. I was her husband? Yes.

I went through my pockets. I was worried at the loss of my wallet. In my fob pocket I found a receipt for the evening meal. It had the name of the hotel. A phone call to the manager confirmed that a man answering my description had taken a meal a few hours ago, had paid in cash and had left immediately. A waitress had found a wallet. The name on the driving licence and other documents was MacDonell. A black Wolseley saloon was in the car park.

The officer on night duty invited me to spend the night in a cell and offered to drive me into Northampton the following morning. He let me phone Chobham to say I was delayed

Next day, I drove south alone with my thoughts. I was inevitably shaken by what had happened. I pulled my mind away from the numerous 'black-outs' that I had handled while a POW. I tried to analyse, as I drove my Wolseley towards Surrey, why this thing had happened. I remained disturbed by my 'black-out' which must have involved at least two or more hours – the police station was six miles from the hotel – and I began to analyse, rationally and chronologically, the events which led up to this temporary loss of memory. At the wheel of my Wolseley, I came to terms with myself. I rejected the idea that I was unhinged, neurotic or bonkers. I was overstressed and had suffered delayed shock. I settled even more comfortably into the driving seat and felt immensely relaxed. I had worked it out. It was all behind me. I wanted my children and my home. I wanted Stella's comfort but, above all, I wanted her sister, Mike's, company.

Mike was becoming a need. Back in Chobham I regained my peace of mind. My leave was drawing to a close and I was in contact with the authorities at Cranwell in preparation for my new appointment. The children were thriving. Stella was cheerful and purposeful. Lady was holding a watching brief. The lawn needed mowing.

CHAPTER THIRTY

Cranwell Revisited

I had mixed feelings at leaving HQ Flying Training Command. While I was happy to be back in the RAF proper, I had missed the thrust and urgency of an operational unit. Even under Cochrane the Command Headquarters lacked the impulse and purpose that I had found in my pre-War and wartime years in the service. Probably I was expecting too much. The War was over. The hopes, fears, anxieties and sheer dogged determination to win through personally and collectively no longer existed and were slowly but surely being eroded by a huge national sigh of relief followed by a lethargy – it's all over, I couldn't care less.

There were good officers with good brains in Command Headquarters but for many their hearts were not in their jobs. Preoccupied as I was with my domestic troubles I was not really aware of what was happening though, with hindsight, I can see that this nation-wide sense of inertia and release from tension was only to be expected: a God-given sedative. People let go the reins. In Command Headquarters, staff officers were away 'visiting' subordinate units in their cars for which they were entitled to petrol coupons. Often their routes were suspect. Occasionally their destinations were fudged. Black markets abounded: money could buy anything. We were becoming a dishonest and self-interested society. People travelling by train smoked in non-smoking compartments and no one complained. Pubs remained open well after licensed hours, and remained so until the drink ran out.

At Command Headquarters there was a hard core who drank their lunch at the bar in the Officers' Mess. One, a colleague of mine on the Air Staff, wrote excellent reports in the afternoon, though he was a bit inarticulate on the telephone.

Inevitably the end of the War meant a drastic reduction in the size of the Armed Forces and the RAF was no exception. As the Air Staff Planner,

I was faced with a pitched battle between the Air Ministry's policy directive to Cochrane, which was progressively to reduce the size of his Command, and the opposition from his subordinate Group Commander who, for a variety of reasons, which ranged from personal animosity to fear of early retirement, fought back tooth and nail to keep what they had; to oppose amalgamations and to play for time.

Meanwhile the output of pilots, navigators and air gunners from the RAF training schools in Canada and Rhodesia in particular, though drastically cut back, was surplus to the requirements of the operational squadrons. Aircrew who had not long got their Wings were absorbed into non-flying backwater jobs or, more commonly, were put in holding units pending redundancy. Morale became badly affected.

My final report to Cochrane, which became known as 'The Five-Year Plan' had taken me the better part of two years to complete. He had briefed me tersely, succinctly, and with his legendary clarity and absence of sensitivity. And I had to do it in concert with his Group Commanders. I was to negotiate an agreed course of action to conform with his directive. I was his envoy but without his clout. I was well and truly in the firing line.

Several years later, when he had retired, I met Sir Ralph Cochrane in the British European Airways marquee at the Farnborough Air Display. He greeted me warmly and led me to the bar for a drink. He looked at me hard and said, 'You're too thin. You are probably working too hard'. We talked for a while and then: 'Your final report was a good one. I sent it to the Air Council with only a few alterations. Don't use clichés in service writing'. He smiled and moved off to join a group at the entrance. I never knew what he meant but I felt rewarded and enjoyed the show.

I was of course no stranger to Cranwell. Apart from the two years I had spent there as a Flight Cadet in the early thirties, I had visited the RAF College as a guest, for Old Cranwellian reunions, and as the Air Staff Planner from Command Headquarters. Since the end of the War, Cranwell had been rapidly – too rapidly – restored to its previous status as the pre-eminent training establishment for the permanent commissioned cadre of officers for the Royal Air Force, the Navy had the Royal Naval College, Dartmouth, and the Army had Sandhurst. A healthy element of rivalry existed between the three. The Air Force Board was determined that Cranwell should not be the lame duck. So the pressure was on. Three and a half years after the end of the War, my posting in 1949 as Chief Flying Instructor at the age of thirty five was to be no sinecure.

A number of changes had been made to the layout of the station. The old wooden huts which we had occupied as Flight Cadets had gone. A large, two-storey administrative block had been built. There was well-trimmed grass with paved pathways between the buildings and young trees which blossomed in spring and lent the camp an atmosphere of suburban, middle-class dignity. Only the names of the little intersecting streets dispelled the illusion: Trenchard Terrace, Dowding Close, Portal Place, and so on. These names serve to describe the Cranwell habitat as I found it on my return in 1949. Royal Air Force Cranwell was essentially focused on the Royal Air Force College. There were other units on or subordinate to the Station for which the whole composite command was vested in Air Commodore George Beamish.

As Commandant of the RAF College – his principal role – Beamish was to me a surprising choice. Bearing in mind that the College was by now much in the public eye and that several foreign countries, particularly in the Middle East, were seeking training for their burgeoning armed forces, particularly their air forces, George Beamish didn't seem to me to be the best 'presenter' of the post-War Royal Air Force.

He was a burly, slow-moving man with a boxer's face – he had been one when younger – who walked ponderously and came onto parade lurching and lacking in any sort of ceremonial élan. Nevertheless he was a man of high principles who took his command responsibility very seriously. He was attentive to me but was not a pilot of any significance and we were not in tune on certain aspects of flying training. Being a bachelor, and probably lonely, he was somewhat out of touch with the reality of the hang-ups and aspirations of the young cadets for whom he was *ipso facto* maestro.

The Assistant Commandant, the Chief Executive as it were of the Cadet Wing, was a dynamic, unpredictable, highly decorated Group Captain known as 'Doggie'. To his lot fell the overseeing of all flying training, the standard of discipline, drill and ceremonial of the Cadet Wing and the organisation of the numerous visits paid by foreign delegations, parliamentary representatives and endless, time-consuming groups of VIPs with whom we were plagued.

'Doggie' was into everything. The antithesis of George Beamish, he was hyperactive, thrusting, disturbing and restless. He did everything at the double. His sturdy figure would erupt without warning into every activity of the Cadet College. His parade presence was dynamically impressive and he was dedicated and single-minded. To 'Doggie', the Royal Air Force College was a mission: he would carry everybody with him in ensuring its fulfilment.

He drove his staff car with its pennant streaming from its little mast on the bonnet as though he was competing in a Grand Prix. He screeched round corners, screeched to a halt, and screeched away in pursuit of other ports of call, emitting a trail of blue smoke from the exhaust. The car was in dire need of an overhaul. Small wonder! His staff car was not all he wore out. There were those who fell by the wayside.

I was directly responsible to 'Doggie' for the Flying Wing and the standard of flying training. I was somewhat out of breath before he and I got our act together and I admit to serious misgivings about the future. But life is full of contradictions and the unexpected. In the event, 'Doggie' and I made common cause and within a few weeks were working harmoniously and effectively together. For this I owe a great deal to my predecessor, Julian Pritchard, a much respected and first-class officer who commanded the Flying Wing as Chief Flying Instructor with distinction. A bachelor, Julian was a quiet, deep-thinking man with a ready wit. We flew together during the week's handover before he was posted. He helped me enormously. It was Julian who had got 'Doggie' taped: he never thwarted him and always gave him unstinting support while protecting his own flying instructors from most of 'Doggie's' more extravagant demands. But what impressed me most about Julian was his uncanny gift of predicting 'Doggie's' daily excursions to any of the units in the great, widespread establishment of Royal Air Force Cranwell.

Undoubtedly, Julian had his 'informers'. They were two extremely capable Staff Officers who serviced 'Doggie's' office in the Cranwell Headquarters. They were, of course, privy to their master's daily programme but there was no breach of security in letting the Chief Flying Instructor know if 'Doggie' was planning to visit any section of his responsibility.

So it came to pass that when 'Doggie' was tearing into the Sergeants' Mess, or the Officers' Mess or the kitchens in the College, or any other part of the campus, Julian would relax and fly and be with the Flying Wing, but when the red light appeared he would forestall 'Doggie'. Be it in the Control Tower, on the tarmac or even in the Maintenance Hangar – 'Doggie' knew nothing about mechanics – 'Doggie' had Julian ready waiting for him. Even on one occasion when 'Doggie' screeched away in his staff car and fetched up way down the airfield, looking indignantly at the tattered windsock which yesterday's gale had shredded, Julian was there with a team of maintenance men who were unloading a replacement from the back of a truck. Julian left a week after my arrival and I was officially appointed Chief Flying Instructor and Officer Commanding Flying Wing.

Diana was in St Andrew's Hospital as a voluntary patient. The news from Chobham was uninformative. Stella was a hopeless letter writer. I was relying more and more on Mike, to the extent that I found my need for her was no longer under control. I sought every possible means of seeing her but to little avail. The College routine involved Church Parade which I was required to attend. That put paid to a weekend in Chobham and a stopover in Mike's flat in Cranley Gardens where I was always welcome and, given notice, her flatmate Pat would be out for the evening.

But there was a break between courses and I took a week's leave. I visited Diana who seemed in worse shape than when she had been admitted. I had notified the hospital that I was visiting, so they had 'prepared' Diana, who was sitting in the lobby, heavily and hideously made up and staring fixedly at the floor. I drove Diana to a neighbouring village for tea. She hardly spoke except to ask when she could come home. We finished our tea and Diana left ahead of me while I settled the bill. The waitress was slow and it was several minutes before I reached the car. Diana was not to be seen. I found her striding down the road. She got in when I pulled up beside her and we drove back to St Andrew's in silence. She didn't say goodbye.

I drove to London, saddened and depressed. I needed to unburden to Mike, to feel her understanding and compassion and her hand in mine as I rid myself of mixed feelings of inadequacy, guilt and, dare I admit it, self-pity. It was Mike's flatmate who answered the bell when I reached Cranley Gardens. She was to tell me that Mike had gone to Chobham, as her father was seriously ill. I then drove on to Chobham and the children. Mike had to spend the weekend with her family but we spoke on several occasions. She gave me comfort and courage as well as she could. 'Lady' had noticed that I was seeing a lot of Mike and felt I was neglecting Stella. She gave me four weeks' notice to leave the property.

I drove Mike back to her flat and, after a brief farewell, I drove on to Cranwell and my room in the Officers' Mess, where I found a note from 'Doggie' who wanted to see me at 8.30 the following morning immediately after Parade. I put Chobham out of my mind, addressed myself to the Cranwell merry-go-round and went to bed. My last thought before sleep overtook me was how wonderful it would be were it possible to put together into one frame the different pieces of my life's jigsaw.

My batman woke me at seven o'clock with a cup of tea, but I fell asleep again. It was eight o'clock when I came to and, by the time I had washed, shaved and dressed, I was too late for breakfast and just made 'Doggie's' office in time for the meeting, which was basically a run-through of the planned activities for the new term. We sat and listened and made notes. Still half-asleep, I realised 'Doggie' was addressing himself to me. 'Mac, have you got that one?' I had drifted away. With half my mind I was listening to 'Doggie', watching his Biro going up and down, stabbing his blotter with tiny spots.

During the previous term, when 'Doggie' had been away I had stood in for him and had been puzzled by the constellation of dots which covered his blotter. It was his Staff Officer who tipped me off. It was the way he conducted his conferences. A sort of emphasis to what he was saying, it was 'Doggie's' way of doing his business. So I was watching his Biro going up and down and I was letting my mind wander from what he was saying to what I had left behind: the tragic and tearful parting from Ranald and Paddy; the drive to London with Mike, who gave me, as always, courage and hope; the realisation as I drove north to Lincolnshire that she had become all important to me, omnipotent as a counsellor and as a woman. I needed her as I had never needed any woman before. 'Doggie' broke through my introspections.

'Sorry, sir,' I replied. 'I'm afraid I missed that.' 'Doggie' gave me a long look and then repeated what I had missed. A French Air Force delegation was visiting Cranwell in the near future. The delegation would arrive by air, lunch in the College, visit the Flying Wing, which was my command, and watch a flying display. I was to conduct the delegation through my training squadrons, following a formal parade on the tarmac when the senior delegate of *l'Armée de l'Air* would review my instructors and their cadet pupils. I took all this in. We had been through similar exercises before. The colour of their skins and the uniforms they wore varied but the format remained unchanged. There was nothing new in the French visit – indeed I had met two of them a year or so before when they had visited Command Headquarters. I found them effete and with the outlook of civil servants. I hadn't taken to them at all.

I assured 'Doggie' that I would brief my two Squadron commanders and that Flying Wing's contribution to the visit would be up to the mark. He resumed stabbing at his blotter and shortly afterwards the meeting came to a close. I returned to the Flying Wing where my Adjutant arranged a meeting with my two Squadron commanders.

Squadron Leader Bruce Cole, in charge of the Advanced Training Squadron, and Squadron Leader John Owen, in charge of the Basic Training Squadron, were two of the finest officers I ever had the privilege of commanding. I only hope that my various inadequacies as their Wing Commander were compensated in some measure by the trust which I placed in them. Bruce and his crew were tragically killed a year after he had been posted from Cranwell to an operational squadron, when a runaway tail trim on his Canberra drove it out of control into a crash dive. John remained in the Service for several years but I lost touch with him. The flying instructors they commanded were of an exceedingly high calibre. I flew with each in turn and rejoiced in the standard they displayed: there was nothing I could teach them, indeed I learned a lot at their hands and was not ashamed to admit it.

So we flew day and night. In the air I was at home with my environment and released from the earth-bound domestic and service problems. I felt the freedom which only those who fly and whose opponents are the elements can fully understand. I no longer fly but I find something of that earlier sense of freedom when driving my car, not fast but within my gift to respond to my will and to behave as I demand. That great French aviator and writer Antoine de St Exupéry has encapsulated this incredible sense of wholeness and aloneness in *Vol de Nuit*. The affinity which I had with his writings comes through in a description I wrote of a flight over mountains in the Middle East.

Lincolnshire is a flat, featureless country. But there was a benign quality in flying over the checkerboard farmland and professional comfort in the knowledge that the Cranwell 'beam' could bring you home safely should you be caught by bad weather. I flew regularly with my instructors but frequently and daily with the cadets to assess their progress and note any particular weaknesses that needed correction.

Inevitably we had our setbacks. Six months after my appointment as Chief Flying Instructor, Flight Cadet Black, who was Lord Tedder's stepson, was killed in a Harvard which he was flying solo. He had plunged at speed and at forty-five degrees into the ground. Both mainplanes had been fractured upwards just inboard of the ailerons. With the Wing Commander in charge of engineering, I visited the site. We agreed that the wing structure had collapsed under excessive 'g'. But why, neither we nor the subsequent court of enquiry were able to decide. Low aerobatics, a black-out recovered too late? It was anyone's guess. But it was a tragedy that marred my first six months as the new Chief Flying Instructor.

THE SEVENTEEN FORTY-FIVE ASSOCIATION

Shortly after my appointment to Cranwell, an Air Commodore Macdonald visited the College from the Air Ministry. He was the first person to address me as 'Glengarry', the title which I had inherited following my father's death in 1941. Dad had upheld the traditions and obligations of his Chieftainship until poverty and ill health had made it impossible for him to travel to Scotland to attend the annual dinners of the Glasgow and Edinburgh Clan Donald Societies. He and I were too remote both geographically and personally for any form of 'handover' and, when I was repatriated in 1945, my domestic and service preoccupations gave me little time or inclination to offer a Glengarry presence in Scotland. But I made contact with Ranald Macdonald of Clanranald, a young man of considerable charm who had recently been granted the Arms Armorial of Clanranald, following the death of an elderly and distant cousin who had been a contemporary of my father. Clanranald and I were invited to the Annual Dinner of the International Clan Donald Society of London. The function was held in the Waldorf Hotel in the Aldwych. The President was preoccupied with his arrangements and I was received with scant courtesy. Clanranald and I dived into the bar and, by the time dinner was called and we were lined up to be piped in, we were feeling no pain at all.

An indifferent meal served with an inferior wine – the War had ended only a few years ago – and I was called upon to respond to a toast to the Society, which I did adequately and honestly. I pointed up the existing schisms and enmities between many of the Highland clans and suggested, probably unwisely, that there were far too many 'isms', not only in our country but throughout the world. I called for a hard look at our post-War society and I challenged – most unwisely – the interdenominational wrangles that were making news headlines at the time. The top table gave me muted applause but I got a standing ovation from a group who flanked the dining room. In his reply the President stated that he had 'little in common with Glengarry's views'.

Clanranald and I moved to the bar where a young barman was serving short measures of brandy. Clanranald sorted that one out. 'Fill them up,' he said. 'You're dealing with Scots!' He showed then the qualities, which did not exclude arrogance, that led him to success and considerable wealth in the business which he set up several years later in North London.

On another occasion, I was invited to be the guest of honour at the Annual Dinner of the Seventeen Forty-Five Association in Edinburgh. The Association – a collection of eccentric, elderly, avowed Jacobites – dedicated itself to the memory of Prince Charles Edward Stuart. Donald John Macdonald of Castleton, the Honorary Secretary of the Clan Donald Society of Edinburgh was also at the Dinner which turned out to be rather a bizarre affair.

The Chairman, I had been told, was one Lieutenant-Colonel Gayre of Gayre and Nigg, apparently an unusually accomplished man some eight years older than me. I looked him up in *Who's Who* and was immediately impressed, indeed bewildered, by the length and complexity of his entry, which ran down the whole length of the page. His accomplishments were so various and numerous that I won't attempt to record them. The one common theme seemed to be ethnology but throughout this extraordinary c.v. was a plethora of high offices held in the classics, literature, art and music, together with distinctions held worldwide and an honour as a Grand Commander of the Order of St Lazarus. I looked forward to meeting the Gayre of Gayre and Nigg.

Donald J – as he was known to his friends – met me in the foyer of a small hotel which backed onto the upper reaches of the Royal Mile. There he was, erect, rugged and dignified, with his crooked smile and twinkling eyes. He received me warmly, made me feel welcome and invited me to join him for a dram in the bar. He explained that the Chairman would be arriving shortly and that there would be a brief committee meeting in private before we went into dinner. He hoped I wouldn't mind being on my own for a quarter of an hour or so. I assured him I would not.

We were getting to know each other when the Colonel arrived with a retinue of elderly ladies who flocked to the powder room. Donald J introduced us. I detected a coolness in the chairman's greeting. Small, dapper, sharp-featured with a permanent frown, he fidgeted with his hands while we exchanged small talk. He drew Donald J aside and they spoke rapidly and quietly for a short while. The ladies reappeared refreshed. Donald J bought me a 'top up' and what I assumed was the committee moved into an ante-room leading off the foyer. Donald J smiled at me as they left.

I sat alone and sipped my drink while other elderly couples in Highland evening dress filtered into the bar, bought drinks and fell into conversation with each other. No one addressed me, so I sat contented and relaxed. I watched the guests as they arrived and tried to pretend that I belonged. I noticed they all wore a white cockade, the historic emblem of adherence to the Jacobite cause.

The door of the committee room opened and Donald J and the Chairman joined us in the bar, and then dinner was announced. There was one long table, lit with silver candelabras and set with fine linen and beautiful cut-glass. I sat on the right of the Chairman at the head of the table. On my place-mat was a white cockade. I pinned it on the lapel of my jacket and we stood for grace in Gaelic. The meal was a good one but I was not at ease. I had not been introduced to those present and the Colonel and I exchanged a few wartime anecdotes, but for the most part I ate in silence. Then the coffee was served and it was time for speeches.

Gayre of Gayre and Nigg struck with his gavel. He stood and called for all to be upstanding for the toast to 'His Majesty the King'. There was a stunned silence from these dedicated Jacobites. Glances were exchanged and then, fumbling with napkins, all stood up. Staring fixedly ahead, the Chairman gave the toast: 'His Majesty the King'. Muted and with heads bowed, the table mumbled 'the King' and held their glasses to their lips. But two elderly ladies stood defiantly with no glass in their hands. We then sat down in silence. Cigars and cigarettes were lit. No one, apparently, had given any thought to my position as a serving officer in His Majesty's Armed Forces.

I was then billed to propose the toast to the Association. This I did with deliberate caution lest I further compound what was evidently an historic and emotionally charged situation where even angels, let alone simple Wing Commanders, dare not tread. As I ended and sat down I caught an encouraging smile from Donald J and accepted a more than welcome dram from the bottle poured by my host.

There was then certain business announced by the Chairman, followed by a welcome break before further speeches. I followed the kilted brethren downstairs where we queued for the inadequate facilities. One man who had evidently dined well asked me if I knew a cousin of his who had been in Bomber Command, I confessed that I didn't. Fighter and Bomber pilots had seldom met. He looked at me and said, 'A-ha, yes of course. I see.' We remained in silence until we attained our destination, when he observed 'Better out than in, don't you agree?' We returned to the table.

When all were assembled, Gayre and Nigg who had 'dined well' rose to his feet to give the speech of the evening. He had no notes and was never at a loss for words. After a few introductory remarks and without any reference to me, he related the well-known saga of the Young Pretender's triumphant march south and the tragedy of the subsequent withdrawal of his army to the culminating defeat at Culloden. At this point his audience had begun to behave emotionally. Many of the elderly ladies were in tears; the men sat silent and huddled over their brandies. Someone began to sing:

> Bonnie Charlie's noo awa
> Safely owre the friendly main;
> Mony a heart will brak in twa
> Should he ne'er come back again.

The Chairman stopped for a moment and then, sensing the mood of those present, began to rant. 'We will never forget,' he bellowed. 'We will never forget,' wailed the ladies. 'We will never forgive,' roared Gayre and Nigg. 'We will never forgive,' growled the men. 'God's blessing on our Prince,' spluttered the Chairman. 'God's blessing – blessing – blessing,' chanted the congregation.

I sat stupefied and fearful. The whole event was beyond me. It was rapidly becoming too Orwellian and a ghastly reproduction of Animal Farm. At last the wailing died down. Gayre and Nigg, with a wild light in his eye, turned to me and said, 'Glengarry, the fiery cross can still be carried by those who remember!' I replied weakly, 'Yes, I understand.' The party then broke up.

Under the gentle guidance of Donald J, I found my feet as one of the Chiefs of Clan Donald. I found time to attend Annual Dinners in Edinburgh and, in 1960, I was invited by Reginald Macdonald of Kingsburgh to be his Guest of Honour at the Ligonier Highland Games in

Idlewild Park, not far from Pittsburgh, in the USA – my first overseas visit as Glengarry. Years later, in 1973, accompanied by my bride of a few months, Lois, I was a guest of honour at the Scottish World Festival in Toronto. We were similarly honoured on several occasions at Highland Games in the US and I was one of the Chiefs at the first Scottish Week in Sydney, Australia, in 1981. This was on top of far greater involvement with Clan Donald in Scotland and in particular the Clan Donald Lands Trust on the Isle of Skye.

But I have jumped ahead in time ....

CHAPTER THIRTY-ONE

More of Cranwell

B ack at Cranwell, the visit by the French Air Force delegation went well. Flying training continued during the forenoon but my Wing was grounded and formed up, instructors, NCOs and airmen together with their aircraft for the afternoon review by the French visitors. The weather clamped down around midday. We probably would not have flown anyway during the afternoon, so nothing much was lost. A formal introduction and they were spirited away to pre-lunch drinks with the Commandant, 'Doggie' and the Station Commander. My lunch-time neighbour was a member of the French legation in London who exuded bonhomie and *Soir de Paris*, or was it *Eau de Nil*? I was excused the 'port and cigars' finale to the luncheon and returned to Flying Wing where everything was in apple-pie order.

Twenty minutes late on the schedule, the delegation arrived at the tarmac with the Commandant and 'Doggie', the latter hopping around, gesticulating and giving a brilliant demonstration of an excitable Frenchman – or perhaps a high-spirited doggy! I called my Wing to attention and marched forward to salute the senior French officer of *l'Armée de l'Air*. He returned my salute, shook my hand and I was then introduced by name, rank and appointment by 'Doggie' who added, in parenthesis as it were, that I had commanded a Spitfire squadron during the Battle of Britain. I was congratulated in French and passed down the line. *Soir de Paris* and *Eau de Nil* were by now well mixed with Napoleon brandy.

I was being introduced to a beaming officer with several medal ribbons on his tunic. 'Doggie' did his Battle of Britain piece and left me gripped by the officer with both hands. He held onto me and said, 'You were a fighter peelot?' I replied that indeed I was. 'Then you are a 'ero. You are brave man – Mon brave!' And with a final blast of Napoleon brandy he exploded, 'I honour you and love you. Oui!' Whereupon he planted two juicy kisses, one on each of my cheeks and released my hand.

In some confusion I took up my position in front of my Wing. 'Doggie' was staring at the sky but George Beamish was smiling broadly. I felt a ripple of suppressed laughter from the ranks behind me. The delegation moved off to tour the Station. The fly-past had been cancelled, so I dismissed my Wing and sought sanctuary in my office. My impeccable Adjutant gave no sign whatsoever of what he had witnessed. We got down to administration and that was that.

Courses graduated with due ceremonial and new courses arrived. I visited the children whenever possible and found them healthy enough under the wing of Stella. Ranald was at a private preparatory school in East Sussex and had settled in quickly, and Paddy took his place at the junior school up the road. Lindsay was a happy little three-year old. I took my annual quota of leave during Ranald's holidays whenever possible. Because he alone of my children remembered Diana, I would talk to him about his mother and encourage him to believe that she would one day be well again and come home to us. For much of his early life there was only Stella to comfort him, for I was so often away.

Mike remained ever ready to support and advise me. Our relationship stabilised but tongues had begun to wag. Together we drove to Northampton and took Diana out to tea. Afterwards I asked Mike if she thought Diana would ever recover. For a while she did not reply. Then she said, 'I am afraid I very much doubt it'. We continued our journey back, silent with our own private thoughts. She put her hand on mine as I held the wheel and I felt a strength flow to me which was both comforting and sustaining . . . .

I and a first-year Flight Cadet walked across the tarmac to where the Percival Prentice basic trainers were lined up for the afternoon's flying training. His instructor had doubts about him and had asked John Owen, the Squadron Commander, to check him out. John had decided to refer him to me, the final arbiter. The boy knew this was his last chance. We walked in silence, our parachutes slung over our shoulders, until we had crossed the tarmac and reached our Prentice with the ground crew waiting for us.

He was a tall, rather awkward young man of about nineteen. His reports from his instructor spoke of lack of confidence and a tendency to 'clam up' when things went wrong. His academic reports were good, his bearing was acceptable and he was clearly trying hard to make the grade. He played tennis very well but didn't mix with his peers and was obviously a loner. I felt these occasions very deeply. Mercifully they didn't happen often but I knew I was too soft and the knowledge that the boy's future lay in my hands, in my assessment, weighed heavily upon me and challenged my responsibility for making an impartial and professional judgement.

When I turned to him to speak and saw the look in his eyes, it was as though I was looking at myself.

'Right,' I said, 'I want you to carry out the pre-flight checks, then start up, taxi down to the end of the airfield and make a normal take-off. I will be sitting beside you. If you are in any doubt about anything, just ask me. When we are airborne, I'll tell you what I want you to do next. Okay?' 'Yes, sir,' and he carried out the checks and drills, taxied to the downwind end of the airfield, waited while another Prentice took off ahead of him, made his final checks, opened the throttle and took off. Elementary, but he performed competently.

'Climb straight ahead to five thousand feet,' I said, 'and then fly over to Rauceby. We ought to have that area to ourselves and you can show me what you can do.' He looked at me and nodded, and we continued to climb. I sat beside him with my hands on my lap and my feet resting lightly on the rudder pedals. The Prentice was a side-by-side, dual control trainer with a third passenger seat behind the pilot's. It was an uninteresting aeroplane but safe and easy to handle and met the requirements for a basic trainer well enough.

We reached five thousand feet. He levelled out, throttled back and turned towards Rauceby. The area was relatively free. A few Harvard advanced trainers were around but we had plenty of airspace, so I began to put him through my usual routine, steep turns, climbing turns, stalling and recovering and other manoeuvres, all of which he carried out satisfactorily.

At Rauceby was one of our practice forced landing grounds, a largish flat field with a windsock and no trees on its boundaries. We were flying away from it when I closed the throttle. 'Okay, now try a practice forced landing.' He hesitated for a moment, then peered down, went into a glide, trimmed the aircraft and made a gliding turn towards the field. A Harvard crossed well below us and began to climb away. Another had landed on the field and was taxiing to the downwind edge before taking off. We made another gliding turn which brought us to the downwind leg of our approach. The Harvard took off and we turned cross-wind. Too high but better than too low. He turned into wind at a thousand feet but we were overshooting. 'Sideslip off your surplus height,' I said calmly. We went into a sideslip. I had one hand on the throttle and the other resting lightly on the control column. We continued to sideslip. Come out, I thought, you are okay now. But the sideslip continued. At three hundred feet our gliding speed was nearing a stall and we were now undershooting badly. 'I have control,' I said tersely and, correcting the sideslip, opened the throttle fully. We cleared the hedge and climbed away. It was a near thing.

He stared ahead as I flew round in a climbing turn. 'Sorry, sir, I can do better than that,' he said. 'Can I try another, please?'

I agreed and continued to climb. I chose a different position at a different height, handed over the controls to him and shortly afterwards cut the throttle. I heard him breathing heavily through the intercom but he positioned the aircraft well, made a faultless approach and when I said 'Well done, go ahead and land', he did so like a veteran.

We sat for a while at the far end of the field with the engine throttled back as we discussed what went wrong. Why had he continued to sideslip almost into the ground? He sat beside me, his long body drooped over the control column and his legs bent with his knees drawn up. Then, very slowly he said, 'I wouldn't have done that on my own, sir. I sort of seized up because you were with me checking me out. I had to do it again and to pretend that you weren't there. I'm sorry, sir.' 'Never mind, let's go and enjoy ourselves. Taxi back to the downwind hedge and take off. Watch for the Harvards.'

We took off from the field and climbed to just below the cloud base at about six thousand feet. We then went through a simple aerobatic routine, a loop, stall turn and a barrel roll. He looked much happier and began to talk to me slowly and quite naturally as we flew back to Cranwell, joined the circuit and made a good landing opposite the hangars. I passed him. I confess my decision was partly a gut feeling that it would be wrong not to. John Owen was loyally non-committal. But the Cadet passed on to his second year and to advanced flying training on Harvards. He graduated and several years later, when I was on a jet conversion course, there he was – a flying instructor!

For a whole week during the late summer, it rained heavily. The cloud base over the whole area was about a thousand feet or even lower. Flying training was limited to dual instruction only and for two days the conditions were so bad that no flying took place at all. The rain poured down vertically through a near tropical atmosphere. Gutters were blocked, the tarmac was awash and it was decided to cancel the Saturday cricket match on the 'Orange', the circular area of immaculately tended grass in front of the College, with a straight edge along the parade ground, which from the air was the shape of an orange. Hence its name which goes down in history.

On the days when flying was impossible the Cadets reported to Flying Wing where ad hoc lectures on the theory of flight, air traffic control and other air forces were somehow cobbled together. 'Doggie' sprang a surprise visit on one of these lectures. He wasn't impressed and addressed a scathing Minute to John, the Squadron Commander concerned. John brought it to me and I undertook to deal with 'Doggie'. I invited him to give us the benefit of his greater experience by talking to the next group who were grounded by bad weather. To my surprise, he agreed and chose a group of the senior term cadets who had nothing to lose by speaking their minds. Long before 'Doggie' had got into his stride they began to chip in to pose awkward questions. Within half an hour they had made mincemeat of him. He gave us no further trouble!

When the rain began to let up, a torrid belt of low pressure took over which drove most of us to the bar in the Officers' Mess. Some went off for weekend leave but most of us were lounging around, drowsy and bored by the time supper was served. Bruce, John, myself, several of our bachelor flying instructors and a group of the Station's administrative officers, went off in convoy to Grantham for a few drinks. I took four passengers in my Wolseley and John had three or four in his car. Another carload joined us. We ploughed our way along partially flooded roads to Grantham where we visited several pubs and painted the town pink, if not red. We got back to the Officers' Mess in fair order around midnight and then proceeded to perform a sort of mechanised dressage, weaving in and out the trees planted on the grass lawns around the Mess. Mercifully, we avoided any serious damage to either our cars or the trees but the tell-tale marks of our tyres on the sodden grass were a sobering reminder of our wantonness when we lurched, bleary eyed and feeling dreadful, towards the College church the following morning.

I shall never forget that service. We filed in rather on the late side. The Commandant and 'Doggie' and his half-French wife, Irene, were already seated, as was the entire Cadet Wing. We took our seats and the organ began to play. We rose as the RAF Chaplain entered and the service began. I stole a glance along our row. Bruce was the colour of a Chinaman, John had his eyes shut as though in prayer. Perhaps he was? The rest of us were doing our utmost to uphold the tradition of our commissions and to maintain a semblance of dignity, though each of us was suffering in his own private way. When we opened our mouths collectively to sing or to answer in response or simply to yawn discretely behind our hands, the breath of stale alcohol swept down our ranks and must have been obvious to 'Doggie' and the senior staff sitting in front of us. Once, during the unutterably boring sermon by the RAF Chaplain, Irene turned and smiled at us. She always had a roving eye.

The last hymn was announced. We rose while the organist played the first bars mournfully and dragged every note. We brayed our way through, but the line 'We love the sacred font' was too much for us. We exchanged glances. Bar – yes, soda water fountain – possibly, but sacred font – no!

We hurried back to the Mess where our hangovers were despatched in quick order. We had lunch and then slumped into the relaxing comfort of the deep armchairs in the Ante-room where most of us slumbered until tea, after which we were restored to normality.

A few days later I had a frightening experience with a Cadet in the air. The Prentice trainer was a safe aircraft except that when put into a spin it tended, after about five turns, to go into a flat spin from which it was difficult to recover. Spinning therefore was limited to dual instruction and confined to no more than three turns. I was carrying out a routine progress test on a Cadet in a Prentice and at six thousand feet I told him to throttle back, stall and initiate a spin. He did so and after three turns I told him to recover. He pushed the control column forward, applied power and opposite rudder and came out of the spin satisfactorily. But after the recovery the nose of the aircraft was down and our speed was building up. I told him to raise the nose and reduce power. He then said he couldn't move the control column back. I took over at once. He was right – the elevator had jammed. With reduced power the nose tended to drop even further; with increased power it came up but not to level flight. He and I both made the same decision: wind back the tail trim. 'Wind the fucking wheel back!' We did so and, with half power, we had the Prentice flying level. I called base and told them to stand by for an emergency landing. Gently, ever so gently, without use of the elevators, I eased our aircraft back to base and to a safe landing. As we came to a halt, 'Doggie' in his staff car, followed by the fire tender and ambulance, rushed out to us. We climbed out, me and my Cadet pupil. We looked at each other and laughed. I slapped him on his shoulders and he slapped mine. 'Doggie' looked speechless! The technical staff found that a bolt had sheered and jammed the elevator controls. Lucky!

CHAPTER THIRTY-TWO

Diana Declines

Diana was discharged from St Andrews Hospital, Northampton, 'on trial' and spent some time with an elderly relative but her bizarre behaviour proved too much and the housekeeper threatened to leave. I shrank from the option of persuading Diana to return to St Andrews: it seemed an admission of defeat. While in hospital, she had been taught to weave by the Occupational Therapy department. We found a weaving family who would provide lodging and further instruction in the craft she seemed to enjoy. But within a fortnight the school wrote saying that Diana was making no progress and was a disturbing influence on the others. I took three days' compassionate leave, and we spent the time in a small hotel near Norwich. She was far from well.

I discussed the problem with the Medical Superintendent. To my astonishment he disclosed that Diana was 'certified' and that the few months she had spent at large with the weavers had been a provision in the Section under which she had been 'released' from hospital, provided the 'domicile' was prepared to accept her. I had never been informed of this provision and we had a row. Dr O'Connell, separated us, took me into his office, gave me a substantial whisky and sent me off in better humour for the journey to Lincolnshire. I returned to Cranwell more able to give of my best than hitherto.

'Doggie' was understanding and gave me far more time off than an officer holding the rank and appointment I had could reasonably expect. In retrospect I perceive a much deeper compassion and understanding in this task-oriented little man than I was aware of at the time. Also, 'Doggie's' wife, Irene, gave me comfort and solace, though my need for Mike remained.

Diana's readmission to St Andrews was, in effect, final. At a review panel a year or so later, her case was recommended for the relatively new brain surgery of bi-frontal leucotomy. The operation, I was told, was intended to stabilise her condition and to relieve the severity of her schizophrenia. It was not held to be a cure. Aunt Nellie, Diana's sister Frida and the Hursts all agreed that I should give my consent. Her affairs were already in the hands of the Court of Protection. I gave my approval and the operation went ahead.

I saw Diana while she was convalescent. Her head was still bandaged but she smiled broadly when we embraced. Her responses were bland and impersonal but she had acquired a tranquillity which I had not seen for a long time. She never mentioned the children. She looked at the clock in the lobby where we were seated and said she ought to leave, otherwise she would miss her favourite TV programme.

I sensed a heavy load lifted off my shoulders. I had long lost Diana but now I saw this as a shaft of light penetrating a fog of uncertainty. Diana was safe and I was safe from her. The surgeon's scalpel had fundamentally changed both our lives. I had been freed from concern as to what I should do to reconcile Diana's illness with the upbringing of our family and my ability to perform adequately in the RAF.

One out of three incompatibles had now been removed. But I still yearned for the married life which I had so much longed for during the barren years as a POW in Germany. This yearning was to be ever present but unrequited for many years to come. Perhaps, who knows, it may have accounted for the cynicism which crept into my relations with those women who served as stopgaps until I found complete and lasting happiness many years later.

CHAPTER THIRTY-THREE

Concerns of a Chief Flying Instructor

B ack at Cranwell and living in the Officers' Mess, I found myself better able to concentrate my thoughts and energy on the job in hand.

I had discovered that, while my primary function was the attainment of the highest possible standard of flying by the Flight Cadets on graduation, I had, in fact, a far wider unspecified remit for the development of these young men into high-quality junior officers. True, the academic-cum-technical training of the cadets was in the hands of specialists. Patrick Johnston, an erudite and highly qualified professor in natural sciences, was the Director of Studies and a more able and stimulating 'headmaster' would have been hard to find. He managed his specialist team with just that blend of understanding and authority which brought the best out of them. I got to know Patrick well. I learned a lot at his knee, as it were, for he was an inspired conversationalist and just half an hour in his room drinking sherry was intellectually and personally uplifting.

But the development of a teenager into a junior officer in two years cannot be achieved by the sort of syllabus one associates with any secondary education. To transform an intelligent and carefully selected school leaver into not only a competent pilot but a leader with the strength of purpose, imagination and courage to command the respect of men for whom he is to be responsible requires an entirely different approach. Yet the old 'sixth form' tradition still lingered in the two-year syllabus at Cranwell. There was no provision for leadership training. 'Leadership is innate. It cannot be taught. A man is either a leader or a follower.' So went the official dogma.

'Successful entrants to the Royal Air Force College were assessed on their leadership potential.' Assessed against what criteria? What means had been employed, and by whom, to decide which of the applicants would develop the skill of leadership and which would not? I didn't know the answers, but to say that leadership cannot be developed by training and experience is nonsense. Many years after the War and following my retirement, I ran leadership seminars for the Industrial Society. There is no doubt whatsoever that those who attended them were far better able to discover their own potential as leaders of their teams in industry and commerce than those who didn't.

In the Royal Air Force we extol, justifiably, the brilliant leadership of men such as Bader, Malan and Leonard Cheshire. Three totally different personalities, ranging from the flamboyant to the strong and silent mystic. What selection board could possibly have foreseen the leadership of Malan, let alone Cheshire? Yet, of the three, it was Bader who learned leadership the hard way in commerce and industry after losing his legs in an aircraft crash in 1931 and bludgeoning his way back into the RAF as a pilot in 1939. There was at Cranwell no form of debating society; no forum in which these young men in their late teens and early twenties could argue, discuss and express their points of view. Officially their development consisted of flying training, drill and ceremonial, and 'other subjects'. There was also considerable emphasis placed on games and athletics. In short, nothing very much had changed during the seventeen years since I had gone through the system before the War.

Flying an aeroplane, climbing into the sky, possibly through mist or clouds, into a world of unlimited upper space, is a unique experience. It is quite different from occupying a seat in an airliner with a smiling stewardess proffering drinks as an anaesthetic against any absurd obsession that the thing might blow up or crash. Even now, with my tally of several thousand hours flying as pilot of some forty different aircraft types, I still have a moment of panic when I hear: 'Good morning/ afternoon, ladies and gentlemen. This is your captain speaking ...' But alone with the flight cadets on a routine check, an instructional flight or a final test, there was always a personal affinity with the young men I flew with. They caught the indescribable sense of immensity that came from the great domed sky, its inscrutability and omnipotence. We would often fall silent as we broke through the cloud layer into this world above our world. When we had completed the training routine and were slanting down towards Cranwell and all things earthbound, I would often talk to my young pupils of my days as a flight cadet. It was surprising how many would drop their guards and open up on ideas and personal problems which made me think deep and hard about the way we, the staff of RAF Cranwell, were handling the future cadre of officers of the Royal Air Force.

It was during these airborne conversations, often as we waited our turn to join the circuit or sometimes as we sat with the engine silent at the edge of the apron before climbing out, that I formulated my somewhat radical views about the extent to which the syllabus was circumscribing the essential personal development of the young men in our charge. I had discussed my concern with my two Squadron Commanders, who shared my views. Bruce, in particular, was strongly of the opinion that some of the flight cadets needed 'toughening up'. He suggested what is now called orienteering, or survival exercises, and was admittedly influenced by certain aspects of the training courses for the SAS and Commandos. We agreed that was going a bit far but I was worried when he instanced certain cadets of the senior term whom he regarded as bordering on 'lack of moral fibre'.

This was serious and I decided to tackle Patrick Johnston. He was sympathetic and to some extent in agreement, but rightly suggested that we should discuss the whole matter with 'Doggie'. Patrick made the point that what we were suggesting was a radical rethink as to how, in two years, a mixed educational and social bag of young men should be brought up to the highest standard possible in flying and officer qualities. This couldn't be done overnight or by the stroke of a pen. Did I think I could prepare a paper setting out the problem as I saw it and making proposals for its solution? Did I have enough time? Wasn't I already stretched to the limit of my resources? I pondered this. Patrick was right, of course. Other than by working at night, in no way could I take on any further heavy commitment. My responsibility for the standard of flying training was hemmed in by morning parades, church parades, passing-out parades and ceremonies, dining-in nights in the College, and frequent Guest Nights. Endless conferences – all necessary – further truncated the working day. I mixed with the cadets during their games, matches and sporting events, went beagling and ran the cadets' Gliding Club. All out of hours. Small wonder my splendid Adjutant looked aghast at the mountain of paperwork which accumulated in my in-tray day by day. Somehow it all got done. Heaven knows how.

I did have an opportunity of talking to 'Doggie'. It was in the context of an adverse flying report on a cadet of the graduating term. 'Doggie' was concerned that his shortcomings hadn't been dealt with earlier – much earlier. We both got rather worked up. I showed 'Doggie' the cadet's regular reports which he, 'Doggie', had seen and signed. I drew his attention to my own written caveats and we then moved from the particular to the general and I spoke my mind to 'Doggie' frankly and freely. He heard me out, his arms on my desk – he was sitting in my chair – and his Biro stabbing into my blotter. When I had done he looked away out of the window at the busy tarmac apron and the airfield beyond. 'What you are suggesting, Donald, is impossible.' He paused for a while. 'It would require a total stoppage of all cadet training for probably a term at least. Even if the Commandant agreed, Command and the Air Ministry would kill it dead. It just isn't on, Donald.'

He got up from my chair. 'We can't suspend this cadet either. He'll have to graduate with the rest of his term. For God's sake, don't let a thing like this happen again.' He grabbed his cap, muttered something about all of us making mistakes at times and ran downstairs from my office and screeched away in his staff car. He never again mentioned my doubts about the syllabus. The cadet graduated: his only distinctions being a taxiing accident in a Bulldog and a bloody nose from a brawl in Grantham. So that was that. We just carried on, except I became much tougher in my progress tests of cadets, particularly during their first year of basic flying training.

Further developments were put paid to, as far as I was concerned, when I developed a form of glandular infection in and below my left armpit. At first I tried to ignore the discomfort – and of course one salutes with the right arm – but after a couple of nights when I barely slept for the pain I saw the Station Medical Officer, who took one look at me, said I must be ill, examined my swollen glands and promptly despatched me to the Cranwell hospital, where I was put to bed, sedated and operated upon under a local anaesthetic that evening. I fretted in bed for a fortnight or so, made friends with the Matron and suffered, none too graciously, the indignity of further incisions and drainage tubes until whatever it was had been cleared up. I was discharged on a fortnight's sick leave, after a homily by the Station Medical Officer on looking after myself, and set forth for a quiet hotel under the South Downs near Ditchling in Sussex which Mike knew about.

She joined me a few days after I had settled in. Bruce Cole had taken over command of the Flying Wing during my absence. I began to unwind. Within a week, walking over the Downs with Mike, sleeping like a log and eating far too much of our host's excellent food, I was ready to return to Cranwell. Mike went back to London: I saw her off by train from Ditchling with a lump in my throat. We had been happy in an unemotional and unprofound way which was both restful and unusual for us. I spent a night with Stella, Paddy and Lindsay at Chobham. One of my instructors flew down to collect me from the nearby flying club on the following day.

'Doggie's' message about spotting duffers early in the course had sunk in and we all tightened up on routine checks, with far more referrals to me than ever before. Command Headquarters became involved and the Senior Air Staff Officer, well known to me, convened a meeting which

'Doggie' and I were bidden to attend. We flew down to Woodley, just outside Reading, where a staff car met us to take us to HQ Flying Training Command, my first visit to my old stamping ground since my appointment to Cranwell. We chose a Prentice for the trip so that 'Doggie' and I could sit side by side and talk.

He said he would like to do the flying, to which I readily agreed. The weather report was not too good but it was acceptable: there were plenty of diversionary airfields on our route and the cloud base was nowhere less than 1,500 feet. We taxied out from the apron at Cranwell, at least 'Doggie' did, with somewhat violent bursts of throttle which resulted in our proceeding to the take-off point in a series of leaps and bounds. We got clearance for take-off and away we went, leapt into the air and climbed uncertainly from the Cranwell circuit, and settled down more or less on course for our destination. We remained at full throttle until I thought it prudent to draw 'Doggie's' attention to the engine temperature which was fast reaching maximum. He reduced power and we proceeded at an acceptable cruising speed towards the London Control Zone, when I took over. We landed at Woodley, the small grass airfield just outside Reading, where the staff car from Headquarters awaited us.

The meeting was held in the office of the Senior Air Staff Officer (SASO), Air Vice-Marshal Fogarty, who had always been a good friend to me. He took the chair and we got down to business. The importance of identifying 'duds' during the basic training first year was emphasised. Those judged unfit for commissions were to be recommended for suspension. Flying Training Command would take the decision. 'The buck stops here,' said Joe Fogarty, 'but we've got to have regular reporting and factual assessments.' Joe then steered the discussion towards the question of the cadet who had shown good officer qualities, was sound academically, was judged to be a potential leader but wasn't making satisfactory progress as a pilot. Could we afford to make an exception and graduate him into the second year in the hope that he would pick up? A late starter?

'Doggie' felt we should. Joe was dubious. He saw progression into the second year as representing a crucial step towards a commission, a step that should be taken only if all concerned were satisfied that the cadet had measured up to all criteria laid down for the first year. We found a partial solution. Accepting that a 'dud' could and should be weeded out during his first year, an otherwise acceptable cadet who was judged to be below average only in pilot training could be offered a commission in the Navigation Branch, if he so wished. We settled for this. It meant, in effect, that my judgement and that of my Flying Training Wing had to be spot on, lest wrong recommendations be made. We had one year in which to reach our assessment on each and every cadet who came through. From then on, for better or worse, his future was decided. We broke up and had lunch together in the Officers' Mess. I flew 'Doggie' back. The weather was closing in and he wanted to talk. We picked up the Cranwell beam and I made an instrument landing with a cloud base of about 800 feet.

The Navigator option was explained to my two Squadron Commanders who accepted it as a fair compromise and, during the following term, I suspended three senior cadets from pilot training and offered to recommend them for training as commissioned Pilot Officers in the Navigation branch. All three accepted and at their Passing Out Parade they were duly awarded the half-wing badge of a Navigator in the General Duties Branch of the Royal Air Force. One had ended the fourth term as a Flight Cadet Sergeant, one rank below an under-officer. His parents attended the ceremony and I met them in the College after the Parade. He introduced me and explained who I was. His mother smiled and shook my hand. His father looked at me, hostility blazing from his eyes. And then he let me have it. He was very angry and very offensive. I wasn't fit to command a troop of boy scouts far less to judge his son's competence as a pilot. He would take up the case with the Air Council – he never did – and I should be ashamed of myself. I heard him out. I explained that not everyone could become a pilot in the RAF; that his son had won his commission as a Navigator which was an essential and very responsible component of the aircrew of multi-engined aircraft in Bomber Command, Coastal Command and Transport Command. He had done well and would do well. I wished him the best of luck. At this, his father hooked his finger round my tie and pulled it out from under the top of my tunic. Neither of us said a word. I took a step back and looked him straight in the face. I unbuttoned my tunic, replaced my tie and, still looking him straight in the face, buttoned up again. I turned on my heel and walked away. I felt very sorry for the son.

CHAPTER THIRTY-FOUR

Breakdown of Health

A few months later I became ill. It began with a persistent headache which no amount of aspirin would dispel. I lost weight and couldn't sleep. Once, on parade, I began to sway and had to be led off by my Adjutant. I reported sick and was given eye tests, as my vision was becoming blurred. The MO spoke with 'Doggie' and I was grounded for a week. But the headache remained and if anything got worse. I began to behave oddly and people in the Mess would say, 'It's all right, Mac, just take things easily.'

I had made friends with the two resident RAF chaplains, one a Roman Catholic. We used to spend long hours after supper in each other's rooms and had fascinating discussions not only about Christian ethics and behaviour but about the philosophers and the beliefs of Marx, Engels and Lenin. They were stimulating messmates and I valued their knowledge and open-mindedness. They lent me books and, though of different persuasions, never quarrelled. Others often joined us; it was good talking. Then one evening when I was feeling decidedly groggy, the RC chaplain accompanied me back to my room. I had been talking rather wildly, so he said, and he wanted me to take a sleeping draught and insisted I see the MO in the morning. I cannot remember what followed. I presume I slept but I only recall being visited in bed by the Senior Medical Officer, who sent me straight into the Sick Quarters and, by the afternoon, had me packed up and, in the company of his subordinate, on my way to the RAF Hospital at Halton, near Aylesbury, where I was bundled into the psycho-neuropathic wing and put to bed.

So I was mad? I made a fuss. I said that I was okay, just a bit overtired. They were kindly and condescending. They gave me an injection and said I would be seen by a Squadron Leader the next morning.

The Squadron Leader, presumably a psychiatrist, was a few years younger than me. He must have been about twenty when the War had broken out. But he did his best. He asked me questions about the Battle of Britain and clung onto my recollections of being a POW. He had a report from Cranwell which spelt out the pressure under which I had worked as Chief Flying Instructor. He seemed to be looking for a neat formula to encapsulate my condition. I don't think I was very cooperative. I asserted that I was not mentally ill, that I had been under a lot of strain and simply needed a break. I probably used words and phrases with which I had become familiar when talking to the staff at St Andrews Hospital. He picked me up, 'You seem to understand a lot about mental disorders.' So I told him about Diana. This made him really sit up and we had a long session mainly centred on my reaction to my wife's illness. I became bored and made a stupid remark to the effect that, as paranoid schizophrenia wasn't catching, there was no connection between my wife's condition and mine. He didn't like that and said a few days' rest would be all to the good. Why couldn't I rest at home? He closed his file with a snap and asked me to return to my ward.

I spent a further ten days or so with my fellow RAF 'loonies'. One was in a bomb disposal unit and had heebie-jeebies every night. Another wandered about or sat on his own, mumbling to himself. One of the nurses told me he was saying his prayers. There was a young pilot who seemed perfectly okay to me. But one afternoon when he was resting on his bed, which was next to a glass partition between the wards, he suddenly bent his knees and kicked the glass; it shattered, and his feet and the calves of his legs were in shreds. He was carted off to Casualty and we didn't see him again.

I was a bloody minded patient – fed up, demoralised and thoroughly uncooperative. I was discharged following an angry exchange with the young MO, who finally acknowledged that I was not psychotic, that I could return to duty after fourteen days' sick leave, but that I could not expect to have my full flying category restored until I had a further medical examination a month or so later. At this I blew my top. I demanded an interview with the Commandant of the hospital. By the time this was arranged I had calmed down. He was considerate but insisted that I report to the Central Medical Establishment before my flying category was granted. I packed my few belongings, dropped in on Mike in London and returned to Cranwell to sort things out and obtain my leave warrant.

I was grounded and at a pretty low ebb.

After a fortnight's sick leave which I spent hitchhiking around the southern counties with Peter, I felt a different person and faced my return to duty philosophically. Inevitably this proved an anti-climax, as I had anticipated. Everyone was welcoming and sympathetic. A new Commandant had been appointed whom I knew well of old. He was good looking, tall and erect and physically everything his predecessor wasn't. He greeted me warmly and we immediately got down to what part I should play in the scheme of things.

I was to be the head of a new Long Range Planning Section, a similar post to the one I had held two years previously at Command Headquarters under Cochrane. I was no longer Chief Flying Instructor and Officer Commanding Flying Wing. I had done a good job. The new Commandant knew of my domestic problems and 'Doggie' had stood up for me. I must try to put it all behind me. I was still needed on the Staff – and so on. Bruce and John and the instructors were embarrassingly supportive, but for quite a while I detected the sidelong look or the cold remark which told of lingering doubts as to whether I might not do something peculiar. I was still suspect.

The remaining six months I spent at Cranwell with my planning team were mundane. Then out of the blue came an Air Ministry circular calling for nominations from officers of my age and seniority for pre-selection for appointment in the rank of Air Commodore as Air Attaché at the British Embassy in Moscow. The man selected would attend a special crash course in Russian at Cambridge, followed by six months living with a Russian emigré family in Paris. The whole exercise would last some eighteen months and the Moscow appointment was scheduled for 1956, some six years away.

In the event, I was selected for the Russian language course. I can still imagine the civil servant sifting through the files of the short-listed candidates and reading – 'Wing Commander A.R.D. MacDonell DFC, place of birth – Baku, southern Russia'! I am sure my file was at once put on the top of the pile. So I had approximately six years to gain promotion to Group Captain, from which the acting rank of Air Commodore would be reasonable. But first I had something under eighteen months to learn Russian.

1. Pilot Officer MacDonell, 1934

2. *Above*: RAF Cranwell - 'D' Flight Atlases in 1932

3. *Left*: Young Donald, Aged 5, in a sailor suit

4. *Below*: L-R Cousin Maurice Hartford, Mother, Father, Donald and brother Peter at home in Swanage in 1932

RAF Cranwell 1932 - 'The Crabs. Bless 'em!' (Crabs is the naval nickname for RAF personnel)

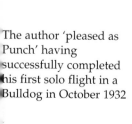

The author 'pleased as Punch' having successfully completed his first solo flight in a Bulldog in October 1932

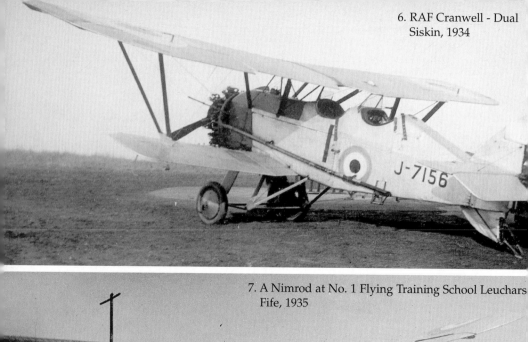

6. RAF Cranwell - Dual Siskin, 1934

7. A Nimrod at No. 1 Flying Training School Leuchars Fife, 1935

8. A Demon of No. 29 Squadron being erected in Abukir, Egypt, prior to moving to Amriya, November 1935

10. *Above*: A Valentia, November 1935

11. *Left*: The Author in Egypt in November 1935

12. *Below*: Al Amriya from the air, showing No. 29
    Squadron in tents and the general bareness and
    desolation of the whole place

13. *Above*: The Pool's first Nimrod in November 1935 - 'a little trouble with the windscreen'

14. *Left*: The Author at RAF Amriya early in 1936: note the black armband worn on death of King George V

15. *Below*: The convoy on route to Amriya in November 1935: 'Please adjust dress before leaving'

16. *Bottom*: RAF Amriya in February 1936

17. The Author in the cockpit of a Hawker Nimrod in March 1936

18. The Author takes off from HMS *Glorious* in a Nimrod in March 1937

19. The Author in dress uniform with his first fianceé, Jocelyn, 1937

20. Diana Keene, the Author's fir wife

21. Squadron Leader MacDonell just before war broke out

64 Squadron 'At readiness at Hawkinge' in 1940 - Author 3rd from left, Richard Jones far right.

23. Messerschmitt Bf110 of DG 26 - shot down by the Author on 18 August, 1940 - after crash-landing. *(Copyright RAF Museum)*

'FREEMA SQUADRON SCRAMBLE!' - Painting of 64 Squadron take-off of 8 Spitfires on 18 August 1940, by J. Mitchell. *(reproduced by kind permission of the artist)*

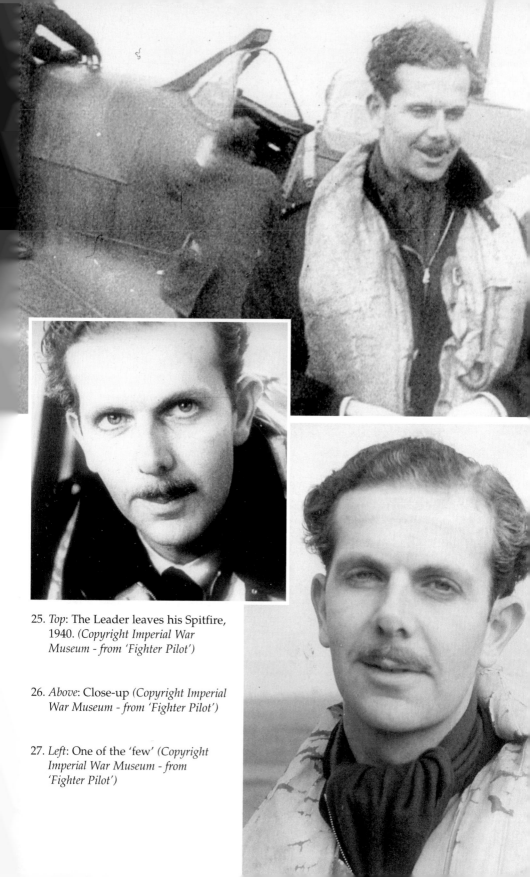

25. *Top*: The Leader leaves his Spitfire, 1940. (*Copyright Imperial War Museum - from 'Fighter Pilot'*)

26. *Above*: Close-up (*Copyright Imperial War Museum - from 'Fighter Pilot'*)

27. *Left*: One of the 'few' (*Copyright Imperial War Museum - from 'Fighter Pilot'*)

No. 64 Squadron members outside the Officers' Mess at Hornchurch in November 1940: L-R: P/O Norman Howkins, P/O John Lawson-Brown, F/Lt. James Thomson, F/Lt. Don Taylor, P/O John Rowden, P/O Alan Towers, P/O E. G. Gilbert, P/O A. R. Tidman, S/L A. R. D. MacDonell, P/O Euan Watson, P/O Richard Jones, S/L Jamie Rankine, P/O John Pippet, P/O Percy Beake, P/O Trevor Gray

The pilot gives 'Thumbs up' from the cockpit *(Copyright Imperial War Museum – from 'Fighter Pilot')*

The Author leads 64 Squadron off the airfield at RAF Leconfield, September 1940

31. Embassy Staff accompanying His Britannic Majesty's Ambassador to present his credentials to the President of the Union of Soviet Socialist Republics in the Kremlin: L-R Ken Scott (now Sir Kenneth), Christopher McAlpine and RAF, Army and Naval Attachés. *(reproduced by kind permission of Christopher McAlpine)*

32. *Right*: Lindsay, Paddy and Ranald at Dodds Grove in May 1953

33. *Right Inset*: 1954 portrait of Lindsay

34. The Author before departure for Moscow in 1956

35. US and British Military personnel in Moscow, c1957

36. Air Vice Marshal Calum Macdonald with Air Commodore Donald MacDonell at No.1 Training Squadron, South Cerney, in 1959 (copyright MoD - 4527G)

37. The Commanding Officer of RAF South Cerney with the RAF Cross Country Champions Division 1 in 1959 (copyright MoD - 4279G)

ROYAL AIR FORCE CROSS COUNTRY
CHAMPIONS DIVISION I 1959

REAR   o/c EVANS   o/c WENNELL o/c SIMMONS o/c STAPLES o/c DAVIES

38. *Right*: Dame Vera Lynn
with Donald MacDonell,
Douglas Bader, Hugh
Dundas, Paddy Barthropp,
Tom Gleave and other
Battle of Britain veterans at
the Battle of Britain Ball in
Grosvenor House in 1973

39. *Left*: HM The Queen greets the Chairman of
the Battle of Britain Fighter Association in
Westminster Abbey on the 25th anniversary o
the Battle of Britain, 15 Sept., 1965

40. *Below Left*: The Author at the time of his
marriage to Lois Streatfeild in 1973

41. *Below*: The 22nd Chief of Glengarry with
Reginald Macdonald of Kinsburgh at Ligonie
Highland Games in the USA, in 1960

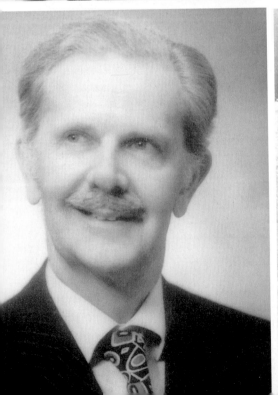

The Chief of Glengarry and Lady Glengarry at the home of Mr. & Mrs. Ellice McDonald, Jr., CBE (Hon), 'Invergarry' Montchanin , Delaware, USA *(Reproduced by kind permission of Mrs Ellice McDonald, Jr)*

43. The Chairman of the Battle of Britain Fighter Association and the Spitfire which he unveiled at Muzeum Lotnictwa I Astronautyki, Krakow, Poland, on 7 Oct. 1977. *(Reproduced by kind permission of the Museum)*

Clan Donald Chiefs and their Ladies attend a Clan Donald Society of Edinburgh dinner, 16 November 1969. L-R Lady Clanranald, The Captain of Clanranald, The Lady Macdonald, Mr. Norman H. MacDonald (standing in for the Society's President), Mrs. Alan McDonald (The President's Lady), The Lord Macdonald, Lady Glengarry and the Chief of Glengarry *(Reproduced by kind permission of Mrs Ellice McDonald, Jr)*

45. Donald MacDonell's
80th Birthday: a uni[...]
gathering with Lois [...]
his children. L-R sea[...]
Lindsay (Cuthbertsc[...]
Donald, Lois, Penelo[...]
standing: Ranald, Ja[...]
Patrick. (Reproduced [...]
kind permission of Iai[...]
Rhind)

46. The 'Raven's Rock' memorial to Air Commodore
Donald MacDonell of Glengarry, CB, DFC, at the
Clan Donald Centre, Armadale, Isle of Skye.
(Reproduced by kind permission of Emma Lavender
and Gerald Laing)

47. 1959 caricature of the Author by Pat Ro[...]

CHAPTER THIRTY-FIVE

Russian at Cambridge

T hus it was that in September 1950 I found myself in a Cambridge taxi, with a copy of the local paper, visiting one after another the addresses offering B&B and supper for undergraduates – mostly freshmen. No one had told me I would need to find my own accommodation. I spent a fortune on that taxi but the driver was agreeable and indeed helpful. Towards suppertime I settled for a room with a German Jewish family called Strich, who were to counsel, support and guide me through an academic year which, without their kindness and understanding, would have been pretty hellish.

I was 'signed on' with St Catharine's College and required to wear a short gown and to attend 'Hall' for a statutory number of dinners each month. I had to be off the streets by 11 pm and to wear my gown when in town. I rebelled at the curfew and gown. Probably a mistake, but I was not going back to school. In no way!

The Senior Tutor of St Catharine's was Tom Henn, an ex-brigadier and a man to whom I could talk frankly. It all seems very petty now and in retrospect I perceive a large chip on my shoulder as I found myself drawn inexorably into the customs and traditions of a great university. Tom Henn let me talk and when he had heard me out he advised conformity with the rules. He agreed I need not wear a gown in town: he invited me to talk to him if ever I felt like doing so and he encouraged me in the hope that I would soon settle down and enjoy university life.

I was one of a group of about eight 'mature' students, consisting of five Naval officers, an attractive young woman from the Foreign Office, and a slightly sinister man around my age who was probably from Military Intelligence. He kept himself very much to himself and was way ahead of all of us in his ability to learn Russian. The oldest in our group was a retired Lieutenant Commander who alone enjoyed the acknowledgement of his rank. He was always referred to as 'The Commander'. Of his Naval colleagues, Pat was a Lieutenant and a submariner, Mike was another Lieutenant from the Engineering Branch, and two other Lieutenants were from the Executive Branch.

The head of the faculty who ruled our academic lives for almost a year was Professor Elizabeth Hill, the daughter of a Scottish engineer and a Russian mother. Her rule was law; she was dynamic, tireless and very demanding. She hammered her tutors and staff, particularly one Peter Squire who had married a Russian girl while in the Soviet Union shortly after the War only to be told that she would not be allowed to leave. He came home alone and grieved for several years. His lectures were often taken by a colleague because, 'Mr Squire was unwell'.

My supervisor was Dr Saulus, an Austrian, who made sucking noises and picked his nose while I struggled through my set translations with him each week. Thus our group was thrown in, to sink or swim. We just managed to keep afloat though the 'Silent One' very soon displayed his outstanding talent for this daunting undertaking. For we were required to attain in one academic year, plus two extra months, a standard equivalent to an Upper Second in Part I of the Modern Language Tripos in Russian. Dazed and bewildered by the ever increasing load heaped on us by Professor Hill (Liza) we lurched from one problem to another: the Cyrillic alphabet, the inflected syntax, the daily vocabulary of words learned one day and forgotten the next.

The group reaction was interesting, for not only did we close ranks but, as a pack of small animals forms a defensive circle when threatened by predators, so we detached ourselves as a body from the undergraduates who attended lectures with us. We sat in a group, we met in pubs as a group and we developed group disciplines and tactics. The Commander and the Silent One were not part of our group. Very soon Pat, the submariner, became our acknowledged leader. He had a penetrating dry sense of humour and was an equal in riposte to even the most hardened lecturers who had to deal with us. He was extremely good looking, lean and athletic, and not surprisingly captured the affections of Jill, the Foreign Office girl, though it must be admitted she tended to wear her heart on her sleeve. The rest of us lived our separate lives within the group, sometimes sharing our private thoughts, often quarrelling over matters of little consequence. It was perhaps the psychology of the self-made prison in which we worked. I truly believe it was Pat who kept us going.

I was luckier than my Naval colleagues who, except for the Commander, were accommodated in rooms in Downing College. I alone lived with a family and, though most nights I worked late in my room, I would breakfast and have supper with Mr and Mrs Strich and their elder daughter

Sabine, who was reading some aspect of medicine at the University. The younger daughter, Laura, was away for most of my stay with the family and I had her room. The Strichs accepted me from the start as a member of their household. Never was I made to feel that I was 'the lodger'. They were kindly, helpful and understanding to an extent which was both sustaining and at times bewildering. They spoke excellent, if heavily accented, English. He had been a professor of philosophy before they had left Germany in the mid-1930s, and he spent long hours upstairs in his room writing some learned thesis in German which Sabine would translate and type into English. Mrs Strich must have been very beautiful in her youth with her magnificent dark-brown eyes, wide generous mouth and thick grey hair. Unlike her parents, Sabine was withdrawn almost to the point of shyness.

They were an intellectual family, conversation was always stimulating and the sitting room was a frequent rendezvous for professors, scholars, musicians and artists from the university. At their hearth I began to unwind. I made friends with Sabine, in whom I discovered a depth of understanding and wisdom which too often lay hidden beneath her shyness. So, from this secure domestic base, I set about the task which faced me: to learn Russian.

Towards the end of the first term, our group had begun to disintegrate. I spent much of my leisure time with the Strichs, either walking or attending concerts, lectures or musical performances. Often Sabine and I would spend an evening together, undemanding and at peace. At the end of term I made my duty call on Tom Henn for my 'Exeat', the official permission for me to go on leave, and was encouraged by the extent of his knowledge of my progress and difficulties. Our Tom was nobody's fool.

The situation at Chobham was tense. We had engaged Margaret, a twenty-two-year-old girl with good references, to help Stella run the family during my absence at Cambridge. Margaret was joined by her elder sister with a small boy who had been fathered by the Station Warrant Officer of an RAF unit where she had served as a WAAF. The two sisters, with Stella nominally in charge, ran the home and managed my family.

At about this stage two things happened which were to have important consequences. Margaret, who had been courted by a local lad, decided to marry him. 'Lady' informed me that she had offered the house to a family due back from abroad in a little under a year's time. My lease really would end shortly after the six months I was to spend with a Russian family in Paris. Stella would not accompany my family to whatever new home I chose.

Mike came up to Cambridge. She had previously told me of her concern for the young daughter of two friends of hers, John and Joan, who had been her contemporaries at RIBA. John and Joan had married and a daughter Joanna had been born. Joan died several years later and John had taken Joanna to Scotland. We were walking along the towpath of the Cam and paused as we crossed a bridge and looked down the peaceful stretch of the river. She then told me she was going to Scotland for a few weeks to do what she could to help John. She looked me straight in the face. In the silence which followed I felt closer to her than ever before, yet pulled myself away for, though I had long foreseen this, I found myself unprepared for its impact.

We met in London after her return from Scotland. John had asked her to marry him and she had agreed. I remember little of that meeting. Mike saved me from myself and in so doing saved my children. What she, with her unquenchable spirit, gave of herself I can never repay.

At Cambridge we ploughed on and I began to make progress and even to enjoy my studies. It was not long before I found myself able to read Russian works by Pushkin, Lermontov and Dostoevsky with the aid of a dictionary. My ability to accumulate a substantial vocabulary steadily increased.

I spent part of the Easter vacation with an eccentric Russian couple near Swanage, where I had spent most of my childhood. Princess Troubetskoi and her husband, Sergei Chafchavadze, had been friends of my father. Emigrés from Russia, they had settled in a bungalow a few miles inland from Swanage, where they lived out a bizarre and threadbare existence. The Princess, who claimed to have been a lady-in-waiting to the Tsarina, was known as 'Mooshka'. Her husband was known as 'Chuff-Chuff'.

'Mooshka' was a tyrant. She spent most of the day on her bed, propped up with pillows and waited on hand and foot by a small, pitiful and elderly spinster known as Mimi. Mimi was treated abominably by 'Mooshka', who expected her to spend hours reading to her, fetching her meals, making her bed and cleaning the room. She was a slave, paid a pittance, starved and abused. I found her plight more than I could bear and did what I could to help her. She had no other home, no close relatives and was terrified of 'Mooshka'. Chuff-Chuff was hardly ever seen. He cultivated a vegetable patch at the end of the property and would pile his produce into the back of an ancient Morris Cowley saloon for marketing in Swanage.

I was despatched on frequent errands by 'Mooshka': to the chemist for medicines, to the grocer for the minimum of provisions but regular small bottles of brandy – 'for my stomach, Donald. You understand?' These commissions were delivered in Russian imperiously and with sweeping gestures of her left hand. I was never given any money for her needs. I received no Russian tuition so I studied in my room until a timid knock on the door by Mimi would summon me to the presence of 'Mooshka'.

Inevitably 'Mooshka' discovered that I had been bringing food back for Mimi from my visits to town. She was furious. She rose from her bed, not entirely sober, and called me treacherous and unworthy of my father. She threatened me with the stick which she always had with her, more for effect than assistance. We both climbed several octaves during the battle, she calling me no better than a peasant – all this in Russian – and I denouncing her as a wicked woman who was working and starving Mimi to death – in English.

The next day I paid up what I reckoned I owed for board and lodging. 'Mooshka' took my cheque and threw it on the floor. I sought Mimi who was in tears. She implored me not to write as 'Mooshka' opened all her letters and, of course, telephoning was out of the question. Chuff-Chuff saw me off and carried my bag to my car. He tried to make amends. He kissed me on both cheeks and hugged me and blessed me in Russian. He smelt abominably. I was told a few years later that Mimi had died of 'malnutrition'.

Back at Cambridge I did my best to put our departure from Chobham out of my mind and to come to terms with the fact that Mike was leaving for Scotland and John. I had left her flat in Cranley Gardens and only once looked back and up at the window which faced the pavement. I trudged to the Underground. I saw her figure and then continued on my way round the corner which hid me from her view.

The last term before the exams was the worst. I had been home at Chobham during the preceding break when Paddy and Lindsay had both contracted mumps. After a week back at Cambridge I began to develop ominous symptoms. Though my illness was a mild one, I told the Strichs who very sensibly called in their doctor, who confirmed my condition. This was some four weeks before our exams! I was immediately quarantined in a room at the top of one of the colleges and visited by another young doctor, a few days later, by which time the symptoms had abated considerably. He suggested offensively that it was not mumps from which I was suffering but 'the jumps'. In effect I had the wind up over the exams. I am afraid I went for him and he ran down the stairs with his medical case banging the banisters while I called him every name I could think of. Poor chap. I was released from quarantine and we sat Part I, which all of us, except the Silent One, failed. I did at least pass the oral exam and was accorded a 'Certificate of Competent Knowledge'. I had a month before leaving for my six months in Paris. We had been given names and addresses of 'approved' Russian families of the *Staryy Rezhim*, the Old Regime, who had been vetted for security but not much else.

CHAPTER THIRTY-SIX

The Advent of Nan

Nancy Joyce Ashley Phillips – known as Nan – was born in India in 1914, shortly before the outbreak of the First World War. Her father was a major in the Indian Army and served in India throughout the War. Nan, who had cared for my father for several years before his death in 1941, had then joined the WRNS in the transport section for the rest of the War. She had twice been selected for a commission but on each occasion had turned it down, claiming that she was not a leader and much preferred driving trucks to commanding units of female ratings. After being demobbed, Nan completed a course in horticulture and gained her Fellowship of the Royal Horticultural Society. She found a job in London with the Roads Beautifying Association in a by-street running down past Charing Cross station to the Embankment. When Mike left for Scotland I turned to Nan. Not on the rebound; never again.

Since my repatriation in 1945 Nan had visited from time to time. It came as no surprise when she put it to me quite bluntly and unemotionally that I had got to face up to a very long-term problem in the upbringing of my children. We decided I should advertise in the national press for a suitable person to replace Stella as housekeeper and guardian of my children. So it was that *The Times* and *The Daily Telegraph* both carried notices which, in effect, sought 'a suitable and mature lady who is prepared to run the home of a serving RAF officer and help in the upbringing of his three motherless children'. 'Lady' was furious and again withdrew Stella to the family home. Several relations of Diana's and mine wrote outraged letters but none offered practical alternatives.

The replies came in, dozens of them. They ranged from the ridiculous – 'I am only twenty-two and my boyfriend has let me down. I have a kid of two. I think I could make you happy . . .' – to the somewhat sinister – 'I am

a handmaiden of the Lord. I am fifty-five years old. I would happily, with
God's help, bring up your family in the true Christian faith. I always lock
my door at night'. There were offers of 'friendship with a view to a
permanent arrangement', outright invitations to 'partnerships' with many
photographs of all shapes, sizes and ages of women, most of whom had a
child or two. Clearly none was suitable.

Nan and I met for lunch a few weeks before I was due to leave for Paris.
Nan came up with a totally unexpected offer to spend a few months with
me settling the family down in wherever the new home might be. She had
always said she was a selfish person and that she found children tiresome.
I was at a loss for words. She made it clear that the offer was on the table
and that it was for a trial period with no commitment on either side. A
week later we met once more. I said yes. The trial lasted eighteen years.

CHAPTER THIRTY-SEVEN

Paris – *Borscht*, Vodka and Russian Taxi Drivers

My train pulled into the Gare du Nord during the afternoon of a September day in 1951. I was met by a Group Captain who was also in Paris learning Russian, though his lodging with a totally French family and his refusal to have any regular Russian tuition made no sense whatsoever. I never understood Alfie B.'s remit but he was to prove a delightful companion, spoke fair French and was as untypical a senior RAF officer as one could possibly imagine. Lonely, eccentric and forever acting the part of the dandified Victorian beau; he wore bow ties, had an abundance of silk handkerchief cascading from his breast pocket and affected a white panama hat and a furled umbrella. His Oxford English accent overlaid his French. His humour and idiosyncrasies were infectious and before long we went about together, calling each other Burgess and Maclean, whose defection to the Soviet Union was at that time a topical scandal.

Alfie chartered a taxi to take us and my luggage to the Champs Elysées where we drank iced Pernod at a table near the pavement. He suggested we then pay a courtesy call on the British Embassy before proceeding to my destination in Asnières. This seemed sensible. Alfie hailed another taxi and we were whisked away to the Embassy.

The Air Attaché was on leave but his deputy received us. It was quite evident that not only was Alfie very *persona grata* but also was regarded as a curiosity and a welcome diversion from diplomatic business. He exuded bonhomie and I was introduced with a flourish and much waving of his panama hat. He sat down elegantly in the only armchair in the room while I made do with an upright hard-back. Young men and women began to filter in: the buzz had gone round that Alfie had dropped by. The bottle of sherry was opened and we spent half an hour or so while Alfie went through his routine of whimsy and anecdotes. An official car was provided for my drive to Asnières. Alfie and I thanked our host and I departed on my own with a British driver at the wheel.

No. 12 Avenue Pinel, the residence of Mme Klotchkoff, was an elegant three-storey house in a narrow cul-de-sac. A low stone wall carried a wrought-iron fence and the entrance gate, also of wrought iron, suggested late nineteenth or early twentieth century. The driver and I began unloading my bags from the boot. The front of No. 12 opened and a long-legged, black-and-white mongrel dog tore down the short paved path to the gate, barking furiously. We decided not to open the gate. Then a small elderly woman appeared in a black dress with a white apron. The house-maid, I muttered under my breath, searching for the correct way to address a servant in Russian. The driver looked at me and nodded: 'She'll help us with the bags.' She scuttled towards the gate, shouting at the dog in Russian, '*Bobka, Bobka. Idi syuda sukin syn!*' (Bobka, Bobka. Come here, son of a bitch.) Bobka took no notice and began to orbit the small front garden at high speed, barking furiously.

The gate was opened but communication was made difficult, if not impossible, by the accompaniment of barks and yelps from seemingly every dog in every garden of every house in Avenue Pinel joining Bobka as a sort of canine backing group to his performance. The lady in black looked at us, smiling and wiping her hands on her apron. She greeted my driver formally: 'Mr Colonel, welcome. I am very pleased to meet you. Come with me.' She took one of the cases and trotted beside him towards the house, chattering in Russian. The yapping died down. Bobka lifted a leg against the gatepost and then sat down on the lawn with his tongue hanging out.

Mustering what Russian I could, I explained that I was *Polkovnik* (Colonel or Wing Commander) MacDonell, that the other *gospodin* (gentleman) was a chauffeur, and would the lady please inform Madame Klotchkoff that I had arrived. Dead silence. Then she threw back her head and laughed and laughed, wiping her eyes with her apron. This set Bobka off again, with the Avenue Pinel canine chorus joining in. Somehow we got sorted out. The lady opened her arms in a dramatic gesture and said, 'I am Madame Klotchkoff and you' – pointing at me – 'are the *Polkovnik*! What a stupid mistake. Well, well, the samovar is boiling and tea is ready. Come in, come into my home.'

The driver smiled his thanks but said to me he should be off back to the Embassy. My hostess, now busy with cups and plates, wiped her hands once more, kissed him on both cheeks and bade him God's blessing: all in

Russian, of which he understood not one word. I thanked him and, with a wary eye on Bobka, he left. Madame Klotchkoff and I sat down in the kitchen and took stock of each other. As we drank our tea, such fragrant tea, and ate our *bliny* (Russian pancakes), she told me of her life.

Yevgenia Vladimirovna Klotchkova, whom from now on I shall refer to as Yevgenia Vladimirovna, had been brought up in St Petersburg where she had trained as an actress and a singer at a drama school. Her stage personality and a voice of outstanding timbre and strength for so small a person quickly endeared her to the Franco-Russian theatre-going aristocracy of the light operatic stage of Russia's capital. She became a star and, shortly before the Revolution, married a Tsarist officer, Boris Klotchkoff, and bore him two daughters. He was killed by the Bolsheviks in 1917. With her two small girls she fled to France. She had lived in Paris for over twenty years. Of her daughters, the elder had never married and was now teaching in a school in England. The younger, Marina lived near the centre of Paris. She was married to the son of a famous Tsarist general, Wrangel. (The family name had been changed to 'de Vrangel' in France.) They were coming to meet me later that evening.

I spoke of my father and mother and of my brother and how the two of us had been born in Baku, where my father was British Vice-Consul. He had played a significant role in negotiating between the warring factions in 1917 and 1918. I told them about my mother bringing me home to Grannie in England in the Spring of 1914. Also of her hazardous journey home with my brother in 1917 during the Great War and the bloody Russian Revolution – via Archangel and Finland and the U-boat infested waters of the North Sea to Aberdeen and so to Sevenoaks in Kent.

Yevgenia Vladimirovna helped me with my stumbling Russian and on occasion we would resort to French, but never English. Bobka decided I was acceptable and sat with his paw on my knee. I felt tired, but I knew things were going to be all right. There was a warmth and sense of serenity in the house which was a comfort and a benison. I went to my room and unpacked. It was one of the two first-storey bedrooms facing Avenue Pinel, spacious, well furnished and spotlessly clean. The walls were devoid of pictures but there was a crucifix above my bed. The windows had lace curtains, the floor was carpeted with two Astrakhan rugs. Bobka had evidently adopted the room as a place of rest; he was frequently in residence as the door didn't close and he could push his way in. I welcomed him and we soon became friends.

The other front room was occupied by a Mme Valentina Driot, a very attractive, young Russian-born woman of about my age, whose marriage to Driot, a Frenchman, had foundered. Valya, with her nine-year-old son

Sergei, lodged with Yevgenia Vladimirovna and became a good friend of mine.

Marina and her husband, Boris, came to supper. We sat down to *bortsch*, an excellent spiced chicken casserole, followed by *blini* and cake, accompanied by a most acceptable Georgian red wine. We drank tea from the samovar and spent the rest of the evening talking and tippling a pretty rough brandy which I was to regret the next morning. Marina ran a dressmaking business in Paris. She employed two young women, identical twins, to work the sewing machines and make dresses in the one large room upstairs on the second floor of the house. Only one of the twins, Musia, was in Paris at the time. I would meet her on the morrow. Marina was an attractive, extrovert blonde. She spoke a little English but we established that only Russian was to be spoken to me and anything else was taboo. There was, of course, a lot of French throughout the day but to me all members of the household spoke only Russian – the Russian of the pre-Revolutionary days, as I was to discover when I arrived in Moscow a few years later.

Apart from the kitchen, with an annexe in which growled an old-fashioned solid-fuel stove which heated the water system and the two noisy radiators in the downstairs rooms, the ground floor consisted of a bedsitter in which Yevgenia Vladimirovna slept. During the day it served as a sitting room, with an icon on a pedestal in one corner where a candle burned. The room was tastefully furnished and heavy with incense, which in a strange way suggested silence and contemplation. There was a great peace in that room. We sat there after supper, the four of us. Marina spoke of her dressmaking business, of Musia and Julia. She told me how the two cut and sewed the garments and sang in Russian as they worked. She spoke of her sister in England, of Valya – and what a lovely person Valya was. She winked when she said I would probably fall for her: most men did.

I liked Marina. I liked her open wide-eyed Russian face, her smile and her friendliness. Boris was gracious and welcoming but there was something about him, a reserve and hesitancy that I was never able to break through. Dark haired, dark eyed, a little under six feet, and about my age, I judged him a Georgian. His aristocratic family had been among the elite of St Petersburg before the Revolution when the Wrangels had graced the balls and receptions of the Tsars. At that time, Karl Marx, Engels and Lenin were sowing the seeds of a revolution which was to rock the world. The Wrangels had fought and fallen in defence of a cause which had long since been lost through despotism and a refusal to accept and accommodate the emergence of an intellectual philosophy based on equality, the abolition of privilege and the teaching of a new creed called dialectical materialism.

I looked at him across the small table while the candle before the icon threw flickering shadows. I noted his dark, dark shining hair, his steady dark-eyed look and the well-cut suit and elegant tie. He spoke to me softly and slowly in a graceful acknowledgement of my halting Russian. He seldom smiled but there were overtones of humour and warmth in his talk which I was to find characteristic of the old regime. He had retained what must have been no more than a few years of his early upbringing in Russia. He never spoke to me of how or when he came to the West.

Marina yawned and said behind her hand, '*Spat khochu*' (I want to sleep). The evening broke up and I was conscious of a subtle change in the mood. A silence fell. Then Yevgenia Vladimirovna spoke a silent prayer kneeling before the icon. We lowered our heads and I was wished God's blessing while in her house and my hands were taken by each of them. I was very moved.

We walked down the garden to the gate, accompanied by Bobka sniffing and lifting a leg. Marina said she felt a little tipsy. I said that I did too. Boris laughed for the first time and commented, 'Donald Ranaldovich, that was only child's play.' I was to discover before long just how true that was!

CHAPTER THIRTY-EIGHT

Paris: Valya

I slept deeply and awoke late. There was no sound from Valya's room, so I washed and shaved in the bathroom and, while dressing, I heard a lovely, soft woman's voice singing a Russian song on the floor above. There was also the sound of a sewing machine. Musia had arrived and was busy with her dressmaking. I made my way downstairs. Yevgenia Vladimirovna brushed aside my apologies for being late and bade me sit down for breakfast, chattering away about the evening before. She then served me a large beefsteak. 'Englishmen like a good breakfast. Eat well!' I did my best but later explained that I had a small appetite and that coffee and French bread would be quite enough. She took the point without offence and merely remarked with a smile that I needed feeding up.

Musia came down to meet me. A lovely girl in her mid-twenties with large slanting eyes, a graceful figure and an abundance of brown hair done in a bun low on her neck. Her voice was soft and her Russian was musical. Yevgenia Vladimirovna watched us as we spoke and smiled at one another. Musia dropped her eyes and said she must return to her work. As she went upstairs, Yevgenia Vladimirovna looked at me: 'You will be good friends but she is a *chistaya* (pure or clean) girl. You understand, Donald Ranaldovich?' I took the point.

I fell into the domestic routine happily. Musia would arrive at about 8.30, having had her breakfast – I never did know where she and her sister lived – and then she and I would take Bobka out to join his numerous neighbours in the daily routine of fouling Avenue Pinel. There were frequent scuffles, but only once did we have to intervene in what was rapidly erupting into gang warfare. Bobka was then put on his lead, which he detested, and sulking would accompany us to the boulangerie where we purchased *deux ficelles*, which would be served with delicious coffee for breakfast. Musia would drink a cup with us and then run upstairs to her sewing machine. I would go to my room or to Yevgenia Vladimirovna's where the candle, alight before the icon, flickered as I sat down to study.

Three times a week I went for tuition with an interesting Russian, Zinaida Borisovna, perhaps in her fifties, who spoke very good English, having been a governess to an English family in Russia. She proved to be an excellent teacher. We related well and with her help I began to speak and write Russian confidently and competently.

The French *vacances* had ended. First Valya and then Musia's twin sister Julia rejoined the *ménage*. Valya really was a knock-out. I was watched with amusement and speculation, particularly by Yevgenia Vladimirovna, whenever Valya and I met. As things turned out we became good friends, saw quite a lot of each other and shared common interests such as art galleries, music and the theatre.

But Musia had first claim on me, for had we not from the very beginning dealt with Bobka's morning needs, bought the bread for breakfast and helped with the washing up? I would have to pick my way warily for, as I soon discovered, the Russian woman is by nature very possessive. The incredible similarity between the two sisters was in many ways helpful. I confess there were occasions when I was at a loss to know which was which: they were utterly identical in appearance, dress, voice, hairstyles and mannerisms. Neither wore make-up. I found myself relating to and treating them as one; a sort of double vision.

This went down well enough but it was Musia who gained on points. She knew what I liked and what I didn't. It was she who gave me the embarrassing nickname of 'Donald-dushka', best translated from the Russian into Donald darling, or even, little darling! The sort of name one might give to a baby boy or a pet cat. The rest of the household picked it up at once and soon all but Boris had dropped the formal Donald Ranaldovich in favour of this pet name. I was flattered at being so warmly linked with the household but somehow felt that I had been relegated to the Second Division.

So, from the day Julia returned from her *vacances*, I was careful to take both the sisters out to the cinema, the theatre or even a restaurant for an evening meal. Thus they shared me and I shared them, and Yevgenia Vladimirovna approved and smiled and wiped her hands on her apron. My relationship with Valya, though platonic, was also not without its problems. She became a more regular lodger and her small son, Sergei, shared her room off the common bathroom next to me. Personal privacy seemed to be of no importance to Valya. On several occasions I found her in the bathroom, once on the bidet. On another occasion, she and Sergei were in the bath together. She hardly ever locked the door to the landing and always slept with her own door wide open. She was a very desirable woman and I judged her not unwilling, should the occasion arise. That it never did was all to the good, for Yevgenia Vladimirovna had sharp ears and was a light sleeper.

So Valya and I seldom went out alone of an evening. She had many friends in Paris and her looks, shining personality and beautiful singing voice were worth all the restraint that our relationship involved.

I often took the Metro into Paris. I had not lost touch with those of our Cambridge group who were scattered round its outskirts. I enjoyed the carefree evenings in their company; they with their girlfriends, I on my own. A cabaret, a casino, an expensive meal in Montmartre. Why not?

Once I asked Valya if she would like to spend an evening in Paris with my friends. She was enthusiastic and left Sergei with Yevgenia Vladimirovna. We all met up at a casino on the Left Bank. From then on she dominated the party. I will never forget the impression she made and the fun we had. It was midnight before she guided us to a restaurant where she was well known. We drank wine and ate hot bread and onion soup. Valya then sang and everyone in the place cheered and applauded. The restaurant was close to a meat market and several butchers arrived in bloodstained aprons and white caps. No one minded and an hour later we were escorted to the pavement by an enthusiastic crowd of late-night revellers who seemed loath to let us go. Valya had won them all over and I bathed in reflected glory. We dispersed amid laughter, clamour and embraces. Valya and I hailed a taxi. She was warm, exciting and wholly woman. We said very little but she snuggled into my arms and was relaxed and drowsy as we were driven across Paris and north to Asnières.

The house was shuttered. We went in using her key and trod silently past Yevgenia Vladlmirovna's room where the flicker of the candle was just visible under the door. On our landing, we looked at each other and then she was in my arms. We kissed passionately. It was she who broke away with a shudder, 'There are people,' she whispered in English. We went to our separate rooms. It was a near miss but they say a miss is as good as a mile. If nothing else, it established a line of demarcation between the two of us which stood me in good stead for the remainder of my stay. We went frequently to the homes of her friends in Paris. She took me to the Louvre and showed me Paris, and it was with Valya that I first attended the unforgettable Russian Orthodox service in the Rue Daru.

A huge congregation of the 'Old Believers' thronged the church, all talking to each other quietly but earnestly. Then immediate silence when the Metropolitan and his attendants took their places at the high altar. In his magnificent deep bass voice he intoned the prayers, which were responded to by a congregation singing as a choir – perhaps two hundred and fifty men and women worshipping God in a harmony which came from deep within their souls. I have never heard anything so moving. Valya led me from the church out to the dark overcast of autumn in Paris.

I am not a religious man, though I hold strongly to my belief in an Almighty, but never before or since have I experienced the depth, sincerity and nostalgia of the wonderful service of worship attended by many who had lost virtually all but their unremitting devotion to the God in whom they so devoutly believed. Valya had held my hand as the taxi drove us to Asniéres but it had been in comfort and understanding: it had been spiritual and in no way physical. I sought my room and remained remote, with Bobka stretched out beside me on the bed.

Alfie B. and I dined together in a very upmarket restaurant in Montmartre. He eschewed the can-can and cabaret type of evening and, as he was obviously a great deal better off than I was, his choice for the evening was fine. He was dining me out! He had chosen a quiet, pleasant place on the first floor above a nightclub in the area of Montparnasse. Alfie was immediately recognised by M. le Patron and we were seated in a corner and fussed over by waiters. Alfie's French was elementary but, spoken loudly and confidently in his embarrassing accent, he had the staff doing his bidding as though we were royalty.

It was a splendid meal which we enjoyed to the full. I was somewhat aghast when he chose a vintage champagne but it was after all his party. Following several glasses of a brandy which Alfie chose after much loud consultation with M. le Patron, we were replete, fairly drunk and utterly at one with the world. Alfie called for *l'addition*, which he studied at length through an eye-glass not seen before. Alfie produced his silk handkerchief – more for effect than necessity – and waved the bill in one hand and the handkerchief in the other. M. le Patron appeared and Alfie, very slowly, proceeded to add up the account item by item. Diners at neighbouring tables stopped talking and threw glances in our direction. The handkerchief was then returned to the breast pocket. Alfie opened and spread his wallet beside the bill, with all the reverence of a parson opening the Holy Bible, and slowly looked up and smiled. M. le Patron smiled, the waiter and I smiled – and the neighbouring diners resumed their conversation.

After a short speech of thanks, which was received by M. le Patron with a gracious inclination of the head, Alfie laid out bank notes methodically as though dealing a hand of cards. He then stood up and dealt a second hand beside the first. I sat watching, fascinated. Alfie bowed slightly and handed the notes to M. le Patron who took the offering with a deep bow. Alfie then proffered the second 'hand' to the waiter, who appeared stunned at the generosity of his gratuity. I got to my feet and, with a final flourish of his handkerchief, Alfie led me with great dignity from the table.

At the door he made another speech, shook hands with M. le Patron, with the waiter, the doorman and two elderly ladies who had just entered. I added my thanks. We all bowed again and then, with linked arms, Alfie and I strode none too steadily towards the nearest taxi rank. This ridiculous pantomime remains etched on my memory, so I have included it in my story. It was of no consequence whatsoever ....

CHAPTER THIRTY-NINE

The Home Front

The situation in Chobham seemed reasonably stable but my lease ended in May and Nan would take over.

She and I would find somewhere to relocate. I was sure of it. She wrote to say she had answered an advertisement from an American family in the southern outskirts of Paris who wanted a 'mother's help'. They had two small children, a boy and a girl. Nan thought that a bit of experience before taking my lot would not come amiss. In her practical way she was probing the future. She was a brave woman. When I had told her of Mike, she had heard me out, not looking at me but relating silently and with an occasional glance which conveyed understanding. She asked no questions.

So Nan came to live with the Garzaros family in a southern *arrondissement,* and we met in Paris and dined together or tippled *fine à l'eau* (brandy and water) in cafes and grew to know each other. We found much more in common than I had dared to expect.

CHAPTER FORTY

Paris – *Vecherinka*

Yevgenia Vladimirovna was making coffee for breakfast. The croissants were on the table and Valya was breaking hers and spreading jam. I looked at her across the table. A lovely woman – dark haired, dark eyed and desirable. What had Driot done or not done to lose her? I bathed unashamedly in her loveliness. Her eyes were on her plate. Yevgenia Vladimirovna poured the coffee. '*Vecherinka!*' she said. 'We will have a vecherinka. Donald-dushka, you will laugh and sing and become a Russian. You who were born in old Russia will meet many who were also born and lived there.' Valya looked up. 'A vecherinka is an evening party. In France it is a soirée. There will be poetry and much love and laughter. You will lose yourself in the depth of it. It is truly Russian and we will always cherish and preserve it.'

For the next week the house was full of talk of the vecherinka. The girls upstairs sang less and talked more as they worked at their sewing machines. The furniture was polished, floors were scrubbed, plans were made, discarded and remade as to who should recite, sing, dance or make music. Yevgenia Vladimirovna was holding a vecherinka. The word was on everyone's lips. Bobka caught the spirit of the thing and ran around the garden barking. It spread up Avenue Pinel, to the boulangerie, to the dustman and the postman.

The guest list was agreed. The menu was agreed. I was despatched – to the chemist, I think – to purchase alcohol, pure and colourless, which Yevgenia Vladimirovna mixed herbs and flavouring into and then diluted to produce her own brand of vodka, which was delicious to taste but had a kick like a horse!

Pyotr, who drove a taxi, would recite Russian poetry; Misha, who had served in a Cossack regiment and now ran a restaurant in Montmartre, would sing – he had a fine bass voice – and Xenia Uvarovna would also sing in her fine contralto. There were the two Semenov brothers, younger and more French than Russian, but they played the balalaika splendidly – though they tended to become *pyany* (tight) rather too easily. And, of course, Valya would sing and the girls upstairs too. And Yevgenia Vladimirovna conceded that she might do her song and dance act. What could Donald-dushka do? What on earth could I do? I knew no suitable song. My Russian was totally inadequate for telling a story. I explained I was a poor entertainer and asked to be let off. Yevgenia Vladimirovna gave me a mischievous smile and said: 'Who knows what you may do when the time comes.'

Xenia Uvarovna was the first to arrive. In her thirties, grossly over-weight, she had a bad cast in her left eye which was a sad blemish on a very attractive face. She greeted me warmly and I detected a whiff of alcohol on her breath. Next came the brothers Semenov, small, well-knit and full of chat. Vodka and wine and brandy were poured. Food convoys from the kitchen were unloaded in the dining room and all the while guests were arriving.

For the first time since our meeting, the twins wore different dresses, Musia in brown and Julia in green. They looked enchanting, excited and wildly happy. Valya looked quite lovely. Under her apron Yevgenia Vladimirovna had a dark blue dress, full length and cut well in at the waist. She wore jewellery, a star in her short hair, and a faint hint of make-up. She was supreme: in command and radiating welcome, warmth and immense personal charm. I noticed that she wore ballet shoes which made her seem even smaller than usual. But her personality remained un-diminished.

Most of the male guests wore suits. Pyotr shed his duffel coat to reveal a vast expanse of chest and stomach and a button missing from his white shirt. Two elderly sisters wore hats throughout the evening. They remained inseparable and conversed in French. An aged Russian was helped in by an enormous woman with a mountain of blue hair pinned on top of her head. He wore a battered suit which hung in folds on his withered body and his left chest was adorned with several rows of medals which clanged as he tottered to the seat which was immediately offered by Yevgenia Vladimirovna. He was introduced as General someone.

As each guest arrived, I was presented. Donald Ranaldovich, Polkovnik, a Scotsman born in Baku. I was embraced and kissed on both cheeks and made a fuss of. I was quite obviously the raison d'être for the vecherinka. Born in Baku in 1913? '*Zamechatelno!*' (remarkable); '*Nevozmozhno!*' (impossible).

Was your mother Russian? No, she was Irish. What was your Scottish father doing in the Caucasus? Here I dropped a grammatical brick. I used the wrong tense and said, in effect, that he is – not was – the British Consul in Southern Russia. A stunned silence was broken by the General, who coughed, spat on the floor and stated with his gongs a-ringing, 'There is

NO British Consul in Azerbaijan!' Boris de Vrangel came to my rescue
and corrected my grammar. There was loud conversation, laughter and
greetings as more guests arrived and I was introduced time and time again.
I said my piece, was complimented on my Russian and the vodka was
flowing. I put mine on a small table as already I was beginning to feel a
mite unsteady.

Yevgenia Vladimirovna clapped her hands and announced that the
meal was served. I stood aside and the guests, vociferous, back slapping
and laughing, proceeded into the dining room. I hung back. The two old
hats rose in dignified silence and accepted my escort to the table: '*Merci,
monsieur vous êtes très gentil.*'

Pyotr took the head of the table. The two French hats found seats under
the window and the heavily breathing presence of Xenia was at my elbow.
The General was eased into an armchair and I took a seat next to Misha
the restaurateur. But this was not to be. It was Marina who firmly evicted
the taxi driver from the head of the table and installed me in his place.

Bortsch was brought in – two huge tureens – and placed on the
sideboard. There was silence. All looked at me and then lowered their
heads. I did likewise but then felt eyes on me from under half-closed lids. I
was expected to say Grace! My mind went blank. I had never before said
Grace in Russian. Frantically I tried to remember, to look composed.
Then I spoke in Russian: 'Thanks to God.' 'Thanks to God.' came from
all round the table. I raised my eyes. Everyone began talking at once,
touching each other and tucking paper napkins into their collars.
Yevgenia Vladimirovna laughed as she and the twins served the bortsch.
Spoons were lifted; toasts were drunk. I was praised by those at the table –
molodets (splendid fellow) – and the sound of slurping bortsch, belches
and a mounting wave of sheer joyous release pronounced that Yevgenia
Vladimirovna's vecherinka had indeed taken off.

I was getting the hang of the thing. Conversation per se was unnecessary. A toast, a remark, a laughing comment with the mouth still
chock full of food, required no more than a glass raised in acknowledgement, a shouted and smiling '*Khorosho*'. Towards the end of the meal,
Pyotr called for silence. Slowly the hubbub died down. Xenia swayed over
to where I was standing by the entrance to the sitting room. Pyotr raised
two massive arms. His sleeves were undone. He wore a bracelet on his left
wrist and the backs of his hands and his forearms were covered in long,
black hair. He stretched his hand towards me. His eyes shone, his mouth
was open and his stainless steel teeth glistened like jewels.

'Donald Ranaldovich,' he began in his deep, resonant voice: 'You who
live here alone with lovely ladies to keep you company. You are a Scot
who was born in the Caucasus. You are learning to speak Russian and we

greet you as a friend of Old Russia. But you must tell us which of these ladies who surround you is your favourite. Speak, Donald Ranaldovich, and tell us truly who is your favourite, your choice.' At this point he was interrupted by someone who said his question was not in order. I was a married man. But Pyotr was not to be gainsaid. 'So Donald Ranaldovich is a married man. And he loves his wife. But married men can love their wives and yet fancy other women!'

The ancient General said 'Absolutely true' and was immediately quelled by his large wife. More babble broke out. 'Speak, Donald Ranaldovich!' shouted Pyotr above the uproar. Within seconds the room rang with a mounting demand that I answer.

I thought furiously. I had to get this one right. I went through a process of rapid elimination. Valya? No – undoubtedly my choice but to admit to it publicly would upset Musia and Julia. Marina? No – not in the presence of her husband, Boris. Musia or Julia, or both? I knew Musia best but I shrank from the possibility of hurting Julia. Xenia? No – I had seen far too little of her. Then, like a flash of lightning, I had it. I clapped my hands for silence. I adopted the arms raised posture of Pyotr and then, with my right hand lowered, I pointed across the room and announced: 'Yevgenia Vladimirovna!'

The reaction was instantaneous. A roar of approval filled the room, drowning everything like an erupting volcano. And there was handclapping, hugging, kissing, leaps and jumps, and calls for vodka and wine – and for music, music for dancing. Yevgenia Vladimirovna and I were hoisted shoulder high and borne around the room on the surge of emotion with everyone laughing and calling our names. Then the voice of Pyotr above the tumult: 'Donald Ranaldovich must dance with Yevgenia Vladimirovna!'

The Semenov brothers stood by the window tuning their balalaikas. Then, as they raised their heads, they struck three long, quavering and liquid chords which melted into the minor key. A moment of silence. A shout of joy and the two brothers broke into a cascade of music that only the balalaika played by Russians can create.

We were led to the centre of the room, Yevgenia Vladimirovna and I. She blushed as she put her hands on her hips and then, tossing back her head, she laughed and began to dance to the irresistible. She danced with an insolence and arrogance and a fierce defiance of everything that had blighted what she had been forty or more years before, when she had delighted the audiences in St Petersburg. We touched hands and she was away, skipping and beckoning, her eyes flashing, a woman transformed. 'Dance, dance, Donald Ranaldovich,' they cried, so I went with Yevgenia Vladimirovna and followed her movements and everyone cheered and shouted afresh. So we swung round each other, not touching but with our eyes on each other, and the balalaika music held us captive.

The tempo changed, to that of an eightsome reel. I set to Yevgenia Vladimirovna and stepped the *pas de bas* with my arms by my side. She laughed and came close to me. She watched my movements and copied them. We set to each other: I crooked my right arm and linked it with hers. We swung and reeled, and everyone roared afresh and clapped in time to the music. The balalaikas ran up to a final quivering chord, and then silence. Yevgenia Vladimirovna took my arm and we paraded round the room to be embraced again and led back to the table where more drink was pressed on us. Exhausted, we sank onto a settee.

Then Pyotr recited poems by Pushkin and Lermontov, and Valya sang my favourite and most poignant song. Then we all sang the ballad of Stenkorasin, or rather Misha sang the verses and the whole company filled the house with the full-blooded chorus singing in parts like a trained choir. I have never heard the like since.

The vecherinka began to lose cohesion: or perhaps I was slightly drunk. The General had taken off his shoes, complaining that he had *douleur* in his toes. The Semenov brothers were hitting the vodka: Bobka made a brief appearance, showed every sign of disapproval and removed himself with his tail between his legs. The twins had gone upstairs and Xenia was not to be seen.

My glass was empty. Misha said we should drink and took it for a refill. I scuttled to the downstairs loo. It was locked – and a soft male voice from within singing what sounded like a hymn. Upstairs to the bathroom, where light was shining from under the door. It wasn't locked so I opened it cautiously. Pyotr was shaving at the hand basin, his shirt off and his chest and arms bare and hairy. He greeted me with a wink and a grin. 'My lover likes me smooth. Tonight I join her after the vecherinka. Ha!' and he gave his chin another flourish with the shaving brush. Xenia lay fast asleep in the bath, snoring. I apologised and backed away but Pyotr waved his shaving brush at the lavatory basin and said go ahead. I did so with enormous relief. I don't recall finding the situation in the least embarrassing.

I do not remember the rest of the vecherinka very clearly except for the conga. One of the Semenov brothers was plucking his balalaika when a rhythm emerged, hard and dominant – one, two, three, pause; one, two, three, pause – a conga! I stomped it out across the floor and was soon joined by Musia who took my arm. I motioned her to dance behind me and hold my hips. I shouted to others to join and then we had an ever-growing snake behind us, laughing and calling for yet more to come until it seemed that everyone had joined the conga. We wound through the dining room, the kitchen – where we collected Valya, Marina and Yevgenia Vladimirovna – plunged into the sitting room and circled beneath the icon, then upstairs, where Julia and the General's wife had sought refuge. Down again – a shambles on the stairs as we squeezed past those going up. Then where? Outside! went the cry. Into the garden! So we stumbled down the steps, down the path and then someone opened the gate. The balalaika was with us. Along Avenue Pinel we stomped and wove, intoxicated and utterly oblivious to the doors and shutters that were flung open as we passed. From some houses we were joined by young people and the snake of our conga grew longer. Back we came, back to No. 12 and up the steps and there the conga ended in sighs, gasps and hugging and backslapping.

The vecherinka was over. Everyone began to leave after they had bade farewell to Yevgenia Vladimirovna and those of us who remained. I escorted the twins to the bus stop. Xenia was tucked up in Valya's double bed, and Marina and Boris stayed until we had put the house to rights. The General left without his right shoe and Boris and Marina drove him and his wife home across Paris.

Valya, Yevgenia Vladimirovna and I sat awhile in the kitchen drinking tea from the samovar. We were tired but triumphant. And then the three of us went silently into Yevgenia Vladimirovna's room and stood before the icon while she spoke a prayer. We embraced and bade each other goodnight and God's blessing. I went to my room and began to undress, when Bobka emerged from under the bed with the General's shoe in his mouth and wagging his tail. I fell asleep with Bobka on my bed and woke the next morning feeling like death.

CHAPTER FORTY-ONE

Christmas at Home

We were given a fortnight's leave over Christmas and the New Year which I spent with the family in Chobham. Peter came to spend a few days with us, staying over Christmas and was planning to bring Ranald to Paris for a week after I had returned. So Ranald got a suitably wrapped return ticket by BEA amongst his presents. He didn't like the idea at first but we talked him into it, reassured him that he wouldn't be left alone in a 'foreign land' and painted glowing pictures of the Eiffel Tower and the Paris buses all travelling on the wrong side of the road. I explained that there would be a boy called Seryozha of his own age in the house whose mother, Valya, had promised to take them to an early evening cabaret of singing and dancing in French. She spoke English. That clinched it. Ranald warmed to the theme: he was nine years old.

Mike telephoned from Scotland; it was a call constrained and restrained by both of us but I was glad she did. Stella was not happy. Poor Stella, she had espoused Lindsay as a foster daughter who, like Paddy, called her 'Mummy'. The tenancy was due to expire in five months' time; I was to sit the Civil Service examination in Russian in April which left little time for Nan and me to find a new home. I had no idea whatsoever where or when my next appointment might be, but I was determined that no more should I be an absent father, that the strain and inhibitions of being beholden to a surrogate mother of my children must end and that I should share with Nan jointly the full responsibility of parenthood. This we had agreed: she had no one looking over her shoulder, she would be 'Nan', not Mummy, and I as Daddy would be a visible presence.

CHAPTER FORTY-TWO

Last Days in Paris

Ranald enjoyed his week in Paris. He and Seryozha made friends and communicated, I know not how, in a mixture of basic French and English. I bought them both elastic-driven model aeroplanes which fluttered all over Avenue Pinel, so the two boys had to make common cause and knock at doors to ask to retrieve their toys.

Alfie B. and I had a farewell dinner together, this time at my expense, and then it was time to take my leave of the many people who had been kind to me, including the British Ambassador and his lady and those of his staff I had met from time to time. The Air Attaché threw a drinks party and Zinaida Borisovna, my fat tutor who had never featured in my social life, bade me a sad farewell and presented me with a volume which she had inscribed very touchingly in English.

Very shortly the car from the Embassy was to take me to the station for the boat train. We were seated in a circle in Yevgenia Vladimirovna's room. She said prayers in Russian and my journey was blessed and, as the car drew up at the gate, each one kissed me in turn – Yevgenia Vladimirovna, Valya, Musia, Julia, Marina and then finally Boris. Bobka sat at my feet and put his head on my lap: he ran barking to the door when the bell rang. The driver was ill at ease, not knowing what to do in the presence of so many emotional Russians. He opened the door to the rear seats. Boris, of all people, came forward, said something in Russian which I didn't quite catch and threw his arms around me in a very masculine embrace. I was kissed again by the ladies while the driver, with admirable tact, took the wheel and stared ahead through the windscreen. Hands waved, Russian blessings were incanted, the girls leading the singing, and we were about to move off when Valya, who had arranged to return to the city with Boris and Marina, opened the rear door saying, 'I come, I come. I will travel with you to the station.' She climbed in. I moved across the seat to the far side, embarrassed and confused by the turn of events which I didn't know how to handle. An anticlimax, a provocation; I was aware only of her presence and the cries of farewell and God's blessing from those who came through the gate and onto the pavement and thronged around the car.

'Carry on,' I said to the driver. The sounds were left behind and we joined the traffic south to the Gare du Nord, neither speaking and only once glancing at each other. I felt betrayed and yet not humiliated. Valya did not possess me though she had won on points. On the platform was a noisy group of four of my Cambridge Naval colleagues and their fiancées-cum-girlfriends. We stowed my heavy luggage in the guard's van and walked back to where they had taken over a compartment. Valya was greeted warmly but stood apart when I joined the group in the false and stupid heartiness and un-funny humour which the British are prone to when being seen off or seeing others off. 'Don't forget to write', 'See you in a month or so', 'Don't do anything I wouldn't on a bicycle', 'Behave yourself – remember what I said', Laugh, laugh, ha ha! The guard blew a whistle. We crowded into the compartment. There were embraces and kisses and shouted valedictions. I waved to Valya, who was sobbing. She was the only Russian present and was typically emotional. We flopped onto our seats, and no one spoke until Pat broke the silence: 'Will you see Valya again, Mac?' 'I doubt it,' I replied. One of our group had a bottle of vodka in his case which enlivened the proceedings.

Later I wrote to Valya, as indeed I wrote to Yevgenia Vladimirovna, Musia, Julia, Marina and Zinaida Borisovna. Yevgenia Vladimirovna and I corresponded regularly for a year or more. Valya sent my letter back with the mistakes ringed in red ink and their corrections written in the margin. Nothing else.

CHAPTER FORTY-THREE

Coulsdon or Bodmin?

O ur group sat the Civil Service interpreters' exam in London. I found it easier than I had feared though I made several foolish mistakes in the oral, largely due to nervousness I suspect. All but one of us passed and I was well content with a good Second Class which was telephoned through to me from my contact in the Air Ministry while I was on leave in Chobham. The letter of confirmation – in classic Civil Service impersonality followed – a week later. I was now a Russian interpreter.

Not knowing where my next posting would be created a serious problem; Nan and I needed to look for accommodation that would not only suit her and the children but also would be within commuting distance of my place of work. I began to badger the postings people in Whitehall; I explained my predicament to them, emphasising that time was fast running out and asking that my case be considered as a priority, and even suggesting quite forcibly that I be told what options were open to me. Extra leave or compassionate leave would be of no avail unless I could be told where I was to be posted. I pulled every string I could.

Nan came to stay and we discussed the problem, while Stella fluttered around and was unhappy. Nan and I had agreed that if my tenancy ended before my new posting came through she would take Paddy and Lindsay to stay with her father and maiden aunt near Chippenham. Ranald would join them when the summer holidays began. It was a bolt-hole, but it would provide a breathing space; there was a kindergarten in the neighbourhood and 'Aunty' was said to be good with children.

Then I had two calls: the first was from the Air Ministry postings people who wanted to see me the following day and the second was from the Staff Officer to the Director of Military Intelligence in the War Office who informed me – in a series of staccato bursts like a machine gun – that he had been in touch with 'my chaps' in the Air Ministry and had been given the 'okay' to ask me to report to the DMI after my meeting with them. He gave me the room number and his rank and name, told me to ask for him and said that my identity card would get me into the building. A further short burst from the machine gun and he hung up. I was intrigued.

Nan and I mulled over this extraordinary involvement of the Air Ministry postings with Military Intelligence. Air Intelligence fair enough, but why Military Intelligence? So I put on my best suit, took my bowler hat and furled umbrella, and caught the train to Victoria and a bus to the Air Ministry.

This was in May 1952. I was thirty-eight years old and still a Wing Commander. My prospects did not seem too promising as I went through the main entrance of the Air Ministry building, showed my RAF identity card, and took the lift to the Directorate of Personnel Services to the office where a Group Captain, a civil servant and a Squadron Leader from Air Intelligence were expecting me. The latter, Mike Forter, was a tall, grey-haired, expatriate Russian who had slipped away some time after the Revolution and had been commissioned in the RAF. Forter, whom I already knew, was a great character. He was to become a close friend and colleague some years later.

The Group Captain led off by explaining that the Korean War was escalating, as was the 'Cold' War. Russian translators were required in considerable numbers by the three Services as quickly as possible and two Joint Services Schools had been established to take in National Service-men and to teach them Russian up to the standard required to qualify as translators. One school was at Coulsdon, near Caterham in Surrey, the other was in Bodmin in Cornwall. Each school was established for a qualified Russian interpreter to fill the post of Director of Studies. The teaching staff were being recruited from suitably screened Poles, Czechs and Russians, together with a nucleus of university graduates who had taken Russian as a language. The civil servant explained that the selection of the teaching staff would be conducted by himself – he was a Chief Executive Officer – Mike Forter and, surprise, surprise, Professor Elizabeth Hill of Cambridge University. With her backing I had been selected as Director of Studies for the Bodmin school in Cornwall! Heavens above! I took a deep breath and became very angry.

Did the powers-that-be not realise that I had a motherless family of small children, that they had had for almost two years neither mother nor father at home, that I had set out my domestic situation fairly, squarely and officially on several occasions? Where were the letters I had written to DPS? The civil servant fidgeted in his chair and muttered something about exigencies of the Service, as though he minded a tinker's rap about me and my problems. For the rest of the meeting I was utterly selfish. They could terminate my commission: I would accept early retirement with all the financial penalties with regard to my pension. I had friends in Surrey and the Home Counties. Bodmin was out in the sticks. How could I, without a wife, relocate my family so far away? Why couldn't I be given Coulsdon in Surrey? Who was to be appointed Director of Studies there?

I think I behaved very badly. Bear in mind that my Service record was in the hands of those who interviewed me: Prisoner of War 1941 to 1945 – suspended from duty as Chief Flying Instructor, Royal Air Force College, Cranwell, on 'medical' grounds – lost to the RAF for one and a half years learning Russian – and now blowing my top at a posting which didn't suit me domestically. My future was probably in tatters. There was silence for a moment. I realised that I had been on my feet pacing the office. I sat down. The Group Captain looked at me and it was a kind look from a good man, 'We understand, Mac,' he said.

The Civil Servant mentioned something about Coulsdon being a possible alternative. Mike Forter made comforting noises about so-and-so probably being agreeable to staying at Bodmin – so they had a Director of Studies there! I discovered later that he was fairly ancient and wasn't a Russian speaker but content to stay where he was in Cornwall. I was to be posted as Director of Studies of the Joint Services School for Linguists at Coulsdon, Surrey but I did not know this when I left the Air Ministry and crossed Whitehall to the War Office.

The 'machine gun' received me. The DMI had been called away, he informed me, but if I cared to sit down he would tell me about the set-up at Bodmin and Coulsdon. Had I been selected for either of them? I said that I had no idea but that I had strong reservations about Bodmin. Why was DMI involved? He appeared to suffer a short stoppage, which was cleared by a high-speed rearrangement of pens, pencils, blotter, notepads and the two telephones on his desk. A short, sharp cough and the mechanism was once again in full working order. Had I worked for Air Intelligence? No. Ah well, the output from the Joint Services Schools for Linguists was required for Russian translation work for the three Services both as at present and – here he coughed loudly like an ack-ack gun – more importantly in the event of an international crisis. He looked at me fixedly for a moment. This important job had been entrusted to Military Intelligence as, should any crisis escalate, it would result in a land war. The two establishments were to be under Army command with the Navy providing the administration and the RAF responsible for the standard of Russian. I said that I was aware of this and repeated my question as to why DMI had wanted to see me. To ensure that you are suitable, he snapped back.

It had been a bad day. I was angry, frustrated and worried. Somehow I managed to control myself and in cold, silent anger I picked up my hat and umbrella, gave the machine gun a curt nod, opened the door and left. Halfway down the corridor I heard his voice: 'It's all right, Wing Commander. It's all right, I assure you.' I took a look back and went out to the spring sunshine and a bus to Victoria. Two days later I received an official telegram confirming my appointment to Coulsdon.

So I accepted an extra week's compassionate leave and with Nan searched for accommodation. The Joint Services School for Linguists, JSSL for short, was a small hutted Army camp close to the Caterham valley and the A22 running south through East Grinstead, Forest Row, Uckfield, Lewes and over the South Downs to the Sussex coast. Someone put us onto an estate agent in Forest Row and within four or five days we had struck oil. There was a house to be let furnished on the edge of the Ashdown Forest, just south of the village of Nutley and a hundred yards or so from the main road where it was intersected by a steep lane called Cackle Street which crossed a narrow stream before climbing steeply into the Forest and a junction with the road to Crowborough. We fell for it. The house was called Dodds Grove.

The owner was a widow whose husband had been an army officer and there was a son, a major, who was about to be posted overseas. There was an agreed lease for a year with an option of six-monthly renewals if mutually agreeable. A bus service from Forest Row ran regularly to within an easy walk of the JSSL. The times were acceptable both ways and the journey took about forty minutes. Nan could drive me to Forest Row each morning and meet my bus there in the evening. Within an hour we had signed the lease, having explained the domestic situation to the owner who was understanding and helpful. We had established a safe haven and drove back quite excited at what lay ahead.

Nan and I described the new home to the children. Ranald was back at school but I telephoned him. He was overjoyed. Paddy, who was seven, looked forward to living in the country and seeing foxes, badgers and frogs in the streams. Lindsay alone cried her heart out and clung to Stella, 'Mummy', when she was told of the change. Stella too was understandably distressed.

Thus it was that I climbed into the passenger seat of the small removals van that I had hired with a driver for our heavy luggage, toys and all the paraphernalia that accompanies a young family, while Stella drove her Hillman with Nan and Paddy and Lindsay in convoy to Sussex and to our new home on the Ashdown Forest. It was the early summer of 1952. Though neither Nan nor I realised it at the time it was the beginning of a long joint endeavour, a crusade if you like, but neither of us expected to return from it with a Saracen's head.

CHAPTER FORTY-FOUR

Joint Services School for Linguistics

N an was an unusual woman: to many she was a contradiction, if not an enigma. She wore her dark-brown, shoulder-length, lank hair in a low bun for the first few hours of the day, after which it fell down. With her huge eyes, slightly bulbous nose and stooping, shambling gait, she looked for all the world like a gypsy. She was not one to dress up except on special occasions, when she could transform herself. She gave the impression of being shy and something of a nonentity. Yet, she had an excellent and penetrating mind, an iron will and an indifference to trivia. At times she was embarrassingly outspoken. A passionate and exciting person to live with, she chose her friends with care. The children took to her readily enough. Nan treated them at first with impartiality, though later Ranald became the favoured one, to be overtaken by Paddy when Ranald rebelled as a teenager.

Stella had gone, my leave was up and the routine at Dodds Grove had been established. Ranald was at school at Cumnor House some few miles away and Paddy and Lindsay were at an infant school nearby. I was ready to take up my appointment as Director of Studies, Joint Services School for Linguists, Coulsdon. This was to be the nadir of my career. Thank God it lasted for no more than nine months.

The unit was an Army one commanded by a brittle and unimaginative Lieutenant Colonel who had not the slightest interest in or understanding of what his job involved. He was the Commandant. Teaching Russian to National Service conscripts from the three services was totally outwith his ken. He was in command of an Army camp and it would be run according to the inflexible rules of War Office Instructions. So, there was to be no heating in the classrooms or the canteen, let alone in the barracks, until November. For six weeks in the coldest autumn on record we froze, until I had my first stand-up row with the CO. I insisted we had heat. Even the

Officers' Mess was like a refrigerator, but he refused to be budged. His Adjutant, an alert and cooperative Captain, while obedient to his CO, did his best to give me support. The unhappy Station Sergeant Major, with whom I developed a warm working relationship, was unable to resolve the problem and it wasn't until I demanded an order in writing forbidding the heating of the buildings that the Commandant finally conceded and stoves were fuelled and lit.

It was a total disaster as far as joint service cooperation was concerned. The Army commanded the camp. The Russian language students, while under my command for instruction, were paraded daily under the Station Sergeant Major and drilled and marched about and inspected and once a week the Commandant mounted a rostrum and took the salute while the conscripts marched past, eyes right, and fell out behind the NAAFI. It was farcical. And everybody realised it, except perhaps the CO who was doing what his Instructions required.

The administration of the unit was in the hands of a Naval Lieutenant Commander, weary and very probably passed over on the promotion ladder. He muddled through the accounts, the roll calls and the inevitable problems of supplies, food, fuel and laundry, difficulties which were compounded by the inter-service wrangles as to who paid for what. He had as his assistant a Flight Lieutenant who, thank God, was not responsible to me, for he was absent on numerous occasions for reasons which were usually suspect and were covered by travelling expenses which the Lieutenant commander signed with benign regularity. I was responsible to the Commandant for the standard of Russian language training of the intakes of National Servicemen who attended the JSSL for courses lasting six months: a very short time to acquire a working knowledge of the language unless they had learned it previously at school, which very few had. I was also responsible for their conduct when under instruction.

I had no terms of reference. I was simply told by the Commandant what my duties were and where my responsibilities lay, namely to him. His Adjutant was made privy to all that I did. I was also responsible for the conduct, punctuality and standard of teaching of the instructional staff. There were some ten to twelve 'instructors' on the strength of the JSSL. I had as my Deputy Director a very intelligent young English graduate in Russian from Cambridge. Peter Broomfield spoke excellent Russian and supported me loyally through the year I struggled with the conflicts of red tape, ethnic differences and sheer bloody mindedness at Coulsdon in what was in fact an inter-service cock-up.

The instructors were a motley group of multinationals, among whom was an elderly Russian lady who always dressed in black and was dubbed 'Black Death'. She ruled with an iron will and a ruler which I had reason to believe she used from time to time to enforce obedience on the most stubborn of her pupils. There was Kosa Gavrilovic, a member of a wealthy and influential Yugoslavian dynasty who had followed the example of their royal family and fled to England when Tito overthrew the monarchy. Kosa was young, attractive and also a graduate of Cambridge, where she had met Peter Broomfield. She set her cap at him but he had other fish to fry and Kosa fretted and fumed. She spoke impeccable English and very good Russian. She was a great asset when she wasn't having tantrums over Peter.

As to the rest, their lot was a sad reflection on the post-War plight of expatriates from Eastern Europe. There were a few Poles whose English was deplorable and Russian mediocre. Two young Russian women who had married British servicemen in the Mediterranean towards the end of the War, only to be deserted on coming to England, struggled to justify their lots and find other partners. Their roving eyes were not unnoticed by the young National Servicemen and there were emotional complications and night escapades which were visited on me until I made it absolutely clear that the 'students' were not my responsibility after the classrooms were closed.

Owing to poor instruction and the course being too short for the syllabus, an unacceptable percentage of students failed their end-of-course exams. Anticipating trouble from the Commandant, Peter and I drew up two charts. One showed the percentage passes by Service: I was delighted to see that the RAF led the Navy Coders by a narrow margin, with the Army trailing behind. The second chart, which we kept to ourselves, related the success or failure to the instructor concerned. This was immediately revealing.

'Black Death' and Kosa were almost equal at the top and the three Poles Peter and I had been unhappy about were well down. Most of our instructors were incompetent. There had to be sackings. I submitted the end of term report and the examination results to the Commandant with a footnote about the standard of the instructors. I suggested that we discuss this problem as it was crucial to the whole operation. He called me to his office. Previously he had had the Adjutant and often the Sergeant Major present whenever he saw me. On this occasion we were alone. For the first time he called me 'Mac', invited me to sit, offered a cigarette and became a different person. We were communicating as brother officers of equal rank.

I suggested Peter Broomfield join us, to which he agreed. Peter spoke of the poor Russian of most of the Poles and their incompetence as teachers. We ended our meeting in agreement that we should call for a discussion with the Staff Officer from Directorate of Military Intelligence and his colleague, Mike Forter, from Directorate of Air Intelligence. They came separately, which was a pity. I would have enjoyed 'Machinegun' and Mike together expressing their views. 'Machinegun' fired several belts but hit no sensitive target and, to his great credit, the Commandant sent him packing. I had warned Mike Forter that the Commandant was inclined to be defensive. Mike handled the meeting superbly. In his well-tailored RAF uniform with a double row of medal ribbons, several of them Russian, on his left breast, his close-cropped grey hair and finely chiselled features, he stood erect until the Commandant bade him be seated. He spoke slowly and quietly in his excellent English, only slightly accented, and made no attempt to go on the offensive. Rather he took the line that the Commandant had a problem not of his making but that bad selection had resulted in the teaching staff falling down on their jobs.

The Commandant listened and relaxed while Mike and I went through Peter Broomfield's reports on the unsatisfactory teachers. Mike explained that many of the more suitable candidates had been eliminated for security reasons. It seems ridiculous in retrospect. What possible information of interest to Soviet intelligence could be gained from a bunch of Eastern Europeans teaching Russian to classes of young National Servicemen or from an Army unit of no military consequence whatever? But bear in mind that McCarthyism and Russiophobia were in fashion. The Cold War, the Berlin Airlift and the knowledge that the Soviet Union had the atomic bomb were giving everyone the jitters. Burgess and Maclean had defected. It was 'Reds under the bed' – and later 'in the bed' as well as the news broke that a British Secretary of State for War, John Profumo, was sharing a mistress with the Soviet naval attaché in London.

A decision was made to dismiss three of the most ineffectual instructors: they were all Poles with young families. Though I knew it was right, I felt sorry for them. I went through the anguish of informing them that their contracts would be terminated. One by one they stood before my desk. Each one stiffened to attention as if receiving a death sentence. One said to me: 'Thank you, sir, for what you have done for my people. It is not your fault; it is not mine but it is the fault of a third.'

When he had gone I realised he was laying the blame on Peter Broomfield. There was nothing I could do about it. Before Mike Forter left the camp, we drank a cup of tea together in my office. He cleared his throat: 'Sir, the Colonel is a very unhappy man. He feels that he has not shown you the respect he owes you for what you are doing and he is concerned that he is not in favour with the Director of Military Intelligence. He has never commanded a joint service unit before and is worried that his annual confidential report will not look good on his CV. He is a lonely man, Sir, and I think he needs your help.' We looked at each other in silence, while the impact of what Mike had said to me sank in. It had never occurred to me that the Commandant needed my personal support. To me the Colonel represented an unimaginative middle-of-the-road soldier with no further promotion prospects. I hadn't, I confess, given much thought to him other than to ensure to the best of my ability that I fulfilled my part of the joint service task. Mike Forter gave me much food for thought. I drove him to the station. We stood on the grubby suburban platform with a huge poster behind us showing a sun bronzed bikini-clad Aphrodite advertising same tourist trap on the Costa del Sol. He saluted me as the London train drew in. Mike was an aristocrat: a Russian of the old regime.

I continued my journey south to Dodds Grove, Nan and my family. In the early months I had travelled to Coulsdon and returned by bus but later found the cash to buy Nan an ancient but roadworthy Austin 7 saloon which left me with the equally ancient and reliable family Lanchester coupé to drive to the JSSL and back.

That evening, after I had read to Paddy and Lindsay, I told Nan what had happened. Though she knew little of my career in the RAF, she had a keen sense of judgement as far as people were concerned, as I was to discover as our relationship grew closer. We discussed what best to do about the Commandant and his wife. We knew that we couldn't effectively entertain them, so we agreed that I should set up some sort of social occasion in the Mess. It could be a drinks party which I and my instructional staff would host for the Commandant, his Adjutant, the Naval Administrative Officer and their ladies. I had this all planned with Peter Broomfield right behind me when the whole scenario was changed dramatically. I was to leave the JSSL and to take up an appointment as the RAF member of a team in the Joint Planning Staff of the War Cabinet Office.

So the tables were turned. The Commandant organised a farewell party for me and my polyglot staff. He and the Lieutenant Commander brought their wives, but Nan decided it would not be prudent for her to attend. The Commandant and I exchanged introductory speeches. I did my best to acknowledge his support and praised his success in running a truly joint service unit. We were on very much better terms than hitherto.

The Colonel, his lady and the Lieutenant Commander and his, looked and must have felt completely out of place in what slowly became an Eastern European form of a vecherinka. The Poles got mildly pissed and began singing sentimental songs, which was fine until Kosa tried to make an emotional speech about freedom for Yugoslavia. 'Black Death' said she would recite a poem by the great Russian poet Lermontov. She struck a dramatic attitude and in her deep, husky voice began: '*Pechalno ya glyazhu na nashe pokoleniye ...*' (Sadly I look upon our generation). I remember hoping fervently that the emotions would not get out of control and, thank God, they didn't. But it was a close shave!

CHAPTER FORTY-FIVE

Home Life and the War Cabinet Office

I had a fortnight's leave before taking up my new appointment as a Joint Planner in the Cabinet Office. Nan and I put the time to good account. We drove south in the Lanchester to the South Downs, Brighton and Eastbourne, and walked over the Ashdown Forest – a forest only in name since the trees had long since been pillaged for burning in the iron foundries or for boat building on the coast. Wildlife abounded: we watched hares boxing in the bracken, and ponies that kicked backwards and galloped away snorting with tails and manes flying as we came upon them. Magpies and jays called from the scattered clumps of trees and foresters and their small children waved to us from their garden gates. Paddy and Lindsay were happy with their new, free life and Ranald would come home on Sunday after school lunch and perhaps bring a friend. Diana was well settled in Northampton and I began to live in the present.

Once, when walking in the forest, we met a man with a puppy on a string. It was a mongrel, mostly I would think a dachshund but with a strain of cocker spaniel. It was black with a docked tail and very short legs. It leapt ecstatically towards us. Lindsay took cover behind Nan but the man assured us it was harmless and friendly. Its name was Bruce. We continued our walk: there was talk about Bruce. Could we have a dog? The following day I crossed the forest to the cottage where the man and his family lived. Was the puppy for sale? Yes. I gave him a pound and brought Bruce home. We were all delighted. Nan had a slight speech impediment which made it hard for her to pronounce her 'r's. She would call 'Bwoocie, Bwoocie!' when she wanted the puppy to come. Perhaps we smiled, perhaps she detected our amusement but, for whatever reason, she decided to call him by a variety of names such as Toddle and Pooh. It was Pooh she preferred and, for the remainder of his seventeen years, he was Pooh.

Inevitably Pooh took over the household. Why families become pathologically pet-centred I have never understood, but thus it was. I recall a whole day when none of us was fed and we scoured the neighbourhood and quartered the forest in search of Pooh who had gone missing since his early morning 'out'. Worn out, famished and desperate, we returned to Dodds Grove. There he was, the little bugger, wagging his stumpy tail and leaping at us, barking in welcome. He was enfolded by Nan while Paddy and Lindsay sobbed in relief. We ate a huge meal and Pooh was the guest of honour! What fools we are.

Nan made friends; the children made friends from their schools. Ranald was doing well at Cumnor House and Paddy joined him soon after we came to Dodds Grove. Lindsay went to a dame school run by a Miss Punt who was understanding and very good with her.

Nan and I settled into a routine which was domestically of her ordering but based on an understanding of each other's needs, likes and dislikes. She smoked heavily. I smoked but moderately. The house stank of tobacco smoke. For not only did Nan smoke in bed and throughout the day but also when bathing. Nothing is worse than the acrid stink of tobacco in a steam-filled bathroom. There was even an ashtray on the bathroom windowsill. But I took it in my stride and I imagine that the children regarded it as a fact of life and accepted it accordingly. Though an excellent cook, Nan was not one to serve meals at set times, other than when there was a deadline like catching a train or entertaining guests. I was the one who made breakfast.

Following my mother's precept that the day should be started on a full stomach each morning I prepared bacon and eggs and fried bread. It was ritualistic, not to be varied, and was the tocsin that heralded each new day. It was known as 'Daddy's Morning Service' and was continued for thirty-five years or so until it petered out in favour of cereal and toast. I admit to a sadness at its going. I miss the rich smell of bacon spitting and the eggs slowly closing their eyes and the bread just crisp on the outside but juicy with fat as you bit into it. We didn't worry about cholesterol levels or health foods in those days.

With the home front established, I was able to address myself to my new appointment as a Joint Planner in the Cabinet Office with a clear conscience and peace of mind.

So I drove to Hayward's Heath, took the train to Victoria and walked across St James' Park to the impressive block of early Georgian buildings at Storey's Gate. I worked in an office with a Naval commander Norman Scarlett-Streatfeild, a tall, sardonic-looking mariner with an excellent mind, a shrewd sense of the ridiculous and an infectious and spontaneous laugh. We hit it off the moment we met. Our Army colleague was Major

Harry Thuillier, the scion of a distinguished military family liberally
sprinkled with generals and others who had achieved high office. He was
the youngest of us, possibly the ablest but a mite too Army-orientated to
fit easily into a joint service team.

The Joint Planning Staff – JPS – was three tiered. We who were the
draughtsmen of the various plans were known as G2 (General Staff
Officer Grade 2). We submitted our drafts to the next level, G1, consisting
of a Captain RN, a Lieutenant Colonel and a Group Captain. They in
turn reported to the Directors of Plans, also a Captain, a Brigadier and an
Air Commodore. Their submissions went before the Chiefs of Staff
Committee. In essence our job was to come up with a five-year estimate of
and costing for the military forces required and available for the United
Kingdom's contribution to the North Atlantic Treaty Organisation,
NATO. A daunting task.

We were briefed by the G1s, collectively and then individually, which
resulted inevitably on each returning to the office with a specific non-joint
slant on what form our draft should take. This was when the fur flew.
Hours of heated argument frequently degenerated into personal abuse.

'Mac, that's utter balls and would be totally unacceptable to the
Director of Naval Plans.'

'Norman, you know bloody well the Navy can't sink every Soviet
submarine that puts to sea. For God's sake, be your age.'

'Harry, do you honestly believe that a couple of tank Divisions can hold
the northern flank of the old Maginot Line? Look what happened in
1940.'

So it went on but when the time came, we submitted to our masters
well-prepared drafts which were usually accepted with only minor amendments.

Often we had to work late and to a deadline dictated by an unscheduled
meeting of the Chiefs of Staff Committee. So I would phone Nan whose
response was usually unsympathetic. I would have to make my own
supper.

I scrounged a week flying jets at the Central Flying establishment at
Manby which did my morale, health and self-esteem a lot of good. It had
not been easy to keep in flying practice but the authorities were charitable
and from time to time I had been released from the bondage of desk jobs
and sent on 'refresher' courses. So it came about that I had qualified on
Meteors, Vampires and Mosquitoes, albeit with no more than twenty
hours or so on each. But at least I could fly them solo and my log-book
was beginning to look considerably more respectable.

It was when away on these refresher courses that I realised the extent to
which flying was in my blood, how much I had missed it during the four

and a half barren years behind barbed wire and how badly I needed the release and fulfilment of the upper air and space to compensate for the earth-bound constraints of my daily life. My Uncle Jacko, the one who had persuaded my parents that I should go into the RAF and had made it possible financially, had urged me to follow his wild Irish passion for the air. In doing so I found the escape which only those who fly alone above the clouds seeking height to the limit of their machine can ever know. I have actually wept in the cockpit of a Meteor because it couldn't reach any higher. There was an infinite firmament above, which laughed at me and challenged, and I was unable to accept the challenge.

While I was away at Manby my promotion to Group Captain was gazetted. My CV was beginning to look a lot better though my years as a POW, with so much lost experience, inevitably held me down on the promotional ladder compared with my earlier contempories. I remember shortly after I had been repatriated in 1945 being offered a drink at the bar of the RAF Club by the 'silly-billy' of my entry at Cranwell wearing the four stripes of a Group Captain while I was still a Squadron Leader. I refused to address him as 'Sir', but there were many of my old contemporaries who were far more senior than me. I knew my feelings were jealous and bitter and I didn't like it. At least I had survived the War. So many of my friends and colleagues hadn't. And now I was within striking distance of Air Attaché, Moscow: I was slowly catching up.

By 1955 our tenancy of Dodds Grove was coming to an end. Ranald was thirteen and had won an exhibition to Bryanston. A new headmaster by the name of Coade had been appointed who transformed the school from an aimless conglomerate of philosophies to a liberal but clearly oriented pattern of development moving far closer to the ethos of Kurt Hahn, the German founder. The change came while my brother Peter was in his senior term and I suspect it threw him off balance. When Ranald went to Bryanston many years later, in 1955, the philosophy and structure were well established. It was an excellent school and I had hopes that Ranald would develop and become broader in outlook. To this extent my hopes were fulfilled.

Ranald's school reports told of a well-behaved, steady boy whose work was good and who was developing into a useful oar; rowing it seemed being the extra-mural activity in which he took most interest, though he spent a lot of free time riding horses which belonged to a family who had befriended him. He just missed becoming captain of his House.

Ranald was a loyal supporter of Nan with all her idiosyncrasies, including her obsession with Pooh who had grown into a spoilt brat. Once, when Pooh had taken up his favourite position on the sofa, Ranald went to sit down beside him. Pooh snarled and bit his bottom. Ranald's tears were more from injured pride than bodily pain. As the oldest of the children, he cooperated with Nan and gained her approval. I often wonder what he had suffered early in his life when his mother became mentally ill.

He was very tall for his age and had many physical similarities to his mother: the same long limbs, the same wide mouth and the same stoop. But he was a thinker and something of a romantic. Paddy, four and a half years younger than his brother, did not remember his mother. Physically and emotionally he was more like me. From being petted by Stella the transition to the impartiality of Nan could have been the reason for a certain lack of self-confidence. He was prone to omissions and unnecessary blunders which Nan handled fairly but sometimes severely. By comparison with Ranald, that much older, he had a somewhat raw deal. Lindsay, with her mother's eyes and auburn hair adapted easily to the new home and the new regime. She later admitted to a certain fear of Nan who once said, 'You had better not. I've got eyes in the back of my head!' At the age of five, Lindsay was certain that beneath the dark mop of Nan's back hair lurked a pair of beady eyes that missed nothing that went on behind her. But the family was united: we did things together; the children were encouraged to invite their pals from school for meals and outings on the weekends. I found a new sense of security.

We moved from Dodds Grove during the short leave I was granted following my promotion in July 1954. I bade farewell to my fellow joint planners, was lunched expensively by my Director of Plans, who said encouraging things about my work, and got my marching orders from the postings people. I was to be the senior RAF member of the Directing Staff at the Joint Services Staff College at Latimer in Buckinghamshire. I had mixed feelings about it.

Our new house, 1 Maresfield Close, Maresfield, was half a large house in the middle of the village, a couple of miles down the road from Dodds Grove. The owner of our half was a Major in the Intelligence Corps who was on the way to the Far East for a two-year tour overseas. The other half was owned and occupied by a Squadron Leader with his wife, two sons and a daughter about Lindsay's age. Each half had its own garden.

CHAPTER FORTY-SIX

Senior Directing Staff (Air) Joint Services Staff College

It was September 1954. Group Captain Donald MacDonell stepped onto the platform at Chalfont to be greeted by Group Captain Duncan Macdonald, the man he was taking over from at the JSSC: 'Mac' succeeding 'Mac'. Duncan and I knew each other of old. On the drive to Latimer House in the RAF staff car he lost no time in explaining the set-up: whom to cultivate, whom to avoid and what he reckoned was needed to ensure that the paramount importance of airpower was rammed home. It didn't sound very joint service to me but I held my peace.

As Duncan droned on – he had a slightly sing-song voice and a habit of inclining his head a shade ingratiatingly as he spoke – I found my mind wandering. Perhaps the country through which we drove brought back to me the long story of Latimer House in the fifteenth and sixteenth centuries and the many well-known families who had lived there. Sir Wyles Sandys, whose brother was the Archbishop of York, occupied the great estate in the mid 1550s. Then the Cavendish family owned it through the Civil War (or the 'Rebellion' as the Royalist chroniclers liked to call it), right down the line to the Boer War in 1899. In that distasteful conflict a detachment of yeomanry under Lord Chesham distinguished itself, but Chesham's eldest son, the Hon. Charles Cavendish, was killed in 1900 at the age of twenty-one. The chancel arch in Latimer Church is dedicated to his memory. Lord Chesham – a Privy Councillor and a KCB – was killed hunting in 1907 and his second son inherited the title while still a schoolboy at Eton. He was the last of the Cavendish family to live at Latimer House.

At the outbreak of war in 1939 Latimer House was requisitioned, first as a convalescent home for Metropolitan Police air-raid casualties. There were, in fact, no such casualties. Later in 1942, Combined Services Detailed Interrogation Centre (CSDIC) moved in and high-ranking German and Italian POWs were held there. Latimer House itself was the CSDIC Officers' Mess. So I mused as Duncan talked on.

We checked in at the Guardroom, drove past the long row of bungaloid cells in which the POWs had been accommodated for their period of interrogation. The story goes that a group of German generals, cultivating a plot in the grounds, insisted: 'Ve do not dig vor your victory but for de victory of our dinners!'

In the interrogations at Latimer no duress was employed. Dr Mervyn Brigstocke, the unit medical officer, recalled one occasion when two Italian officers had been put together in a cell, which was bugged, in the hope that some secret information might be divulged. The staff were astonished to overhear a homosexual exchange!

The intelligence-gathering was of great value to the war effort. It helped to complete our knowledge of the German V2 rocket. Of value to the understanding of the German psychology was the number of POWs who were found to be carrying a suicide kit – often cyanide capsules. These were cleverly concealed in with whatever baggage they were carrying. How different from my kit which consisted of a compass, a map and a Colt – the latter for shooting my way out rather than for self-destruction – when I was made a POW in March 1941.

The concept of inter-service or 'joint' study of the economics, strategy and tactics of war did not become a reality until after the Second World War. For centuries Britain had been essentially a maritime power: its numerous land campaigns had been waged, often with European allies, in the knowledge that Britannia rules the waves and that the heartland was invincible. The idea that officers of the Navy and Army – there was of course no air force – should be trained to think beyond their immediate function as sailors or soldiers was never considered. Far from it: in 1783 Francis Grose offered this gratuitous advice to officers of the British Army:

> 'Above all be careful never to promote an intelligent officer; a brave chuckle-headed fellow will do fully as well to execute your orders. An official that has an iota of knowledge above the common run you must consider as your personal enemy; for you may be sure he laughs at you and your manoeuvres.'

And a century later the following comment was attributed to the First Sea Lord about the Second Sea Lord's proposal for a Naval staff college: 'The other officers of the Royal Navy would be deeply suspicious of any officers who were trained to think.'

Despite the long-preserved notion that sailors and soldiers, whether commissioned or not, were no more than brainwashed hired assassins brought up to obey the orders of the High Command unquestioningly, shortly following the First World War a Naval Staff College was established at Greenwich, an Army Staff College at Camberley and, when the Royal Air Force emerged as a third independent service in 1921, an RAF Staff College at Andover, later to be moved to Bracknell. The three service Staff Colleges preached their own specialised doctrines. It was the Second World War which brought home to the Joint Chiefs the need for a far greater integration in philosophy and training.

This was not as revolutionary as it appeared to some sceptics. Back in 1921, General Sir Ian Hamilton had said:

> '*The Staffs of the Army and Navy will always be brought up to think in a different way until they are brought up together. But the sooner they are brought up in the same way, the better for all of us. I declare here that it would be better to trust to motherwit than to have separate Staff or War Colleges for each of the services. If we wish to breed discord and confusion that's the way to do it.*'

Yet, it was not until 1951 that the mandate for the establishment of the Joint Services Staff College at Latimer was given government approval. Field Marshal Viscount Montgomery – going somewhat over the top as was his wont – envisaged the three services being brought more closely together, even to the extent of combining them into one. By September 1954 the concept of the early visionaries had become a reality. The Imperial Defence College produced the top brass; the JSSC at Latimer provided the grist for its mill.

I was introduced to the Commandant, Rear Admiral Kaye Edden. Tall, sharp-featured, with red hair greying at the temples. His handshake was firm as he welcomed me. He paced slowly round his office, with Duncan and me invited to sit down. Despite his habit of shooting his cuffs from the sleeves of his uniform I took to him and felt that I had made first base without difficulty.

And so began my appointment as Senior Directing Staff (Air) – SDS (Air). The structure of the JSSC was pyramidal. Under the Commandant and responsible directly to him were the three Senior Directors – Navy, Army, and Air. I was introduced to each of them. There was also a learned professor who ranked equally with the Senior Directors each responsible for a team of subordinate officers known as 'Directing Staff'. Mine were Wing Commanders: three were pilots, the fourth was from Secretarial Branch. All were graduates of the RAF Staff College; the one from Secretarial Branch had been my instructor when I was a student in 1946.

When I arrived the course in session was coming to a close and a good deal of 'end of term' frivolity was apparent. The final exercise of the course had been issued to the 'syndicates'. It was a set-piece combined operation, fictional but clearly set in the context of a NATO war against the Soviet Union. The student voted to present the final operational plan was a Naval officer. He addressed the course members, the Commandant and the Directing Staff with a presence and a command of idiom and history the like of which I have never heard since. It was the quintessence of parliamentary debate: it was Palmerston, Churchill and Macmillan – laced with humour. It was brilliant. With great tact and skill he reshaped the whole concept and concluded with a solution that opened up new strategies that, had we but known it at the time, were to prove visionary.

The silence which had attended his presentation was broken by a hubbub which continued as he collected his notes and walked back to his seat. Then, as was the tradition, SDS (Navy) moved to the rostrum. In the circumstances he did well: he disagreed with the criticism of the setting – the Navy had drafted it – but was generous in his praise of the detailed thought expressed in the presentation. SDS (Army), as I had expected, pitted his wit and skill as a speaker against the presenter. He neither criticised nor praised: indeed he said nothing of much relevance but in five minutes he had us all laughing. He sat down and it was Duncan's turn.

I thought, next course this will be me. I tried to imagine how I would handle such a situation but my mind went blank. Duncan was reading from prepared notes. The students were fidgeting in their seats and then it was over bar the Commandant's summing up. He stood up, shot his cuffs and, stiff-lipped, strode onto the platform and faced us. We awaited a broadside. He didn't fire a single gun. War, he said, like so much of life, was often a paradox and the parody of a paper operation which we had just heard was not likely to be forgotten by Latimer for a very long time. Indeed it would give future members of the Directing Staff a lot to think about. He was right. It bloody well did.

On the final dining-in night, there were speeches – some amusing, some abysmal. The drinking went on into the early hours. Next morning the students left. We, the Directing Staff, spent the afternoon in an assessment of the course and how it could be improved. But our main preoccupation was the presentation of the day before. We agreed to tackle that when we came back from leave a week before the next course assembled.

CHAPTER FORTY-SEVEN

Holidays and Cousin Lindsay

Everyone was in good heart at Maresfield Close. All three children were on holiday from school. Pooh was as repulsive as ever and Nan was complaining that the weather was making gardening intolerable. She either had a grouse against something or somebody or was in a state of enthusiasm or even euphoria. A woman of extremes, she kept us all guessing.

It was during my leave that a teenage cousin joined the family. She was the daughter of my first cousin Elizabeth Gordon. When we moved to Swanage in 1921, my father's younger sister, Aunt Dorothy – Auntie Dee as we called her – with her ailing husband Edgar Gordon and their two young daughters came with us. Uncle Edgar died soon after they left Swanage and a year later Auntie Dee also died, only to be followed a few years after by her elder daughter, Lindsay. So Elizabeth, the remaining daughter, at the age of fifteen or fourteen was an orphan. Some distant relatives took her on and she visited us in Swanage during school holidays. She and I became close friends. In our late teens when I was a cadet at Cranwell, Eliza came to one of the Graduation Balls. She was living with an older unmarried woman whom I should have identified as a lesbian for that was what she was. But Eliza had always been more than interested in boys. Later, when I was newly commissioned she would accompany me to the wild parties in Edgware. Song, drink and sex were the order of the night. I lost touch with Eliza when I went to the Middle East and she married an actor – and a poor one to boot. When I heard of her again, she had two daughters, Sarah and Lindsay, her marriage had broken up, war had been declared, and she had acquired a boyfriend who was called up and conscripted into the RNR as a gunner on a minesweeper based at St Peter's Port, Guernsey.

With her two very young daughters, Eliza followed him and was living on Guernsey when his ship was sunk and he was killed. Shortly afterwards the Germans invaded the island and Eliza joined what today would be called a pop group to entertain them. She was an attractive, uninhibited young woman as I had reason to know. But in 1942, she, her children and a number of other 'undesirables' were rounded up and transported across Europe to a civilian internee camp at Biberach in Germany near the Swiss border. I was then in *Stalag Luft* III. We corresponded through the International Red Cross and I organised a collection of wool in any form, which was what the internees seemed to need.

We met again when we were repatriated. I think Eliza and the girls were back with the lesbian. Then, a year or so later, I found myself faced with Eliza being in a London hospital with TB and a collapsed lung. Sarah, the elder daughter had joined the WAAF but Lindsay was homeless.

Thus it came about that Nan, who had heard me tell of what had happened, put her hand on mine and said 'Of course Lindsay must come, but she must conform with our lifestyle.' I looked hard and long at this extraordinary woman. I had expected a violent refusal: I found it very hard to express my feelings. But Lindsay joined us and became 'Lin Mark I' while my daughter was now 'Lin Mark II'. She remained with us for a year, during which she adjusted well considering what had befallen her. She went to the local secondary school until she was old enough to become a live-in student nurse in a London hospital. Later she married an RAF corporal in the MT section. They ran a pub in Cornwall.

So Nan took on a fourth child as a surrogate mother and it seemed to me that she was pleased to do so in her strange, often inscrutable way. She passionately wanted children of her own which in the circumstances was denied her. Instead she made the best of those who were not of her body. Only once in our long relationship, before she left for Malta did she confess to me the agony of not having a child of her own. I think perhaps we men don't always understand these things.

Lin Mark I became an elder sister to Lin Mark II. Paddy took to the newcomer and only Ranald showed, at times, an unease in her presence. We took a picnic to our favourite vantage point overlooking the London to Brighton road for the annual run of the 'Old Crocks' Race'. When the bulk of the competitors had clanked and grunted by to the accompaniment of wild cheering from our party, led by Nan, we would pull out into the road and follow the stragglers south in the old Lanchester which was almost old enough to qualify as an entrant. We found the 'White Steamer' in trouble outside a pub, so we too stopped and had drinks all round.

Nan organised a bonfire in the garden for Guy Fawkes Night. We didn't have an effigy as neither of us cared to be reminded of that dreadful method of execution. Indeed Nan observed that it had been a pity his gunpowder plot hadn't succeeded, so little did she think of Parliament and the politicians who governed the country! We had a number of children at the bonfire. The daughter of a retired brigadier fell over the ha-ha and was recovered muddy but uninjured. Sausages and potatoes were sizzled in a homemade barbecue and the fireworks all went off according to plan. My leave drew to a close and I returned to Latimer. It was the winter of 1954.

CHAPTER FORTY-EIGHT

JSSC and the Visiting General

I had no active experience of the development of airpower, of saturation bombing, ground attack or long-range fighter escort of day bombers, let alone the concept of mass wings of fighters, 'Balbos' or 'Beehives' as they were called, crusades against the ever-weakening fighter defences in the West as the *Luftwaffe*'s resources were turned to the East to confront the Soviet Air Force. It concerned me that I had begun to see myself as posturing as an expert when my operational experience was limited to the Battle of Britain and its aftermath.

I called a meeting of my staff. We agreed that a radical review of the last joint exercise in the syllabus should be handled later with the Commandant and the SDS having a go at it in the first instance and then involving the whole Directing Staff. I then steered our meeting to the substance of the RAF presentation for the opening session of the new course. I was at pains not to impute any criticism of the script my predecessor had left me, of which they all had a copy, for loyalty is a strange, abstract and often changeable quality.

We have hereditary loyalty. My ancestor, the infamous 15th Chief of Glengarry, was an arrogant, bullying braggart but I tend to defend his behaviour. In business or in the Services, it has become virtually ritualistic to support the boss, be he inept, a shit or a bully. A squadron in the RAF unites under its commanding officer for better or worse, and so on up the scale. It was ever thus.

When I took my place at the rostrum for my opening presentation, I was very nervous. I referred to my secondment as a pilot in the Fleet Air Arm and to my service in the Cabinet Office as a Joint Planning Officer. I explained that my active service had been limited to the command of a Spitfire squadron in the Battle of Britain and that I had spent four and a quarter years as a POW. I looked forward to working with the students on the course. After a few relatively simple questions, it was all over.

The students included members of the armed forces of Canada; a splendid, self-opinionated extrovert from the Australian Civil Service; a highly decorated Major who thought he knew it all but didn't; a Wing Commander from the Indian Air Force and another from the Pakistan Air Force who avoided each other throughout. A sad reflection on Mountbatten's independence of Imperial India and its separation into two autonomous countries.

Also from India came a bouncy little man who held high office in the Civil Service. Dapper, well dressed, of small stature, with his attractively accented English he quickly established himself as possessing a penetrating and lively mind but his personal cleanliness left a lot to be desired. It was not long before he was dubbed 'UN' (Underarm Neglect). At a reasonable distance he was admired as an original thinker who served to uplift and enliven the course. There was also a graduate of the Trenchard Police College at Hendon, a lonely man whom I spent a lot of time talking to. Inevitably, he became known as KGB. To the astonishment of all, he put on a brilliant if somewhat inebriated one-man show during the farewell guest-night.

It was not long before old inter-service jealousies and rivalries were melded into free and easy banter and leg-pulling, though there were the exceptions. I recall Latimer as an academy of wisdom, learning, adjustment and, above all, a place of humour. It was the latter which kept the circus on the road. It was a standing Latimer joke that in the routine syndicate business the Navy did the thinking, the Army did the work and the RAF did the typing. This, while good humoured, smacked somewhat of calumny. I felt it was up to me to demonstrate that the Junior Service had brains and intelligence equal to those in the Navy and Army. Maybe we had a mild inferiority complex. Who knows?

We imported several outside lecturers of various callings and persuasions to point up the core messages of certain exercises. Among these speakers was General Sir Brian Horrocks, the Commander of the British Land Forces during the drive up the spine of Italy and the assault and final storming of Monte Cassino, the last bastion before Rome. The General gave a splendid talk delivered in a free and easy, pulling-no-punches style with a lot of body language which included placing his bottom on the edge of a table and twisting and untwisting his long legs when the battle got hot. At first I thought he was bursting for a pee but as time went on I reckoned it was just a mannerism. He spoke at each subsequent course and still twisted up his legs, so I was reassured.

But when he began to lampoon the air bombardment of the German positions at Monte Cassino and really slated the bombing force – which incidentally had been the USAF – I began to get hot under the collar. He had a point to make: the bombing had not been as accurate as it could have been. Agreed – but the message he was putting across was that it had been useless and a hindrance to our ground forces. Moral: bombing in tactical support of land forces is a waste of time, so don't do it. I glanced at my RAF team and they didn't look happy. I decided to wait for question-time.

We finished our coffee, wiped the biscuit crumbs off our uniforms and took our seats again. The Commandant put the first question. I stood up next. 'Could the General explain more fully in what way he considered the very concentrated bombing attacks on the German defences at Monte Cassino to have been a failure?'

Horrocks stopped leg twisting. He walked to the edge of the rostrum. 'Because they were damned inaccurate. They were all over the place. They did far more damage to our own ground forces than to the enemy. In my experience they usually do!' He threw out this last charge on a note of contempt. The audience began to fidget.

'But, sir,' I went on, 'wasn't Monte Cassino virtually a pile of rubble and weren't the German defences demolished when your ground forces took the place? It was, I would have thought, a good example of the effect of saturation pattern bombing.'

'Pattern bombing my foot!' The General was beginning to splutter. I was in trouble, I reckoned. 'It was just bloody bad bombing! Yes,' he barked 'the place was a shambles when we finally took it. But the enemy had evacuated it BEFORE these last strikes took place. And the Air Commander didn't know he was bombing a deserted target! What a waste of effort! Where was the communication between the air and the ground? There wasn't any! Disgraceful – wasted effort – pattern bombing!'

He strode back to the podium and looked balefully around his audience. The RAF looked unhappy, the Army looked smug and the Navy smiled and made notes on their pads. I was glad when Kaye Edden wound it up, thanking the General for a stimulating and 'thought-provoking' presentation, shot his cuffs, shook the General's hand and led him out of the hall. Perhaps I imagined it but as Kaye Edden passed me, I thought he gave me a wink. Nevertheless, I ordered a large gin and tonic before lunch.

General Horrocks made no mention whatsoever of the USAF air strikes when he gave his repeat performance during the following course.

HOME AGAIN

I spent every other weekend at home. I was becoming aware that Nan might be drinking too much. There was a bottle or two of whisky in the larder whenever I was home and the 'off-licence' grocer's bills were becoming heavier and heavier. Not that I begrudged her her cigarettes and liquor. She had virtually no income of her own. She was running a family of three during term-time and five during the holidays. But my pay as a Group Captain, even with the RAF allowance towards education and the standard rent for my accommodation – which fell short of what in fact I paid – barely met the cost of supporting the family. I received nothing from Eliza for Lin Mark I. I was in and out of overdraft with Lloyds Bank pretty frequently.

Just up the road, at the intersection of the route to Haywards Heath and the A22 to Uckfield, Lewes and Brighton stood a pub. A Sussex firm had recently marketed a fierce brew of cider under the name of 'Merrydown'. A wickedly deceptive drink, it went down smoothly and with no initial impact but suddenly it hit you; like scrumpy from the West Country. I pulled away from it but Nan took to it and was too often wobbly after a session in the pub. A bit further down the Haywards Heath road was the Army Intelligence Corps camp. The soldiers were not long in discovering the merits of 'Merrydown' and, when the pub closed and they reeled back to their barracks, their obscenities and vomitings disturbed our evenings. After a group had invaded our garden and fallen over the ha-ha, I phoned the CO who came and saw me. He agreed to ask the publican to limit the sale of 'Merrydown' to no more than one pint per person, an undertaking that was honoured more in the breach than in the observance, if the continued antics of the Army in retreat were anything to go by.

At some time during this period of our family life in Sussex we built a punt, or rather a half-punt, on similar lines to the one in which Maurice, Peter and I first put to sea during the Swanage days. It was about six feet long with a centre thwart and had two single paddles. Representing a family effort, it was christened 'Doncyrapalinto' (*Don*ald, Nan*cy*, *Ra*nald, *Pa*ddy, *Lin*dsay and *To*ddle, as Pooh was called at that time). It was launched on Piltdown pond with the ceremonial breaking of a bottle of lemonade and the honking of horns by the owners of the cars which parked most sunny afternoons facing the water with their elderly owners either dozing in the seats or slumbering in deckchairs by the water's edge. It was a great success.

One Saturday evening, Nan and I talked over a wide spectrum of subjects, not all concerned with the welfare and future of the family. I remember the log fire and Nan, curled up like a cat on the sofa, her long shapely legs tucked up under her bottom and the inevitable bottle on the table. We spoke of our future: we agreed not to fix a deadline nor to pledge each other to a lasting relationship. We were both too independent yet in need of each other. We had my children at heart. I didn't realise then just how much they had become an essential part of her life. We talked about religion and its part in my children's upbringing. Nan had no time for the church, judging its ministers men of closed minds, brainwashed by theological college into accepting without question all that was written in the Scriptures. I was at that time uncertain as to what I believed. My experience on the freezing march across Germany in January 1945 when I was convinced we were accompanied by someone walking in the shade of the forests lining the route, who seemed to beckon and encourage, was still a vivid memory. I had long lost the teenage euphoria of the high church, the magnificent choral seduction of my schooldays at Hurstpierpoint. As a half-starved prisoner-of-war, bodily needs had been obsessive to the exclusion of anything else. Nan and I compromised. We agreed that, as Ranald and Paddy were taken to church each Sunday when at school, we would not compel them to attend church during the holidays. We decided that as a family we would attend the Easter and Christmas services.

In the event, after I had left the family in her exclusive care and gone to Moscow, Nan reneged and on one Christmas sent the three of them off alone to the nearest Church of England service while she combined a morning's boozing with old friends who dropped in while cooking a much-belated Christmas lunch. Ranald, Paddy and Lindsay returned, exhausted and hungry, to what Paddy described – much later – as a monstrous travesty of Christmas.

CHAPTER FORTY-NINE

Stories and Visits

T he Mess occupied the superb and elegant Latimer House. I remember with affection and admiration the Mess Secretary, Bob Grimley, a retired Major, who was the epicentre of all that was gracious, nay even luxurious, in our domestic lifestyle. He was always helpful yet ever ready to pounce should the staff fall short of his high standards. There were WRACs who served behind the bar, supervised by Bob but commanded by a young WRAC officer whom I shall call 'Captain WRAC'. Small, dark haired and physically well endowed, with brown, deep-seated eyes, she had a certain 'come hither' charm attracting a coterie of students and Directing Staff. I didn't pay her much attention. For several months Captain WRAC had sniped at me, always observing the rules of address to a senior officer. 'I believe you had a rough ride in this morning's session – Sir?' 'We enjoyed watching you running all over the field during the cricket match – Sir.' I had been press-ganged into taking part in the Directing Staff versus the course, an annual cricket match. Not having played since my prep school, I made a complete ass of myself as a fielder. I did, however, score 12 when I went in to bat! Captain WRAC became a pest; like a fly that won't let you alone when walking in a wood, she was buzzing me all too often. I had had enough ....

Following a Mess dinner, when good food, wine and port had loosened tongues and released constraints, I moved with a few of my team into the bar. Captain WRAC was there with a small group of admirers. I moved across the bar from them and we ordered whisky. The annual cocktail party was shortly to take place when DS and students and the permanent staff, together with their ladies, would be the guests of Kaye Edden and his charming wife. Local residents friendly towards the Joint Services Staff College, together with the appropriate Service senior officers, were on the invitation lists. Somehow Captain WRAC manoeuvred along the bar towards my group. Then she was next to me. She said something like 'Hello, sir, are you enjoying yourself?' I said yes I was and waited for it. 'I expect you are inviting a lovely girl to the cocktail party – Sir?' Something snapped inside me ... 'Oh no,' I replied, smiling. 'You see I'm a homosexual!' I had no more trouble from her for the rest of the tour at Latimer.

Senior ranking officers, freed from the shackles of their Naval, Army or RAF duties for a blessed six months, often let themselves go in a manner which we as their benign overseers truly delighted in. Two gems which I remember were:

> 'Tornadoes are flying around at 200 feet at night over West Germany and in four years' time they'll be able to see where they are going ...'

> 'We must stamp out pacifism.'

During my tour as SDS (Air), the Directing Staff were encouraged to spend a week or so of our breaks visiting NATO establishments in Europe, at the MOD's expense. My first visit was as an 'observer' for an exercise in the US sector of what, I assume, was a reconstituted Maginot Line in Western Germany. The second was to an obscure diplomatic-cum-administrative unit in Izmir in Turkey.

My companion on the visit to Germany was a Naval Commander called Henry. After a stormy crossing of the English Channel, we reached our destination and were met by two GIs with a jeep. We were told to get in the back. There was precious little room for our bags. The GIs chewed gum and drove far too fast to a guardroom at the edge of a barbed-wire enclosure with US Army notices saying, STOP! WHO ARE YOU? DOCUMENTS! WE ARE FULLY ARMED! A warm welcome! We were led to a bunker, one of many built into a hillside. We were shown bunk beds and told to take our pick. I asked for the Commanding Officer. No one knew where or who he was. However, we were shown where to eat, which we did fairly early, but totally ignored by the crowded, noisy and evidently hungry US Army personnel. We dossed down in our bunker and I was on the verge of sleep when a loud voice woke me. 'Who the goddam Hell are these guys?' A hushed voice answered, 'They're British observers, General. They came in today.' 'Why the Hell haven't I been told? Tell 'em to report to me tomorrow. I need to hit the sack!'

Throughout the night there had been strident sounds of drunken GIs coming home to roost. After a high-speed breakfast we sought the RAF liaison officer. A fussed, chain-smoking man, he had a sort of schedule for our visit but had not received any notice of our arrival time and had taken a 'lot of flak' from the General. Eventually, a junior US Army officer produced a brief with a 'C' on the first page and gave a perfunctory, standard resumé of the exercise – which made no sense to either of us. As a mission it was a complete waste of time and money.

My visit to Izmir was well planned and properly managed. I went alone, flying by civil airline to Istanbul, where I stopped overnight in a very comfortable hotel, and then on by internal feeder airline direct to Izmir, a flight of about an hour and a half.

The UK presence in this small NATO enclave was an Army Major with a few other ranks. There was an American Colonel and a Turkish officer who spoke some English and wheezed asthmatically. The weather was sultry and the temperature in the eighties. My accommodation was in the only hotel of any respectability in the town. I was invited to join the Major and his wife for supper in a local restaurant. Shortly after I had washed and shaved next morning, the earthquake struck. It was relatively low on the Richter scale but as I moved towards my wardrobe I was suddenly hurled back against the wall. The whole world seemed to be shaking: my first reaction was that I was having a fit or a stroke but there were rumbles outside and cries in the street. Next I was hurled forward against the wardrobe to which I clung until the shock abated. I felt very frightened. Then the world, my solid world, stood still again. I walked across the room: I put on my uniform and went into the passage. An old woman in black, possibly a cleaner, was on her hands and knees, moaning and praying. There was little damage to Izmir. I had my meeting with the Major who seemed quite unmoved by the shock in the night. 'Fairly regular occurrence, Sir,' was his comment. Oh well!

The Commandant had been notified that I was earmarked as the new Air Attaché in Moscow with effect from April 1956; it was then the summer of 1955. I was required to be relieved of my post in late November in order to undergo a two-month course of indoctrination with the Directorate of Air Intelligence and the Foreign Office before embarking for my new assignment. Kaye Edden saw me on my return and said how sorry he was at my going. He was complimentary about my service and invited me to dinner in his house at the end of the course. I told my colleagues I was leaving and was quite moved by their obvious disappointment.

The emblem of the Joint Services Staff College was a cormorant, representing a creature equally at home on the sea, on land and in the air. The Cormorant Club, which all those who served at Latimer were entitled to join, has remained true to its members. The journal lies on my desk beside me as I write and, peering haughtily down its long beak, sits the silver model on its base: my reward for serving on the Directing Staff. Its wings are spread and it beckons me to get going ....

CHAPTER FIFTY

Preparing for Moscow

The next few weeks were spent helping Nan to relocate for my absence in Moscow. Nan wanted a smaller, cosier home, so we looked around the area. She had made a number of friends and I was concerned that the move should not be too far away. We found a small gate lodge at the entry to the long drive into an estate dominated by Stroods House on the road between Maresfield and Crowborough. An agreement was proposed for a period of two years at a very modest rental for furnished accommodation which consisted of three main rooms downstairs, a kitchen and 'utility' room as a back extension with a bathroom and loo, and two small bedrooms upstairs. The idea was to have a double bunk in one of the downstairs rooms for Ranald and Paddy while Nan and Lin would sleep upstairs. Lin Mk. I had already gone to a nursing training college in South London. I got the Air Ministry's okay to sign the agreement with the owners, and turned my attention to a month of indoctrination and briefing by the Directorate of Air Intelligence, the Foreign Office and whatever branch of Military Intelligence was concerned. I was, in effect, on my way to Moscow.

The administration, travel, passport and visa, advance finance and everything other than the actual intelligence-cum-diplomatic briefing were handled by a remarkable civil servant, one J.B. Hogan. JB, as he was called, together with a very competent staff, masterminded the entire management of every British air attaché worldwide. In his late forties, broad-beamed and solid, JB sat enshrined in his mahogany, well-padded chair behind a huge desk just opposite the Cenotaph in Whitehall Gardens. Unruffled and absolutely foot-sure, he ruled the likes of us most competently and with understanding and immense wisdom. To me he represented the best of the Civil Service. Knowing my domestic situation, he asked to meet Nan which was no problem as he lived with his wife and ailing son near Chichester in Sussex. He called on us in Maresfield one weekend and undertook to look after the service aspects of the family, should Nan ever need help during my absence. 'Just give me a ring in my office,' he said. That was typical of JB.

We lunched together in the RAF Club. There he sat tucking into his steak and onions, his napkin stuck into his collar and his deep, soft Cockney tones telling me many things about my tour in Moscow which were of great value. I knew he liked a glass of port with his coffee, so we repaired to the Cowdray Room where he lolled in a deep chair, belched contentedly and smiled his thanks. I chartered a taxi and he sped off up Piccadilly to his office in Whitehall Gardens. He was a good friend even long after he had guided me through my tour in Moscow. His son died, and he and his wife were never the same. Unsung and unrewarded, he was possibly the strongest and most loyal link between Whitehall and the men of the RAF who served in British Embassies, particularly those behind the Iron Curtain.

I had been in communication with the current Air Attaché, Air Commodore Peter Donkin who had been a year senior to me at Cranwell. His letters had been much to the point. He told me I would need a good quality dinner service for twelve and appropriate cutlery for my dining room . There was, he wrote, a large quantity of tinned foods and other things in the fridge and the larder which he would sell to me when we had taken stock of what he had to hand over. Fair enough.

The lease of Maresfield Close was not due to expire for three months after my departure, when the tenancy of Stroods Lodge, Herons Ghyll, Uckfield, East Sussex, would commence. I had reservations about leaving Nan and the family to make the move on their own, but she was content enough and, with the help of local friends, it apparently went smoothly enough.

My briefing began with a 'lecture' from a Secretary in the Foreign Office who made it very clear that he had more important things to do than tell me how to comport myself in diplomatic surroundings. I heard him out: he was twice interrupted by a messenger who handed him something written on a notepad and even more frequently by phone calls. I was glad when the briefing was over. Next I was instructed to report to an office situated near Regents Park. I was kept waiting in a lobby for twenty minutes before the man at the desk invited me to go down the corridor to Room whatever. Seated behind a desk was one of the loveliest women I have ever seen. Well dressed, beautifully groomed and with the palest of blue eyes, she smiled and offered me a seat. There were no preliminaries.

'Good afternoon, Air Commodore. You are going to Moscow unac- companied and unattached. How do you feel about living celibate for two years?' Had this come from a man, I could have accepted it without embarrassment but, looking at this lovely young woman poised behind her desk with her pencil tapping on her blotter, I was woefully disadvantaged. But I took her on. 'As you probably know,' I replied, 'I was a POW in Germany for four and a half years.' I was ready for the next one. 'Have you ever had a homosexual relationship?' I managed a smile. 'No, never.'

She nodded and rifled through some papers in a file. There was a long silence, then she looked me very straight in the face. 'You are an attractive man. You are very likely to need sex while you are in Moscow. I'm sure you've thought about that.' She stood up and moved from behind her desk with her hand outstretched. I rose and we shook hands. 'Just be careful,' she said, opening the door, 'Please be very careful.' There was something almost maternal in her farewell. I desperately wanted to kiss her. She was so bloody lovely. Instead I said 'Thank you, I will' and hurried out. I pulled myself together, consulted my notebook and looked for the remaining room on my visiting schedule. According to my notes, this was to be a briefing on electronic and radio interception. It was just that. Two men in shirtsleeves received me: one did the talking, the other produced gadgets. They were practical, factual and the antithesis of the lovely lady I had just left. We discussed 'bugs' and a whole range of electronic listening devices known to be used by the Soviets. I was much impressed with the extent to which the KGB had evidently developed eavesdropping on all the missions except those from within the Soviet bloc – and who knows whether or not they too were bugged. The message came across loud and clear. Keep your mouth shut indoors, don't trust your Russian domestic staff, your chauffeur or any guide in a museum, church or ancient monument. In short, trust nobody.

I pondered this as I made my way back to the Directorate of Air Intelligence (DAI) with whom I was spending a week being briefed on Soviet aircraft recognition, surface-to-air missiles (SAM) and other professional matters which were clearly important to my mandate as the senior air adviser to our Ambassador in Moscow. I was to be a spy in disguise, with diplomatic immunity. Like my father in Baku over forty years earlier, I would be suspect.

I joined a team which consisted of five Air Attachés-designate escorted by two extremely able and deeply committed members of the Civil Service element of DAI. We travelled by train to ICI in Billingham where we were shown what we needed of the huge chemical complex, dined luxuriously and then sent on to an iron foundry in Wales, where we watched red-hot, molten metal pour forth down a channel on the very edge of which stood hard-faced men in overalls and tin hats, nonchalantly stirring the boiling mass as it hissed past them. A false move and they would have fallen in. I didn't much care for it.

Then back to London – trotting up and down the train corridor identifying likely landing areas for airborne forces for all the world like train-spotting schoolkids – and a week or more working with the Directorate of Air Intelligence and I was judged sufficiently informed, forewarned and forearmed to be allowed home to Maresfield for a few weeks before my departure for Moscow in April 1956.

CHAPTER FIFTY-ONE

Moscow: First Impressions

Packed, with my heavy luggage, crockery, pictures, cutlery and an assortment of bits and pieces which Nan had advised me to send out by ALTRANSPORT, a lumbering Anglo-Russian company, I was seen off on the evening train from Liverpool Street station by two of JB's staff – a kind gesture. The press were present: *The Times* and *The Telegraph* of the following day had a short piece about the new British Air Attaché and a shot of me in a trilby hat and a raincoat smiling out of a first-class carriage on the boat train to Ostend. There was also a bit about my background and Scottish title. As usual they spelt my name wrongly in both papers.

My connection with the train to West Berlin was made without hassle and I settled down in my traditionally 'continental' buffet seat, ate good meals and drank good beer until the great steam locomotive gave its final hoot and pulled to a stop. West Berlin. On the platform was the Group Captain from the staff of the quadripartite Control Commission, accompanied by a grey-haired man, a Squadron Leader from Donkin's staff, known as Dennis, who was to accompany me to Moscow. We were driven first to an RAF headquarters where I was welcomed by a Wing Commander who gave me a personal message from home, a series of forms to sign and a special telegram from JB. We were very well cared for by the Group Captain and his wife overnight and on the morrow the Group Captain, Dennis and I were driven through the Brandenburg Gate into the shambles of East Berlin to the Ost-Bahnhof and the awaiting train to Moscow.

I cannot describe the mixture of excitement and apprehension. The atmosphere, once we had entered East Berlin, was tense. Escorted by a posse of East German guards on motorcycles, we were virtually herded onto the train lock, stock and barrel while our host, the Group Captain, looking strangely incongruous in his RAF uniform, saluted formally as the great ten-coach train pulled out for its destination, Moscow.

Dennis and I had a double-berth sleeper to ourselves: he offered to take the top bunk. We had been advised to go into the restaurant car by six o'clock before provisions and service petered out. So we did and were treated to a mediocre meal, a vicious Russian wine and lukewarm coffee. Our waitress was dilatory, bloody-minded and elephantine. I suspect she had been drinking and I got a good slop of borscht onto my lap on which I luckily had my napkin. She was to be our guardian for the remainder of the journey and only softened when I tried out my Russian on her in the loo. This happened when she broke in when the coaches were being changed to the new rail gauge at the Polish–Russian frontier at Brest-Litovsk. I was on the throne and she laughed at my discomfiture. Dennis and I had decided to remain on board as we were both tired, so we did not see the unique early-morning operation in which the locomotives move into sidings, the eastern one backing up to pull the coaches which have been hoisted by hydraulic rail-borne ramps over the Soviet frontier and then bolted onto the bogeys of the new gauge. An hour or so later the operation was completed and we pulled away. Late that afternoon we reached the suburbs of Moscow and then – with much ceremonious tooting – we rolled to a stop in the capital of the Union of Soviet Socialist Republics. I remember feeling excited but Dennis was silent as he leaned out of the window, opened the door and stepped onto the platform. I followed.

I knew who they were at once. Standing slightly apart from the noisy throng pouring from the train and being greeted by those waiting, there were two men: one tall and thin, wearing a heavy overcoat and battered trilby hat, his face set in a frown and looking slightly away from us, Peter Donkin. I recognised him from our time together at Cranwell twenty-four years back. His companion was younger, good looking and in a duffel coat and an astrakhan hat. Dennis said 'There they are' and seemed to stiffen. Then Donkin said something to his companion, who nodded and came quickly towards us. He was John Deverill, the senior of the three Assistant Air Attachés and also a Squadron Leader. Donkin remained where he was, now looking at us but giving no sign of greeting, let alone coming forward to meet me.

Bloody Hell, I thought, two can play at this game. Our hand luggage lay around us. I had my briefcase in my hand. Dennis went to the rear of the train where I had a wardrobe trunk in the luggage wagon, so I turned my back on Donkin and began a conversation with Deverill. It was several minutes before Dennis rejoined us, accompanied by a padded and muffled female porter with a barrow containing my trunk among other pieces of luggage. We followed them down the platform and I stopped in front of Donkin. He nodded, extended a weak handshake, spoke sharply to Dennis about bringing my luggage to 'the flat' and then strode off ahead of us to the barrier where a flaccid Russian whom he addressed as Misha was waiting.

Donkin and I had barely exchanged a word by the time Misha, his chauffeur, had opened the rear doors of a black Humber Snipe into which he climbed, followed by me. Misha, breathing noisily, drove off and the two of us in the back sat silently side by side as the city of Moscow, its inhabitants still clothed against the savage winter which was barely breaking into spring, slid speedily past.

What I have related may seem trivial, but for months I had lived in anticipation of arriving in Moscow, the Russian city in which my grandfather had contracted typhoid and in which my father had met my mother. So, possibly my sense of anticlimax can be excused. Rather than try to break through this barrier of silence with the man from whom I was to take over, I too remained mute and observed the people, the streets, the buildings and the traffic – very little traffic – as Misha drove us to the flat in Skatertny Peryulok (Carpet Lane) which was to be my home for the next two and a half years.

It had indeed been a savage winter, the severest for a long time. People had passed out from hypothermia while crossing the broad boulevard of Sadovaya, the 'Park Lane' of Moscow. I saw pedestrians barely recognisable as human beings in all the clothes, wraps and clouts they wore, seeming like convalescents from long illnesses so drawn and pale were their faces. They shuffled along the sidewalks which were surprisingly free of snow while slush still remained in the gutters and breaking ice lay on the city streets, making Misha fidget nervously as he swept down Gorky Street and drew into the little sidestreet where presumably carpets had been fashioned or sold in the days of the Tsar.

We stopped outside a three-storey block of flats with a policeman in a sentry box alongside the entrance. Misha handled my baggage and followed Donkin and me up a flight of stone stairs to a first-floor flat. Misha took off his fur hat, looked utterly miserable as he deposited my baggage in the hall, and left. I then met Klava, my cook and friend to be. Dear Klava – a superb cook, a lovely person in her forties with the face of a Botticelli angel and straight, blonde hair drawn back into a bun – greeting me warmly and, so like Yevgenia Vladimirovna of Asnières, wiping her hands on her apron before taking mine in both of hers. We made friends from that very moment. Donkin had gone into the flat and I was left to follow him.

Strange man. Decorated for outstanding leadership in the air, he seemed desperately impatient to be out of this diplomatic mission. Klava gave him a sidelong look when he arrived. Later I grew to recognise this as doubt about the reaction of the man. Would he smile or would he scowl? No one ever knew. She served an excellent meal, cleared it away and took her leave. Donkin had shown me over the flat, which consisted of a sizeable drawing room leading into a small study which in turn gave into a large dining room with a table for twelve places. All these rooms had windows which overlooked the street. There was a central corridor through the flat: on the other side were two small bedrooms, the kitchen, a bathroom and loo, and the master bedroom at the very end. The whole was adequately furnished with decoration and drapes very much à la Ministry of Works. Whitehall had crept into Moscow. But it was spacious and warm.

We sat in the study and drank whisky. Donkin had relaxed somewhat over the meal and had given me a useful introduction to the personalities I would be working with in the Embassy. I let him make the running and was impressed by what he said, his deep, rather soft voice contrasting with his almost hostile look. He spoke of Sir William Hayter, the Ambassador (H.E. – His Excellency) and Lady Hayter; made some pithy remarks about other members of the Embassy staff and then turned to his own team.

John Deverill spoke good Russian, was unmarried and much sought after by the many young secretaries among the Diplomatic Corps. He was, observed Donkin, too prone to become involved with students from Moscow University and had to be watched lest he compromised himself. He had a 'guardian' in the Consular section of the Embassy: Daphne Park – now Baroness Park of Monmouth. Daphne was a plump, highly intelligent person who exercised a degree of maternal restraint over John: they were close friends and she paid us the great compliment of travelling only with the RAF. Her Russian was excellent: she was a most refreshing companion. But I should keep an eye on John all the same. Donkin confirmed my impression of Dennis as being a man of balance and stead-fast loyalty whose integrity and intelligence were invaluable – something about 'still waters running deep'.

The junior Assistant Air Attaché was a Flight Lieutenant, Peter Lewis, from the Technical Branch. Donkin hesitated for a while, looking down at the whisky glass in his hand – then: 'He has a lot of potential but he is very unsure of himself. I'll leave it to you to do what you can. He and I don't relate very well.' We left it at that. There was a youngish Warrant Officer to deal with the secretarial side of the office and a communal Embassy typing pool which was understaffed and overworked.

Donkin stretched his long legs, offered me another whisky, poured himself a freshener and pointed to the ceiling. 'Every building occupied by Western diplomats or their staff is probably bugged.' He looked hard at me. 'Never forget that! We've had this place swept by the electronic boys from London and their verdict is negative. But don't accept that. Just don't talk shop to anyone anywhere except out of doors.' He drank. 'It's bloody awful living like this month after month for two or more years. I hate these people and their regime. Thank God I shall be gone in a few days.' That was all he ever said to me about his personal feelings though I shared his flat for the better part of a week before he left for Helsinki to fly home to rejoin his wife and two daughters who had gone ahead of him the day before I had arrived.

The next morning I was presented to Sir William Hayter. In William Hayter and Patrick Reilly, his successor, I found two men who not only commanded my respect and admiration for the manner in which they represented the United Kingdom during the worst period of the Cold War but also for their warmth and friendship to me who – without a wife and hostess – was faced with a formidable task of entertainment often long into the night and the full day of 'business' to follow.

Donkin and I were received by HE in his office in the British Embassy, a well-designed three-storey building originally built for a tea magnate, standing back in a courtyard with a wrought-iron fence and main gate on the embankment of the Moskva river almost opposite the Kremlin. A guard in a sentry box was on duty outside the gate twenty-four hours a day. After I had metaphorically presented my credentials, we drank a glass of sherry and discussed East-West relations. Tall, well proportioned and with a strong face, Sir William spoke in simple direct terms. And he listened. Later I was to meet another British ambassador who was known as 'Walkie-Talkie' for reasons which immediately became obvious. HE was joined by Lady Hayter, Iris, who had a vague charm which concealed a shrewd mind. She was a close friend of the wife of 'Chip' Bohlen, the US Ambassador, whom the Kremlin hated and feared.

I was invited to a simple lunch for the next day. Donkin and I took our leave. He opened the door of his office. A rich odour of tobacco smoke greeted us. I was a smoker then and recognised Gauloises. A sad-looking man wearing glasses, with a cigarette in a long holder, stood up as we came in. This was the Assistant Military Attaché, a Major who, I learned subsequently, had been offered sanctuary by Donkin because working with the Military Attaché in the same office had been driving him to drink. Donkin moved to his own desk, the Major excused himself and left, and then Donkin explained. Seemingly the Military Attaché, a very small, eccentric and totally unpredictable Brigadier was, to use Donkin's words, 'as mad as a March hare!' The Major, who had a background of nervous collapses due to a broken marriage, had a first-class brain which the Brigadier did not. Donkin had taken him in, Gauloises and all. So that was to be my lot!

We visited the office of the three Assistant Air Attachés and I took special interest in the Flight Lieutenant, Peter Lewis. It was immediately apparent that he was terrified of Donkin, and it was not until he and I were alone that I found what I was looking for, a very intelligent and highly technical mind, a low-key but friendly and often amusing personality and, above all, an extremely shrewd appreciation of the whole abysmal trough of so-called International Relations. We called on the Military Attaché, who looked up from his desk, eyes darting hither and thither, and quacked like a duck. 'You see what I mean,' said Donkin as we left.

Next was the Naval Attaché, a Captain with an excellent War record and a holder of the Distinguished Service Cross and Bar. Adrian Northey was a big man, somewhat portly and a shade deferential, addressing me as 'Sir' when we were introduced. Donkin didn't really hit it off with him and had warned me that he tended to come 'the Senior Service' and to recommend that all of us should troop in together at National Day functions or propose when we should all wear what. I was also warned that his wife, Betty, would try to take over and organise my social activities. Beware, said Donkin. They detested each other.

We met the Secretariat, the people who did all the hard work, and Dick Slater, Head of Chancery. He and his wife Barbara were to become firm friends. Many years later we discovered that Barbara and I were related and Dick was related to my second wife, Lois, whom I married in 1973. From the Secretariat we moved through to the Consular Department, and thence to a small office off the courtyard where a sinister official of Greek parentage, married to a Russian, headed the Soviet-controlled administrative functions of the Embassy – heating, lighting, telephone exchange, cars, chauffeurs, cooks, maids and mail deliveries. His name was Kostaki and the organisation he represented was BUROBIN, the acknowledged KGB cell in every embassy from west of the Iron Curtain and probably from inside it as well. Kostaki was an enigma: he knew far too much and had almost certainly a deep involvement in the Vassall affair and, subsequently, in the compromising of my Warrant Officer. But I am jumping ahead.

John Deverill, Dennis, Peter and I saw Mike Donkin off on the Aeroflot flight from Vnukovo Airport. Donkin looked morose and almost ill. I tried to thank him for his help but he didn't appear to take it in. A disillusioned man, he boarded the aircraft and somehow managed a smile and a wave before the door closed behind him and the plane began to taxi out for take-off.

Misha drove me and John back to Moscow. A new Misha who smiled and showed his dreadful teeth and no longer fidgeted behind the wheel but even hummed a little as we entered the new housing estate which was going up twenty-four hours a day on the western outskirts of the city. We arrived at the Embassy, where I asked John to accompany me round the small back garden with its tennis court and garages so that we could talk together. I foresaw problems with the Gauloise-smoking Major sharing my office and I needed advice and more background. John was very helpful; behind his outrageous good looks was a shrewd mind and a deep-rooted belief in the renaissance of a real Russia free from the despotic nihilism of the Communist state. He was sincere: like Donkin, he hated the 'system' but, unlike Donkin, he loved the people.

He unburdened himself as we strolled round the Embassy garden. He told me a lot I wanted to know about our standing as an RAF team in the diplomatic scheme of things and I was pleased to learn that, while Donkin had been regarded as an 'odd one', his professionalism and security had earned him high praise from HE as well as from his American and French colleagues. We discussed the main object of the RAF team's appointment – the provision of Intelligence about the Soviet Air Force, its capabilities, its future developments, its nuclear potential and the extent to which we, together with our American colleagues, could penetrate the security which our hosts had erected around almost all our movements.

The moment one of us left the Embassy we would be followed: if on foot then a 'goon' – I soon introduced the old POW term – would walk behind at a discrete distance. If by car, then the obvious KGB Pobeda, clean and shining, was astern.

John emphasised that the statutory forty kilometres radius from Moscow was the absolute limit of our travel without special permission from the OVS, the Department of External Relations – permission which was never in fact acknowledged positively, so that unless we were refused a request to make a journey outwith the limit we could assume we were free to go. And of course, unless Kostaki of BUROBIN had booked our accommodation along the way, we knew that the trip was a non-starter.

John and I returned to the Embassy, closed up our offices and had Misha drive us back to my flat for the evening. We talked well into the night, carefully avoiding shop but getting to know each other. I hoped that I could depend on John for much of what I had to do and I needed to know the man. He left some time after midnight and as I saw him out at the ground floor the sentry was on his phone. I was beginning to get used to another, more exciting form of imprisonment.

Protocol demanded that all newcomers of senior rank make formal calls on their opposite numbers in the missions to which their government was accredited. In my case the only outsider was East Germany. In the case of the United States, it was China. But by common consent this round of tedious and time-consuming alcohol-swilling was not expected to begin until the new arrival had spent a fortnight sorting himself out and settling into his new surroundings. I used the first two weeks getting to know my colleagues in the Embassy and finding my way around Moscow either on my own or with John.

So much has been written about Moscow, Gorky Street, the Kremlin, St Basil's Cathedral and Red Square that I have no intention of competing with Thomas Cook, Intourist or any other tourist guide. I spent two and a half years in Moscow. I discovered hidden wonders in this urban contradiction of the very, very old and the horribly new. I loved the Moscow which lay beneath the foundations of the concrete, stereotypical five-storey blocks of flats which disintegrated ten years after they were erected. I loved the simplistic philosophy of the Russians which emerged, often in drink, from beneath the brainwashed exterior of the Soviet 'comrade'. I loved the deep, sadly hidden belief in God which moved as a spiritual groundswell among the older people, including Klava. I loved Moscow.

The Cold War persisted. Anthony Eden was Prime Minister and leader of a Tory government in Westminster. The Soviet Union, with its KGB tentacles well established throughout the 'Free World', was hellbent on becoming the political and ideological leader. Communism was being insinuated with success into India, Korea and other countries whose constitutions were none too stable. Where the advance of the Soviet dose of medicine was rejected, force was often used and bloody civil war was cynically planned as in Afghanistan; while the newly appointed President of Cuba, Fidel Castro, bowed to Moscow in exchange for an offer of nuclear missiles and declared Cuba a Communist state. Others followed, seeing the Soviet Union as the rising star.

Nikita Krushchev, the volatile First Secretary of the Communist Party, was a man of the people. Of peasant stock, he spoke execrable Russian, was usually well into his vodka and had as his back-up group Bulganin and the sly Armenian, Mikoyan, whom Eden in Westminster never understood.

The Diplomatic Corps in Moscow was fairly clearly defined politically: the United Kingdom, the United States, France, Holland, Norway, Sweden, Canada and Australasia were to be expected to work together and present a common front against the Kremlin's most arrogant proposals. India was pro-Communist but still 'played squash' with the West.

Indeed the Indian Military Attaché was a friend of mine and a mite better than me at squash! I was beginning to put on weight.

The Poles were in a parlous situation. Overrun and virtually annexed by the Soviet Union, their historic arch-enemy, they were inevitably schizoid in their international relations. I established an abiding and warm friendship with the Polish Military Attaché, whom I respected, and we both observed the necessary cautions throughout our contact. I found myself on less sure ground with the Finnish Military Attaché who, with a Russian wife, would too often call on me. Also, he was wont to offer somewhat spurious counsel as, for example, during the Suez Crisis when we were in diplomatic trouble. I soon discovered which side he was on: it wasn't ours.

So, when my fortnight's grace was over, I had my staff set up a programme of formal visits to my *chers collègues*. I survived I am glad to say without defeat, though my call on the Yugoslavian Military and Air Attachés – with its accompaniment of slivovitz – very nearly laid me out. Somehow I managed to retrieve my service cap and gloves, say how grateful I was for their hospitality and ease none too gracefully into the back of my car for Misha to drive me home. The Yugoslavs who saw me off – in more senses than one – appeared completely sober. I wonder whether my drink had been laced.

There was a paradox in that a Communist state, with its denial of religious belief, took so much care in restoring and maintaining so many of the old, disused churches. Quite apart from national tourist attractions such as the multi-coloured St Basil's in Red Square, throughout the Soviet Union great care was being paid to the maintenance and beauty of churches insofar as their exteriors were concerned. True, many of them were closed to the public, either being used as warehouses or for small business enterprises, but they were cherished as works of architecture and beauty. A few were open for worship, particularly the better-known such as the monastery of Zagorsk some fifty miles north-east of Moscow and the great co-cathedral in Moscow itself. But it was the 'Old Believers' who worshipped and always, it seemed, the Metropolitan had a magnificent bass voice and the congregation sang the responses in sympathetic harmony. A well-attended Russian Orthodox service is to me the ideal form of communal worship, but I admit it is the music that enthrals me.

While the Soviet Union's conduct of external affairs was offensive to the West, with its overt endeavour to hold the nuclear clout over the head of the USA in particular, there was of course a defensive element. Russian internal affairs were undergoing a fundamental change when I arrived in Moscow in March 1956. Krushchev, at the recent Party Congress, had pronounced a denunciation of Comrade Stalin. He, Krushchev, exposed the dead leader's tyranny, genocide and self-aggrandisement. The 'Cult of

Personality' was out! So was the legacy of Stalin. His embalmed body was removed from the mausoleum under the wall of the Kremlin: he was publicly reviled in *Pravda* and his statues were demolished throughout the Soviet Union. Krushchev preached a new form of freedom, freedom to speak in open forum.

The students in the University on the hill overlooking the city were the first to test out this freedom as, world over, students will. They were obliged to put their questions in writing to the professor or lecturer who was in charge of the session. Only those which were uncontroversial were accepted. The students objected violently and there were stormy scenes within the precincts of the University. Krushchev had allowed the safety valve to open too far. It was shut down and a number of students were expelled. We never knew what happened to them though John Deverill's contacts said they had been taken into custody. So much for freedom of speech.

The news from home was reassuring. Nan wrote excellent letters in which her literary skill, humour and depth of human understanding all came through. She and I had discussed how to minimise Lin's sense of loss at my going. As the youngest, while she still clung to Nan, she missed me and Nan worried. So a New Forest pony was bought at an auction in Lewes and 'Brownie' was corralled in a field lent to us by the family who farmed the estate down the lane. Being a stallion, he rampaged around and did his utmost to break through the fence to get at the mares until he was delivered to the vet and dealt with appropriately. But Lin and Brownie became friends and Ranald schooled him into a semblance of passive behaviour. Lindsay rode him across the forest and was happy in his company. Brownie and I never saw eye to eye.

It was time for me to host a dinner party. The problem was who was to be my hostess. Donkin had given me the gypsy's warning about the Naval Attaché's wife and her predatory social ambitions but it seemed to me both tactful and interesting to give the lady precedence in what was bound to be a long queue of hostesses during my tour of office. So I asked her and she accepted with grace: indeed she offered many useful suggestions and helped me to select my twelve guests in the best interests of protocol.

I had informed Klava of the occasion and the date. She inclined her head in the characteristic Russian token of agreement and asked were the guests *prostyye* (simple), *srednyye* (medium) or *bolshiye* (big/important). This was of importance since the standing of guests dictated the level of culinary effort she would put into the occasion. I told her *bolshiye* as I had in mind the French Military Attaché, who was a General, and his wife, and the American Air Attaché, Colonel Chuck Taylor, and his wife, together with a smattering of senior diplomats from other missions. I was reserving the top diplomatic echelon for later dinners when I had gained experience: this first one was a dress rehearsal and I needed a cast I knew.

My hostess, Betty, and Adrian arrived well in advance of the invitation time. We ran over the seating plan, he gave me several useful hints about the male guests and Betty offered to look after the one who tended to drink too much. In the event my first dinner party was a success. People arrived; Klava was confined to the kitchen; my daily maid, Tanya, an illiterate but attractive young woman, together with another helper imported by Klava, immaculate in black dresses and white aprons, ushered in my guests, and the party got off to a good start. Everybody spoke English, Chuck and his wife were on top form, and Betty was charming.

Klava served a magnificent meal, we drank champagne and ended with Klava's *grande finale* – a beautifully modelled swan made of meringue and ice-cream and laced with crème de menthe. The last guest left, the boozy one more or less under tow by Adrian, at midnight and I closed the shop having paid Klava, Tanya and the extra help. The following morning. I phoned Betty to thank her warmly. She said, 'Well done! You don't have anything to worry about.' She and I and Adrian became friends. But we hardly ever spoke of Mike Donkin. Something had gone badly wrong there.

Klava once asked me – we always spoke in Russian though I fancy she knew some English – 'What do you do in the British Embassy, Mr MacDonell?' What did I do? Obviously I could not tell her that I was concerned to discover as much as I could about the size, location and capabilities of the Soviet Air Force, and yet the question begged an answer. I pondered for a moment. Then I explained that in the Embassy there were men and women who had come to the Soviet Union to do what they could to understand the mutual problems of the East and the West; that Great Britain was an old and once powerful country; that we and the Soviet Union had fought together against Nazi Germany but that unhappily we no longer seemed to trust each other. I was here in Moscow to work for a better understanding between the Royal Air Force and the Soviet Air Force. Because I was an airman, I was the adviser to our Ambassador on all matters affecting our two air forces. I was proud to serve in Klava's country, a country in which I had been born before the Revolution. Klava had been seated in the kitchen while I spoke my piece. Not until I mentioned Baku, my birthplace, did she show any interest. Then she looked up sharply, stood up, smoothed her apron, and said, 'So you are a spy, Gospodin MacDonell?'

'No, Klava,' I replied. 'I am not a spy but the more our two countries know of each other's armed forces, the easier it will be for our governments to understand the importance of finding solutions to our problems without using force.' I spoke slowly because my Russian, though fair enough, was put to the test. Klava smiled slowly and said, 'You are a good diplomat, Gospodin MacDonell.' She then turned the conversation to the matter of my next dinner party, which was why we had been sitting at the kitchen table.

CHAPTER FIFTY-TWO

Sightseeing and Military Intelligence

I t was time to get travelling, as this was what yielded the most fruitful information about the Soviet Air Force, provided always that one's journey incorporated an air force or military base with a possibility of photography, in which context we had been instructed to be sensible and take no 'obvious risks'. This injunction was typically Whitehall in its off-loading of responsibility and ambiguity. I settled for an invitation from Chuck Taylor and his No. 2 to accompany them on a 'clean run' by rail which merely passed by a Soviet fighter base. This was in effect a dummy run for me which Chuck had set up to help me get started.

Our destination was Kharkov, a few hundred miles south of Moscow in the Ukraine. We booked a four-bunk compartment on the night train which suited us fine as our goon had a berth further down the coach. As I was to discover later, three male travellers overnight were often joined by a Soviet fellow traveller who, if he remained sober, was obviously there to keep an eye on us. But our fourth bunk was vacant and gave us the space we wanted for our bags, cameras and other paraphernalia. Hank, Chuck's No. 2, was a good companion with a fine war record in the Technical Branch of the USAF. Chuck was a Colonel in the best tradition of his service. He and I and his wife became close friends until his tour expired a year after my arrival. We slumbered on, though the train clanked and groaned and stopped, it seemed, at every station on the way. We woke and ate from provisions we had brought with us and the samovar lady in the corridor brought us piping hot tea. We were nearing the Soviet airfield beside the railway. Chuck and Hank had their cameras 'readied'. We slowed down as the airfield came in sight.

Then our compartment door was opened by a uniformed guard who asked us, none too convincingly, for our *bilety* (tickets). We at once recognised him as our goon. Chuck pretended not to understand and put down his camera. The man turned to me. I fumbled in my pockets and played dumb. Hank, camera at the sling, said in English – he had virtually no Russian – 'Toilet' and left the compartment.

The goon looked nonplussed. He made a move to follow Hank but by then I had my diplomatic pass and my ticket. He glanced at them, muttered something about cameras not being allowed in the Ukraine – which was rubbish – and then inspected Chuck's documents, which included some toilet paper and a receipt from the Moscow liquor store where we had bought our wine. By the time the charade was over, Hank had returned ostentatiously adjusting his flies. The goon left. Hank had got several good pictures of the air base from the toilet window. I admit I was impressed. Round One to Chuck and Hank.

It was pouring with rain when we reached Kharkov. We stood outside the station looking for a taxi but none came. People, hunched against the weather, slouched off carrying their baggage. Then a Pobeda stopped opposite us and the driver asked where we wanted to go. We gave him the name of the hotel which BUROBIN had booked for us – 'the best hotel in the town' – and climbed aboard. Chuck reckoned it wasn't a taxi: it had no meter and unusual registration plates. We arrived and checked in, and were handling our luggage when the driver came up to the desk. From the manner in which he spoke to the concierge and the length of time he spent with him, we came to the conclusion he was our local goon, though not the one we had with us on the train.

If our hotel was the best in the town, one speculates on the standard of the others. We received no service, the lift was not working, the toilets had neither seats nor paper – we always travelled well supplied with the latter – and our rooms had no keys. As was customary, we also had our passports with us which were impounded on arrival. Kharkov is, or was then, an attractive town full of historic and architectural interest with old battlements, several beautiful churches and a populace who looked healthier and less downtrodden than the people of Moscow. Possibly the terrible winter of 1955–56 had struck less harshly. The rain storm had passed and we wandered through the streets with the Pobeda never far behind. There were two occupants in the front seat. We were right: it was our 'taxi'!

Our plan was to spend the next day sightseeing as there was nothing of military interest in the place and then to take the late-evening train for which BUROBIN had reserved a four-berth sleeper, thus allowing us another view of the Soviet air base the following morning. We agreed that a good look would be enough, particularly as we were now clearly suspect.

So we returned to our hotel for an early supper and a good night's sleep. Soviet rail sleepers were even worse than those in the UK at that time.

Back in our hotel we went into the restaurant where a small band – two balalaikas and an accordion – were playing. Near the band sat several women of indeterminate age, brazenly made up and dressed in blouses and short skirts. They were the dancing partners for whom you paid a few roubles a dance, rather more for a drink and considerably more to go upstairs. We three agreed the last option was most definitely out.

We ordered our meal and Chuck chose a Georgian red wine which was very acceptable, although we had time to consume two bottles before our meal was served. However, it was a good one. On Chuck's advice we avoided brandy; they had a wont to lace it, he said. Instead we bought a bottle of Stolichnaya vodka unopened and sat smoking, replete and relaxed until Hank said he wanted to dance. Chuck and I didn't think it was a good idea but we had drunk a fair amount, so he said, 'Okay, but no funny stuff.' Hank chose his partner, at which the band really came to life and bashed out an old English dance tune.

Hank swayed and rocked to the rhythm while his partner, about half his size, struggled to follow. The music stopped and the couple crossed the floor to our table. She spoke no English so we made polite conversation in Russian. She was at least forty, drenched in some pungent scent and seemed nervous and fidgety, frequently looking across the restaurant. And there, as we should have expected, were seated our two goons. So Hank paid the lady her fee, thanked her, shook her hand which obviously embarrassed her and, with assumed gallantry, escorted her back to her table, waving a greeting to the goons as he passed. Good for Hank – we were scoring points.

Next morning we went to check out, to be told that the train on which we had been booked that evening had been cancelled. Our bookings had 'luckily' been changed to a much earlier and very popular one which was an express to Moscow. It left in mid-afternoon. All was in order; here were our passports and it was hoped we had enjoyed our stay in Kharkov. At first the import of this changed schedule didn't strike me and it was Hank who, when we had left the desk, said, 'That means we pass the air base at night during darkness.' And thus it was. Clever! There was a taxi waiting for us after an early lunch. Our goon helped us into the booking office and smiled, but not benignly. Score to date – one all.

CHAPTER FIFTY-THREE

Diplomatic Circles

Back in Moscow with no car to meet us, since we had been unable to get through to let the US Embassy know of our change of plan, we took a taxi and I was dropped off at our Embassy where I joined my team. A short report to the Directorate of Air Intelligence – with copies to Chuck (we always exchanged everything, including photos) – and to our Head of Chancery for information for HE, and then I went back to my flat.

Klava informed me that two men from BUROBIN had been in to check the wiring circuits which were 'due for inspection'. They had spent some time in the sitting room and in my bedroom. They had made some repairs but had reported that the system was now *vse v poryadke* – all in order. I smelt a very large rat. I thanked Klava, had a drink and went back to the Embassy where I discussed the situation with John who was working late. We agreed to inform HE the following morning.

The Ambassador got the message and sent a telegram in code, which was probably broken, to London and, as a result, I had two British electronic engineers as my guests within a week. They found the bugs but warned me that they were relatively unsophisticated: there might well be others of far more dangerous capabilities deeply hidden in the walls or ceiling. They repeated the Whitehall warning – don't talk shop to anyone in the flat – thanked me for my hospitality and took their leave. I drove them to Vnukovo Airport where their bulging cases – brought in under diplomatic immunity – were regarded by the baggage handlers with evident suspicion and disappeared into a separate area for, at the very least, an x-ray, though I would not myself trust the honour of our hosts to respect the immunity of all who travelled as diplomats. The Soviets were not easily fooled – certainly not the KGB.

For obvious reasons I shall not chronicle my exact service activities as Air Attaché. I don't care for the readiness with which those who held positions of security spew out, often profitably, their stories – warts and all – once the thirty-year embargo date has passed. Much has changed since I left Moscow in 1958. The Soviet Union has been dismembered into what is likely to become a copy of the United States of America for better or worse. But I foresee always the shadow of yet another revolution if economics, food distribution, prices, ethnic loyalties and the absence of central control by Moscow of this vast country cannot be handled effectively. Here at home in 1992, as I write of this fascinating period of my career in the RAF thirty-six years ago, my mind inevitably reacts to these momentous events.

The months passed. I became accustomed to the regime in this fascinating environment. I grew to know Moscow if not street by street at least in terms of places of historic interest. I was invited into the Kremlin where a museum housed treasures and artefacts from generations of khans and tsars. I drove up to the Lenin Hills overlooking the city where Moscow University, impertinent in its modernity, dominated the site. I shopped in GUM (General Universal Store) where you queued to choose your purchase, had it channelled to another department where it was priced and where you paid, and then moved again to a further one where you presented your receipt to have it packaged and pushed to you across the counter. One transaction could take up to half an hour or more.

I studied the people of Moscow, gloomy, silent and shuffling in the manner they were wont to during the long, bitter winter that they still remembered. Their eyes fell on me as I passed, looking at what I was wearing and especially at my shoes. Shoes were at a premium. There were several pairs on display in Gorky Street and I passed a group of young men looking at them and at the prices. 'That's three months' wages,' said one. 'They wouldn't last more than a year, and then what?' said another. They moved on. I saw few smiles and heard little laughter in the streets of Moscow.

Our work in the Embassy, mine in particular as the senior RAF adviser to HE, was sandwiched between journeys to places of 'interest' from which our best intelligence might be obtained and the relentless social demands of lunch parties, cocktail parties or dinners, whether as host or guest, together with the annual round of 'National Day' receptions held by every mission in the city. There was of course the May Day Parade on Red Square when the Soviet Union's armed forces marched past and flew over in salute to the political leaders who stood limp and grim-faced on the battlements of the Kremlin while we from NATO tried to spot new equipment and remember what we had seen. Photography was out but the Americans all carried cameras slung round their necks: they were surrounded by security men and never to my knowledge got a single picture. But they took the heat off us and we did manage a sly snap or two with our Minox. It was the receptions which were the hardest work on the social round. My dinners with or without an imported hostess were voted a success, very largely due to Klava's excellent cooking, and a regular supply of wines and spirits made drinks parties no problem.

But it was not long before the fact that I had been born in Baku spread round not only the diplomatic arena but the senior Soviet admirals, generals and air marshals who attended the receptions and formed, as always, a defensive circle usually in the middle of the reception room. The size of the circle determined their proximity to the other guests but the further away the better, it would seem. There they were, never with their spouses, bemedalled and beribboned, together with the top echelon of the Politburo, knocking back the vodka and exchanging guttural jokes as they ate from the platters carried round by the waitresses and dug at their teeth with toothpicks. We made polite greetings in Russian and then joined our friends.

Then, on one occasion when I had strayed from John Deverill and Chuck Taylor, none other than Marshal Zhigarev, Commander in Chief of the Soviet Air Force, caught my eye and beckoned to me, saying, 'Come here please, Mister Military Air Attaché of Great Britain'. So I walked over to the group, who stopped talking and looked at me. Zhigarev introduced me. 'Here is a man from Baku' – 'vot Bakunitz' – and then explained that I had been born there before the Revolution. There were exclamations of 'Good heavens! Not possible! Is he of Russian parenthood?' And it was left to me to explain how it came about.

They grinned and shook my hand; they called for more vodka and more to eat. Thus began my interesting, if unfortunate, discovery that I had a very high tolerance for this pernicious Russian spirit. I am not a big man; I don't carry much fat and I was at that time a very moderate drinker. But that evening I was toasted by one and all and, as is the Russian custom, I returned their toasts. I know not how many they were but after a while and a lot of talk things were becoming muddled as all seemed to want to speak at the same time. I was let off the hook and returned to my group who, understandably, asked how I was. In fact I felt fine, was steady on my feet and, though feeling no pain at all, was in no sense drunk. The Soviet top brass left, giving me a grin and a small wave of the hand. I had evidently passed the test and was still alive to take part in this unusual form of Russian roulette.

CHAPTER FIFTY-FOUR

Suez and a 'Spontaneous' Demonstration

In July 1956 Gamal Abdel Nasser, who two years before, at the age of thirty-six, had become the first native independent ruler of Egypt since the Persian invasion in the fifth century BC, nationalised the Suez Canal, a concession owned by the Paris-based Suez Canal Company, the supreme symbol of Western exploitation in the eyes of the Arab world. In Westminster, Anthony Eden, the Conservative Prime Minister, was furious and his Party carried a motion to use military force against Egypt to enforce a return to the status quo. Eden sought and secured the support of France and Israel and squadrons of Canberra day-bombers were deployed to Cyprus. The White House in Washington strongly opposed force; India in particular and many other countries gave diplomatic support to Nasser, as did the Soviet Union. The bombing of Egyptian radar stations, TV installations and other targets began.

Feelings in the British Embassy were mixed. HE called us to a special meeting and explained the reactions to be expected from other missions in Moscow. He had already been summoned to the Kremlin and given a strongly worded condemnation of this 'act of naked aggression'. He asked us to give him any information from our Service ministries as soon as we could. None of us received anything of the slightest significance: indeed the Directorate of Air Intelligence (DAI) sent me a memo in that week's diplomatic bag instructing me to find out what I could about the possibility of intervention by the Soviet Air Force. So we sat and waited and read reports and listened to the News. Joe Parrott, who as the Minister was second in command to the Ambassador, was visibly upset and throughout the whole sorry affair would ask me when I thought the bombing would stop. I had to say I didn't know because I simply didn't know. The Indian diplomats and their ladies, with other supporters of Nasser, refused to shake hands with us at receptions – protocol required this form of greeting even though you might have met the person at a lunch party that day – and sides were taken wherever and whenever the diplomatic corps met collectively. The United States moved their Mediterranean fleet into a position effectively blocking our naval forces from any sea borne assault and Chip Bohlen, while making it quite clear to William Hayter what Washington's views were, still grinned at us and shook hands. The French Military Attaché, General Vigan-Bracquet, strutted up to me saying 'We are allies again', and the Israelis kept a low profile but were obviously delighted.

Nasser sank blockships in the Canal, the whole operation ended in fiasco and Eden resigned in favour of the elderly Harold Macmillan, but not before the citizens of Moscow had been given an opportunity to demonstrate their contempt for what was taking place. It was a heaven-sent chance to make capital out of a British capitalist-cum-colonialist cock-up and they relished it.

Some two weeks after the Suez operation had begun we got wind of what was being referred to by the University students as a 'spontaneous demonstration' against our Embassy. Indeed, so good was our contact that we were forewarned not only of the date of the demonstration but also of its timing and where and when on the day before those selected to take an active part would be briefed. So we decided to attend the briefing, but we didn't want the goons to follow us and cause trouble. We pondered this.

Behind my block of flats was a yard where a Service car was frequently parked. Each flat had a back door leading into the yard. Our chauffeurs normally went off duty at about 6 pm. It would be no problem to have someone either lying on the floor in the back of the car or in the boot and for the driver and front-seat passenger to move out quite openly past the guard on duty at the front entrance without the stowaway being spotted. Only the two front-seat occupants together with the number of the car would be reported by phone. We rehearsed this and it worked. We decided to abandon the boot scheme as being too obvious when the occupant was released and too uncomfortable. But by driving deviously and stopping immediately after several sharp turns in narrow streets when the Pobeda would pass only to stop some distance away, 'our man' could slip out and, suitably clad, mingle with the pedestrians.

So, on the evening of the rehearsal and knowing the time and the venue, we carried out our plan and it worked perfectly. Our man was away, shuffling along and inconspicuous, before our Pobeda raced past, recognised the car and screeched to a halt some fifty yards ahead. We drove off and were escorted from behind to Skatertny Peryulok where we parked the car and went into the flat for a drink. The rehearsal for the 'spontaneous demonstration' was conducted with skill and efficiency in a square in the north of Moscow and was thronged with people, mostly young, who were sorted into Kollektivs – employees of Soviet enterprises – and marshalled in chattering groups.

A voice rang out through the public address systems. Kollektiv Number One would leave at such-and-such a time, then each would follow on orders. They would gather outside the gates of the British Embassy. The gates would be shut but the fence could be climbed into the Embassy forecourt. There was to be no violence unless attacked. Comrade whoever would be on guard duty outside the gates which he would open after fifteen minutes. The British workers would be inside the Embassy, which was not to be broken into. Any vehicles were to be left undamaged. There was to be no drunkenness. The 'spontaneous demonstration' was to express the Soviet Union's unanimous outrage at the British attack on a friendly defenceless people. The comrades could shout 'Britain out' and 'Down with colonialism'. There would be police on duty to control the operation. 'Glory to the Soviet Union!'

The crowd was dispersed. Forewarned, the Embassy prepared for a siege. Only those essential for its operation were to come in on the following morning. The Chancery guards were instructed to man the entrance hall and all cars were to be locked in the garages. Joe Parrott had a lunch engagement which he said was very important and wanted to know how long the demonstration would last. We didn't know and told him so. He went back to his office looking miserable.

Sure enough, on the following morning at about 11.30 the first group of demonstrators appeared outside the gates. They chanted, waved clenched fists and unfurled banners. They were joined by more and more until the pavement and embankment road were choked by an ever-increasing stream of people of all ages. Then they began to climb the railings and surround the entrance porch of the Embassy. We had closed and locked both glass-fronted doors, through which we could see what went on. The mob – which it had now become – was being orchestrated by a long-haired man with a megaphone. But no one was paying much attention. We saw a sprinkling of police in the forecourt and realised that the main gates had been opened.

The crowd in the forecourt grew larger and more and more vociferous. There was banging on the entrance doors and we spotted a senior police officer who had arrived and seemed to be in authority. He came up the steps and gestured that he wanted to be allowed into the hall where HE, the Service Attachés and four Chancery guards were 'on station'. So we let him in together with a long-haired man who handed us a large petition with pages and pages of signatures from 'The People of Moscow'. Not bad for a spontaneous demonstration! We took the document and they left peacefully. Someone asked the police officer how long this intrusion was going on. He consulted his watch and replied 'Fifteen minutes', saluted and walked down the steps into the forecourt.

Joe Parrott was bent on attending his lunch appointment and wanted his chauffeur to drive him as soon as possible. But there were no chauffeurs on duty that morning. It was well after midday and the throng in the courtyard was larger than ever. Joe put on his dark overcoat and astrakhan hat and got the garage key from the Chancery guard in charge. Adrian and I did not like this at all. We assumed that Joe had informed HE of what he intended. We, together with the heftiest of our staff, formed a sort of military escort for him and managed to get him down the front steps with nothing more than a surge of mostly young people towards our group as we came out from the Embassy building. Adrian, being the biggest, led the group. John was on one side of Joe and I was on the other; we left the Brigadier to bring up the rear. The others did their best to stay alongside but before we had got halfway to the garages, we were literally mobbed: there was no violence but at Joe's appearance there were calls of 'Is he the Ambassador? Ask him to speak with us. We have much to tell him!' We were hemmed in and inevitably separated from Joe. He stopped and made a gesture with his right hand, two fingers crossed in the manner of a bishop blessing his flock, but remained silent. 'Speak!' cried the crowd.

A young woman put her arm in mine and asked: 'What Kollektiv are you from?' I paused. She was an attractive blonde. 'Scottish Kollektiv Number One,' I replied. She disengaged and looked hard at me. 'There is no Scottish Kollektiv. You are a foreigner?' She left me and merged with her comrades.

Joe gave up. We got him back into the Embassy with nothing worse than some hands-on from a gang of youngsters who had certainly been drinking. The Chancery guard locked the two doors behind us and we were all inside intact and unhurt. I had been quite frightened.

A quarter of an hour later the police officer in charge blew a whistle. The hubbub subsided, the throng left peacefully through the main gates and the demonstration was over. There had been no damage, other than some trampled flowerbeds. HE offered sherry and that was that. Joe got away to his lunch appointment half an hour late and the Brigadier explained why our presence had deterred an 'attack in force'. Adrian and I left him to it.

CHAPTER FIFTY-FIVE

Activities of an Air Attaché

AEROFLOT AND BEA

For some time before my arrival in Moscow, Aeroflot, the state-controlled Soviet airline, had been operating the new Tupolev 104, a twin-jet, medium-range airliner very similar to our Comet on internal routes and to neighbouring friendly countries. Tentative negotiations had been conducted between the Soviet Union and London for an exchange agreement whereby Aeroflot and BEA would have reciprocal rights to operate flights between Moscow and Heathrow. As the negotiations proceeded towards agreement in principle, I became involved. I was instructed to return to the UK to discuss with Sholto Douglas, a retired Air Marshal and Chairman of BEA, certain aspects of the proposal. A delegation from Aeroflot was flying over shortly to sign a 'protocol', which in Whitehall parlance is a provisional draft agreement but to the Soviets was mere prevarication. I was required to attend.

I met Sholto in his London headquarters and we sorted out certain problems. He was very much his old RAF self, portly, affable and on the ball. The Aeroflot delegation together with the extras – probably KGB – and an interpreter arrived. Two cars from the Soviet Embassy met the aircraft. The visitors were looked after for a day or two before the official meeting with BEA and an Assistant Under-Secretary from the Ministry of Aviation took place in Whitehall. Mike Forter was present as an interpreter. This was a relief for I had understood that I was to do the job, which I didn't relish as my technical Russian was none too good. We all shook hands and sat down at a long table in the conference room; BEA with the 'Men from the Ministry' on one side, the Soviet delegation on the other and Mike and myself at opposite ends of the table.

The meeting went well, thanks largely to the Chairman who, after a warm welcome, applauded the initiative and cooperation of Aeroflot in bringing the proposal to the conference table. He explained what the protocol was – namely a draft which the meeting could amend by agreement before signing it as an intention to enter into an binding agreement. He spoke slowly, giving the Soviet interpreter plenty of time to translate. There was a copy of the Protocol before each of us. Aeroflot's was in Russian: their interpreter's was in both English and Russian, which was a thoughtful gesture.

Mike Forter and I said nothing until we both noticed that on several occasions the Chairman's remarks, particularly in relation to the meaning of the Protocol, were being subtly twisted by the Aeroflot interpreter to imply that the British government were not prepared to sign without certain concessions. Mike then spoke up, first in English and then in Russian. In short order he restored the confidence of Aeroflot, shot a dirty look at their interpreter, who was clearly astonished at Mike's impeccable classical Russian, and then sat back in his chair. We had no further trouble. Amendments were agreed and the meeting ended cordially with signatures from both sides and an undertaking to have the final document on its way to Moscow within a week.

BRIEF HOME VISIT

I went down to Sussex again. Lin was back at school and the boys were away boarding. I visited Paddy at Cumnor House and spoke with Ranald at Bryanston on the phone. All seemed well though I thought Nan was hitting the bottle a bit and seemed to spend too many evenings in the local. I also took the opportunity of buying a new car. It was a 1956 model Ford Consul, a basic four-door saloon with a well-proved 1.7 litre engine with no frills. I had no difficulty in raising a loan from Cox and King's, the Lloyds Bank branch favoured by RAF officers. With a concession for diplomatic use and an allowance for export from the UK, the price I paid was unbelievably low. I arranged to have the Consul shipped to Leningrad and thence by rail to Moscow.

DIPLOMATIC LIFE

Back in the Embassy, we celebrated the wedding of Peter Lewis to Lisa. Sir William and Lady Hayter were due to end their appointment within months. They had been very kind, inviting me to informal family meals and to Sunday afternoon walks in the woods outside the city. We would be driven out in the Rolls Royce by the Russian chauffeur to places where the peace and quiet of the woods was broken only by the cry of birds and small animals. While we were crossing a stream on a flimsy wooden bridge HE told me in confidence that Dick Slater was to be replaced by Christopher MacAlpine from our embassy in Peru. Christopher was the brother of Mary who had married my brother Peter. I looked forward to his arrival in some six months' time.

Ever since my appointment to Moscow had been confirmed, I had nursed a fierce longing to visit Baku, the town of my birth. I discussed this possibility with John and Daphne who both agreed it would be a wonderful trip but had doubts whether one of such length and time would be agreed by the Department of External Relations (OVS). So I decided to sound them out.

Of the four OVS officers we dealt with, we all warmed to and trusted Colonel Chuvilsky from the Technical Branch of the Soviet Air Force. Chuvilsky was a gentleman, spoke 'educated' Russian and was open-handed in his dealings with us, showing great tolerance when we did stupid things, which happened from time to time. So I asked for a meeting and put my request to him. He knew I had been born in Baku and I made no bones about my desire to visit the place of my birth, probably the only opportunity in my life. He smiled and explained that such a journey would involve a great deal of organisation, reservations by air, train and in hotels. How did we propose to travel from Moscow to the Caucasus?

We planned to fly down to the Crimea; one of the drivers would take the Standard Vanguard Estate to Mineralnye Vody (Mineral Waters) where we would rendezvous. The driver would return to Moscow by air and we would drive over the Georgian Military Highway to Tblisi where we would leave the vehicle, fly to Baku and spend the night in a hotel and return by train to Tblisi the following day. We would then drive back to Moscow.

Chuvilsky listened with interest. 'Gospodin Air Commodore,' he said. 'I understand your wish to visit Baku. Long visits such as this depend on the behaviour of the 'military diplomat'. Higher authority will consider how he has observed the diplomatic rules. You have been of good behaviour, though your American friends have often broken our trust. Also will be considered the treatment and freedom of movement accorded to our Air Attaché in London. It may take time to obtain a ruling on this from higher authority.'

So we waited and hoped. I admit that the intelligence potential of the visit was virtually nil, though Adrian asked that we keep a 'weather eye' open for submarines in the Caspian Sea! How the hell did they get out? But J.B. Hogan, in London, had given us his blessing and we informed Kostaki of BUROBIN. I would guess that he was already privy to our plans.

After several months, during which – I learned later – exchanges had taken place between Moscow and London and Colonel Constantinov, the Soviet Air Attaché, had been satisfied with his reciprocal freedom to travel within the UK, our journey to Baku was officially approved. Usually, when permissions were sought for journeys out of the forty-kilometre limit from Moscow, we received no replies. Trips were always buggered up by the Soviet authorities.

To give an example, Pskov to the north-west of Moscow had a beautifully preserved sixteenth-century church. I asked Peter Lewis and his bride Lisa if they would care to accompany me to Pskov in the Vanguard. I told Klava where we were going. She smiled, confirmed that Pskov was a nice place and described the road as a 'fine Soviet highway' – it proved to be a tarmac road with potholes and broken surfaces all along the route. A Soviet Air Force base about half a mile off our route was the only place of any significance to Air Intelligence. About a mile from the airfield the road further degenerated into single track and led across low-lying agricultural land intersected by narrow dykes crossed by heavily planked bridges. We approached one of these only to find a team of Soviet soldiers, under the command of a Captain, pulling up the planks and effectively blocking our progress. I went to investigate and was told tersely that it was a routine maintenance operation and that we should go back and take a detour to Pskov. The Captain clearly knew our destination.

I asked how long the operation would take. He muttered something about all day. He looked uncomfortable. I consulted Peter and Lisa. We decided to sit it out as, by now, several other vehicles had drawn up behind us, their drivers giving the Soviet Army colourful indications of their opinions of military exercises on public highways. We sat in the Vanguard, ate the good things Lisa had provided and drank a bottle of wine.

The soldiers had a lunch break and looked sullen. The Captain came and spoke to me: why hadn't we gone back as he had suggested? We were on holiday and in no hurry, I replied, but there were others who needed to get home. Perhaps he should advise them to take the other route? He didn't like that and said we should obey his orders. I said he hadn't given any and that we were diplomats and were not impressed with his behaviour. He returned to his team. The beams were put back over the dyke – the whole thing was a pathetic charade.

Then a motorcyclist arrived. He and the Captain spoke and the man returned, head down and his exhaust roaring with no silencer. We crossed the bridge, followed by a large tailback of cars and trucks. As we neared the airfield we were surprised to see large banks of grey-green smoke curling upwards. They had lined the nearside perimeter with smoke candles so that nothing of the base was visible.

This episode exemplifies the petty lets and hindrances which were visited on us wherever we went. Had our reciprocal treatment of Constantinov in

London been comparable, I would have said 'Fair enough', but I learned later that once his journeys had been approved he travelled unfollowed by road or rail only to be checked into his destination by police with no training in counter-intelligence. He was virtually free to go where he pleased. He was even allowed through the guardroom of an RAF station by saying that he was an 'Allied' colleague. Little wonder the KGB had penetrated so far in the UK. It certainly wouldn't have been so in the USA.

We visited the church in Pskov the following day. The interior of the cupola dome had murals covering the entire inside of its onion shape, the like of which we had never seen. A wooden stairway led up to a circular viewing balcony and it was then I realised for the first time that I suffered from vertigo. And me a pilot! Lisa helped me down. Next morning Peter went to get the Vanguard which was in the yard behind the hotel. He was back within minutes saying that the brake system had been severed. I blew my top. The Director of the hotel denied any knowledge of what had been done. The police, whom I insisted be called, pretended to know nothing and when I said I would phone the British Embassy in Moscow there was a complete black-out and 'all lines to Moscow were engaged'. Giving vent to a torrent of indignation – which I frankly enjoyed – I demanded to know how we were to return to Moscow. The answer came pat: a car had been ordered, free of charge, to drive us to an intersection with the Leningrad-Moscow road where there was a coach stop. We would then travel on to Moscow. All prearranged without seemingly any knowledge of our vehicle's immobility!

We agreed to act bloody-mindedly. I told the Director it was an outrageous way to treat visitors to the Soviet Union! The poor man, his hands shaking, protested it wasn't his fault. Whose was it then? He didn't know – perhaps *khuligany* (hooligans). I said the best Russian equivalent to 'balls' and we left the hotel to board a dilapidated Pobeda which had arrived at the entrance. Our driver took us on a route away from the airfield and then rejoined the 'fine Soviet highway' along which we bumped and lurched until we reached the junction with the Leningrad–Moscow road where, not surprisingly, awaited an inter-city coach with a very angry group of passengers who had been kept sitting there for over an hour. Forty-eight hours later our Vanguard was returned to the Embassy with a written apology from the police of Pskov and all damage to the brake system repaired. Misha, my driver, was in trouble with the authorities. I knew nothing of this except that he was withdrawn and moody.

DRIVERS

A few days later Misha was driving me out to Vnukovo Airport to meet the RAF Hastings which was bringing the Hayter family back from the

UK when I noticed that Misha's shoulders seemed to convulse and that he was driving erratically. I said, 'Misha, what's wrong?' He just shook his head and went on hunched over the wheel. I told him to stop. He pulled into the side of the road and I climbed into the front passenger seat beside him. His flabby face was creased and he was crying like a child; Misha, who had always joked with me, was in tears.

'Misha,' I said. 'Why are you so unhappy?' He just shook his head. Then he said: 'Gospodin MacDonell, tomorrow I am to leave you. Another driver will come.' He gave me a tear-stained look and then wiped his nose on the back of his hand. 'But why have you to go, Misha?' I asked. He shook his head again. 'I cannot tell you, Gospodin. But I have been ordered to another job. I cannot tell you.'

Back in Moscow, I shook Misha's hand. He shambled out of the Embassy compound and I only saw him again, by chance, when he was working for the Thai Embassy. I sought out Kostaki and asked why Misha was leaving. He gave me a blank stare and said drivers were often given different employment. I would have a new driver tomorrow. Back in the flat I told Klava that Misha had gone. She looked stony-faced and mumbled something about him having done his two years' service with our Embassy.

Viktor Romancha was probably in his early thirties. Lean, good looking and speaking a fair amount of English, he drove the Humber to my flat at nine o'clock the following morning. He wore a cheap grey suit and a large floppy cap such as I see men of the Black Isle wearing in the old sepia photographs of the villagers which hang on the walls of the local pubs. We spoke in Russian and I confess I took to Viktor. He told me that, as a teenager in Leningrad during the long siege in the winter of 1942, he had queued for many hours for the barest of rations and had fainted twice from under-nourishment and hypothermia. After the War he had moved south to Moscow. More than that he wouldn't say. His driving was impressive, as was his care of the ageing Humber Snipe which he lovingly washed and polished. He didn't smoke and never smelt of drink. But then vodka doesn't smell on the breath. Viktor gave every impression of being less a Communist than a seeker after other political philosophies, but I never lowered my guard.

Kostaki informed me that my Ford Consul had arrived: there were certain import formalities and documents which I had to sign. Viktor drove me to the railway station where my car was in a shed. Its appearance left much to be desired for it had, sensibly enough, been covered in grease against the brine of the sea and the chrome wheel hubcaps were packed in the boot. Its appearance aroused a lot of interest and it was soon surrounded by quite a crowd. Why was it so dirty? It wasn't very well 'chromed'. What make was it? Wasn't Ford an American factory? Why did a British diplomat have an American car?

I explained that while Ford of Detroit was indeed an American company my car had been made by a British subsidiary. The young men crawled underneath. Some praised, some poured scorn on such a dirty, unchromed car. The Soviet cars were much better: they were made by dedicated comrades, not like the British workmen who had to strike for a minimum wage! I left Viktor to arrange the Soviet diplomatic registration and the delivery of the Consul to the Embassy. I drove back in the Humber Snipe, followed by the ever-present Pobeda.

CHAPTER FIFTY-SIX

Cold War

I began to feel if not at home at least at ease in this extraordinary environment of diplomatic protocol – often quite false but not to be dispensed with whatever the circumstances – and in the main purpose of my post, the search for intelligence about the Soviet Air Force. While the everlasting shaking of hands with *chèrs collegues* on every formal occasion, together with the restraint required to avoid telling a repellent and drunk little pest from another mission to 'get lost' was almost irresistible, I managed to curb my often intemperate nature and produce the 'MacDonell charm'. Thus was I judged and declared *persona grata* by the diplomatic corps in Moscow. At those official functions which were graced by Krushchev and Bulganin – 'Crush and Bulge' – with Mikoyan inevitably in tow, I would be required to join their senior military circle. I would be smiled upon, plied with vodka and obliged to drink far too many toasts to anything from *mir i druzhba* (peace and friendship) to the health and prosperity of their families and mine. It was always Mikoyan who broke it up and, smiling, let me off the hook with a polite 'Goodbye Mister Air Attaché of Great Britain'.

I was usually received back in the Western camp with approbation but I detected a certain envy from some members of embassies who were toadying for special attention from the Kremlin. Joe Parrott was a mite disapproving though he merely warned me not to be trapped – an odd expression as I thought at the time. But it was Daphne Park who made me realise that behind the diplomatic glitz, protocol and ceremonials were the ever-watchful eyes of the KGB. The goons were no more than the tip of the iceberg. I usually walked to the Embassy each morning and the goon was not far behind. When in my own car, the Pobeda was astern. When driven in my official car by Viktor, he alone was my custodian. The arch-enemy of the Soviet Union and the main target for their propaganda and KGB infiltration was of course the United States. The Cold War was practically at freezing point.

When Chip Bohlen took over as American Ambassador in Moscow, a new Embassy was under construction, quite separate from the Ambassador's personal residence. Finding the half-completed building liberally sprinkled with bugs, Bohlen put a stop to the work and only allowed it to be continued after security personnel had been stationed on the ground floor during the day and the bugs removed – as he thought. At night the KGB 'swallows' – ladies of easy virtue – got to work. Something like a dozen US security men were seduced and then shown 'photographs' of their activities in attempts to blackmail them into becoming KGB recruits. All confessed to Bohlen and were out of the country within twenty-four hours. I wonder how many others there were who did not confess.

In the French Embassy Maurice Dejean, the Ambassador, and his Air Attaché, Colonel Gibaud, were seduced by KGB swallows in an elaborate plan under the control of a Soviet general in their counter-intelligence department. Dejean was attacked and beaten up by the furious, so-called 'husband' of the lady concerned, and Gibaud was shown the customary photos of his sexual activities whereupon he committed suicide. Dejean was withdrawn but the KGB man who had organised his compromise defected to the West. The story of John Vassall is well-known. He was recruited by the KGB when in a junior post in the Admiralty and was then posted to Moscow as a clerk in the office of the British Naval Attaché, Adrian Northey. A self-confessed homosexual, Vassall soon fell for the blandishments of members of the KGB with similar proclivities, but it was not until his tour expired that he confessed, insisting that he had leaked 'nothing of security importance to the Soviets'. He maintained to the end that he had only endeavoured to encourage the Soviet Union to believe that an exchange of information about 'weaponry' would create a greater understanding in the East/West impasse. I believe he did what he thought right; he was a pretty simple-minded man, under duress. In his memoirs he confesses that the photos he was shown of his homosexual activities – almost certainly montage – with him having oral or a complicated array of sexual acts with a number of different men, made him feel sick.

Poor Adrian Northey. Inevitably, when Vassall confessed in London, he was inundated with enquiries concerning Vassall's behaviour while serving on his staff. Before he and his family left about a year later, he had further trouble. A young, well-spoken English girl had joined the family as a mother's help. She was both attractive and sociable. She had one or two days off a week. Neither Adrian nor Betty was concerned how or where she spent these days until she informed them, within a few months of their leaving Moscow, that she was engaged to a Russian and was to be married. There was nothing that could be done. The Soviet authorities approved the wedding, she was accorded Soviet citizenship and that was that.

I too was not without my problems. Shortly after Donkin's departure my telephone rang and a female voice, well spoken in English with a slight accent, was on the other end. Was Mr Donkin there? No, he had returned to the UK. She was speaking for BUROBIN – they had a pair of ski boots which Mr Donkin had left for repair. They were ready. Could she bring them to the flat? My defences went up. Bring them to Mr Kostaki at the British Embassy, I said, and hung up. Neither the caller nor the boots ever reached the Embassy. Next a male voice on the phone. He had agreed with Mr Donkin to write a joint account of a visit to Zagorsk, the Russian Orthodox theological monastery in which Mr Donkin and his family had shown great interest. He, the caller, was involved in arranging visits to Zagorsk. Could he please call and discuss a programme with me? I said yes and asked him to come to my office in the Embassy. He never turned up.

On another occasion, I was on my own in Red Square. I had wandered into St Basil's to get a close-up view of the paintings in the dome, which was reached by a wooden stairway leading to a circular platform which gave visitors an excellent view of the splendid murals. I was, as I thought, alone. I looked at the work of craftsmen of centuries ago and then became aware of a woman opposite me who faced towards the Biblical paintings but occasionally shot me a glance. She wore a long, light-coloured rain-coat. Her hair was blonde and long. She was instantly attractive. I looked at the paintings. She moved round the balcony in my direction. I too moved round, away from her. She began to walk round towards me, so I moved to the wooden staircase leading to the ground floor. There were others coming up but I managed to squeeze past them. I left St Basil's and crossed Red Square to the GUM department store where I went in by the main entrance, turned left and stopped, looking over a counter where they were selling wooden dolls.

The woman came in a few minutes later, saw me and walked across to the opposite counter selling cosmetics. There was a mirror behind the counter and she was watching me. I moved down the main concourse of the store to where the staircase ran up to the upper level; I hastened up it, hurried down the length of the floor and then ran down the stairs at the end. I went out by a side door, turned left in Red Square and used a number of side streets to regain the area of Skatertny Peryulok. It occurred to me that I might have been followed by a female goon but there was a male goon, shuffling along some fifty yards behind me, stopping to do up his shoe laces whenever I paused in my tracks. I never saw the blonde again.

There were more troubles to come at the hands of the KGB. Sir Anthony Meyer was appointed as a First Secretary in the Embassy towards the end of 1956, to be joined later by his wife Barbadee. Some time in the new year, he was to attend a meeting in a Moscow hotel. Anthony rang for a taxi – a mistake. On the way to the hotel a woman, well dressed and with a shawl over her head, stepped off the pavement, raised her hand and shouted, 'Anthony!' He told the driver to stop. She flung open the door, flopped down beside him and the driver took off at speed. She then ripped her blouse, raised her skirt to above her knees and began to scream and struggle. Anthony hadn't touched her and had never seen her before. The taxi drove up to a police station where the driver and the woman told of an assault. After a perfunctory investigation, Anthony was detained for an hour and then returned to the Embassy where he immediately reported to HE. He and Barbadee were out of the country in forty-eight hours. HE's outraged protests were brushed aside by the Soviet Ministry of Foreign Affairs.

While I was back in Sussex on my annual leave in 1956, JB phoned and asked if I could come up to Whitehall the next day: he didn't want to tell me why on the telephone. I found JB looking unhappy. My Warrant Officer Clerk had been compromised and was on his way home. Seemingly my clerk's predecessor had been running a highly profitable business. We were allowed a clothing parcel each month by the diplomatic bag; once a month a suit bought from the 'Fifty Shilling Tailors' had been sent out to be flogged on the black market for enough roubles which, when exchanged for US dollars, represented an enormous profit. The racket, unknown to me, had been handed on to my Warrant Officer a substantive sergeant in the RAF Accounts Branch, who had been spotted by the KGB as a likely candidate for recruitment. Foolish though he was, when presented with the inevitable photos of the 'transaction', he went straight to HE who signalled the Foreign Office and DIA (Directorate of Air Intelligence). Within a fortnight I had a new warrant officer join my team. He drove the whole way to Moscow in a replacement Vanguard Estate.

But I had enjoyed four weeks in Stroods Lodge, Herons Gyll, near Uckfield, Sussex – what a splendid address – and, apart from a sense of anxiety about Nan's drinking, everything was in apple-pie order. The little lodge suited everyone and the old Lanchester was still bumbling along at a steady 50 mph. I returned to Moscow for my second year with plans well laid for Nan to bring out Ranald, Paddy and Lin during the summer holiday of 1957.

CHAPTER FIFTY-SEVEN

VIP Visits to Moscow and London

There had been changes in the staff of the Embassy. The Ambassador, Sir William Hayter, was due to leave, as was Adrian Northey. Dick Slater, Head of Chancery, and his wife Barbara had left in November 1956. Joe Parrott had been replaced as Minister by Hilary Young. Christopher McAlpine, Dick Slater's replacement, 'Christo', was on his way to Moscow, preceding his family by a month or so. The Gauloise-smoking major had been posted back to UK, so I had my office to myself. His replacement, Major Tony Hall, a noisy man who had lost an arm at Dunkirk, had made an unfortunate first impression on arrival by getting drunk at a reception held by the mad brigadier. But he was happy to share his boss's office, thank God.

Sholto Douglas – later Lord Douglas of Kyrtleside the Chairman of British European Airways – came to Moscow with a small delegation as guests of Aeroflot. An RAF Transport Command Hastings landed at Vnukovo and the crew, with a wing commander as captain, were accommodated in Moscow. I had the two officers as guests in my flat. There was a reception for them in the Embassy and I organised a dinner party at which Klava my cook excelled herself. Sholto and his wife Hazel were in cracking form. She lavished kisses on all the males when they left and Sholto sought out the ladies and did likewise. The airline inter-flight agreement had been signed and everything would have been fine but for the fact that the Hastings, which was to take the Aeroflot delegation for a flight round the Moscow area, was found to be unserviceable and remained grounded for two days before a replacement component was flown out. I think there were some red faces back home!

Another delegation of a very different genre, also as guests of the Soviet Union, was ecclesiastical and headed by the Archbishop of York, Dr Michael Ramsey, with the Bishop of Derby as back-up. They were supported by an austere clergyman who said very little and a younger priest with a splendid personality and sense of humour who was clearly enjoying the visit, his food and drink and thought the Archbishop a shade over the top! I agreed with him. They were off to Zagorsk on the morrow but what I hadn't bargained for was being asked by HE if I would take over as interpreter from the secretary who spoke really good Russian, as he had a tummy bug. Ye Gods, literally! I spent most of the night mugging up the Russian for transubstantiation, the Eucharist, Pentecost, the Risen Christ and anything and everything I could rake from my rudimentary memory of scripture classes.

We drove to Zagorsk. Doctor Ramsey and the Bishop of Derby were in the large black Zil with two Soviet officials, and I was with Viktor, with the boot-faced cleric and the cheerful young one in the back. We arrived and were received by the Metropolitan, a small group of plain-clothed Soviets and, Heaven be praised, an interpreter who spoke excellent English. Speeches were exchanged. Ramsey nearly put his foot in it when he said how delighted he was to find the 'fountainhead of Christianity in a state which had pronounced itself as atheistic'. This was subtly watered down by the interpreter and a tour of the magnificent monastery followed. We had a splendid meal at which the young priest did pretty well on the wine – there was no vodka – and we returned to Moscow. Ramsey was asleep in the back of the Zil when we arrived but thanked me graciously. I don't know what his visit accomplished.

Several months later the Metropolitan of the Russian Orthodox Church of Moscow, with the blessing of the Central Committee, invited the 'Red Dean', Hewlett, the Dean of Canterbury – a dedicated Communist – to visit Moscow. He arrived and the Soviets took him over. There was a reception to which the Heads of Missions were invited. The Reillys, who had succeeded the Hayters, accepted and I accompanied them. Hewlett was robed according to his office in the Church of England. It was not an easy occasion: we shook his hand and moved on but there were those ladies who swept past him, heads turned and dresses dragged away. I found this offensive and tried to support the Reillys, newly arrived in office, without giving offence to one side or the other. The Red Dean left the following day.

Sir Patrick and Lady Reilly were splendid representatives of our mission in Moscow. Both the Hayters and the Reillys represented the finest possible selection for the Moscow appointments at a time when

Anglo-Soviet relations were at an all-time low. It was a privilege to serve on their staffs.

The mad Brigadier left with Cecily to be replaced by a fat Brigadier Young who spent a fortnight in my flat while his own was being refurbished, and probably rebugged. He tended to drive me mad with a piano accordion which he played frequently and excruciatingly badly. But he was an excellent tennis and squash player at which he beat me into a cocked hat.

When Christo McAlpine was joined by his wife Helen and their small son 'Bobsie' with his nanny, they all occupied the ground-floor flat below mine, which was a great blessing for me as Christo and I had become firm friends and the warmth and affection of Helen gave me a much needed sense of family involvement. Their two older children, Sarah and David came out during the school holidays. I am not by nature a bachelor or celibate but I had accepted both as my part of the bargain in this out-of-the-ordinary appointment. I had been feeling domestically isolated and that I was living a life of make-belief in which at the end of each performance – lunch, reception, drinks party or formal dinner – I would take to my bed exhausted and without solace or companionship. Christo and Helen have over the many years since remained dear friends. I owe more to them than they realise.

The KGB was operating at full throttle throughout the Soviet Missions in the United States and Western Europe, and the Moscow 'Centre' was well-nigh hypermanic about seeking information from its agents as to how close the West was to a nuclear attack on the Soviet Union. All this is set out in remarkable detail in a book by Christopher Andrew and Oleg Gordievsky who was a defector from the KGB.

My team kept the Directorate of Air Intelligence informed regarding the potential of the Soviet Air Force, any new long-range bomber developments being programmed and, ever and always, took more photos. HE agreed that, since being caught photographing Soviet air bases or aircraft factories was almost certain to result in the culprit being declared *persona non grata*, from the RAF point of view it wasn't worth the candle. Thus we did not provide anything like as many photographs as did our colleagues on the Air Attaché's staff at the US Embassy.

The Americans had established at München Gladbach in West Germany, an intelligence base which churned out officers for service in embassies behind the Iron Curtain. They came off the production line like Ford cars. It mattered little if an American service attaché was declared *persona non grata*. He and his family, if he had one in Moscow, were seen off at the railway station by a crowd of colleagues swilling champagne and bidding them farewell. This happened with monotonous regularity and the replacement arrived within a fortnight. But we could not afford to lose staff. There were few if any competent replacements to be sent out at short notice, as had been made very clear to me before I left for Moscow. We had no 'Kwik-Fit' organisation comparable with München Gladbach and I had to be cautious, even though this meant that our undertaking to exchange all intelligence, be it photographic or written, with our American counterparts, was inevitably somewhat one-sided.

With all that was going on, both in my office and outside, I hankered for the chance to visit Baku. I was impatient to try my luck but Daphne Park and John Deverill thought it was premature, bearing in mind the appalling East-West relations and the recent demonstration which Chuvilsky would often refer to as 'the people's reaction to the ugly face of capitalist-colonialism'. However, Daphne was due to be replaced within six months and both John and I agreed that a journey of that length without Daphne was really not on. We three discussed it as we strolled across the Great Stone Bridge over the River Moskva and walked towards GUM to see what new, if anything, was on sale. (Daphne kept a remarkable catalogue of merchandise under various headings.) We agreed that the Baku trip was probably a non-starter. On the inevitable quid pro quo basis, what comparable journey in terms of mileage could be offered the Soviet Air Attaché in London? Twelve trips to John o'Groats and back! But 'nothing ventured, nothing gained'. We decided to sound out Chuvilsky as soon as possible, before submitting a formal request.

The opportunity occurred only a few days later at a reception in the Polish Embassy. Chuvilsky was talking to the Polish Air Attaché who, despite our political stances on opposite sides of the Curtain, was a good friend of mine. The Pole spoke fair English and good Russian, and knew personally a number of the 'renegades' who had joined the RAF during the War. His wink and gestures as he spoke of them were eloquent testimony to his true feelings. He wished he had been with them. They moved apart and Chuvilsky smiled to me in greeting. I reminded him of how much I hoped it would be possible for me to travel to Baku, the place of my birth. He nodded and looked down: elderly, grey-haired, almost fatherly in his manner towards us. I pressed my case. Had I not behaved well, kept to the rules and respected the security constraints imposed on me and my Royal Air Force staff? If I and my senior Squadron Leader Deverill and Miss Park from the Secretariat were allowed to visit Baku, we would accept whatever travel arrangements the OVS laid down, but we hoped to use one of our cars which could be driven to the Crimea by a Russian chauffeur who would meet us at the airport and then return to Moscow by air. We were planning to drive over the Georgian Military Highway to Tblisi where we would leave the car, fly to Baku for an overnight stay, return to Tblisi by train, pick up the car and drive back to Moscow via Novorossiysk. I spoke slowly and gave Chuvilsky time to consider what we had in mind. It would be the journey of a lifetime for me, I said.

We were joined by other senior attachés but, as Chuvilsky took his leave, he caught my eye and I followed him. He turned to me and said, 'Send to me your planned journey, Gospodin Kommodore. Write it to me personally. I will do what I can but it may be difficult. Don't forget, send it to me personally.'

We waited and we waited.

A Soviet Air Force delegation headed by Marshal of the Air Force Zhigarev was invited to the British Aircraft Corporation's annual display at Farnborough. They were to fly to Heathrow in a TU 104 with me as escort. John Deverill would act as navigator/interpreter when the aircraft flew out of Soviet air space and entered the Berlin Air Traffic Control Zone and so to London Air Traffic Control where R/T communication would be in English. My particular responsibility was a Soviet general who spoke a little English and was companionable and obviously in good heart. The others in the delegation were ill at ease. I did my best to assure them that they would be welcome but they were clearly concerned about the visit.

The TU 104 was a fine aircraft, an early jet airliner with two Antonov turbojet engines set into the main planes and strikingly similar to the Comet. The delegation sat stony-faced as we climbed away to the West. John sat with us as we were under Soviet air traffic control. We did our best to make our guests feel at ease but their obvious nervousness was difficult to handle and after a while we gave up. I noticed that one of the party, in the uniform of a Colonel, kept visiting individual members of the delegation at regular intervals. They seemed to agree with what he was saying, replying *Ponyatno* (understood) or *Tak* (so be it). John and I agreed that he was undoubtedly from the KGB. Served by elephantine air hostesses, the delegation drank plentifully of vodka and ate the cold collations served by the cabin staff. Some nodded off. None smoked.

We flew west out and approached the Berlin Air Control centre. I had a map on which I showed our guests where we were. Their fidgets increased as we entered the Berlin area. They began to question us. Would they be searched after landing? We said no, though in fact we were not too sure of this. Would they be welcomed by the English? We assured them they most definitely would be – why on earth not? They looked at each other and their eyes flickered. The KGB Colonel watched us the whole time. Would there be a reception for them at the airport? Would they have to make a speech? This was a difficult one, as neither John nor I had been briefed.

We compromised by saying there would be a warm greeting but probably nothing else. Would I be with them during their visit? Yes, I said. And my colleague, John Deverill, also? Good, they replied, *On khoroshiy paren* (He is a good fellow). But they were by no means at ease, frequently visiting the toilet, drinking a large amount of vodka and staring silently out of the windows, sucking their teeth and muttering to each other in undertones. John, who had been on the flight deck, came back to explain that we were now crossing the English Channel and would be landing at London Airport in about thirty minutes. They accepted this, stony-faced and mute.

Out of my window I saw two aircraft in formation converging on us from above and to starboard. They were RAF Meteors and their presence created near panic among the delegation. The Meteors took up station one on each side of us, some fifty yards from the TU 104. I tried to explain that this was an RAF escort in honour of the Soviet Air Force but my words did little to restore calm and it wasn't until the Meteors broke away and waggled their wings in salute that the delegation settled down.

We lost height over the coast and approached Heathrow Airport where we landed with somewhat of a bump, ran the full length of the east-west runway and came to a halt as the van with the parking marshal arrived and escorted us round the perimeter to the apron immediately in front of the arrival entrance of the international terminal. The two engines whined down to silence. The gangway was in position and the huge stewardesses opened the door. I stood up and said something like 'Welcome to Great Britain' which was greeted with more fidgets and a few words of acknowledgement. But nobody moved from their seats. I went to the open door. On the apron was a group of uniformed, senior RAF officers, a few immaculate, pinstriped men who were quite obviously from the Foreign Office/Civil Service and, standing apart, two heavily built, black-suited bruisers, clearly Soviet security men. Each had his right hand in his jacket pocket!

The bruisers came aboard and moving down the rows spoke barely audibly to the delegation. They said something to the KGB Colonel, nodded to me and left. The delegation rose and then made their way down the gangway where they were greeted by several Air Marshals, a representative from the Foreign Office and the media with their cameras and microphones. We disposed of the media in short order and I was escorting my General towards the reception party when I saw her.

Nan! She was there with Ranald, Paddy and Lindsay behind the wire-net barrier between our parking area and the public enclosure. They were waving and jumping and shouting. It was an ecstatic welcome which I could not ignore. I grabbed my General, saying in Russian, 'This is my family, please come and meet them'. He grinned and followed me across the apron. We exchanged handshakes through the wire. I introduced the General who said 'Plees tomeetoo', to which Nan replied, as I had schooled her, *Ochen priyatno*, which crossed the wire netting with clapping of hands and 'Bravo, bravo'. Then one of the black-suited duo called us back. I told Nan I would phone her that evening from our hotel and, with more waving, jumping and calling 'Bye Daddy', we rejoined the delegation who were being escorted to the entrance of the airport building.

We were ushered through Immigration and Customs without any delay and even our guests' baggage was given priority and was outside in the car park when we all settled into three black Daimler saloons for the drive into London. There was a spot of bother when the men in black suggested that Zhigarev and Colonel Konstantinov, the Soviet Air Attaché in London, should travel behind in a Zil, a soviet saloon provided for the members of the Politburo in Moscow. I decided to put my foot down.

No, I said, Marshal Zhigarev was our guest. He would travel with us. In no way would he travel with his 'security guard'! The black suits looked daggers but after the customary whispered consultation, they agreed to comply and Zhigarev sat in the rear seat of the leading Daimler with my General next to him. I sat in one of the fold-down seats in the rear and tried to make conversation with Zhigarev, pointing out the very few objects of interest, mainly factories or high-rise, glass-faced office blocks with the names of their firms – Glaxo, Marconi or whatever – in large lettering on their roofs, but he wasn't interested and sat mute, merely acknowledging my remarks in monosyllables. It was mid-afternoon. The traffic built up at Hammersmith and Zhigarev began muttering under his breath. He was impatient for the journey to end and by the time we had crawled to Piccadilly Circus he was clearly about to blow his top. My General too was taciturn and on edge. We inched our way into the maelstrom of taxis, buses, private cars and every sort of vehicle creeping clockwise around the statue of Eros. Then Zhigarev exploded. Thumping the palms of his pudgy hands on his knees, he turned to me. 'Absolutely uncontrolled!' he spluttered in Russian, 'Better to go on foot!' My General made no reply. I made no reply. The Foreign Office man in front didn't hear as the glass partition was closed. We crawled on in embarrassed silence to our journey's end, the main entrance to the Savoy Hotel.

Zhigarev was out in a flash. Brushing aside all overtures of welcome, he dashed into the hotel shouting '*Tualet*', hotly pursued by the hotel manager. With an uncomfortably full bladder the interminable journey to the Savoy must have been misery. In Moscow any car or convoy of cars with the Red Flag on the bonnet meant Soviet officials. All lights go green; all other traffic – of which there is little enough – is held by red or halted beside the route by the police motorcycle outriders while the Soviet VIPs, unidentified behind tinted windows, sweep without interruption from the city outskirts to the Kremlin.

The men in black emerged from the second car and strode into the foyer followed by Konstantinov. I grabbed him. The security guards were not our guests. He had best get them off the premises without delay. I spoke in Russian without remembering that he spoke fair English. He replied in English that the two 'escorts' had been provided by the Soviet Embassy. I gave him one more chance. If the 'escorts' were not out of the hotel and away in their Zil in five minutes, I would abandon the delegation. He, Konstantinov, could take over the visit and I would explain to the Air Ministry and the Foreign Office that I was not prepared to act as host unless the KGB kept out of it. I was tired and very angry and the message must have got through, for the men in black in their black Zil pulled out. We only saw them once more during the visit, at the reception in the Soviet Embassy.

I explained to Konstantinov that single rooms 'with facilities' – not so easily translated into Russian – had been booked, as had a reception room or lounge and a private dining room. Breakfast would be served in their suites and there was a Russian-speaking lady on the telephone exchange to look after anything they needed. I suggested – it was late afternoon – that our guests rest awhile before refreshments were served in an hour or so. Then the man from the Foreign Office explained that an evening meal would be served at 7 o'clock; that seats had been booked at a local cinema for the late evening screening of a 3-D film which had never before been shown in the UK; the delegation would be met by the manager outside the cinema at 8.15. Cars would be provided.

I took a deep breath. The Foreign Office representative was only doing what he had been told. I explained that the Soviet delegation had been on the move since 7 am our time – 5 am their time: that the last thing they wanted was a rushed meal and a film in English. A senior British Air Marshal, in a dark suit, arrived with a Wing Commander who had limited Russian. We went into the bar. The delegation had taken to their rooms and were changing – at my suggestion – into suits.

The Air Marshal asked: 'How is it going, Mac?' 'Not too well. It's early yet but the delegation is suspicious and the security men have said something to them that has rocked the boat. They are also very tired and, frankly, I think this outing to the 3-D film is a mistake.' Konstantinov joined us. In fair English he confirmed that his comrades were tired and were relaxing in their rooms. We exchanged toasts and got down to business. Centred on the SBAC display at Farnborough, we discussed the associated events during their week's stay as our guests in the UK.

We had a programme which had been translated into Russian, together with the customary 'bull' which purported to explain our liberal way of life and the freedom with which each and every citizen could vote according to his view. The Church came in with a plea for freedom of religious expression which I found difficult to understand; the Russian translation was incomprehensible. There was even a plug for the London Underground system which, defiled by litter, undignified by graffiti and manned by unhelpful staff, was the worst possible introduction to the capital of the United Kingdom.

I had changed into a suit, had rung Nan and said that things were more or less under control. She wished me a somewhat boozy 'Good luck' and I hung up. The delegation came down, each wearing the standard suit for non-ceremonial occasions. Bereft of their multi-medalled uniforms, they presented a very different image: no longer were they 'Heroes of the Soviet Union' but elderly peasants unused to the social behaviour of the West.

The evening meal was a good meal but our guests were tired and in no mood to be hurried. Russian meals are leisurely. Official functions in the Soviet Union are frequently held up because the speakers haven't finished eating and drinking. But we were hustled out into the cars before the brandy and coffee had been served and were late at the cinema. The film had started when we threaded our way along the front row of the circle to the seats which had been reserved for us. The delegation reacted immediately to the smoke-laden atmosphere of the auditorium. They were frankly appalled. Smoking is simply not allowed in Russian theatres or cinemas. The 3-D presentation was technically very good but we had missed the beginning of the film; it was in English and the stench of tobacco smoke was too much. After ten minutes or so, Zhigarev rose from his seat, said '*dostatochno*' (enough), and we all filed out of the front row of the circle. I made my apologies to the front-of-house manager. We walked back to the Savoy as our official cars were not to be seen. A disastrous evening.

I apologised as best I could and suggested we have drinks in our private lounge before going to bed. Zhigarev shrugged this off and left with Konstantinov. The others followed me into the lounge and I ordered drinks. We drank a lot, mostly brandy, and were joined later by Konstantinov who said Zhigarev had a headache and had gone to bed. The Soviet Air Force delegation to London had got off to a bad start.

I phoned J.B. Hogan, gave him a brief account of the situation and asked if he could persuade the Director of Air Intelligence to release Mike Forter for the day which was programmed as 'Sightseeing'. Dear JB, within ten minutes he was back to say that Mike Forter was on his way, as was also an Air Vice-Marshal who spoke fair Russian. The AVM arrived, then the young man from the Foreign Office turned up and Mike Forter, looking immaculate in his dark-grey pinstripe suit, made his appearance.

We drove our guests to St Paul's Cathedral, Westminster Abbey, the Tower of London – where we were received by the Governor and the usual glass of sherry – and thence to a dockland pub where the Cockney proprietor, being pre-warned, served Stolichnaya vodka, a recent import from the Soviet Union, which was followed, in a private room, by an excellent meal and more vodka and very acceptable wine. The drivers then conveyed their noisy passengers to the Savoy where they repaired to their rooms and slept, until the evening when a formal dinner was on the programme, hosted by the Vice Chief of the Air Staff.

This was the breakthrough. Our guests relaxed. We lingered over the vodka, caviar, smoked salmon – you name it – which was served in abundance before dinner was announced. We had enough Russian speakers to keep the conversation going and the Savoy management served an outstanding meal which combined the most traditional of Russian cooking with British beefsteak and a choice of French or Russian champagne followed by brandy, liqueurs and coffee.

International barriers were down. Someone produced a balalaika and there was singing and hugging and much emotion when the guests one by one tottered up to their rooms. I fell into my bed, fairly drunk but content. The KGB Colonel, however, who wasn't staying in the Savoy, had been silent and uncommunicative throughout the evening. He left at about 11.30 pm and we didn't see him on the morrow.

We flew the delegation to the Central Flying Establishment at RAF Manby where they were warmly welcomed and well fed. Unfortunately, the weather was poor and the flying display had to be curtailed. On the way the pilot of the fairly antiquated Transport Command aircraft had flown us directly over a US Air Force bomber base, whether deliberately or otherwise I never knew. Our Soviet guests went crazy, rushing from window to window while Konstantinov, maintaining as dignified a calm as possible, wanted to know the name of the base. I told him. Why not? The Soviet intelligence obviously had it plotted. He grinned at me and said in English, 'I think you fool me, Mr MacDonell.' I grinned back and left it at that.

Next we flew the delegation to the Royal Air Force College at Cranwell. The Flight Cadets were on leave, but the Commandant and his staff, together with the Chief Flying Instructor and his squadron commanders, received our guests. We drove round the precincts of the College, the Flying Wing and the married quarters where our motorcade stopped at a pre-arranged sergeant pilot's married quarter into which we were invited. It was immaculate. The sergeant pilot instructor, his wife and two small girls showed us over their home. The sergeant pilot conducted himself with great dignity and hospitality: his wife, a sweet dark-eyed young woman, had prepared for her guests with warmth and grace. The two girls were charming and showed off their dolls and teddy bears in wide-eyed silence. They were somewhat taken aback when Zhigarev, in true Russian fashion, chucked them under their chins. In Russia this is a gesture of affection; the girls were not at all sure what it meant. I was interpreting more or less non-stop. Zhigarev wanted to know the rank of the occupant. I told him. He froze and muttered something about only a colonel would have such a 'flat'. It wasn't a flat, which gave rise to even more tooth-sucking. I thanked the sergeant and his wife who both smiled and she said, 'I hope that was what was wanted?' I reassured her it was exactly what was wanted. She said, 'Thank you. I'm afraid they had mud on their shoes and didn't wipe their feet.' My heart went out to her.

After lunch in the Mess, we looked in at the library, inspected an unoccupied Flight Cadet's room and then drove to the Flying Wing – memories of my command as Chief Flying Instructor nine years before. Then the Russians were escorted through the hangars and viewed a line-up of some ten Jet Provosts of the Advanced Training Squadron, each aircraft with its pilot and ground crew in attendance in full operational kit. Each member of the delegation was invited to climb into a cockpit and handle the controls. Communication was by sign language until I was free to explain a technical point. But Konstantinov was helpful, as his English had improved considerably. Zhigarev was offered a flight by the Squadron Commander but declined somewhat stubbornly, which suggested he was under orders not to go joyriding. I asked Konstantinov if he would accept a flight with the Chief Flying Instructor. He looked at Zhigarev and spoke to him in Russian. Zhigarev stiffened and faced his group: 'No one is to fly with the British pilots. These are the regulations.' The Commandant asked me to translate, which I did. Why, he asked me, had this embargo been imposed on Cranwell when the Soviet Air Force delegates had been flown up by Transport Command? I had no answer. We were flown back to RAF Northolt. Cranwell was always good at presenting itself and our guests had been well impressed.

We met later in the evening for drinks, dinner and after-dinner drinks until, one by one, we retired to our rooms. Tomorrow was the highlight of the visit – the reception by the Society of British Aerospace Companies at their annual air display at Farnborough. It was well past midnight when I got to bed. I simply could not keep pace with the drinking of vodka and brandy and I was not in the best shape at breakfast. However, I had a job to do and shortly after the cars arrived I had the delegation, all in uniform, sorted out to their wishes – the KGB Colonel with Zhigarev,

Konstantinov with me, and my General and the others with a sprinkling of members of the Foreign Office and a Wing Commander from the Directorate of Air Intelligence. Our convoy toiled westwards slowly and to the obvious frustration of its passengers until we reached the entrance to Farnborough where we were held up for at least twenty minutes because the Secretary of State for Air was due to arrive. Eventually we were admitted and driven to the SBAC marquee.

We were received by the Chairman and his staff, by Sholto Douglas and many others who spared no pains to make our Soviet Air Force delegation most welcome. The caterers did us proud: there was vodka, brandy, whisky and champagne with caviar, salmon and a splendid variety of cold meats and savouries a truly magnificent buffet. Within ten minutes our guests were smiling and hitting the vodka and brandy. Two interpreters arrived and helped to take the load off me. When the flying display began, I suspect there were few of us who took our seats in the enclosure and weren't feeling on top of the world – except the KGB Colonel and the two in black suits who had materialised some time during the meal and just stood, refusing food or drink.

Despite the sky's being overcast and the cloud cover being about 3,000 feet, the flying display was carried out with impeccable precision. Our Soviet guests were genuinely impressed, jabbering to each other and following the aerobatics with wild-arm gestures, grunts and nods of approval. I sat at the end of the row and felt content, if not entirely sober.

Conspicuous in their uniforms, which Konstantinov had advised them to wear, the Russians were objects of curiosity. Who were they? Where had they come from? What language were they speaking? And so on. We moved into the static display area where a few aircraft but mostly components were being presented by their manufacturers, each with a team of dark-suited salesmen with well-rehearsed patter and a brochure for any potential client. There was a relatively new turbojet engine on display, complete with its nacelle and tail pipe.

Konstantinov showed immediate interest. He walked round, peering into the front and then into the tail pipe. Something caught his attention and he heaved himself up and crawled inside, only his bottom and waving legs visible. The Press had been following us and at this juncture they had a field day with their cameras. Then we bade our hosts farewell and with much handshaking and good humour we climbed into our cars and were driven back to London and the Savoy. It had been a good day. Zhigarev and his colleagues spent the evening at the Soviet Embassy so the rest of the day was free.

I was about to walk to the RAF Club for an evening meal when I was called to the phone. It was Nan. Could I come down to East Grinstead tomorrow? Lin had fallen off her bicycle and had cut her chin very badly. She was in East Grinstead Hospital for surgery. Nan was clearly upset though she assured me that Lin had not sustained any more serious injury. She would, however, always carry a scar, Could I manage a short visit? There was nothing of much importance on our programme for the morrow: a visit to the War Memorial at Runnymede and theatre in the evening. We were flying back to Moscow on the following day.

'Yes, of course,' I said. 'Give me half an hour and I will call you back.' She sounded reassured. As JB had just left to catch his train to Sussex, I called the Staff Officer of the Air Marshal in the Air Ministry who was to be tomorrow's host. We knew each other and after I had explained what had happened he agreed immediately that I could be let off the hook. Mike Forter would join in and I wasn't to worry. He suggested I explain the situation to Zhigarev and hoped my daughter wasn't too badly injured. I called Nan and we agreed on a train that suited the hospital visiting hours. I took a taxi to the RAF Club where I ate alone at a table for two in the Buttery and was fussed over by the Head Waitress to whom I told of Lin's accident. I know not why, I simply remember an over-whelming need to share my concern with someone.

Back at the Savoy I made contact with Konstantinov who was in conference with the rest of the Soviets in Zhigarev's suite. I was not invited in but Konstantinov said he and the Marshal completely understood and were sure they would be well looked after. There was a lot of background noise and laughter at the end of the phone and I reckoned the dinner at the Soviet Embassy had been well up to standard. I slept deeply that night.

I caught an afternoon train to East Grinstead where Nan met me. We drove to the hospital. She said she wouldn't accompany me to see Lin. I detected something strange in the way she made her point. Lin was in a ward of her own with a television and the usual collection of fruit juices and sweeties. She was bandaged and looked pale and frail. We fell into each other's arms. Her tears welled out and she spoke with difficulty telling me that Nan had scolded her for falling off her bike and had said that Daddy would be very angry. She had dreaded my coming to see her. I would blame her and she couldn't bear to have me visit her if I were angry with her.

Poor Lin. I comforted her. I told her I loved her, that I didn't blame her at all and that Nan had probably over-reacted. Lin was only nine and a half: she clung to me and we talked lovingly. I described how I had arranged for Nan, Ranald, Paddy and her to come to Moscow in the summer and that we would all go to Yalta in the Crimea, where we would bathe in the Black Sea and have picnics on the beaches. She began to smile and when I left she was hugging me in real happiness.

It would not be long before we were together in Moscow. But I had misgivings about Nan's treatment of Lin. There was something wrong which I was unable to identify before she drove me to the station for my train to London. Why had she not wished to see Lin in hospital? I pondered this back in my room in the Savoy and went to bed with a heavy heart. It would be five months before the summer holidays and the family visit to Moscow.

We were driven to Heathrow in the morning where a farewell reception was held in the VIP lounge, hosted by senior government and Royal Air Force representatives. Neither the KGB Colonel nor the men in black were in evidence and after the customary toasts to our respective countries and a speech or two from either side we were invited to board. We took off appropriately from the west-east runway. The KGB Colonel was on board before we arrived. The same stewardesses were in attendance and the delegation settled down silently to the food and drink that was served.

Only when John came back from the flight deck to report that we were we were '*nad rodine*' (over the home country) did our passengers come to life. They crowded to the windows but we were flying above cloud and no land was visible. They laughed, hugged each other and called for more drink. John and I were thumped on our shoulders and even the stewardesses managed a smile as they plied us with glass after glass of champagne.

It was a joyous if somewhat disoriented party that tottered down the steps onto the apron at Vnukovo where a small reception committee immediately took over. The senior representative from the British Embassy and one of my Assistant Air Attachés were virtually ignored. Zhigarev shook my hand and nodded to John. No other member of the delegation gave us a word of thanks. They were hustled to their waiting Zils and swept away, prisoners of their own making and back behind the bars of the KGB's surveillance.

We arrived at my flat to find it locked and empty. But the policeman in his duty box at the ground floor had my key. I was too tired to question his right of entry to my residence, so I let him open the door and without further ado I undressed, took a shower and slept for the better part of twelve hours.

CHAPTER FIFTY-EIGHT

To Baku and Back

The next day Daphne told us that our journey to Baku had been approved with no restrictions. We could leave within a fortnight! Unbelievable!

We made our plans. Daphne took charge of the commissariat on the understanding that she could bring her fishing rod: this was the first John and I knew of her interest in the sport.

Leaving my two Assistant Air Attachés in charge of the office, we loaded the Standard Vanguard with luggage and confirmed the Aeroflot flight from Vnukovo to Mineral'niye Vodi for the first leg of a journey that had been so long in my mind – the journey to Baku, my birthplace.

The Vanguard had left two day's earlier and was there when we landed. The driver, Vasili, saw us off on the first stage of our journey over the Georgian Military Highway to Tblisi. He then returned to Moscow by air. I have often wondered whether the expense involved in these journeys was justified but we played the game according to the rules, which seemed remarkably flexible.

John did the driving. I sat in front while Daphne occupied the back in supreme command of the food and drink, which she dispensed at regular intervals, and maintained a running commentary on our whereabouts and what lay ahead. We climbed the highway towards the towering height of Mount Kazbek while half a mile or so behind a small cloud of dust reminded us that the goons were following our trail.

The Georgian Military Highway was a single carriageway, roughcast in tarmac which was too often broken into potholes and craters. We wound our way up the great strategic road which the Russians had started building some two centuries ago across the towering mountain barrier of the Caucasus. A remarkable feat of engineering, the highway, 120 miles in length, connected Ordzhonikidze (now once again called Vladikavkaz, 'key to the Caucasus') to Mtsheta, the old city close to Tblisi.

Even Daphne, who was, and still is, a great conversationalist, fell silent as the sheer grandeur of the landscape unfolded. No longer were the hill-sides wooded; indeed any form of vegetation other than sparse grass and the occasional shrub was left behind. The hills were rock-strewn and barren, of the colour of sand, and crowded in on our passage. Occasionally a valley revealed a distant landscape with mountains towering as though in menace with snow-capped peaks breaking through the rain clouds that were gathering ahead of us. We saw an occasional shepherd with a horse or donkey, a few dogs and a weary flock of goats or sheep. There were no habitations for mile upon mile and it began to get cold as we climbed. Nevertheless we stopped for an alfresco meal and an opportunity to stretch our legs; we ate little for Daphne had fed us copious snacks from the back and the odd tot of vodka. We ate enough to keep us going and relieved ourselves behind the rocks.

The goons passed us, pulled up in a lay-by a few hundred yards ahead and then one of them appeared head and shoulders above a rock where we were sitting. We waved and shouted 'Greetings' in Russian, He disappeared. John drove off in style, honking the horn as we passed.

Thus we proceeded up the Georgian Military Highway to Kazbegi for our overnight stop which was accorded the status of a 'good hotel with a restaurant and facilities'. We drew up outside a rundown building with a sign *Gostinitsa* (Hotel) hanging from a rusting bracket above the entrance.

There was a small desk in the entrance hall but no bell. John banged his hand on the desk and an unshaven and none too friendly man emerged from an office behind. John explained who we were. We were told all rooms were occupied. The man was drunk. He spoke in a Georgian dialect which we found difficult to understand. Our explanation that two rooms had been booked for us from Moscow, that we were British diplomats, had no effect, He withdrew and a dark-haired, dark-eyed youngish woman appeared. John repeated that we had been booked in for the night by BUROBIN from Moscow. Was there another hotel in the town?

No, there wasn't. She looked at a ledger and said, 'Yes, there was a three-bedded room booked for visitors from Moscow'. What were our names? We gave them. She sucked her pencil and said *'Ponyatno'* (Understood) and managed a smile. We said that two rooms had been booked for us. We were in no way prepared to sleep all together. She looked at Daphne, John and me, muttered something and went upstairs.

At this stage the goons arrived; at least we reckoned they must be from the way they looked at us sideways and slunk into an annexe.

The young woman came down and shook her head. Only one three-bedded room had been reserved for us. She shrugged her shoulders, implying that we could take it or leave it. Daphne said she would happily share a room with us. She spoke in English but John would have none of it and, addressing the woman in well-articulated Russian, he informed her that he was a British diplomat who with his two companions had travelled all the way from Moscow to visit Tblisi and Baku. He was furious that now the accommodation was not available. How disgraceful ...! We had practised this approach on a few previous occasions with considerable success. I added my usual tailpiece to the effect that the whole business was making a very bad impression on us.

She glanced towards the annexe and then went in. We heard her speaking softly and a man's voice answering. She reappeared and said 'It can be arranged. There will be one room for the lady and another for the two gentlemen.'

We unloaded the Vanguard and were shown to our rooms. Daphne's was twin bedded, ours was triple. Where was the toilet? We were shown into a very small shower room with a wash basin, no mirror and no toilet. Where was the toilet? The woman looked blank so, without undoing my flies, I mimed doing a pee. Ah yes, she understood. I then used the Russian word *ubornaya* which I had heard on previous trips outside Moscow. '*Na dvore*,' she said – outside. We exchanged glances as we followed her downstairs. Out through a back door and there down a few steps was a low stone building with its front open to the four winds. We peered inside. Two undivided earth closets with fixed stone seats covered with excrement, the whole place stinking and crawling with flies. 'Christ,' said John. 'In no way,' said Daphne. Words failed me.

Daphne duly joined us in our room; we knocked back our vodka, agreed we had no option but to accept what was on offer – used bed linen, unopenable windows, the unspeakably dreadful outside privy and whatever the establishment had to offer us in the way of an evening meal. We decided to be on the road by no later than 9.30 next morning as we wanted as much time as possible to see something of Tblisi, the capital of Georgia.

We were in good humour when we went downstairs to the small restaurant. Against the far wall at a table for two sat two po-faced men who looked down at their food when we appeared and acknowledged our 'Good evening' with grunts. Without doubt our goons, who probably had to double up in consequence of our outrage at the accommodation that had been offered us. They left the restaurant shortly after we sat down and we saw nothing of them for the rest of the evening.

The meal was, in fact, very good. The Georgians are fond of their food and wine and cook well. John was tired after all the driving, so we retired early. The sun had gone down over the mountain range to the west and the sky was cloudless with a myriad of stars in all their brilliance, for the moon was not yet up. I was soon asleep.

Someone was shaking my shoulder, I awoke and instantly sat up. It was John with his torch. 'I'm sorry, sir,' he said, 'But there's something I think you should see. I've woken Daphne and she's coming with us.' I scuffled into my socks as the floor was filthy and followed John into the corridor where a bleary-eyed Daphne in her dressing gown awaited us. John led us to the end of the passage and then out onto the balcony.

Dawn was just breaking. The shadows of the mountains of the Caucasus were just visible against the first feeble light in the east but away and above the range a small golden glimmer of light held our attention. John said, 'Mount Kazbek'. We watched and waited. Slowly but dramatically this small light grew in intensity and radiance until the whole majesty of this great mountain was crowned in crimson, a blazing beacon lighting the foothills to the reality of another day. We stood there, on this grubby balcony, while the sun appeared beyond the peak and the world – our world – woke up to dawn in Georgia. I doubt if any of us will ever forget what we saw or what we felt.

There was no hot water in the shower room: indeed the shower dribbled cold when turned on, spluttered, dribbled again and then gave up. Without a mirror we decided to go unshaven, washed as best we could and unashamedly urinated down the shower drain from which the stink of stale pee suggested this was standard practice. We collected Daphne and ate breakfast in the dining room. The goons were leaving and to Daphne's enquiry as to whether they too were travelling to Tblisi they mumbled something which I didn't catch; but she added, 'I expect we will see you again when we arrive'.

John and I managed the outside privy without sitting down. I believe this is a custom practised by Hindus. Very uncomfortable but just possible if you don't take too long. Daphne said she would wait until we were away in the mountains. We settled our bill, loaded the Vanguard and set off for the pass over the summit. The goons took up station a few hundred yards behind.

A while later Daphne asked if we could stop as she 'had to go'. We pulled in by a side-track which ran up between rocky outcrops. Daphne disappeared; the goons parked some hundred yards behind and John and I noticed the passengers get out and move up the slope in Daphne's direction. We sat in the Vanguard and talked. We heard a muffled shout, possibly a shepherd calling to his dog, and thought nothing of it. Then Daphne appeared, elated, adjusting her undergarments and grinning. 'Off we go,' she said as she settled into her seat in the back. She began to laugh.

Then she told us. Seemingly she had found a suitable place to 'go' and was in the process of adjusting her dress when she saw a goon peering at her few yards away from behind the rock where she had chosen to squat. He returned her look without moving. Daphne was not one to take this sort of thing without reacting. She managed to pick up a stone which she hurled with remarkable force and accuracy at the goon and scored a bull, striking him on the back of his neck as he retreated from his bunker. Hence the shout!

We drove on and shortly reached the pass and summit from which we could look down the highway as it coiled through the slopes of Georgia to Tblisi some fifty miles below. The landscape changed dramatically. No longer did we drive through barren, bleak rock-bound scenery. Now we entered wooded hillsides with bushes and vegetation, cultivation and villages, people and cattle and small bands of children with schoolbags on the swing, running along beside us and shouting in their patois, 'Where do you come from?'

The surface of the Georgian Military Highway improved and we ran into Tblisi during the afternoon and registered with no problem in our hotel, where we were greeted with a much appreciated glass of Georgian red wine – 'for friendship'. We rested until the evening meal, checked our flight to Baku for the morrow and drifted into the restaurant, tired but content.

We had a very good meal, after which Daphne changed into a skirt and sweater and said she was 'going out', an explanation which we never questioned. Her London brief was clearly more explicit than was ours: she had her particular business while our much more general remit left the choice of visit very much to us always bearing in mind the requirement to obtain a sighting of a Soviet Air Force base.

I must confess we didn't have much faith in the occasional specifics from Air Intelligence. We received one which involved a two-day journey for which we duly applied to BUROBIN. It was granted. We set off and found that our route passed along the perimeter of the 'airfield' we were required to cover. Somewhat surprised by the absence of checkpoints we pressed on only to discover that the 'airfield' was abandoned and had clearly been disused for several years. My brief to Air Intelligence was to the point and contemptuous. I got no reply!

Daphne returned buoyant and ready for a nightcap. We had a drink but didn't ask her what she had been up to. This was her affair.

We were away early the next morning for our flight to Baku. We landed on a somewhat basic airfield but, as I stepped off onto the tarmac, I experienced an extraordinary sense of *déjà vu*. We had arrived in Baku – the town of my birth forty-four years before. I found myself imagining my parents walking where I stood; the landscape of oilrigs virtually surrounding the airfield; the strong smell of the wells and the still, acrid air which my father had spoken of many years ago. I felt an extraordinary sense of belonging.

We were driven to our hotel. John and Daphne went in while I and the driver unloaded the luggage. A very unpleasant man who claimed to be the 'Director' was in an angry argument with Daphne. We were not to spend the night in Baku; there was no train back to Tblisi on the morrow and we had been booked on the train that evening; a four-berth sleeper compartment had been reserved; the train for Tblisi left in two hours' time and a car would pick us up from the hotel. We would be offered a meal whenever we wished.

Daphne and John were furious. They pulled out all the stops. This was quite obviously not an administrative bungle but a deliberate political move to have us out of Baku that evening. I joined in the argument. Was not I the diplomat who had been granted permission to spend the night in Baku so that I could visit the house where I had been born? What was the reason for making this long journey from Moscow pointless? We would stay in the hotel two nights and take the train back to Tblisi the day after tomorrow.

There was no hotel accommodation for us came the reply.

We produced the outraged formula, adding in this instance that we would report this disgraceful discourtesy to London where no doubt the Soviet Ambassador would be advised that his Soviet Air Attaché would have his liberty looked at very carefully. The man just stared at us and said in Moscow Russian, 'I advise you to leave Baku as you have been told'. Daphne said, 'You are not a Georgian. Our Ambassador in Moscow will be told of what has happened. Good evening!'. He slouched away. The hotel manager came up looking uncomfortable and asked us if we wished to eat. We said no thank you and went into the bar where we had several drinks. Later the manager produced an accommodation bill which we refused to pay. He became abusive, threatened to call the police but pulled out when John said that if there was to be any argument we would refuse to take the train. That would cause trouble for him! He took the hint and we accepted the taxi which drove us to the evening train.

John bought the tickets. He said to the railway clerk, 'I understand the train to Tblisi is not running tomorrow?' 'But certainly it is,' he replied, 'Normal service will operate as usual.' We said nothing but already in my mind I was composing a note to HE in Moscow and a letter to Air Intelligence in London.

Back in Tblisi the Vanguard had been secured in the backyard and was undamaged. We loaded our luggage, Daphne complaining that she hadn't had any fishing and John unable to conceal his fury at the way we had been treated in Baku. I held my peace; I was too upset to say anything and it was Daphne who comforted me. Dear Daphne: she really was at the helm through fair weather and foul. Then we drove off on the long, long journey back to Moscow.

With John and Daphne's help I wrote my report to the Director of Air Intelligence with a copy for HE. I wrote factually of what amounted to nothing more than a motor tour over the Caucasus to Tblisi, a flight to Baku and a few hours later a return to Tblisi by train and thence a long drive back to Moscow. The report contained nothing whatsoever of intelligence value as we had seen only the mountains, hardly anything of Tblisi and virtually nothing at all of Baku. I made no reference to Daphne's evening sortie in Tblisi: that was her business, not mine. Nor could I offer any explanation as to why we had been quite deliberately put on the next train back to Tblisi once we had landed in Baku.

In short, I made no excuse for our failure to secure anything of the slightest interest to DAI. I suggested nevertheless that the extent to which Konstantinov, the Soviet Air Attaché in London, was able to travel unmolested and certainly never 'tailed' be seriously reconsidered.

HE asked me to see him: we discussed what had happened and he agreed to send a copy of my report to the Foreign Office. It went off with the courier in the following week. I never received a reply though what happened to me in Moscow several months later suggests that London reacted to what I had reported and had kept Konstantinov on a much shorter rein.

CHAPTER FIFTY-NINE

A Visit from the Secretary of State for Air

Two further events of consequence occurred before my term of office as Air Attaché came to an end. A Royal Air Force delegation headed by Nigel Birch, the Secretary of State for Air, was invited to Moscow on a reciprocal visit; and Nan brought Ranald, Paddy and Lindsay for a fortnight during the summer of 1957.

To describe the RAF delegation's visit as a flop is not to say that it wasn't worthwhile. Any sort of exchange between the Soviet Union and the United Kingdom was a bonus and for me and my staff to have with us for a week the Commanders-in-Chief of Bomber Command and Fighter Command – Sir Harry Broadhurst and Sir Tom Pike – along with several other senior RAF officers – was an enormous morale booster. And to my amazement and delight who should disembark with the delegation when the Transport Command Britannia came to a halt on the apron at Vnukovo but Mike Forter, back in his native Russia for the first time since he had crossed to the West some twenty-five years before. The delegation was received formally by Zhigarev and his entourage, with me and my team and two senior members of HE's staff from our Embassy bobbing attendance on the tarmac. In due course we were driven at high speed and without any hold-ups whatsoever to a large hotel off Gorky Street where our delegation was accommodated throughout their visit.

Mike Forter disappeared. He had sought permission to make contact with friends and relations of long ago and had been granted, as it were, weekend leave. I thought this exceedingly unwise but it wasn't my business and I held my peace. Nigel Birch, who had arrived in a crumpled raincoat and wearing a battered trilby hat, was complaining that he was ill and asked to see the Embassy doctor. We never knew what the trouble was. He was in evident discomfort and seeking medical advice throughout the visit. I mentioned it to Harry Broadhurst who smiled mischievously: 'Piles I reckon, Mac. Watch the way he sits down'. We left it at that!

The programme of events for our delegation seemed bland in contrast to the lengths to which we had gone to show the Soviet Air Force delegation something of our way of life, not only in the RAF but in our country. Our Soviet hosts depended too much on receptions, interminable briefings and propaganda scenarios.

Inevitably, both the Soviet Air Force and the British Embassy hosted receptions and the first forty-eight hours were devoted to diplomatic and social functions. Our delegation was escorted round the Kremlin, given lunch in the Soviet equivalent of the Air Ministry and, mercifully, allowed what remained of the afternoon to themselves – the lunch had lasted three hours. The Secretary had been plied with far too much brandy and wine and was looking none too well. Harry Broadhurst and the others, however, were soaking it up and giving as good as they got from their hosts; but I was keeping a low profile, interpreting and steering some members of the delegation away from a group of black-suited individuals who seemed bent on getting them drunk. In the end we took our leave in good order though I realised that somehow we had to protect Nigel Birch from what was the usual pattern of 'hospitality' towards a VIP. He simply wasn't up to it.

We were flown down to Stalingrad in a basic Soviet short-range transport aircraft. The seats were dreadful and we flew at about 800 or 1,000 feet, below cloud, which provided the most uncomfortable flight I have ever experienced. The Secretary of State was sick. I advised the delegation not to accept the frequently offered vodka but to eat anything that was passed around; our hosts appeared to relish both food and drink and I found it awkward to explain that *Gospodin* Birch was not very well.

'Brandy,' they brayed, 'Give him brandy. He will soon feel better.'

At Stalingrad we were driven in convoy to one of the few main buildings which stood proud from among the ruins of the rest of the town, where we were greeted by a group of Soviet Army senior officers. Following a prolonged buffet meal during which Nigel Birch was toasted far too often, we were assembled in an auditorium and, after a lengthy introduction, were treated to a ninety-minute presentation of the Battle of Stalingrad, the heroic encirclement of Von Runsted's army and the final capitulation of the enemy in what was undoubtedly the turning-point in the 'Great Patriotic War'. Nigel Birch was asleep for the better part of an hour during the presentation but no one paid much attention. He was wearing his trilby.

Later we shuffled aboard the Soviet aircraft and were treated to another low-level flight back to Moscow. It was mind over matter that brought us to the dinner table in our hotel with Zhigarev, who hosted the meal, and Konstantinov, who had arrived that morning. Nigel Birch had opted out but rejoined us later. I gained the impression that our hosts were very much under the strict supervision of their masters, the KGB. Any suggestion on my part of the smallest deviation from the day's programme, which was only made known to us on the day before, was abruptly dismissed as '*Nevozmozhno!*' (Impossible!).

We were driven out to a Soviet airfield a few kilometres from Moscow for a 'display of new military aircraft'. Photography was absolutely forbidden but we would have a close look at the aircraft. We could ask questions which would be answered.

We left the hotel shortly after breakfast. Nigel Birch was feeling better and was taken over by Konstantinov and Zhigarev's deputy, a general I had not seen before. They travelled in the first Zil limousine, behind which was another with a driver and two men in black suits. There was some problem with seating so, as I had my official Humber with my driver, I offered to take Harry Broadhurst and Tom Pike. The men in black got out and there was a low-key conversation which I couldn't catch but, in the event, my offer was accepted and in we climbed with instructions to my driver from one of the men in black to take up position as number two in the motorcade.

Thus we proceeded and within half an hour reached the main gates of the airfield though they remained closed for several minutes. The unknown general got out of the front car. Two of the men in black emerged from the one drawn up behind us. Further talk with animated gesticulations. Harry Broadhurst and Tom Pike were fascinated. 'What the hell's going on, Mac?' I turned to Harry. 'I suggest, sir, that we three get out and discover what's going on.' He looked at Tom Pike. 'Why not? They can't exactly shoot us.' So we opened the doors and stepped out: it was all very organised and dignified with me holding the door-handle and standing stiff and erect as two Air Marshals emerged, shot their cuffs – memories of Kaye Edden at Latimer – and stepped onto the pavement.

Bedlam! The men in black and the general began to stride towards us shouting and pointing back to the car. We must get back at once. We would be received shortly by the Base Commander – after the gates were open. We had not been invited to get out of our car. *Gospodin* Minister had not left his seat, why had we left ours?

I replied loudly in my most formal Russian so that all could hear. 'Mr General, very senior Royal Air Force officers do not like being kept waiting with no reason. Please apologise to your guests and explain why.'

This was a bull's-eye! The two Air Marshals stood beside me in calm dignity. The general fell to pieces. I repeated. 'Why are we delayed? Why are the gates closed? Where is the Guard of Honour?' Don't overdo it, I thought to myself, keep your cool and don't overplay your hand. Then Konstantinov got out of the first car. 'Leave this to me,' he said in English. 'There has been a mistake. We are not yet expected. All will soon be in order.'

He strode across to the group and suggested to Harry Broadhurst that we get back into the car. We left Konstantinov to deal with the situation. Within minutes there was a lot of stamping, shouting and the sound of motorbike engines from within; then the gates were opened and we drove into the Base serenely and with an escort of motorbikes past a double line of Soviet Air Force personnel with their arms at the salute.

We were received by the Base Commander in an administrative block with no view of the airfield. An address of welcome was followed by the inevitable buffet with lavish servings of caviar, salmon and many other delicious Russian dishes. There was vodka and champagne.

Then we drove round the airfield where, virtually out of sight, was a line-up of Soviet military aircraft, most of which even at long range I recognised as having been identified by the DAI, though I suspected that at least two were unknown. So we drifted around the perimeter track and were halted a hundred yards or so behind the line-up where we were given a further briefing, the theme being the effectiveness of the Soviet Air Force.

We were marshalled into a line which was at right angles to the static display, a position from which we could observe nothing of note about the aircraft. After a further briefing from a colonel, we were driven at a fair pace past the ten or so military aircraft that comprised the static display. There were two short-range bombers which were of interest, the rest were, from an intelligence point of view, old hat.

Would we like to ask questions? Yes, indeed! I did the interpreting. Tom Pike and Harry Broadhurst put the questions, almost all of which were focused on the two newcomers to our compendium of Soviet military aircraft. Questions, mostly from Tom Pike, came thick and fast: top speed, range, operating height, static thrust of engines, armament, bomb load, and so on. Not a single query was answered definitively; all answers were evasive, the most frequent response being, 'The data have not yet been evaluated', or, 'The aircraft is still undergoing flight testing.'

Nigel Birch looked bored and moved back into his limousine. Harry Broadhurst said little: he was busily sketching the two new aircraft on the back of an A4-size envelope. After about twenty minutes we gave up, climbed into our cars and were driven back to Moscow and the hotel.

The Secretary of State called a conference and asked me to attend. Could I give a summary of what had been achieved? He looked me very straight in the face. Very little, I replied, and then suggested that the Soviet Union was not concerned with developing a conventional air force as we understood it. The two new aircraft we had seen were short-range, ground support fighter-bombers probably equipped with fairly sophisticated radar targeting and a high-speed, low-level capability. But what was occupying the minds of the Soviet air defence staff in the Kremlin was the completion of surface-to-air (SAM) missile sites surrounding Moscow and other strategically important centres in the Soviet Union and, of far greater consequence for the West, an intercontinental nuclear missile capability about which we had relatively inadequate intelligence. I spoke clearly and slowly in the knowledge that the Secretary's suite was inevitably bugged and that what was said in the reception room was certain to be recorded. I had decided that to make my views known to the KGB on these issues would serve our policy of pre-emption – for the United States was at that time well ahead in their development of long-range nuclear rocketry – and that no reaction would ensue other than probable further restrictions on my movements and activities.

Nigel Birch, Broadhurst and Pike heard me without comment. Then Broadhurst produced his sketch of which he was justifiably proud. It wasn't half bad: he had the main details well outlined and we fell to discussing the aircraft's potential.

Shortly after we had sat down in the restaurant, the hotel director came to our table and asked if the Secretary would be so good as to speak with a representative of *Pravda*, the Soviet-controlled Communist Party daily. There was a gentleman from *Pravda* in the lobby. It would only be a very short interview. Nigel Birch looked at me and stood up. I suggested that he decline the invitation. He looked me straight in the face. 'Would it not be a good idea if I were to give them a short interview? Good for inter-national relations?'

I hesitated. 'No, sir. I don't think it would be to our advantage. Whatever you say will be misrepresented in the Soviet press. Could I talk with the representative and say that you are very tired and on your way to bed?'

The Secretary of State said nothing for a while. I stood in front of him, unsure of what I should do. I knew that any statement would be ridiculed in the Soviet press. Did this really matter? Already I was beginning to experience the Donkin syndrome. Why did we have to play the diplomatic game when the KGB was persistently messing us about – Pskov and Baku and a mockery of a display of Soviet aircraft at an airbase on the outskirts of Moscow? I pulled myself together. Nigel Birch had his eyes on me. 'Let me talk to the representative, sir,' I said. 'I think I can get rid of him.'

Nigel Birch nodded. I left the room and went down into the lobby where a small group of reporters and a cameraman were waiting. I greeted them with the explanation that the Secretary of State for Air was unwell but that he had sent me to convey his best wishes and to express his appreciation of the courtesy he had received in the Soviet Union. I bade them goodnight and trod the stairs back to the function room.

The following morning *Pravda* had a small column giving a short but biased biography of Nigel Birch – a typical capitalist minister who was not well enough to speak to the Press.

On the following day we made a short visit by air to Leningrad. We were shown around the Hermitage and the Winter Palace, given an excellent lunch in a hotel, and then driven to St Isaac's Cathedral before being flown back to Moscow for our last evening before the return to the UK. I was to accompany the Secretary and the RAF delegation and to take a fortnight's leave during which I would be required to spend several days with JB and the Director of Air Intelligence. I was delighted, phoned Nan, who wasn't in, but contacted Lindsay, who was over the moon with the news.

On our return from Leningrad we were joined by a slightly tipsy, jubilant Mike Forter – quite obviously he had had a ball. Even his usually impeccable English had gone a bit awry. He was accompanied by an old man who was introduced as Cousin So-and-so. I was at once on my guard but, whoever Mike's companion was, it was immediately evident that he was far too drunk to take in anything. Mike had a sort of Gladstone bag which contained several bottles of vodka, a number of jars of caviar and a bottle or two of Georgian wine, all mixed up with his pyjamas and toiletries. He had found several old friends as well as members of his family. He was quite as clearly surprised to be back safe and sound with the delegation as we were to see him. I had, I confess, given him up as lost.

Next morning, when I was driven to the hotel, I found Mike to be his dignified, immaculate self. We were then driven in a motorcade with police escort to Vnukovo Airport and into the VIP lounge. Among those present were several senior Soviet Air Force officers including Zhigarev; also Konstantinov who was flying back with us. Two senior members of the British Embassy were 'looking after' Nigel Birch and inevitably the odd man in black was in the background. We drank toasts in vodka or brandy and tucked into caviar on crisp biscuits and other *zakuski*.

There were smiles and handshakes all round. Zhigarev made a fulsome speech which Mike Forter translated into English, and then the Secretary of State replied. He was ill at ease, wore his battered trilby and held a leather briefcase in the same manner as the Chancellor of the Exchequer in his traditional departure from No. 11 on Budget Day. The whole effect was somewhat bizarre but he made a good speech. Then, after more handshaking, we proceeded to the tarmac where we paraded down a line-up of more Soviet Air Force officers, our own Naval and Military Attachés and my entire staff, all in uniform.

After the Secretary of State had been escorted onto the Britannia, others filed in. I took up the rear and found myself beside Konstantinov. The crew were already on the flight deck; the engines were run up, the chocks were away and we taxied round the perimeter track to the down-wind end of the runway.

CHAPTER SIXTY

With the Soviets to London

W e took off. Konstantinov looked out of his window. '*Do svdaniya, rodina moya,*' he said – goodbye, land of my birth. He slumped in his seat and there were tears in his eyes. We spoke in Russian. 'You will soon be back, and with your family.' He blew his nose and turned to me. 'Who knows, my friend, who knows?' He stared ahead and we fell silent.

A bottle of vodka from Mike Forter was circulating. The WAAFs provided plastic mugs. Konstantinov waved it away. Presently he turned on his side and, from his heavy breathing, I judged he was asleep. For me, Mike Forter's vodka had an effect of revival. I realised I had been very tired so I lay back as we hit some turbulence. My mind drifted back to the year I had spent as my country's senior RAF representative in the Soviet Union. To what extent had I and my staff offered valid and professional advice to our Ambassadors? Daphne had completed her tour and was back in London. Of my own staff John and Dennis had both been repatriated. Their replacements were enthusiastic and loyal but inexperienced, and it had fallen to me to guide them, deal with the inevitable gaffes and weld everyone into a team in which each gave of his specialist background.

John had been replaced by a large squadron leader with considerable pilot experience. Tiny, as he was called, needed guidance in protocol and etiquette. A compulsive smoker, he would enter a reception with a cigarette in his mouth – which was simply 'not done' – and would parade around those he knew with the thing still hanging on his lower lip. His wife, Rita, through no fault of her own, was completely out of her depth, educationally and socially, and unable to make contact with wives of other service attachés. She eventually settled for an unexacting friendship with the wives of two Chancery guards: an unfortunate choice since I had reason to suspect that one of the guards was too often in the company of Kostaki.

Dennis from the Secretarial branch had been replaced by Alan, a somewhat brash, young flight lieutenant with fair Russian who had travelled out with Daphne's replacement: the Hon. Barbara Fisher, the sister of Lord Fisher who owned a large estate in Norfolk. Alan was likeable enough: tall, slim and with red hair. With his musical talent – he conducted our Christmas carol concert – and the fact that he had, so he thought, the Hon. Barbara Fisher in tow, Alan considered himself several pegs above the rank of a junior service attaché. At an informal drinks party, to which he brought Barbara, he called me Donald. I put a stop to that. He had two driving incidents, but the first was not his fault. A young woman stepped off the pavement in front of him. She was mercifully only superficially injured and admitted the fault was hers. The Soviet authorities exonerated Alan. The second, which involved Barbara as his passenger, was due to his careless driving in freezing conditions. The car skidded and hit a bridge entry. Barbara was badly bruised about the face and Alan had a bump on his head. It was with difficulty that we were able to prevent his driving licence from being withdrawn. I had to be rough with Alan: he was inclined to be a damn nuisance!

Peter's replacement, Oliver, was an enigma. Technically he was very competent – his specialism being radio and electronics – but, withdrawn, silent and very much a loner, he was never really part of the team. Socially he was polite but uncommunicative; often I sought him out at receptions to find him apart, blinking behind his rimless spectacles and more often than not getting slightly drunk.

This was the group I had to weld into a team. By the time I left Moscow we were more or less pulling together, but people don't necessarily adapt as circumstances dictate and I still wonder whether I wasn't wasting my flagging energy and patience during my last six months. I longed for home, for a return to all I had grown to love and respect in the Royal Air Force, to be no longer looking over my shoulder lest I drop a diplomatic brick or give the KGB another card to stack against me in their constant endeavours to compromise and antagonise.

So what of me? What had I achieved in my year and a half in this international charade? I know that I was well accepted by all levels of the diplomatic corps in Moscow. My cocktail parties, lunches and dinners had been successful, largely due to the excellence of Klava's cooking. I have a gift for conversation and narrative derived possibly from my father. I have always been able to put people at their ease; possibly I am more prone to concede when it would be more honest to contest. I won my social spurs in Moscow and HE was well pleased. I was happy that he approved. I had kept my nose clean both socially and privately but by nature I was not a celibate. I had chosen my few partners with great discretion. Oftimes I was tempted by someone from a foreign mission but with one exception I backed off. It was not easy but the forewarning the beautiful girl in the London office had given was ever at the back of my mind: without its blunt truth I could well have been compromised, as were many others in my situation.

I was less confident about how the Director of Air Intelligence would judge my performance. My reports had been factual, sometimes critical, but possibly not fulfilling the essential purpose of my appointment. I had not gathered very much intelligence on the Soviet Air Force.

We crossed the Berlin air traffic control zone and the RAF Russian interpreter who had handled the Soviet control out of Moscow joined us in the passenger section. Konstantinov woke up and became conversational. Where were we? I told him and added that we would be landing at an RAF airfield in England within an hour. I asked him about his impressions of England.

There is much, he replied, which I like but much which I dislike. He looked me straight in the face with his slanted and heavily hooded eyes still weary with sleep. The WAAFS brought the vodka round and he took a glass. So did I. He drank his in a gulp and continued. What he did not like in England was the 'uncomradely' behaviour of its citizens in London: the rudeness of the pedestrians who strode towards him and his family and never gave way to them; the 'unpatriotic' attitude of the black staff on the underground stations who pushed passengers into overcrowded trains and spoke in an accent which he couldn't undersatnd; the demands of a 'tip' from a taxi drivers who swore when he withheld what they regarded as their right. He hated the capitalist system which made the rich richer and the *rabochiye* (workers) poorer or even without work. He hated the smell of London. I broke in and asked what he liked about our way of life. I shall always remember how he sat back in his seat, looked out of the window, took a deep breath and stared ahead.

I like the English people as individuals, he said. I have met many and most of them have been kind and have made me welcome. A few have turned their backs on me because I am a Communist, but the *narod*, the people of your country, are 'true' and we understand each other. In your hotels and pubs, when people understand that we are foreign but can speak some English, they are kind and helpful and we feel warm. I love your countryside and especially Scotland though we are often lost in understanding the dialect. He took my hand: 'You are a good comrade,' he said, 'and you speak good Russian, but perhaps we may never share the same true understanding of our ideologies.' Then he smiled: but we are both aviators. That somehow expressed all that needed to be said. The Russian-speaking squadron leader said we would be landing at RAF Cranfield in an hour's time.

Our arrival was greeted by an imposing turn-out of top brass from the Royal Air Force and senior members of the Secretary of State's office and the Civil Service. A Soviet Air Force major and the inevitable black suit homed in on Konstantinov and escorted him to the car park but not before he had taken me by both hands, kissed me on the cheek and said in Russian, 'Thank you for your friendship'. This was remarked upon by my RAF colleagues and it was a while before I lived it down. 'Mac kissing the Soviet Air Attaché! Good for Mac but, well I mean ...'

We bade farewell to Nigel Birch who graciously thanked me. Then the RAF uniforms and pin-striped suits were driven out from the base. I was heading for the RAF Club and Harry Broadhurst gave me a lift in his staff car as he too was spending the night in London. We spoke of the delegation's visit to the Soviet Union but he didn't vouchsafe any opinion as to its value. Instead we reminisced about the War and the operation when I was shot down in 1941 off the top of the Wing which he had led on a bombing raid on the Forêt de Guine. I thanked him for his kindness in personally calling on Diana to tell her I had not returned. He said, 'Mac, she was quite remarkable and seemed certain that you were still alive.'

Diana had held to this belief until the International Red Cross confirmed that I was a POW. Even my somewhat pessimistic father, with whom she stayed in Swanage for the first three months after my posting as 'missing', found her faith in my survival quite extraordinary. Though he died shortly afterwards, I believe that Diana's faith in my survival sustained him until his end. He wrote me one letter before he died which was of enormous comfort to me with its simple message of love and good cheer. It represented everything which was best in my father: his philosophy, his understanding of what faced me, and his absolute belief that I would come through strengthened and matured. I loved him for it though I had often disapproved of his posturing. This was the soul of my father and I had wept when his letter had been delivered.

Other than the frequent letters from Diana and from the 'pen pals' her notice in the London press had created, I had received very few letters, even from relatives and close friends. My brother Peter had never written a single one during my four and a half years in captivity.

I booked into the RAF Club and rang Nan. We agreed on an afternoon train to Haywards Heath, as I needed to obtain my rail pass from the Air Ministry. I thought it prudent to invite JB to lunch in the Club. I reported to DAI who was evidently pleased with my performance: 'Well done, Mac!'

When the train pulled into Haywards Heath I was ready with my two bags and the window open. They were standing on the platform almost opposite my carriage. Nan saw me but Lin was looking in another direction. I jumped down. Nan nudged Lin and pointed at me. She rushed into my arms and for a while we hugged each other before Nan joined us, very heavily made up and smelling of drink. I kissed her and then looked again at Lin. She was pale-faced, thin and emotional. We humped my bags and a package of presents over the bridge to where the faithful old Lanchester was parked. I drove, Nan beside me. Possibly I spoke mainly to Lin because Nan became tucked up and morose.

The week in Strood's Lodge was an eye-opener. I immediately detected Nan's sense of isolation and Lin's obvious nervousness about her. My presence helped to ease the tension but as I lay in the lower of the bunk beds in Ranald's and Paddy's room I found myself more and more concerned at the effect my absence was having on Nan and especially on Lin.

The boys were away at boarding school: Ranald at Bryanston and Paddy at Cumnor House some three miles from Strood's Lodge. We had him home on Sunday. He was in good shape and, though guarded with Nan, full of fun, talkative and much looking forward to the summer holiday in Moscow, a subject which occupied a great deal of the few days I spent at home. Ranald was too far away at Bryanston to come home so we drove over and took him out to tea with Marsali Gifford and her husband who lived nearby. She was a cousin of my father's and was an elderly and kindly relative who had an abiding interest in my family.

Daphne had made contact with Nan and was to be an invaluable friend and help in the planning and execution of the voyage to Leningrad in the *Baltika*. So, if the relationship between Nan, Paddy and Lin left a lot to be desired, the combined support of Daphne and JB made Nan's travel arrangements relatively trouble free.

CHAPTER SIXTY-ONE

The Family Holiday in Russia

So I was waiting for the family to arrive in Leningrad. To my questions as to why the ship was late, the port officials smiled and said, 'What does it matter? The passengers are comfortable and the *Baltika* will arrive in due course'. In due course, a good hour behind schedule, she drew alongside the dock, hooting her siren, her decks lined with a multinational crowd of passengers shouting in their native tongues to the jostling and boisterous throng on the quayside. I spotted Nan, Ranald and Paddy and we waved and shouted. Where was Lin?

'Where do you think?' said Ranald. 'She always chooses the wrong moment.' The gangways were down, the passengers were disembarking in a noisy, jostling surge to be enveloped in hugs and kisses by friends and relatives. Then Lin appeared and my family came ashore. Nan looked near the end of her tether. With them came a stranger, a woman in her late thirties, Elizabeth Ward. She had travelled with them and was, by the most extraordinary coincidence, the sister of Squadron Leader Ralph Abraham who had shared the room with me, Aidan Crawley, Marcus Marsh and others as POWs in *Stalag Luft* III. The family had changed its name from Abraham to Ward by deed poll.

So Elizabeth joined our party and we were driven in two taxis to the hotel in Leningrad where I had booked accommodation for an overnight stay. Elizabeth had no difficulty in securing a room. She was to spend a fortnight with Helen and Christo whom she had known for several years.

I am said to be all too ready to judge a stranger on first acquaintance. This I deny. I show politeness to a newcomer whatever my personal opinion. I had an initial reservation about Elizabeth but I enjoyed her uninhibited opinion of her first impression of life in the Soviet Union. Yet, I felt an undercurrent of disapproval from her of what she perceived to be my job – that of a spy in a cloak of diplomacy.

We were a mite late for our meeting downstairs. She made the point and stressed that she had waited for thirty minutes in a foreign hotel. Oh dear! The dinner was traditionally Russian. Nan, Ranald, Paddy and Lin ate it up with relish. They were all pretty hungry. Elizabeth complained: she didn't care for borscht, chicken Kiev or anything on the menu. She left the table saying that the Russians were peasants and hadn't any social graces whatsoever. I paid the bill!

We saw Ranald, Paddy and Lin to bed and then Nan and I returned to the lounge where I gave her a couple of brandies. She mellowed, said that she had missed me and that Ranald had become critical and at times hostile. I asked her about Paddy. She was cautious: she didn't really know him, he usually complied with her wishes but there was something about Paddy which she couldn't fathom. He appeared to lack self-confidence.

And so to Lin. Here Nan at once became defensive. Why was I concerned about Lin? She had noticed that I gave her a great deal of attention when I was last at home. Was she, Nan, not giving her the care and attention she needed? 'Why was I worried?' Nan asked for another brandy. I hesitated and then agreed. She sipped her drink, her large eyes wide open and staring me very straight in the face. 'Speak,' she said, 'You are not happy about Lin, are you?'

'Not entirely' I replied. 'She is washed out and too thin.' Nan grabbed her drink, knocked it back and said 'So I am a failure: then I had better leave as soon as we get home!' She picked up her handbag, looked at me hard for a moment and left the lounge. I sat silent and very disturbed for a while. When I went upstairs her door was locked and there was no reply to my call.

This was characteristic of this extraordinary woman. Far from leaving my family she continued to look after them for a further twelve years, though there were several temperamental and often none-too-sober forays when she took off in a fury only to return sullen and demanding a brandy, until the next outburst.

But the following morning she was in great form. All had slept well – except me but I kept quiet about it – and were looking forward to a good tuck-in before going out and seeing something of Leningrad. We knocked on Elizabeth's door. She would perhaps join us later; she was staying in Leningrad for two days, while we were booked on the afternoon flight to Moscow.

When we were settling into the taxi to take us to the airport an official from our hotel rushed up, called 'Mees Feeleeps' and gave Nan the passport which she had left behind at the hotel desk. I regarded this as a good mark for the organisation and reported accordingly to Kostaki on our return to Moscow. After a relatively comfortable flight we landed at

Vnukovo where my Ford Consul was waiting. I drove through the outskirts of Moscow to Skatertny Peryulok but, alas, a dog ran under the car
and was killed instantly. We were shocked; Nan repeating time and time
again, 'It could have been Pooh!'

Thus an emotional party was greeted by Klava and Tanya. After I had
explained what had happened Klava – a mother of four – took Ranald,
Paddy and Lindsay into the kitchen and fed them pancakes and gave them
fruit drinks while I poured brandy into Nan. In due course she calmed
down and by the time everyone had eaten Klava's magnificent evening
meal the party was in good heart.

Christo and Helen MacAlpine lived in the flat below and quickly made
us welcome. Ranald had a room in the flat above ours which was being
refurbished against the arrival of Hugo Newton, the new Naval Attaché,
and his family. Paddy and Lindsay shared one spare room in my flat and
Nan occupied the other. Klava, very much at the helm, was concerned
that my family should be cared for and happy. She never questioned
Nan's wishes or whims but vouchsafed one significant remark – 'Ona ne
mat' (She is not a mother). But, though she made a big effort to adapt to
the social environment, Nan was always ill at ease and Moscow was not to
her liking. She would never leave the flat with the children other than
when Viktor was free to drive them. She, Nan, showed no interest in the
museums, galleries or churches and spent far too much time in the flat,
drinking and wandering from one room to another.

While expecting Nan to have difficulty in identifying with the diplomatic
circle, I had not anticipated her self-imposed imprisonment. I sought to
help her, not only for her own sake but also for the children's. But I was
not free to be with the family every day as my duties in the Embassy tied
me to my office from breakfast until six o'clock. On the weekends Christo
and Helen and 'Bobsie' would often take us out to the Embassy dacha, a
small wooden cottage in the woods a few kilometres outside Moscow.

I had arranged a fortnight's leave and had booked accommodation in
the best, if not the only, hotel in Yalta in the Crimea. This was in some
measure a solace to Nan, who expressed interest in the Crimea, in Yalta
and whether or not we might be able to visit the Palace of Livadia where
the Yalta Conference between Churchill, Stalin and the ailing Roosevelt
had taken place in 1945. Meanwhile Paddy and Lindsay were happy
enough in the company of Helen, Bobsie and Nanny and exploring
Moscow with them.

Ranald was finding Nan's behaviour as much as he could handle. At the
age of fifteen, he sought interests outwith those of Paddy and Lin. His
loyalty to Nan concealed a degree of understandable independence which
was for him impossible to satisfy. Fortunately, an American family with a

daughter of his own age invited him out and were only too happy to get the two together. We joined a riding club. Ranald, on an enormous horse, and the American girl were schooled in trotting, cantering and a measure of dressage in a large arena on the outskirts of the city.

All this had been a 'fill in' before the holiday in Yalta. The Assistant Military Attaché, Tony Hall, his wife and two young sons had also booked into the Yalta hotel. We all got on pretty well together. We were to fly down. Viktor would drive my Consul to Simferopol, the nearest airport to Yalta, and would then return to Moscow by air. We would fly back; he would collect the Consul and drive it back to Moscow – all expenses paid!

Thus we took the flight from Vnukovo and endured another low-level two-and-a-half hours to the Crimea, by which time Nan was at her wits' end. 'Why was the bloody fool flying so low? Why didn't I go and tell him his passengers were feeling ill?' My explanation that civil aviation in the Soviet Union was bound to fly below the level of the radar screen made no impression on her whatsoever. The flight was bumpy but we landed and were disgorged into a crowded reception area where we waited a long while for our luggage.

Viktor had not arrived and there was no taxi. We sat in a sordid lounge for half an hour. I bought orange juice for the children. Nan went to the loo and after a while returned saying, 'That's put paid to my bathing'. The children fortunately didn't understand the implication of her remark and before long Viktor arrived. We were driven to the hotel.

Viktor left. He had bought small presents for the children and was most enthusiastic about my Consul. We opted for an early evening meal and were in the restaurant by 6 pm. The Halls hadn't arrived, so we ordered our meal. Nan was feeling better after a couple of brandies. I translated the menu, we ordered and we waited, and we waited. Frustrated and hungry, I looked for our waitress. She was not to be seen.

Some tables had been served but most had not, their occupants sitting mute, smoking and drinking. I went to the cash desk behind which an amply proportioned lady was sitting picking her teeth. Where was our meal which we had ordered half an hour ago? Half an hour ago, she repeated, going for a back molar. That was before the staff change. You now have a different waitress. You will be served in turn. All will be in order. What was the number of our table? I hadn't the least idea. She sucked her teeth and asked what I had ordered. I was about to blow my top when the Halls arrived, Tony – who only had one arm – waving his one good arm and using the most undiplomatic language, furious that his bookings had been ballsed-up with one bed short and no provision for his driver whatsoever. Kostaki had clearly made a nonsense of this one.

Tony Hall in a temper was not easy to handle but I managed to help him get sorted out with my better command of Russian. I then addressed the problem of our meal.

Politely but firmly I demanded to see the *Direktor*, the manager of the hotel, After some delay a weary-looking, middle-aged man came out from a back office and asked why I wished to speak to him. I was, I said, the Air Attaché from the British Embassy in Moscow and my family and I had been booked in for a week by BUROBIN. Would he please check our registration and provide a meal as soon as possible? We had waited over half an hour. He looked at me, consulted what I assumed was his registration book and then said in a Moscow accent, 'You will be given the same consideration as all our other guests'. I asked him if it was usual for guests to be delayed for over thirty minutes after they had ordered their meal. He looked at me and spoke slowly in Russian. 'We have rules in this hotel. We expect our guests to understand them. Please do not be "unfriendly".' I felt that enough was enough. We were to spend a week in Yalta. Better fall in with the 'rules' of the hotel than make trouble. So I smiled and said, 'Thank you, but remember we have small children who are ever ready for a meal.' Nan who was into her third cigarette and second brandy was not best pleased. Why didn't we go to a restaurant in Yalta? Why wait all night for this bloody hotel to produce a meal? The meal arrived. Thank God it was a good one and before long we were all well fed.

This was the service we were obliged to accept from the best hotel in Yalta, the number one among the Black Sea resorts to which weary members of the Politburo came for a fortnight's rest. The feeble and infirm from the Communist Party hierarchy were sent to recover in the 'health centres' there and parties of children from specially selected schools were dragooned in uniforms to centres of correction. One ponders what 'correction' meant in the context of Soviet indoctrination.

The Halls had their driver from Moscow as Tony found driving for long something of a strain. He made quite an impression when he blew his top, waving and gesticulating with his right arm while his left stub rose and fell in unison beneath the shoulder of his shirt. People looked embarrassed and sympathetic, particularly when I said he had fought as a major in the War. He became something of a local hero.

We soon worked out a daily programme. Breakfast as early as possible but not before 8.30 which was when the kitchen staff clocked in. They served nothing for the next half-hour. So we settled for nine o'clock when I would take a seat at our usual table and order our meal. The Halls had brought with them an abundant supply of dry cereals which they insisted on sharing with us. The hotel milk was usually sour but we got by and drank coffee, hot chocolate and *fruktovyy sok* (fruit juice) which was available in abundance. But Nan demanded a more substantial repast. I suggested a boiled egg. She thought this a good idea and we all ordered boiled eggs cooked for four minutes. Again we waited and waited.

The word for egg in Russian is *yaytso* in the plural *yaytsa*, which translates vulgarly in the vernacular as 'balls'. I had taught Nan a certain amount of domestic Russian, and she was an able pupil. Following the better part of half an hour waiting for our boiled eggs, Nan blew her top. As a blowsy waitress came to our table, Nan stubbed out her cigarette and pronounced loudly, '*Yaytsa. yaytsa – yaytsa!*'. The effect on the crowded restaurant and particularly on the waitress was immediate. The *Direktor* strode in. Why had we used bad language? How disgraceful! I said we had asked for eggs. The lady did not understand the *double entendre*. When would our eggs be served? They were on the table in five minutes, parboiled and stale, but Nan unknowingly won that round and from then on we were served with reasonable punctuality.

With the Halls as companions we would drive to the market and buy cheese, bread rolls, fruit, dried fish and bottles of *fruktovyy sok* which the children enjoyed. The adults would buy a couple of bottles of Georgian red wine, so the midday meal was easily catered for, and we then would proceeded to a delightful beach with white sands, rocks and a slowly lapping tide beneath the village of Simyes some four or five kilometres from Yalta.

There we sunbathed, swam, jumped off the rocks and ate our picnic lunches. The weather was perfect, the water was warm and we revelled in blissful days of relaxation and peace. I dozed off on the beach after lunch to be coaxed once again into the water by Paddy, who was learning to swim. Our goons were with us, seated some fifty yards away and wearing slacks and Panama hats and no shirts. Ranald had a butterfly net and a killing bottle which swung at his hip. He would push off into the bushes at the top of the beach in pursuit of a wide variety of butterflies. He had taken up my youthful hobby of collecting butterflies and moths, of which there was a rich harvest on the shores of the Black Sea. But the goons were clearly puzzled. Ranald's lunging through the bushes and his swipes at whatever he fancied were beyond their comprehension. Was this youngster in possession of some sophisticated form of radar or radio? Better find, out and report back. So Ranald was followed and only when he returned to our picnic place on the beach would the goon rejoin his colleague. I think the mystery of Ranald and his butterfly net possibly gave the goons more to ponder than we realised at the time.

We never visited Livadia Palace though I twice made application through the desk at the hotel. The Palace was *pod remontom* (under repair). There would be no visitors for several days. I tried again later with no success. Nan and I decided to give up even though I had it on authority from vendors in the market that coach loads of 'tourists' were being admitted daily. So we drew our own conclusions. We were unpopular and had best toe the line. But our week in Yalta was well worthwhile for all of us.

Ranald was old enough to enjoy the 'goon situation'; Paddy, whose swimming had improved enormously, was a much more confident eleven-year-old than when he had arrived in Moscow three weeks previously; and Lindsay was just lapping it up, getting sunburnt and making friends with the Hall boys who were much of an age with her. Nan seemed more relaxed and accepted the inadequacies of the hotel with reasonable grace. So long as she had her drink. To this day, some thirty-six years later, I treasure my memories of Yalta, the placid, sandy beach at Simyes and the deep-blue waters of the Black Sea. I shall never forget the market in Yalta where we bought our picnic lunches; the cheerful, colourful people, haggling and bartering for bread, cheese, meat and vegetables.

I recall the old man on his stool who stared through dark glasses, his hand outstretched, saying in a sing-song voice, 'Blind, blind, blind ...' I had my doubts, so I put a half-crown – then British currency – into his palm. He stared at the coin, then at me and said what I interpreted as, 'Piss off!' Blind, my foot! but it was all part of the tapestry of life in the Crimea.

An impression which will forever be etched in my memory was that of the fatter of our two goons who, wearing no more than his underpants and his Panama hat, tottered into the shallows and then sat down plonk and splashed with his hands like a small child. He then swam slowly and none too confidently a few yards out where he paused, blew a lot of seawater from his mouth and shouted an invitation to his colleague to join him. Both were badly sunburnt: the colour of boiled lobsters. Both wore their Panamas. Both had large stomachs. The colleague shook his head and lay back on the sand. The swimmer splashed around for a while, came ashore, still wearing his Panama hat, and waddled to where his companion lay spread-eagled in the sun. As he emerged from the sea, his genitals hung out from beneath his underpants. Nan looked at him with ill-concealed interest. He was well endowed. 'No wonder they have large families', she said. I made no reply.

At the end of the holiday, Viktor arrived and drove us to the airport. We flew back to Moscow in relative comfort, albeit somewhat sunburnt, to be met by one of my staff who drove us back to my flat and Klava, who had prepared a splendid evening meal. We took to our beds early and

Tanya, our daily maid, cleaned our shoes of the sands of the Crimea and washed and ironed our laundry.

Then, all too soon, Nan, Ranald, Paddy and Lindsay were on the flight home via Riga where, unknown to Nan, there was a European time change. So they all settled down in the airport lounge, where Nan ordered a meal, expecting to board in an hour and a half. The meal had barely been served before the call came to board. Nan was furious and was not much consoled when the time change was explained to her. But she had managed a drink and, so it seems, the rest of the flight to London Airport was uneventful.

CHAPTER SIXTY-TWO

Mob Attacks and KGB Pressure

So I was back in the office with my diplomatic functions, my correspondence with DAI and my endeavours to combine into a team the three totally disparate personalities who comprised my staff. Several weeks later we had a second 'spontaneous' demonstration. Ironically, while the Americans were vehemently opposed to the Suez affair, they were in this later one nationally involved in a pre-emptive show of force in a Lebanon/Syria dispute which infuriated the Kremlin, who were behind the trouble. So the UK and the United States were the villains and – forewarned by our informers – we were, this time as allies, prepared for what was to come.

As before, the demonstrators arrived outside the Embassy but this time the gates were already open and the throng surged into the courtyard. It was immediately apparent that there was a hard core of vicious and none-too-sober toughs in the forefront of the mob. For a mob they were. Howling and fist-waving and banging on the outer glass-fronted door of the Embassy, they presented a very ugly confrontation and the glass in the door was splintered within a matter of minutes.

Christo was on the phone to the Soviet Department of External Affairs. We saw no sign of police among the crowd now filling the courtyard. Then the Russian girl who manned the telephone exchange in an outbuilding flanking the yard broke through the demonstrators and begged admittance to the Embassy. We let her in, with several Chancery guards slamming the doors after her. Badly shaken and near to tears, she told us that the mob had threatened to wreck the telephone exchange and had broken into the flat above where the young British doctor and his wife and infant daughter were being held hostage. This was very bad news indeed.

Hugo Newton, the fat Brigadier and I spoke with HE who agreed we should take our service staff with us and do whatever possible to bring the doctor and his family from their flat to the relative safety of the Embassy. The Russian word for doctor is *vrachk*, which we agreed to use in an attempt to get through the mob. The other word we agreed on was *obratno*, which means 'back' or 'go back'. All the Embassy guards were assembled in the hallway, unarmed in the military sense but to their credit wielding substantial clubs such as old chair legs. One with a wicked look in his eye swung a heavy chain. 'They'll get this, the bastards,' he said as he and his colleagues opened the doors and let us into the forecourt.

Hugo was tall, well muscled and with a strong and imperious look. The fat Brigadier was a bulldozer probably weighing fifteen or sixteen stone. John Deverill's replacement, Tiny, a huge man much heftier than his rather flabby face suggested, was no coward. The rest of us were, like me, of medium build and not of commanding presence. Hugo led. I freely admit I had serious misgivings, for he was a man with a fiery temperament. A false move, an aggressive reaction and we could be in real trouble, for the mood was very hostile. No more were the young people from the *Kollektivy* there laughing and enjoying themselves. This was a very different ballgame and violence was just under the surface.

But we made it, thrusting, elbowing and shouting '*Obratno*' on our way through. I dare say many of the crowd didn't immediately identify us for whom we were. The staircase up to the doctor's flat was jam-packed. I found myself behind Hugo who simply forced his way past those who had broken in and the often-repeated '*Vrachk*' seemed to prove effective. '*Mozhno*,' they replied – 'Okay' or 'permitted'. So we threaded our way up to the flat and broke through to find the young doctor standing in his front hall with his wife and their terrified little daughter in her arms. Hugo turned and faced those at the top of the stairs. He swore, raised his fists and hurled himself at the invaders. The fat Brigadier was enjoying himself pushing others down the stairs. Tiny did his stuff by grabbing one in each hand and thrusting them backwards and downwards. My adrenalin was flowing. Colin Campbell and the relief of the Residency in Lucknow, or was it Cawnpore, in the Indian Mutiny? So foolish are one's thoughts on occasions such as this.

But the intruders retreated, tumbling and scrambling downwards, and then there began the escort of the doctor, his wife and infant out into the courtyard and across to the Embassy where the guards had manned the entrance. Police had arrived and, though we were cursed, hustled, banged and buffeted, we made it and gained entry to the Embassy. I had my jacket ripped, Hugo got away with a bruise or two, and I had to restrain one of my team from resorting to violence when he was held back by his collar as he was about to be let into the entrance. The diplomatic repercussions lasted several weeks.

The Americans in their main service Embassy were similarly besieged, though having no forecourt they confronted a mob gathered on the street immediately in front of the building. Chip Bohlen was there on the ground floor together with his Marine guards who, unlike ours, were armed. The mob hurled themselves at the closed doors. A few broke in and were immediately clobbered by the Marines. Using a loud hailer, the Americans warned the demonstrators that if they broke into the ground floor they would be arrested. If they came to the first floor – where the cipher and cryptographic sections were located – they would be shot. This warning was repeated in Russian several times. At first the reaction was violent, noisy and vehemently anti-American, but when the import sunk in there was a lull and within a very short time a large squad of armed police raced up in vans and surrounded the building. The crowd was forced back across the main street and dispersed.

Chip Bohlen and his entire staff boycotted every reception attended by Soviet diplomats for a month and made it patently clear why. I think probably at this time East-West relations were at their most dangerously low ebb. The Cuban crisis was yet to come. During 1957 and 1958, both sides were, as it seemed, holding their breath.

Sir Malcolm Sargent came to Moscow to conduct a concert with the Moscow Philharmonic Orchestra in the Bolshoi. He stayed in the Embassy where a reception and dinner were held in his honour. Unhappily, during the first half of the concert there was a murmuring and twittering down our row of seats. Donald Maclean had been recognised seated on the outside of the aisle on the same side as our row. Maclean had served under Sir Patrick Reilly in the Foreign Office before his defection. By the interval Maclean had sensibly disappeared. The concert was a great success and there was much applause, backslapping and kissing. Malcolm Sargent was even then an ill man and spent the following morning in the Embassy but we were able to bid him farewell and to congratulate him in the evening. He was a fantastic conductor and the Russian audience loved him.

Later, I was to experience an incident which, I confess, frightened me.

As was my wont, I was walking from my flat to the Embassy carrying an elderly attaché case which never contained anything of security importance but mostly newspaper cuttings, Soviet journals and odds and ends. My goon wasn't in tow but I thought nothing of it until a Pobeda with a tall radio aerial, the unmistakeable sign of a KGB car, screeched to a halt a few yards ahead. Aha, thought I – late on parade! But oh no! The doors were flung open. Two large and very ugly men jumped out: they wore dark raincoats and Homburg hats. They approached me side by side. The Pobeda sped off. I moved to pass them. They moved to block me. I felt trapped. Was I to be kidnapped, arrested, assaulted? I could expect no help from passers-by. I considered turning back towards my flat but this clearly wasn't on. So I stood my ground and asked in Russian: 'What was this? Did they know I was a British diplomat? Would they care to see my identity card?' For a moment they said nothing. Then, 'Continue to walk', said one. They allowed me to pass and I continued to the Embassy with my two attendants no more than a few paces behind me. At the entrance to the Embassy forecourt they spoke to the guard in his pillbox, saw me cross the courtyard to the main entrance, and withdrew.

Christo was out of the office; HE was on leave in the UK, so I sought out Hilary Young (the deputy Ambassador) and told him what had occurred. He was clearly concerned, asked me what I had been up to and said he would get a strongly worded protest sent to the Ministry of Overseas Affairs as soon as possible.

The same thing happened the following morning except that the 'escort' was waiting outside my flat. Hilary and I had agreed to give it a second run-through before having Viktor drive me to the Embassy and back each day. Viktor was off duty due to a 'chest infection'! So, between my flat and the Embassy I rode with Hugo, the new Naval Attaché, in his car. For a fortnight I never left my flat unaccompanied. The feeling of being a marked man began to tell on me and we tried to contact Colonel Chuvilsky of the OVS but with no success. Then, we began to piece together the sequence of events. It would seem that HE's report to the Foreign Office and mine to DAI of the deliberate sabotage of our visit to Baku and the constant messing up of most of our other 'approved' visits to towns in the Soviet Union had been taken seriously. Konstantinov, for the first time as Soviet Air Attaché in London, had found himself being followed wherever he went. Never before had he experienced surveillance. Never before had he been accompanied by a security man on a train journey. Never before had he been asked for his identity card on arrival at his destination. His previous freedom which was, in my judgement, utterly unjustified was suddenly proscribed. He was being treated as were we, and he didn't like it. Thus, in the typical tit-for-tat language of the West-East dialogue, I was being punished for the 'undiplomatic treatment of Comrade Colonel Konstantinov in London'. It looked like stalemate.

For a fortnight or so I lived with this virtual imprisonment. I used Viktor as much as possible but his hours of duty were laid down and, though overtime was agreed on the basis of extra pay, he was not always available. Neither was our other driver, which left me to drive my Consul to whatever evening function I had been invited. The KGB Pobeda was ever on my heels and every possible difficulty, short of actual blockage of my route, was put in my way. Several times I was stopped by the police and asked for my '*dokumenty*'. I discussed the whole situation yet again with Hilary Young and HE on his return to Moscow. Both agreed that it was intolerable and paid me the compliment of expressing their gratitude for my restraint. We left it that they would make the strongest possible protest at the manner in which I was being harassed. It was Hilary who hit on the splendid idea that I should travel with him and his wife in his official car on a perfectly legal drive round Moscow and its environs. Bearing in mind that the Ambassador and his deputy (Hilary) were by mutual agreement with the Soviets never followed when travelling within the forty-mile limit from the city centre, it would be interesting to test out this agreement with me, the victim of reprisal, as their passenger. So off we went on a cruise round Moscow and then out into the roads to the suburbs. Never did we venture outside the prescribed limit.

Sure enough, after we left the Embassy and were crossing the *Bolshoi Kameniy Most* – the Great Stone Bridge – over the Moskva River, the shiny brown Pobeda with the tall radio aerial drew up behind us and followed wherever we went. We stopped outside a beautifully restored cathedral and strolled out to take a close look. It had been converted into a museum but in no way defaced or distorted: such was the strange attitude of the Soviet Union towards the Russian Orthodox Church that, while ostracising overt Christianity, they sustained the outward evidence of past religion in their painstaking care and maintenance of almost all of the magnificent churches which stood proud and defiant in this atheistic state. While the two toughs were getting out of their Pobeda, I shot off a few camera snaps, though Hilary was not too comfortable about it. We returned to the Embassy. The Pobeda drove off and we joined HE and his wife Rachel for tea.

Rachel was all for making a big issue of the affair. She had never made any secret of her contempt for the Soviet regime, its rulers and certain individuals from other missions, notably the Indian Embassy, who kowtowed to the Kremlin and its leaders. I will never forget her splendidly undiplomatic riposte to the Anglo-Indian wife of the Indian first secretary at a reception when the wretched young woman began to heap praise on Krushchev for some reform he was reported as having pushed through the Supreme Soviet. I can still see the look of horror on her face as the young woman dashed from our group with her sari askew and her slipslop shoes coming off before she reached the sanctuary of her own colleagues.

Prudence prevailed and HE agreed to make the strongest possible representation to the Soviet Ministry of Foreign Affairs. Within three days my heavyweights had gone and we were back to square one with my mute but friendly goon a hundred yards or so behind me.

CHAPTER SIXTY-THREE

Last Days in Moscow

I was nearing the end of my tour of office. Already invitations were being delivered by colleagues from friendly missions to attend farewell lunches, cocktail parties, informal evenings and dinners. My engagement book was rapidly filling up: I drew the line at breakfasts which had just become fashionable with the Americans. My successor had been appointed and would join me ahead of his wife and family within a few weeks. I realised just how tired I was. It was at this stage, within a month or so of my return to the UK, that I threw caution to the winds and fell for the blandishments of a lady from the secretariat of a small European mission. Ironically we had been introduced by Christo, in all ignorance and sincerity. It was one of those affairs that took off spontaneously. She was good looking, spoke excellent English and had a fascinating story of how she had lost an eye – her left one was artificial – when the Germans overran her country.

I cannot explain the complexity of my feelings except that beneath the pleasure of our relationship lurked a sense of self-betrayal. Almost all unaccompanied members of the European missions had partners. It was the rule rather than the exception.

We were happy and relaxed in each other's company but not as discrete as we should have been. Lights on in my flat but no response to the front-door bell; taxis to and fro and sometimes at a very early hour in the morning. We walked together in Moscow arm in arm, visiting churches, museums, art galleries and simply wandering in the woods outside the city, eating in restaurants and lazing on the wooded promontory of Cerebrany Bar overlooking the Moskva River. We were perhaps an embarrassment to those who were planning farewell parties for me. But we did not expect to be invited as partners and only a few who knew us well included my companion.

Of the many lunches, cocktail parties, dinners and receptions given by my *chèrs collegues*, by far the best and most original was the evening organised by Christo and Helen who hired a river cruiser together with food, drink and waiters to spend two hours or more on the Moskva River while we danced to music from a tape recorder, much of which was a variety of Scottish country dances. We had with us, other than my own personal friends and Service colleagues, James Robertson Justice. The actor had come on an Anglo-Soviet friendship visit but had reneged on them soon after arriving in Moscow and had joined us in time to be included among the guests. As we dined and wined from the excellent food organised and served by the cruise-launch staff, gliding down the river, James Robertson Justice provided an added lustre to this memorable occasion.

We danced to the recordings of Scottish country dances. JRJ joined in, not too competently but with uninhibited enthusiasm. An American colleague who had never experienced Scottish country dancing became fascinated and joined an eightsome. He got the idea of 'setting' but found it difficult to unset and cocked up the eightsome, though this didn't really matter as by now the waiters had dropped their KGB disguises and the trays they were carrying and were leaping and shouting in our midst and hugely enjoying the dancing. No one really gave a damn. We had a ball! We returned past the floodlit Kremlin and cruised under the *Bolshoi Karneny Most* where a group of youngsters shouted and waved and threw down what looked very much like streams of toilet paper. In fact they were tracts in Russian, saying '*Mir i Druzhba*' (Peace and Friendship) and they drifted down and landed on our launch. We shouted back and were soon alongside the quay where we embraced and said goodbye. It had been a great evening.

Air Commodore 'Sandy' Sanders arrived a fortnight before my departure. His wife Mary, of Dutch extraction, would follow later. She and I had been in correspondence over what I saw as being the basic needs for the flat – pots and pans and even pictures for the living rooms – unaware that she was herself an artist. I received a very discourteous reply which made it clear that my suggestions were not acceptable. HE gave me a magnificent farewell party at which Sandy was introduced and my two and a half years in Moscow came to an end.

Arrangements had been made for me to drive my Consul home via Warsaw, Prague, West Germany, Brussels and Dieppe, with Hilary Young accompanying me as far as Prague whence he would return to Moscow by air. We agreed that in the circumstances this was a reasonable safeguard.

It was about a week before my departure. Sandy and I were up to our ears in sorting out the flat and its contents. The furniture was Ministry of

Works property and remained in situ but I had accumulated a considerable stock of tinned food, drinks, pots and pans, and a twelve-place set of tableware, together with cutlery, table linen and much else. Klava had laid out for us all the cooking paraphernalia which I had taken off Peter Donkin at a nominal price. We had just about listed those belongings which I did not want to be sent home and were discussing a financial settlement when Klava, who had returned to the kitchen, burst in and announced with a great display of histrionics, 'Viktor has entered the flat by the back door. He is very drunk!' Damn, Hell and blast!

Klava led the way, clip-clopping down the passage to the kitchen where Viktor stood rocking unsteadily, his wide-brimmed and large peaked cap askew and a glazed look in his eyes. Very drunk indeed. Viktor Romancha, in his early thirties, who had lovingly cleaned and cared for both my official Humber and my own Consul; Viktor who had served me unfailingly as my driver; who had bought gifts for Ranald, Paddy and Lindsay and chocolates for Nan – expensive gifts. Viktor who had sat relaxed and talkative as he drove me to and from my engagements; who had asked me about life in the UK and had described the seige of Leningrad during the 'Great Patriotic War' when he was a teenager. How he had twice fainted in the queue for bread, so hungry was he and so bitterly cold the winter. He and I had exchanged jokes and he had practised his English, which was elementary although he understood a lot more than appeared on the surface. Viktor who had become not only a trusted driver and custodian of my cars but something of a friend. Possibly this had been his undoing. He stood there wobbling in the kitchen, broken and drunk.

Sandy was behind me. Klava stood in the door and wiped her hands on the apron she always wore. Viktor put his hand in his pocket and extracted a cigarette. Klava broke through and cried, *Net, net! Kurit na kukhne zapresheno!* 'No, no! Smoking in the kitchen is forbidden.' Viktor stood there, blinking and shaking. He dropped his cigarette on the floor and stooped to pick it up; he fell, and Sandy and I got him up and put him on a chair. I spoke to him in Russian, 'Viktor, what has happened? Why are you here and why are you drunk?' He looked at me from under his wide-brimmed cap and spoke haltingly. 'Gospodin Kostaki has told me that I will not drive for you any more.' He turned and looked at Sandy. 'I will not drive for you or your family. I have been told by Gospodin Kostaki that another driver will come tomorrow.' He looked down and shook his head. 'Why has Gospodin Kostaki told you this, Viktor?' I said. 'What have you done wrong?' I looked back at Klava, who stood in the doorway, her face without expression, her hands clasped in front of her apron. 'Tell me, Viktor, what Gospodin Kostaki said to you. Tell me because I have a right to know.' He looked up at me, bleary-eyed and with great sadness. 'Gospodin Komodor,' he said. 'Kostaki has said that I am too young to be your driver. He told me that I have become too "close" to you. That I have shared some of your ideas about the Soviet Union, that I enjoyed your stories about life in Great Britain and that I needed "cleansing" – the first time I had heard this word in the politico-ethnic sense – 'that I must attend special classes'. He again hung his head and was near to tears. 'My mother is Polish and my father was in a camp in Siberia. We have not seen him since the War.' Sandy and I helped Viktor down the back stairs. We saw him to the police guard of Skatertny Peryulok and returned to the flat. I never saw Viktor again.

I confronted Klava. I asked her who had reported adversely on Viktor's relationship with me. Had she reported something to Kostaki? She was clearly very angry. So was I. She said, 'Gospodin MacDonell, I do not know what you and Viktor have discussed. I am your cook. I am not an informer'. I looked her very straight in the face. 'I hope you are not, Klava, because I have always trusted you. Will you now please leave?' For the first time in our two and a half years together, she gave me a look of hostility. Then she hid her face in her apron, hurried into the pantry and was away down the back stairs in a matter of minutes.

I was furious and wanted to go for Kostaki and say exactly what I thought of him and his Goddamn bloody mischief-making. But it was Sandy who suggested I sleep on it. Would it not perhaps be best if we accepted Viktor's dismissal and Klava's probable involvement, and took a look at the new driver who was due to report to the Embassy on the morrow? I recognised sense in what Sandy said. We ate what Klava had left for us, drank a bottle of Georgian red wine and went to bed. I slept well in the knowledge that in Sandy I had a newcomer fresh and un-inhibited by the imprisonment of the 'System', who was prepared to face the realities of being a diplomat when the whole force of the military development of the Soviet Union was poised in readiness for an attack from the West.

As I write this, some thirty-five years later, with the emergence of *glasnost* and *perestroika* – openness and reconstruction – and the dis-memberment of the Soviet Union into independent republics, it is difficult to take my mind back to the days when the brittle thread of diplomacy was stretched to breaking point. And throughout those dreadful months everyone shook hands. Krushchev, Bulganin and Mikoyan still beckoned me to join them on diplomatic receptions and everybody smiled and made facile conversation which amounted to damn all.

I didn't speak to Kostaki. I told my staff what had happened and the new driver was said to be in the garage checking out our official car. I had him come into my office, though I understand Kostaki was furious. He was very different from Viktor. In his forties, thick set, with small eyes and a mouth full of stainless steel teeth, he represented an unfriendly and somewhat sinister presence. I gave Sandy the stage and let him say what he would. The new driver was rather more self-assured than I would have liked but he was to be Sandy's driver and I left the two to communicate as best they could – I detected a fair understanding of English on the driver's part.

There were a few final farewell parties, all thrown together by my special colleagues. Thus it was that I found myself involved in a 'brunch' with the American Air Attaché and his staff. We got together at eleven o'clock in the morning, consumed waffles with various spiced meats and maple syrup and drank far too much buck's fizz. We were joined by the American Naval Attaché and his wife, a large extrovert couple who 'talked loud' and shared unquenchable thirsts. It was not long before the 'brunch' became a booze-up which tottered to a close some time in mid-afternoon. I was by then as near drunk as makes no difference.

Farewells were shouted. I was driven back to my flat where I collapsed into an armchair and slept for a couple of hours. Klava and I had become friends again and she had left me an excellent salad of cold chicken, caviar and a half-bottle of Georgian red wine. Sandy joined me and we spent the evening together. For my last evening, he and I had organised an informal farewell party for our RAF team and their ladies. He was clearly popular and I relaxed in the knowledge that he would cope both professionally and diplomatically.

On the morrow Hilary called for me shortly after lunch. Klava was her warm and friendly self and our parting was one of genuine sadness. She, a good Communist Party member, in effect wished me Godspeed and blessed me. Such were the paradoxes in Russian society.

CHAPTER SIXTY-FOUR

Journey Home from Moscow

Hilary made the arrangements for our journey, which involved flying to Minsk. My Consul was to be at Minsk where we would stay overnight before heading for the frontier post of Brest Litovsk and so into Poland and Warsaw for two nights with the Air Attaché, with Hilary in the Embassy. We were seen off at Vnukovo airport by a surprising number of colleagues. Our RAF staff were there in force; the US Air Attaché and his wife, and many others to give us a champagne farewell. Way in the background was a lady who just raised a hand as Hilary and I boarded our flight for Minsk. I hoped she saw me smile.

We ate a good meal in our hotel in Minsk, went to a cinema which was showing a badly dubbed film featuring Richard Burton, and had an early night.

Hilary was a perfect companion. I suspect he detected my mental exhaustion for he never broke my silences with trite remarks but the very fact that he was next to me – for we shared the driving – was an enormous comfort. When he was driving I would often nod off.

We drove down the long main road to the West through dense pine forests and then the wild, open agriculture of Belorussia which was being reclaimed after the 'scorched earth' withdrawal of the Soviet forces during the Second World War in 1942. We ate our picnic lunch beside a wide field of recently harvested barley where a farmer joined us with a young man who was introduced as his son. I managed to cope with their local dialect and we shared a bottle of wine and explained who we were, where we were going and spoke of Moscow and its beauty and historic interest. They listened spellbound: they had never been to Moscow and probably never would.

The Consul was a joy to drive. A very basic Ford, it simply cruised effortlessly at 55–60 mph, smoothly and silently, possibly too smoothly as

Hilary and I found our one-hour stints behind the wheel just about as much as we could take before our eyes began to droop. But we made the frontier post at Brest Litovsk.

Suddenly, from the tree-lined main road we found ourselves in a no man's land, scalped of vegetation, with a concrete track leading to a small, white frontier building from which an armed guard appeared, halted us by levelling his Kalashnikov at our car and then demanded our *dokumenti*. We complied with his demands without question and were told to remain in the car. We did so for half an hour. Hilary wisely restrained my inclination to get out and demand an explanation for the hold-up and, in due course, our documents were returned and we were directed to the crossing point where the heavily guarded gates were opened and we crossed no man's land from the Soviet Union to Poland.

POLAND

I was driving and I remember experiencing the same feeling of relief when, thirteen years before, I had been released from a POW camp in Germany and repatriated by the Americans. With the barbed wire and frontier posts with their machine guns behind us, I drove the three hundred yards to the Polish frontier with its machine gun posts trained in our direction. Hilary and I remained silent, each alone with his thoughts. I drew up at the double gates of the Polish frontier post. They remained firmly closed. An armed guard appeared from a building a short distance inside the Polish defences. He had his rifle slung over his shoulder, his uniform was scruffy and his cap was askew. He slouched up to the double gates and waved. 'Hello, welcome to Poland,' he shouted. We waved back. Then one of the guards from the watchtower came down and opened the gates. We were signalled to cross the frontier, and drove into Poland. The gates were clanged behind us, locked, and we were motioned to stop. The guard saluted and climbed back up the tower. What next?

Our 'scruffy' guard leaned against the open driver's window. He smelt strongly of drink and was smiling. He spoke in broken English. 'Where you come?' I got this one right. 'From Moscow.' 'Why you Moscow?' I looked at Hilary who suggested I explain who we were. This I did, emphasising that my friend was the 'deputy' to the British Ambassador and that I had been the senior Royal Air Force 'adviser' to the Ambassador. Our friend shuffled his feet, looked around and said, 'My brother RAF, he killed in bomber.' Hilary and I made appropriate gestures of sympathy. Scruffy looked at me. 'Where you go?' 'To Warsaw, Prague, West Germany, Brussels, France and hence to England'. He pointed back across the frontier to the Soviet Union. 'Rooskis sheets,' he said with emphasis and spat towards no man's land. 'Rooskis attack our land and the Germanskis attack us. Both sheets, but Rooskis big sheets. You go Varsava' – the Polish name for Warsaw – 'You see Varsava. Very beautiful. Now rebuilt. One time all centre of Varsava finished – kaput – by the Germanskis. Now fine city. You see new Varsava. Good place to see.' He lit a cigarette, belched and looked again across no man's land. 'Sheets,' he said, 'Bloody sheets.'

A smartly clad officer then appeared. He, too, smiled, saluted and asked in good English for our documents. He glanced at them, handed them back and wished us well on our journey with a benediction I shall always remember: 'Welcome to our country which will one day be free. We owe much to Great Britain who fought the Nazis to defend us. God be with you'. He made the sign of the cross and waved us on our way.

We rendezvous-ed with the Air Attaché and his wife – and dog – on the outskirts of the city. We cruised in convoy to the British Embassy where Hilary was welcomed and we were invited to have drinks with the Ambassador and his wife at six o'clock on the morrow. The Air Attaché and his wife gave me an early supper and showed me to my room, suggesting I might care for a good night's sleep.

The next two days were wonderfully relaxing. No longer was I tailed by a goon. We drove many miles out of Warsaw without a follower. The Poles had inevitably capitulated to the Nazi-cum-Soviet occupation but their hearts were with us in the 'Vest' and this came through in all our dealings during the two days Hilary and I spent in the Polish capital. That the centre of Warsaw had been wholly restored was not only evident but also a magnificent tribute to the dedication of the preservation of their ancient culture. I like to think that the essential Poland, shorn today of Soviet and German domination, is once more a nation of independence, pride and Catholic faith.

CZECHOSLOVAKIA

We were on our way to Prague, escorted for several kilometres from Warsaw by the Air Attaché and his wife and dog; we exchanged farewells and headed west along the broad, well-surfaced road that led through Lodz and Breslau to Prague, a good day's journey, but we were well provided with food and wine, and even a small bottle of Polish vodka to sustain us. We crossed the frontier into Czechoslovakia without incident and pulled off the road in a pine forest to eat an excellent meal. We were in shirt sleeves, the sun shone from a cloudless sky and the forest rang with the sound of birds, the barking of dogs or foxes, and the occasional cough of some larger animal.

We must have dozed off. I awoke to find a uniformed policeman standing over me, his motor bicycle beside our car. He had his truncheon swinging.

Hilary stood up. The man spoke in his own language which neither of us understood. We tried Russian but the only response we got was '*Nyet*'. He pointed at the Consul and swung his truncheon round and round and then stopped with it pointing in the direction from which we had come. Hilary took over. With hand outstretched, he approached the policeman, who stopped pointing and accepted Hilary's greeting. The word '*dokumenty*' produced nods from the officer, which I followed up with '*Britanskiy diplomat*' as we brought out our *dokumenty* from our hip pockets.

This did the trick. The stamps on our passports from the frontier post were scrutinised and accepted with an immediate lessening of tension. I pointed down the road and said '*Praha*' (Prague). He nodded and slung his truncheon on his hip. His face creased into a grin and he walked round the Consul nodding in approval and running his hand over the bodywork. The road was empty of traffic. I produced the small bottle of vodka and offered it to him. He looked both ways, then took a swig. Hilary and I did likewise. We all shook hands; he then kick-started his motor cycle, waved farewell and sped off in the direction from which he had come.

We still had a long way to go. The vodka and our nap beside the road combined to loosen our tongues. We talked with easy understanding. I hope I didn't monopolise our conversation, for I was eager to have Hilary's professional views on the East-West confrontation. I wish I could have taped our talk. Hilary was a very good conversationalist – and a good listener. Inevitably we touched on the danger inherent in the Soviet fear of attack and the paranoid distrust that the Kremlin harboured of every move and statement from Washington. I can even now see in my mind's eye Hilary's profile as he sat beside me; and I can hear the measured tones of his soft voice as he spoke of the seemingly ever-present danger of armed conflict. I was listening to a very worried man and one moreover who had reason to be, by virtue of what he knew and deduced from his contacts as a senior diplomat with his Soviet counterparts in the Kremlin and also in the Foreign Office in London, as well as from the many friends he had cultivated among the pro-Western missions in Moscow.

I was driving. After a while I noticed the scenery had changed: cultivation and woodlands had given way to broken patches of what suggested small industrial settlements. There were narrow-gauge railways flanking the road, far more mechanised traffic than before, and smoke and steam climbing up from behind the screen of deciduous trees which still lined our route. I looked across at Hilary. He was asleep, almost childlike as he curled in the corner of the front passenger seat. I drew into a lay-by, which woke him up. He yawned and smiled and joined me in studying the route map we had to lead us into the centre of Prague and so to the Embassy where we were to be met by the First Secretary and the Air Attaché.

As we drew nearer to the city I wondered at the beauty and antiquity of the outskirts. Warsaw had impressed us by the wonderful reconstruction and rebuilding that the Poles had accomplished. But Prague had mercifully been spared during the annexation of Czechoslovakia by Nazi Germany in 1939. The beauty and historic background bore witness to the free entry that was given to the invaders in return for the consideration they had shown in sparing the city. Following our street map, we wove our way into the city and in due course found our way to the Embassy where Hilary was to spend the last night before returning by air to Moscow and I was to rendezvous with the Air Attaché.

The Embassy was somehow different from that in Warsaw and even more so from the one in Moscow. I have often pondered on this: I dare say the 'atmosphere' of a diplomatic mission abroad reflects the personality of its head in much the same way as the morale of a squadron or a warship depends on the personality and effectiveness of the leader. Why was it was that the Prague mission seemed wrong, unfriendly – even suspect? I could never put my finger on it. As an old friend of mine once said of a newcomer to our squadron: 'If you tap him he makes an odd noise'. It seemed to me that the Prague Embassy, when you entered and breathed in its atmosphere, also had a strange smell.

Hilary was escorted away by the Ambassador and a senior secretary. I was left in the hall with the Air Attaché, a rather limp, dark-haired man; his assistant preened himself in a long mirror, adjusting his tie and twitching his waistcoat until I, tired, dirty and bored, suggested to the Attaché that we moved on to his home. This was met with a rebuff from the Chancery guard who said that the Ambassador would expect me to be ready to attend him as soon as he was free. I suggested we should be given refreshments – we had driven a great distance and I, for one, was extremely tired. The Chancery guard – who had a squint – took a while to hoist this in. 'HE will receive you shortly. Just sit down and relax.' And he returned to his desk which appeared to have nothing on it.

So we – the junior secretary, the Air Attaché and his assistant, and I – sat obediently in the hard-angled, office-type chairs until I became so tired and uncomfortable that I could take it no longer. The Air Attaché was evidently prepared to sit it out. Not me. I stood up. 'We are going to the Air Attaché's house,' I said. 'I need to wash and change before I am received by HE. I will be back in thirty minutes'. The Chancery guard squinted at me. 'In no way, sir, can you leave the Embassy before HE has interviewed you. He will not be long. Relax in your chair. Perhaps a cup of coffee?' A good idea!

Eventually, the door off the hall opened. Hilary emerged with the Ambassador and several senior secretaries in attendance. They were shown out to the patio. I stood up. Hilary said, 'Good luck, Donald! We will keep in touch by letter'. No one else said anything. I was becoming very angry. However, it was not long before a senior secretary swept us up and escorted us to the Ambassador's office. He was seated behind a large desk in a room festooned with the heads of dead animals, photographs of groups of paunchy people wearing topees and breeches, and clusters of muskets, sidearms and shields. I could see only one family photograph on the edge of the desk.

HE didn't even rise to greet me. He waved to various chairs around the edge of the room and, without a word of welcome, started in on a written brief which he took from a tray on the right of his desk. He had a gold ballpoint pen which he held between his thumb and first finger, and moved regularly from the left to the right of the brief he was reading. For twenty minutes or so, this went on. It was the most impersonal introduction to a foreign mission that I can imagine, consisting as it did of nothing more than a monologue on the past and present of Czechoslovakia. No opinions offered, no explanations – flat Foreign Office stuff which I had heard for many years. I could hardly believe it. 'Any questions?' asked HE. 'Thank you, sir, no,' I replied. The Air Attaché over in the corner didn't even speak. The senior secretary produced his stock one. 'What of the future, sir?' HE closed his folder, stuck his gold ballpoint into his jacket pocket, looked slowly round the room and replied, 'Who knows? Who knows?' With which words of wisdom, the Ambassador rose, smiled to us and bade me a safe journey back to Moscow!

The next morning we toured the centre of Prague and lunched well in the magnificence of Wenceslas Square in a restaurant on the pavement, our scraps being readily consumed by several dogs lying expectantly under the table.

After another excellent meal at Air Attaché's house and a good night's sleep, I set off from Prague, with a plentiful box of provisions for the journey and drove alone with my thoughts across the frontier of West Germany to join the autobahn to Nürnberg. At that time I had no clear idea as to what my future posting was to be. Nor had I decided whether or not to remain in the Royal Air Force. To do so would seem to accept the predominant role of Nan, with me as an occasional father, breadwinner and counsellor; to retire on pension would provide me with the freedom to join my family, a relatively small gratuity of a few thousand pounds, and an annual pension which was, even then, wholly inadequate to maintain the running expenses of the home, the school fees for the boys and the growing extravagance of Nan. Even today, I am aware that this was the juncture at which I moved away from worrying about the extent to which I had served my RAF and diplomatic post in Moscow towards an anxiety about my future. How could I reconcile responsibility for a young family left in the care of an emotional and unpredictable woman with my responsibilities as a senior officer in the RAF? I needed advice and, as I entered the outskirts of Nürnberg, I decided to seek a meeting with the Air Secretary as soon as possible.

GERMANY

My thoughts were suddenly interrupted by a rhythmic bumping from the near-side rear wheel – or so it seemed. I drove into a lay-by. Sure enough there was a large blister on the right-hand rear tyre. I changed the wheel and drove on to Nürnberg where I expected accommodation and garage facilities. The recommended hotel was of a high standard. I parked outside and was met at the entrance by a German manager who scrutinised my dismal appearance in some disapproval – my very grubby, lightweight suit which was badly soiled and with holes in the sleeves.

I proffered my diplomatic card. This produced raised eyebrows. He spoke English. He continued to look me up and down though he consented to book me in. I said I wanted a tyre repaired by the morrow. His eyebrows went up again but he phoned a number and said that the repair would be carried out. I remember I was obliged to lug my bags upstairs to my room, where I bathed and dressed in my dark-blue suit.

My arrival at the downstairs desk produced an immediate reaction. The manager looked me up and down and said, 'Herr MacDonell, what a difference! What a change! What can I get for you?' I was brought a cocktail; I was escorted into the dining room where I was served an outstanding meal and given every attention.

A magnificent breakfast, distinguished by a 'courtesy' glass of schnapps with my coffee, set me up well. My bags brought down and my car brought round to the entrance. The account was a large one but I didn't grudge it and left an ample tip. The manager was affable and beaming, and curious to know where I was heading. I told him Wiesbaden, to spend the night with my American colleagues. He looked less pleased and mentioned *Walpurgisnacht*, the eve of Mayday which, according to German legend, was the occasion of a witches' sabbath. The Americans celebrated the occasion with a national 'bash' – 'No holds barred and lock up your wives and daughters'. I did not at the time take this too seriously.

A mechanic came into the lobby and presented his bill for the tyre repair. It was pretty steep but I paid it and he left without comment. The porter stowed my bag in the boot of the Consul. The manager opened the driving door. I looked at the wheel that had been repaired. The hubcap, which was a carefully moulded press-fixture, was bashed in out of all recognition. I looked at the manager and he returned my look stonily. I asked: 'Why this?' He shrugged his shoulders, drew himself up in a semi-military fashion and said, 'Herr MacDonell, the mechanic is not a diplomat'. He then opened the driver's door wider. The implication was obvious. I climbed in, looked around for any other damage and started up.

I pondered the odd valediction from one who had seemed so agreeable. And then it came to me that perhaps the German mechanic who had repaired my tyre had been a resident of Nürnberg for many years. For the city had been, some fourteen years back, the target for one of the heaviest and most vicious, and in my opinion outrageous, of Bomber Harris's raids. Virtually the whole of Nürnberg had been laid in ruins.

I drew up at the guardroom of the US Air Force base at Wiesbaden. I had driven for eleven hours, was very tired and was not prepared for what was in store for me. I had been invited to spend the night with an RAF couple who were on the American base in a liaison capacity. He was a pleasant group captain and she was a down-to-earth thirty-year-old who had got the American lifestyle well under control. At their married quarters I was immediately introduced to a very noisy party. There seemed to be twenty or thirty guests of various ages and nationalities. I was thrown in at the deep end and, within a few minutes, was feeling very much better after a strong drink which I didn't even bother to identify.

The evening went on and on. We all decided to go 'walkabout' and it wasn't long before I lost contact with my host and hostess. The camp was awash with revellers in various disguises, some in witches' smocks and poke-bonnets; whether they were men or women, young or old, was impossible to say. It became apparent that *Walpurgisnacht* was what would now be called a 'rave' with wife-swapping and getting drunk the order of the day. I recall a large American in a tee-shirt and jeans weaving unsteadily and noisily towards me. 'Boy oh boy! I've laid my driver. Zeez, whacko, whacko! She sure knows how to use the gear stick! Yippee!' And he stumbled off . . . .

Next morning I had a hangover. It was ten o'clock. My host was in no great shape himself but offered a 'brunch' at eleven o'clock. I declined with thanks: I had a long drive ahead to Brussels where I had been booked in a hotel recommended by a senior secretary in the Embassy and confirmed by Kostaki. So we bade farewell and my hostess looked as fresh as could be as she kissed my cheek and bade me bon voyage with a picnic lunch and a bottle of wine.

BELGIUM

I entered the outskirts of Brussels as dusk closed in, found my hotel without difficulty and was unpacking in my room when the telephone rang. How did she know my hotel, my telephone number? And why?

Kostaki of BUROBIN in the Moscow Embassy had made my booking but had no right or reason to disclose it to a secretary from a European mission. Christo had introduced us but would surely not be so tactless as to disclose my route to France. Hilary would be back in Moscow but didn't know her and would never reveal my whereabouts. Why had she pursued me? 'I shall arrive by Aeroflot ... due at Brussels at 6.30 pm. Will you meet me?' 'Yes. Why are you coming to Brussels?' 'I have business in Brussels. You will meet my plane. Please, Please.' 'Accommodation is arranged.'

I spent the day in deep thought, which spoiled my appreciation of the World Exhibition which I had looked forward to enjoying. Even so I found it much better than the Festival of Britain on the South Bank where I had wandered with Stella and the children several years before.

She came through the barrier carrying a small case which I took from her. She had tears in her eyes and clung to my arm but said nothing except that she had no further baggage. She seemed to me like a refugee. We hardly spoke at all as we joined the taxi rank. In the cab she broke down and wept uncontrollably. Our relationship had never been heavily charged with emotion: our love-making had been satisfactory but, in a sense, formal. I held her hands as we drove into Brussels. I asked her to tell me what was wrong. Why had she followed me and what business in Brussels brought her post-haste by air? And how had she found the name of my hotel? I pressed her but she withdrew into her corner of the cab and we fell silent. As I paid off the taxi outside our hotel, I realised that I had not given the driver its name when we left the airport. Nor to my knowledge had she. What was going on?

I was worried as we pushed through the entrance and went to the desk. She moved into a chair in the lobby while I spoke with the receptionist. No room had been booked in her name. Instead she and I had been entered as *M. et Mme MacDonell*. Realising that my room had a bed which could be regarded as a double, I asked for a single room in exchange. My request was declined: there were no single rooms vacant. The manager was brought in at this stage and was surprisingly unco-operative. So it was that the two of us went to my room. I suppose I was too tired and bewildered to raise the roof – and I took her hand and together we went in and I closed the door behind us. We sat opposite each other. She had made up her face and was looking more composed and cheerful. I sought to break through her refusal to explain the extraordinary situation she had created.

We were not in love. We had agreed on that. Neither of us depended on the other: our partnership was one of companionship and physical satis-faction. Her seemingly compulsive arrival in Brussels and the emotional state when I met her at the airport were incomprehensible. We had parted in Moscow as two mature people who had enjoyed the theatre, art and architecture of the city. For an hour or more I strove to break through her refusal to tell me what had happened, why she had business in Brussels, how she knew my whereabouts and what had brought her to book a double room in my name. At one stage I became angry and began to pack my bag, saying I would leave the hotel. Only then did her look of defiance change and she stared sadly into my eyes. 'Do not interrogate me, Donald. You are not the Gestapo.'

You are not the Gestapo. We had often spoken of our pasts: she of the suffering of her family and her people at the hands of the Nazis. The mention of the Gestapo pulled me up. I took her hands and together, silently, we looked out of the windows as the lights went on in Brussels and the evening traffic built up at the crossings as drivers and pedestrians waited their turns to go. She said, 'I wish to have a drink. Ring for the waiter to bring us drinks. Please'. We sipped our drinks in silence, each in a separate chair. Occasionally our eyes met but there was no other contact. I rang the restaurant and booked a table for two. She nodded in agreement and went to the shower room with her make-up sachet. I stood looking out the window as night marched on in Brussels. I was confused.

The restaurant was filling up. Already several tables were occupied and the strong smell of cigars was, perhaps, typical of Belgium in the evening. We had a table in a bay of the main window with a view of the entire restaurant. She had hidden her previous sorrow and was buoyant and smiling as the head-waiter handed me the menu. We had dined together in Moscow on several occasions and I had no difficulty in choosing a meal which I knew she would enjoy.

We drank two aperitifs and began to talk. We spoke of Moscow, of the Soviet Union, of our friends and colleagues in various missions. But much of what we said was the sort of politely restrained conversation that was exchanged between dinner partners who did not know each other at formal diplomatic lunches or dinners. She would from time to time allow her glance to wander in the direction of the door from the kitchen. I followed it and saw a dark-suited, heavily built man seated alone at the table nearest that door. Her interest made me wonder. So I followed her glances as discretely as possible.

Our waiter came in with our final course. The man in the dark suit pushed back his chair and made much of wiping his mouth with his napkin. The waiter looked at him and they exchanged nods. Our waiter left and at the same time the dark suit stood up and followed him out of the restaurant. She paused in her sorbet and then dropped her eyes and drank some wine. It was a very good meal, but I was becoming increasingly worried.

We smiled at each other, watched the television, had another drink and took the lift to our room. The man in the dark suit was reading a newspaper in the front lobby. He lowered his paper as we passed but she didn't appear to notice. As usual we made love but it wasn't really us. I was possibly too tired but when I fell asleep she was no longer in my arms and the lights seemed to be on for much longer than usual. She was fully dressed and her bag was packed when I woke. I had nothing on. She sat beside me on the bed, and put her hand on mine and said in perfect, unaccented Russian, 'Donald Ranaldovich, I am now leaving you. Do not try to write or contact me ever again. We will never see each other again and we must forget each other. Please, Donald Ranaldovich. Please'. She had never before spoken to me in Russian.

I wanted to touch her but she left the room and closed the door behind her. I heard her walk down the corridor to the lifts. I have never heard of her or seen her since.

I sometimes find this episode difficult to believe and wonder if I have dreamed it all. Yet some three years later I was lunching in the Royal Air Force Club in London with a friend who had been the Assistant Air Attaché in Moscow after I had left. Somehow we found ourselves discussing tailing and the extent to which we had been under surveillance by the KGB – the huge display of radio aerials opposite my flat in Skatertny Peryulok, for instance. He looked straight at me. 'Forgive me, but did you ever hear anything more of the secretary from that foreign Embassy?' 'No', I replied. 'Why do you ask?' He looked embarrassed. 'You know she fled her Embassy in Moscow and was picked up in Brussels by the KGB. She was one of their agents.' I said no more but he looked at me strangely. When he left he said, 'Sorry, sir, perhaps I shouldn't have brought it up'.

FRANCE

I drove from Brussels in some confusion and reached St Omer in the late afternoon. I had hoped to find the little estaminet where in March 1941 I had first become a POW but, though I cruised round, the village had become much changed. The battle that had been fought around it had virtually destroyed it. Since it had been rebuilt, I could find nothing which might have been the original estaminet, so I booked in at a small hotel.

I reached Dieppe. The Newhaven-Dieppe ferry was not a 'roll-on roll-off' in 1958 and all vehicles were lifted into the hold by a heavy winch operated from the wharf. They were redeemed on the other side in the same way. I must have dozed through their loading for I seem to remember the sound of engines and movement. We were backing out from Dieppe and by the time I had gone out to the sundeck we were clear of the harbour. The Consul was safe and snug in the hold below.

Much later, when we were entering the narrow channel of Newhaven. I grabbed my bags and went out on deck. I could see them. Nan bent and smoking; Ranald, Paddy and Lin leaping and shouting and waving. 'Daddy, Daddy, well done, Daddy!' I waved back and took a long shot of them with a cine-camera I had brought with me. I came ashore and we melted into each other's arms. Even Nan seemed relaxed. The Consul was swung gently on to the landing stage. One of them climbed in beside me. Nan took the others in the Hillman Husky I had bought for her during my previous visit. We were together. 'Drive on the left, Daddy. Don't forget, drive on the left.' We set off on the well-known road through Lewes and Uckfield to the Ashdown Forest and Stroods Lodge, Herons Gyll.

CHAPTER SIXTY-FIVE

Rockwood

My arrival was dramatic: Nan at her best and the three children, joined by the little black mongrel Pooh, leaping like grasshoppers at what had been set for my return. Crossed over the porch of Stroods Lodge were two banners; one the Soviet hammer and sickle, and the other a splendidly woven banner bearing the Glengarry crest of the Raven's Rock waving bravely in the breeze. It was a hero's welcome. When I think back to that occasion, created by Nan with her imagination and identification with me, my problems and the children, I am ever aware of a sense of inadequacy in that I could never reciprocate the feelings she had for me and my children.

There was much to do. Stroods Lodge was too small for the whole family, with only three bedrooms, one of which had been adapted for the boys by installing a double bunk, and the other two upstairs – small, with dormer windows, and occupied by Nan and Lin – there was no place for me. So I bought a caravan which was parked, illegally, in the field which bordered the tiny back garden. There I slept.

I had six weeks' leave which was uncommitted other than to meetings in Whitehall with JB, the Director of Air Intelligence and the Air Secretary. JB was evidently pleased with the administrative and financial control of my staff in Moscow, and we lunched contentedly in the RAF Club with a bottle of claret and two full measures of the Club's port as a ritual salutation to what JB, belching, described as a job well done. I put him into a taxi back to Whitehall and made my way dreamily into the Club's smoking room where I fell asleep in a sympathetic armchair for a good two hours.

I had certain misgivings when I was shown into the office of the Director of Air Intelligence (DAI) a week or so later. We had known one another for several years and, though older and senior to me, I had never really agreed with or understood the workings of his mind. A strange man. So it was that we spent the whole day mulling over the Moscow portfolio and inevitably the matter of the paucity of our photographic intelligence came up. I explained once again my policy of caution: the need to weigh the dubious value of random shots – seen and reported by the goons – against the strong likelihood of members of my team being clobbered and declared PNG (persona non grata). I faced him squarely with the example of the Americans' contemptuous disregard of the Soviet veto on photography of anything remotely military, and the resultant expulsions from their Air Attaché's staff. Such casualties seemed of little concern to them and were quickly made good by replacements from a apparently inexhaustible supply from Wiesbaden.

He had my terminal report, a copy of which had been delivered to HE before I left Moscow. DAI disagreed with my conclusion that the Soviet Union was running down its long-range bomber force in favour of an ever-growing intercontinental nuclear weapon capability, the stark evidence of which must surely have been well known to NATO and many others outside the Iron Curtain. Following a fruitless discussion, I left, though he did pay me the compliment of congratulating me on the conduct of my tour in Moscow. We parted on good terms and at least we hadn't quarrelled, though I must admit to being a mite fed up by the time I got off the bus outside Adastral House for my meeting with the Air Secretary and the postings people.

Helen, dear Helen, had vowed that she had it on the most reliable authority in Moscow that my destination was to be the Imperial Defence College. But as I suspected, she had got it wrong. A few minutes with the Air Secretary, an Air Marshal whom I knew well and much admired, and I had been appointed as Commandant of No. 1 Initial Training School (No. 1 ITS) at South Cerney, an RAF station near Cirencester in Gloucestershire. I was not surprised. Just disappointed ....

We discussed the assignment. The Air Secretary acknowledged that South Cerney was sixty-odd miles from where my family was based in Sussex. We agreed that the circumstances with Nan made it unlikely that I could move the family into the Station Commander's quarter. He was anxious to help in whatever way possible. In response to his concern for Diana, whom he had met during the early years of our marriage, I explained that her illness was incurable. We agreed the family would be resettled in Sussex and I would go to South Cerney.

I was disturbed that yet again my family and I were to be separated, that my role as a father would be 'offstage' and probably no more than that of prompter in the wings. I was beginning to worry about Nan's ability to maintain stable relationships with Ranald, Paddy and Lindsay. She was drinking heavily and, though they were wonderfully loyal to her and obedient and compliant with her oftimes vague and seemingly strange demands, I found within each of the children a confusion between acknowledgement of Nan's sovereignty and their love and expectations of me, their father.

Nan's dedication to the welfare of my family was outstanding but drink is an ugly business. The progressive degeneration of our relationship, like the breaking down of a marriage, if you will, was essentially drink-related. After two and a half years in Moscow – having developed high tolerance to alcohol, vodka in particular – I found it far too easy to slip into the daily habit of drinking in the morning and evening. If things were to be improved, a great deal would be required of me as a peacemaker and, indeed, active partner in the guidance of three confused and sensitive young people. I had six weeks' leave to start the process. Six short weeks, after which my time and energy would have to be fully given to my new RAF posting as Commandant of No. 1 Initial Training School, Royal Air Force South Cerney, Gloucestershire.

We needed a larger home. So Nan and I called on the local estate agent in Uckfield and were told about Rockwood in Fairwarp on the edge of the Ashdown Forest. It wasn't strictly on the market: the owner had died and the executors were still arguing over the sale price and whether the property was to be sold as a single holding or in three parcels. There was no reason why we shouldn't walk over the grounds and view it from the outside.

I recall that moment when for the first time we saw unfolding like a panorama before our eyes the serenity of the place. The house was on the small side, built of brick in the style of forest cottages in the area. It stood four-square on a narrow plateau from which the land fell away in two sizeable fields to the bottom hedges beyond which a thick mass of trees of the forest climbed away and over the horizon. The strip of cultivation on which the house stood had a shrubbery, fruit trees, a garden of mixed plants choked with weeds, and a sizeable vegetable patch that had long since given up trying. At the end of the property was a barn, partially converted into a studio, and a small brick stable.

Who knows how long we spent looking round, peering into the downstairs windows, striding down the field and across the hedge to the bottom and so into the woodland of fine trees badly choked with hornbeam. Nan was completely absorbed in all she saw, peering at everything in the garden, muttering more to herself than to me that this would have to go, that this and the other would have to be done. She strode here and there measuring areas of cultivation, giving names to plants I couldn't recognise from weeds. Dishevelled, her hair all over the place and her stockings laddered, she seemed inexhaustible. Only the light in her big eyes told of the excitement that she felt.

So it was that the euphoria of my return from Russia was of short duration. Our visit to Rockwood with all that it promised for the future only served to emphasise the difficulties. But, I bought the property, thereby establishing something of a common bond between Nan and myself. It was somewhere permanent in which to bring up my three children, involving them in the creation of a home of our own and it was to be my base for the next fourteen years.

* * * * *

Is retrospection different from, or akin, to memory? In my judgement the two are not always complementary. What I have written of my life, is drawn from a host of memories – which can admittedly be fallible – but is interspersed throughout with comments, criticisms or plaudits which are after-thoughts – the result of much later rethinking, changed attitudes of mind and over-riding experiences. So apart from vanity, why have I put pen to paper with the intent of placing on record my varied but relatively undistinguished career? There are two reasons. The first, and most personal, is that Lois, my wife, has worried that I have never really settled down to retirement since we came to the Black Isle in 1981; the second is that many clansmen, to whom I have from time to time told stories not only of my War years but of other, more personal happenings in my life, have urged me to write it down: 'You owe it to Clan Donald!'

So be it ... *Suas alba.*

Afterword

By Lois MacDonell

Following South Cerney, from where he visited the family every second weekend, Donald went to his last posting before his retirement from the RAF in 1964. This was as Director of Management and Work Study at the Ministry of Defence. For his innovative work in this post he was made a Companion of the Bath. In 1960 Donald became Chairman of the Battle of Britain Fighter Association and remained so until 1978. In 1965 he was presented to the Queen on the occasion of the Service of Thanksgiving for the 25th Anniversary of the Battle of Britain.

The children, having grown up and followed their own careers. Nan was now free to make a life for herself. She bought a property in Malta and went to live there.

Sadly Diana never recovered and lived out her days in St Andrew's Hospital, Northampton, eventually dying of cancer.

On a happier note, in 1973 Donald married Lois Streatfeild, some years his junior. To his great joy they had two children, first James and then Penelope.

Donald continued to maintain contact with the widowed Mike. Both she and her sister Stella have now died.

After retirement from the RAF Donald undertook a number of senior consultative posts in personnel, but in 1981 decided to retire permanently with his second family to Fortrose on the Black Isle in the Highlands of Scotland. This enabled him to play a more active role as 22nd Chief of Glengarry, visiting Clan Donald events at home and abroad. In 1971 Donald had become one of the founding Trustees of the Clan Donald Lands Trust on the Isle of Skye, to which he subsequently devoted much time. He also served as President of Ross & Cromarty Branch of the Soldiers, Sailors, Airmens' and Families Association (SSAFA) for a few years and was a Trustee of the Finlaggan Trust.

On 15 November 1993, Donald celebrated his 80th birthday. This was the only occasion when he and all his five children were together at one time. It was a memorable event. But his health gradually deteriorated until in June 1999 he died. Though he is buried in Fortrose and Rosemarkie Cemetery, in 2002 a memorial was erected – by family, clansfolk and friends – outside the new Museum of the Isles at the Clan Donald Centre at Armadale on the Isle of Skye and was unveiled by Lois, Ranald, James and Penny (Paddy and Lindsay both live in Canada). Also present were The Chiefs of Clan Donald, the Air Officer for Scotland and many friends and clansfolk. Fittingly, the memorial is a representation of the Glengarry clan crest 'The Raven's Rock' in the form of a bronze raven, sculpted by Gerald Laing, on a rock obtained from Invergarry, the Glengarry Clan seat. Emma Lavender's beautiful hand-engravings on the granite plinth incorporate the RAF crest.

Index